POLITICAL PUBLIC RELATIONS

Political Public Relations maps and defines this emerging field, bringing together scholars from various disciplines—political communication, public relations and political science—to explore the area in detail. The volume connects differing schools of thought, bringing together theoretical and empirical investigations, and defines a field that is becoming increasingly important and prominent. It offers an international orientation, as the field of political public relations must be studied in the context of various political and communication systems to be fully understood.

As a singular contribution to scholarship in public relations and political communication, this work fills a significant gap in the existing literature, and is certain to influence future theory and research.

Jesper Strömbäck is Lubbe Nordström Professor and Chair in Journalism and Professor in Media and Communication at Mid Sweden University, Sundsvall, Sweden. He has published more than 30 scholarly articles on political communication and political news journalism, in addition to more than 15 books on the same subjects.

Spiro Kiousis, PhD, APR, is Professor and Chair of the Department of Public Relations in the College of Journalism and Communications at the University of Florida. His current research interests include political communication, political public relations, and new media. Dr Kiousis has published his work in leading journals, including *Communication Research, Journal of Communication*, and the *Harvard International Journal of Press/Politics*.

COMMUNICATION SERIES
Jennings Bryant/Dolf Zillmann, General Editors

Selected Titles in Public Relations include:

POLITICAL PUBLIC RELATIONS

Principles and Applications

Edited by Jesper Strömbäck and Spiro Kiousis

Routledge
Taylor & Francis Group

NEW YORK AND LONDON

First published 2011
by Routledge
711 Third Avenue, New York, NY 10017

Simultaneously published in the UK
by Routledge
2 Park Square, Milton Park, Abingdon, Oxon OX14 4RN

Routledge is an imprint of the Taylor & Francis Group, an informa business

Library of Congress Cataloging in Publication Data
Political public relations : principles and applications / edited by Jesper Strömbäck &
   Spiro Kiousis.
   p. cm.
   Includes index.
   1. Public relations and politics. 2. Communication in politics. 3. Campaign
   management. 4. Political campaigns. I. Strömbäck, Jesper. II. Kiousis, Spiro.
   JF2112.P8P65 2011
   659.2'932—dc22
   2010044232

ISBN 13: 978-0-415-87380-2 (hbk)
ISBN 13: 978 0 415 87381 9 (pbk)
ISBN 13: 978-0-203-86417-3 (ebk)

Typeset in Bembo and Stone Sans by
EvS Communication Networx, Inc.

Printed and bound in the United States of America on acid-free paper by
Walsworth Publishing Company, Marceline, MO

Library
University of Texas
at San Antonio

CONTENTS

PREFACE

While political communication and public relations have always been closely intertwined, public relations strategies and tactics are probably more ubiquitous in political communication today than ever. Still, there is neither much theorizing nor empirical research on *political public relations*. Most public relations theory and research centers on public relations strategies and tactics in relation to the corporate sector, while most political communication research neglects or only briefly mentions public relations theory and research. The same is true of most political science research. Furthermore, political communication scholars are seldom well versed in public relations theory, whereas public relations scholars seldom display a deep understanding of what makes political communication and politics different from other areas of inquiry.

In other words, despite the importance of political public relations, the general rule is that there is not much theorizing and research that manages or even attempts to bridge the gap between public relations, political communication, and political science theory and research.

To remedy this and to encourage integrative theory and research that bridges the gap between public relations, political communication, political science, and other related fields, we decided to edit this book. This is the main purpose of this book, which is intended for undergraduate and graduate students as well as scholars in political communication, public relations, political science, and political marketing. We also hope it will be of interest to practitioners in political public relations

As the first book explicitly focusing on political public relations, we have tried to cover the most important contexts of political public relations. The overview of the content is included in the first chapter, but briefly, the volume includes chapters on political public relations and news management, agenda building, political marketing, corporate issues management, strategic framing, crisis management, relationship management, government information management, public diplomacy and corporate foreign policy, as well as on presidential and digital public relations. Thus, we hope students and scholars within each of these areas of theory and research will find the book appealing.

Acknowledgments

An edited volume like this one only becomes as interesting and important as the contributors make it. As editors, we thus want to express our gratitude first and foremost to all contributors for their efforts and contributions to this book. It has been a great pleasure to get to know and to work together with the contributors, some of the best scholars in the intersection of public relations, political communication, and political science, and we are sincerely grateful for all the high-quality chapters they have provided.

We would also like to thank Linda Bathgate and the staff at Routledge. We are grateful that Linda Bathgate shared our vision of this book, and for all the consistent support we received during the process of conceiving, editing, and publishing this book.

The idea of this book was born during informal lunch discussions during the spring of 2007, when Jesper Strömbäck was a visiting scholar at the University of Florida. As we were both working at the intersection of public relations, political communication, and political science, we were both amazed that there was no major book focused on political public relations. Because we were preoccupied at the time with other projects, it was not until the fall of 2008 and the spring of 2009 that we actually started to work on the book. By that time, Jesper Strömbäck was back at the University of Florida as a visiting scholar. These two visits at the University of Florida proved decisive in making this book become reality. Jesper Strömbäck would thus like to express his sincere thanks to Mid Sweden University, Sundsvalls kommun and Karl Staaffs fond för frisinnade ändamål, which provided the funding for his guest scholarship at the University of Florida in 2007, and to the Sweden-America Foundation, which provided the funding for his guest scholarship in 2008–2009. Thank you very much for your support. Spiro Kiousis would like to thank the Department of Public Relations, and College of Journalism and Communications at the University of Florida for their support in helping make this project a reality.

In the final phases of editing this book, we received some great help from UF doctoral student Ji Young Kim in proofreading and formatting the chapters. Ji Young's diligence and close attention to detail were crucial to the quality and cohesiveness of this volume: Thank you Ji Young for your assistance.

Last but not least, we would also like to thank our families for all their unwavering support and patience when we were working on this project instead of spending time with them. Jesper Strömbäck would therefore like to thank his wife Berivan Mohammed, and Spiro Kiousis would like to thank his wife Jennifer and children Anastassia and Konstantine for their continuing support of his research activities. Finally, we would both like to thank our parents and siblings for their support of our efforts over the years.

Jesper Strömbäck
Spiro Kiousis

1

POLITICAL PUBLIC RELATIONS

Defining and Mapping an Emergent Field

Jesper Strömbäck and Spiro Kiousis

While political public relations as a concept and research field is rather new, the practice of political public relations is probably as old as politics and society itself. If politics is ultimately about "who gets what, when, how," as suggested by Lasswell (1936), and this is decided through processes of communication, persuasion, and information dissemination and processing (Castells, 2009), then politics, political communication, and political public relations are inextricable linked together. As Bernays, one of the major contributors of modern public relations, wrote in 1952: "The three main elements of public relations are practically as old as society: informing people, persuading people, or integrating people with people" (p. 12).

Consequently, traces of political public relations can be found as early as 64 BCE, when Quintus Tullius Cicero offered some advice to his brother, Marcus Tullius Cicero, who was running for election for Consul in Rome. Quintus states that there are two paths to success: the support of your friends and the favor of the people. Among other things, a candidate should thus study his opponents; know their motives and their friends and allies; and gain the favor of the people; for example, through listening to what people are saying (Petersson, Djerf-Pierre, Homberg, Strömbäck, & Weibull, 2006, p. 10). Here we can find some roots of contemporary political public relations strategies and tactics such as, for example, relationship management (Ledingham & Bruning, 2000), targeting and positioning (Baines, 1999), opposition research (Johnson, 2007), rhetoric (Heath, 2006), and persuasion (Pfau & Wan, 2006).

Moving forward to the American Revolutionary War, the campaigns before and during this war revolutionized the tools and techniques of political public relations (Cutlip, 1995). Samuel Adams and his fellow revolutionaries not only pioneered the use of easy-to-remember slogans such as "No taxation without representation," they also realized the importance of getting their side of the story to the public first, managing news media, and they organized one of the first pseudo events, the Boston Tea Party (Cutlip, 1995; McKinnon, Tedesco, & Lauder, 2001). This event featured colonists dressed as Indians, dumping imported tea into the harbor, in order to catch public attention and crystallize public opinion. Samuel Adams was thus not only one of the fathers of the American Revolution; he was also one of the fathers of press agentry and political public relations (Bernays, 1952).

These are just two examples to suggest that although the bulk of contemporary public relations theory and research focuses on corporate settings (Botan & Hazleton, 2006; Heath, 2001a), with many textbooks usually treating public relations in political contexts mostly in passing or as "special cases" (Baines, Egan, & Jefkins, 2004; Cutlip, Center & Broom, 2000; L'Etang, 2008; Wilcox & Cameron, 2006), in practice, politics, political communication, and public relations have always been closely intertwined. A strong case could even be made that public relations strategies and techniques in general were established by political actors and in political contexts, and used for political purposes (Cutlip, 1995; Lamme & Russell, 2010; Newsom, Turk, & Kruckeberg, 2010). It was mainly during the last half of the 19th century and with the rise of the industrial society and modern mass media that public relations became increasingly prominent within and mainly associated with the commercial sector.

Hence, the paradox appears to be that while political public relations has a long and prominent history, and continues to be highly important in political communication processes, there is neither much theorizing nor empirical research on political public relations. Most public relations theory and research centers on public relations strategies and tactics in relation to the corporate sector, while most political communication research neglects or only briefly mentions public relations theory and research. The same is true of most political science research. Furthermore, political communication scholars are seldom well-versed in public relations theory, whereas public relations scholars seldom display a deep understanding of what makes political communication and politics different from other areas of inquiry.

In other words, despite the importance of political public relations, the general rule is that there is not much theorizing and research that manages or even attempts to bridge the gap between public relations, political communication, and political science theory and research.

To remedy this and to encourage integrative theory and research that bridges the gap between public relations, political communication, political science, and other related fields, we decided to edit this book. Thus, this functions as the main purpose of the book and the chapters to follow. In this chapter, we will attempt to map and define the field of political public relations, and discuss its relationship with other fields of theory and research, before outlining the chapters included in this volume.

Toward a Definition of Political Public Relations

When Bernays published his classic *Crystallizing Public Opinion* in 1923, he also provided one of the first definitions of public relations—or the activities of the public relations counsel, as he labeled the position. According to Bernays (1923), the public relations counsel is the one "who directs and supervises the activities of his clients wherever they impinge upon the daily life of the public. He interprets the client to the public, which he is enabled to do in part because he interprets the public to the client" (p. 14). Thus, the boundary-spanning role of public relations was already stressed from the beginning (White & Dozier, 1992).

In contemporary theory and research, there are a rather wide variety of definitions of public relations offered by leading scholars or practitioner organizations. One of the more often quoted definitions is offered by Cutlip et al. (2000) who assert that "public relations is the management function that establishes and maintains mutually beneficial relationships between an organization and the publics on whom its success or failure depends" (p. 6). Another widely quoted definition is offered by Grunig and Hunt (1984) who argue that public relations is about the "management of communication between an organization and its publics" (p. 6). A third influential definition comes from Harlow (1976), who tried to synthesize more than 500 definitions. According to him,

> Public Relations is the distinctive management function which helps establish and maintain mutual lines of communication, understanding, acceptance and cooperation between an organization and its publics; involves the management of problems or issues; helps management to keep informed on and responsive to public opinion; defines and empha-sizes the responsibility of management to serve the public interest; helps management keep abreast of and effectively utilize change, serving as an early warning system to help anticipate trends; and uses research and sound and ethical communication as its principal tools.
>
> (p. 36)

A fourth definition, offered by Coombs and Holladay, highlights the role of influence in public relations processes (2007). According to them, public relations should be defined as "the management of mutually influential relationships within a web of stakeholder and organizational relationships" (p. 2).

These and many other definitions have several traits in common. First, that public relations is a management function; second, that public relations is about the management of communication between an organization and its publics; third, that relationships between an organization and its publics is at the heart of public relations; and fourth, that these relationships should be mutually beneficial (Baines et al., 2004; Cutlip et al., 2000; Newsom et al., 2010; Wilcox & Cameron, 2006).

Having said this, many definitions tend to mix descriptive, prescriptive, and normative elements. This is most evident in definitions that include notions that the relationships between an organization and its publics should be mutually beneficial. While this might ideally be the case, the extent to which such relationships in fact are mutually beneficial is ultimately an empirical question. What public relations *is* and what it *should be* are two separate matters. Normative elements should hence not be included in the core definition of public relations or of political public relations.

Perceiving public relations as a management function that seeks to establish and maintain relationships between an organization and the publics on which it depends highlights that organizations and their publics are interdependent. The boundaries between an organization and its publics are porous; the publics can have major effects on the organization just as the organization can have major effects on its publics. Conceptually, this is similar to the relationship among political actors and institutions, media actors and institutions, and the public in political communication research. Hence, McLeod, Kosicki, and McLeod (1994) define political communication as "the exchange of symbols and messages between political actors and institutions, the general public, and news media that are the products of or have consequences for the political system. The outcomes of these processes involve the stabilization or alteration of power" (pp. 125–126). Similarly, Blumler and Gurevitch (1995, p. 32) contend that "political communication originates in mutual dependence within a framework of divergent though overlapping purposes. Each side of the politician–media professional partnership is striving to realize certain goals vis-à-vis the audience; yet it cannot pursue them without securing in some form the co-operation of the other side" (p. 32).

Hence, both political communication and public relations are about relationships formed through communication, and in both cases, the relationships between various actors are interdependent and shaped within the boundaries set by structural and semistructural factors such as laws and constitutions, cultural norms and values, and the overall media and political systems (Blumler & Gurevitch, 1995; Cutlip et al., 2000; Esser & Pfetsch, 2004; Hallin & Mancini, 2004). Neither political communication nor public relations managers nor practitioners can disregard the cultural, social, political, institutional, or systemic context in which they are located—or existing power relationships.

Related to the emphasis on relationships, both public relations and political communication have also been concerned with the construct of reputation and its impact on stakeholder perceptions and actions (Carroll & McCombs, 2003). For example, public relations research on issues management and perspectives on issue ownership in political communication posit that strong reputations are closely related to organizational and institutional effectiveness (Kiousis, Popescu, & Mitrook, 2007; Petrocik, Benoit, & Hansen, 2003). According to Gotsi and Wilson (2001), "a corporate reputation is a stakeholder's overall evaluation of a company over time. The evaluation is based on the stakeholder's direct experience with the company, any other form of communication and symbolism that provides information about the firm's actions and/or a comparison with the actions of other leading rivals" (p. 25). Elsewhere, Wartick (1992) defines reputation as "the aggregation of a single stakeholder's perception of how well organizational responses are meeting the demands and expectations of many corporate stakeholders" (p. 34).

A useful framework for understanding the roles of the relational and reputational approaches in stakeholder engagement is offered by Hutton, Goodman, Alexander, and Genest (2001) who suggest that the importance of each construct varies according to the level of involvement between organizations and their constituencies. Specifically, they suggest that relationship cultivation and management is more critical for groups that are substantially involved with an issue or organization while perceptions of reputation are more important for peripheral groups. Within political contexts, active volunteers and donors might be best understood from a relational perspective while occasional voters might be best understood through a reputational point of view. Thus, the study and practice of political public relations is strongly concerned with both these constructs.

Another similarity between political communication and public relations theory and research is the central role of the media. Although both interpersonal communication, organizational communication, and digital communications are important in both political communication and public relations processes, in contemporary societies the media in general and mass media in particular are arguably still the most important sources of information in matters beyond people's own experiences (Gunther & Mughan, 2000; Strömbäck & Kaid, 2008). Politics and current affairs in postindustrial democracies have thus been described as mediated (Bennett & Entman, 2001; Nimmo & Combs, 1983). Hence, political actors, corporations, and other organizations cannot afford to disregard the media, what issues they underscore, and how they frame various actors, issues, and processes. The media have a major influence on how the world is imagined (Iyengar, 1991; Kinder, 2003; McCombs, 2004), and as noted by Lippmann (1922/1997), "The way in which the world is imagined determines at any particular moment what men will do...their effort, their feelings, their hopes..." (p. 16). Hence, the increasing importance of digital media notwithstanding (Castells, 2009), communication through mass media has always been and continues to be important in political communication as well as in public relations processes.

A crucial difference between political communication and public relations, however, is that political communication in general does not necessarily have to be purposeful or a management function. Most theory and research on political communication rather stress how ubiquitously embedded communication is in politics, hence making it virtually impossible to separate "politics" from "communication"—regardless of whether the communication is purposeful or not. As noted by Blumler and Gurevitch (1975):

> If politics is about power, the holder's possession of and readiness to exercise it must in some manner be conveyed to those expected to respond to it. If politics is about participation, this consists in itself if "the means by which the interests, desires and demands of the ordinary citizen are communicated to rulers."... If politics is about the legitimation of supreme authority, then the values and procedural norms of regimes have to be symbolically expressed, and the acts of government have to be justified in broad popular terms. And if politics is about choice, then information flows clarifying alternative policy options must circulate to those concerned with decisions, whether as their shapers or as consumers of their consequences.
>
> (pp. 167–168)

Another crucial difference between political communication and public relations is that political communication theory and research, comparatively speaking, is more attuned to questions and conflicts of power, which public relations theory and research sometimes, albeit not always tend to treat as matters that can be managed or resolved through communication. But some conflicts and questions of power are rooted in enduring and incompatible differences between positions or interests, and cannot be resolved through communication (Pfau & Wan, 2006). On the other hand, both power and conflicts of power are at the heart of politics, and hence also of political communication processes. Lasswell (1936, p. 3) thus defined the study of politics as "the study of influence and the influential," whereas Key (1964) succinctly stated: "Politics as power consists fundamentally of relationships of superordination and subordination, of dominance and submission, of the governors and the governed. The study of politics is the study of these relationships" (pp. 2–3).

Again, the notion of relationships comes to the forefront, but in political science and political communication theory and research, these relationships are characterized by opposing interests, conflicts, and the use (or abuse) of power, whereas in public relations theory and research, there is at times an assumption that all conflicts can be solved and that the relationships between organizations and their publics not only should be but also are mutually beneficial. This is not to say that those studying politics are cynical whereas those studying public relations are naïve, but rather that there are both significant similarities and differences with respect to the focus on and perceptions of the nature of the relationships between different actors in society.

While public relations scholars seldom focus on political actors, issues, or processes in political communication research, the purposeful communication of politics is a rather prominent field of inquiry. This research is, however, often decoupled from public relations theories and research, and the term *political public relations* is only rarely used (Jackson, 2010). More often, those who study the purposeful communication of politics refer to terms such as the *communication of politics* (Negrine, 2008; Sanders, 2009), *political campaigning* or *political campaign communication* (Plasser & Plasser, 2002; Trent & Friedenberg, 2004), *political management* (Johnson, 2009a), *political marketing* or *market-orientation* (Lees-Marshment, 2009; Scammell, 1995), or *spinning* (Farnsworth, 2009; Palmer, 2000). Sometimes terms such as these are even used interchangeably, although there are some both theoretically and conceptually important differences between, for example, political market-orientation and political campaigning (Strömbäck, 2007).

When the term *political public relations* is used in political communication research, it is primarily used to refer to purposeful activities by political actors to influence the media, their agendas, and how they frame events, issues, and processes (Davis, 2002; Froehlich & Rüdiger, 2006; McNair, 2000, 2003; Moloney, 2006). Franklin (2004) refers to this as the packaging of politics, but the most common term is probably *spinning*, with political public relations professionals and consultants referred to as spin-doctors (Farnsworth 2009; McNair, 2003, 2004; Palmer, 2000). Oftentimes, those who write about political public relations using terms such as *spinning* and *spin doctoring* do it from a critical perspective, leading McNair (2000) to criticize the "demonization of political public relations."

Needless to say, political public relations should not be equated with news management. While news management and media relations are highly important parts of political public relations (J. Grunig & Hunt, 1984; Zoch & Molleda, 2006), political public relations is much broader than the strategies and tactics for influencing the media. Similarly, public relations strategies and tactics are relevant in many other areas of political communication activities aside from those related to news management and media relations.

Thus, while political public relations as practice is widespread and important, and studied from many different perspectives and through different theoretical lenses, it is seldom properly defined, and there is very little theory and research on political public relations that integrates theory and research from public relations, political communication, political science, and other relevant fields. There are some exceptions but these do not change the overall picture (Jackson, 2010; Kelley, 1956; Kiousis & Strömbäck, 2010; Lee, 2008; Liu & Horsley, 2007; Xifra, 2010).

This situation, we believe, is problematic: If political public relations somehow is about the use of public relations strategies and tactics in political contexts or for political purposes, then a proper definition of political public relations should integrate public relations theory and research with theory and research on political communication and other related fields. In Figure 1.1, some of the most important research areas that are related to, and could inform theory and research on political public relations, are highlighted.

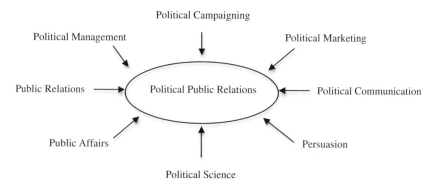

FIGURE 1.1 Political public relations and related fields of theory and research.

While many fields of research are related to and could inform theory and research on political public relations, ultimately, political public relations is about the use of public relations strategies and tactics in political contexts and for political purposes. Hence, a proper definition of political public relations should reflect common definitions of public relations, albeit adapted to the context of politics and political communication. It should emphasize the communication of politics, because communication is at the heart of public relations as well as politics and political communication. It should also emphasize the purposeful nature of political public relations, because attempts to influence others are an intrinsic part of both public relations and political communication. Finally, it should be integrative, because political public relations in both theory and practice can be approached from many perspectives.

Based on this, we propose the following definition of political public relations:

> Political public relations is the management process by which an orga-
> nization or individual actor for political purposes, through purposeful
> communication and action, seeks to influence and to establish, build, and
> maintain beneficial relationships and reputations with its key publics to
> help support its mission and achieve its goals.

This definition can be compared to the few definitions of political public relations offered by others. According to Zipfel (2008), "Political public relations refers to the strategic communication activities of actors participating in the political process that aim at informative and persuasive goals in order to realize single interests" (p. 677). This definition perceives political public relations communication as unidirectional, and expresses a functional perspective on political public relations. Hence, it does not incorporate the transition toward a cocreational perspective on public relations that has been manifest in public relations research over recent decades (Botan & Taylor, 2004). In contrast, we believe the relational perspective is essential for an understanding of all processes that involve politics, communication, and public relations. Hence, we find Zipfel's (2008) definition biased toward a functional perspective that has become increasingly outdated.

McNair has offered another definition. According to him (2003), political public relations is about "media and information management tactics designed to ensure that a party receives maximum favorable publicity, and the minimum of negative" (p. 7). This definition does not have much in common with contemporary understandings of public relations within the field of public relations research, but is typical for how political communication scholars often perceive public relations. In this understanding, public relations is mainly about media management, image management, and information management (Moloney, 2006). This is, however, a narrow understanding of public relations.

In contrast, the definition proposed here reflects contemporary understandings of public relations; it is adapted to the context of politics and political communication; it emphasizes the communication of politics and the purposeful nature of communication for political purposes; and it has the potential to integrate theory and research from different fields of research. It also subsumes the different public relations functions usually highlighted in the literature, such as managing publicity, reputation management, public affairs, issues management, and relationship cultivation.

To further map the field of political public relations, and its association to other fields of research, we will next turn to the issue of organizations relevant in the context of political public relations.

Organizations Relevant in the Context of Political Public Relations

In political science and political communication research, the most important political organizations are political parties. In electoral democracies, they perform a number of functions that no other political organization does. Among other things, they simplify choices for voters, mobilize people to participate, recruit and train political candidates and leaders, articulate and aggregate political interests, organize the government as well as the opposition, and ensure responsibility for government actions (Dalton & Wattenberg, 2000; Montero & Gunther, 2002; Webb, 2002). Thus, it has been said that a "representative system of parties operating within free and fair electoral procedures performs duties that make democratic government possible; without such parties, a democracy can hardly be said to exist" (Katz & Crotty, 2006, p. 1).

Most democracies around the world are party-based, in the sense that political parties are the main actors in political communication and policymaking processes (Newton & van Deth, 2005; Ware, 1996). The United States is partly an exception, as parties there traditionally have been weaker while individual candidates have been stronger than in most other democracies. As noted by Rozell, Wilcox, and Madland (2006), "In most democracies, parties run against each other with the help of their candidates; in the United States, candidates run against each other with the support of their parties" (p. 18). U.S. political parties have even been described as "empty vessels" (Katz & Kolodny, 1994). The partisan realignment of the South and increasing partisan polarization, have, however, made the parties more important also in the United States (Jacobson, 2007), although the electoral system and political culture continues to be candidate- rather than party-centered.

Political parties are not the only organizations relevant in the contexts of political communication and political public relations. Other important organizations are "collateral organizations"; that is, organizations that are linked to parties while simultaneously having their own agendas and interests. Typical examples include think tanks, political action committees (PACs), and a diverse set of nongovernmental organizations such as unions, churches, environmental organizations, human rights organizations, and other interest groups (Poguntke, 2006). The nature of the relationships between parties and collateral organizations, and the formation of networks of collateral organizations, vary across countries, but in all countries, parties "use other relevant organizations that constitute their environment to create linkages to diverse groups of potential voters" (Poguntke, 2006, p. 396). These organizations, in turn, use the parties for advancing the interests of their constituencies, in competition with other organizations and interests (Rozell et al., 2006). When doing so, they involve themselves in political public relations, either in their interrelationships, in their relationships with political parties, or in their relationships with their publics.

Thus, the concept of political actors is much broader than the concept of political parties. All nonprofit or for-profit organizations that operate in political contexts, or are involved in lobbying and attempts to shape political opinions, or have political agendas or linkages with political parties or governments are, at least partially, political actors. The defining characteristic of political actors are not their inherent nature but rather if they have political agendas and are trying to influence political processes.

Hence, not only political parties are involved in political public relations. To the extent that organizations such as unions, interest groups, or commercial businesses have political agendas and try to influence political opinion formation or policy-making processes, they are involved in political public relations activities. The same is of course true of governments and public sector agencies (Lee, 2008; Liu & Horsley, 2007). To some extent, this brings political public relations as theory and practice close to the field of public affairs.

Political Public Relations and Related Fields

Following Harris and Fleischer (2005), there are three broad definitions of public affairs. According to the first definition, the term *public affairs* refers to the "policy formulation process of public and corporate stakeholder programmes" (pp. xxxi–xxxii). According to the second definition, public affairs refer to "the corporate consideration of the impact of environmental (in its broadest sense), political, and social developments on a company and the opinion-leader contact programs which follow." The third definition refers to "the totality of government affairs or relations." In all these cases, it is about a management process by which primarily corporate organizations, for political purposes and through communication and action, seek to influence and to establish, build and maintain beneficial relationships and reputations with its key publics, primarily within governments. Public affairs scholars and practitioners may prefer the term *stakeholder* to *publics* (de Bussy, 2008), but apart from that, the definitions of public affairs and political public relations are strikingly similar.

Still, public relations and public affairs theory and research appear to live largely separate lives, and when public relations scholars do discuss public affairs, the latter is usually perceived of as one specialization of public relations (J. Grunig & Hunt, 1984; Toth, 2006). Whether reasonable or not, the mutual insularity is to the detriment of both fields of theory and research (McKie, 2001), making it all the more important that theory and research in political public relations is integrative.

Another field related to public relations, and hence political public relations, is that of marketing. Similar to the relationship between public relations and public affairs, public relations and marketing theory and research tend to live largely separate lives with different bodies of knowledge, scholarly networks, professional associations, and journals. According to both public relations and marketing scholars, the main reason is that they are conceptually distinct. According to Cutlip et al. (2000),

> marketing focuses on exchange relationships with customers. The result of the marketing effort is quid pro quo transactions that meet customer demands and achieve organizational economic objectives. In contrast, public relations covers a broad range of relationships and goals with many publics—employees, investors, neighbors, special-interest groups, governments, and many more.
>
> (p. 8)

Similarly, Ehling, White, and Grunig conclude (1992) that

> marketing management presupposes a business organization with a single economic purpose, that of producing goods or services for a single constituency (consumers). Public relations management, on the other

hand, presupposes an organization (not always a business enterprise) that is multipurpose in its commitment and serves a number of different constituencies.

(p. 363)

From the perspective of public relations scholars, there is in addition a strong rejection of what is perceived of as "the diminution and finally absorption of the public relations function by marketing" (Ehling et al., 1992, p. 378).

Turning to the marketing literature, theory and practice has changed during the last few decades. In short, there has been a transition from transaction marketing to relationship marketing, and from consumer marketing to nonprofit, social, and services marketing (Christopher, Payne, & Ballantyne, 2002; Grönroos, 2000; Gummesson, 1999; Lees–Marshment, 2004). Hence, marketing is no longer focused only on "giving customers what they want" and singular exchanges. Instead, there is an increasing focus on the need for long-term relationships with different stakeholders. Gummesson (1999, p. 3) hence defines relationship marketing as "marketing based on interaction within networks of relationships" (p. 3). Grönroos (2000) similarly writes that the purpose of relationship marketing "is to identify and establish, maintain and enhance, and when necessary terminate relationships with customers (and other parties) so that the objectives regarding economic and other variables of all parties are met. This is achieved through a mutual exchange and fulfillment of promises" (p. 243).

Hence, neither public relations nor marketing theory, research, and practice is the same today as it was some decades ago, and the changes that have taken place have actually brought the two fields closer. There are still important differences, but the relational perspective is now highly prominent in both fields, and there are other overlaps as well.

Related to this is the development of political marketing theory and research during the last couple of decades (Lees–Marshment, 2001, 2009; Newman, 1994, 1999; O'Cass, 1996; O'Shaughnessy & Henneberg, 2002; Scammell, 1995). Although the parent disciplines of political marketing are marketing and political science rather than communication and political science, there are some clear linkages between political marketing on the one hand, and public relations and political public relations on the other (Newman & Verčič, 2002; Strömbäck, Mitrook, & Kiousis, 2010).

Broadly speaking, political marketing can be defined as:

the application of marketing principles and procedures in political campaigns by various individuals and organizations. The procedures involved include the analysis, development, execution, and management of strategic campaigns by candidates, political parties, governments, lobbyists and interest groups that seek to drive public opinion, advance their own ideologies, win elections, and pass legislation and referenda in response to the needs and wants of selected people and groups in society.

(Newman, 1999, p. xiii)

Although this definition is not explicitly relational and most political marketing literature tends to focus on voters rather than other publics or stakeholders, in both political marketing and political public relations, there is a focus on the management of purposeful communication and action that is intended to help organizations achieve their goals. In both fields, there is also an acknowledgment that political parties or other organizations have multiple publics or stakeholder groups that they have to attend to (Kotler & Kotler, 1999; Ormrod, 2009; Strömbäck, 2007). Thus, the management of relationships and reputations is crucial in both fields.

Again, there is however a disconnection between theory and research on political marketing and public relations. There are some important exceptions (Newman & Verčič, 2002; Strömbäck et al., 2010), but overall, too little cross-fertilization.

To us, this is another argument for why it is important that theory and research in political public relations is integrative. What matters is not whether theories and research originated within public relations, public affairs, political marketing, or any other field, but whether there is theory and research that seek to understand and investigate the management process by which organizations or individual actors, for political purposes and through purposeful communication and action, seek to influence and to establish, build and maintain beneficial relationships and reputations with their key publics to help support their mission and achieve their goals.

Political Public Relations as a Management Process

According to almost all contemporary definitions, public relations is or should be perceived as a management function. While many practitioners are technicians rather than managers or specialists (Dozier, 1992; Dozier & Broom, 2006), for public relations to be effective, it is claimed that top public relations managers should participate in management decision making and form part of the dominant coalition in their organizations (Dozier & Ehling, 1992; Dozier & L. Grunig, 1992; L. Grunig, J. Grunig, & Ehling, 1992).

While it could be argued that the thesis of public relations as a management function is prescriptive as much as descriptive, the literature lists many reasons for this. One of them is that public relations practitioners are supposed to function as boundary spanners and perform the dual function of representing the organization to its publics and the publics to the organization (White & Dozier, 1992). To represent an organization to its environment, the public relations manager has to have access to the top executives, know the rationale for the organization's actions and behavior, and be able to communicate effectively what the organization stands for and why it behaves in a certain way. To represent an organization's publics to the organization, the public relations manager must similarly have access to the top management, and have influence to make sure that the publics' interests are taken into account in the organization's decision making. Everything an organization does has (or might have) implications for its relationships with different publics; if public relations is not a management function, it will hence not be possible for public relations practitioners to help establish, build, and maintain beneficial and mutually influential relationships with the organization's publics.

Related to this is another reason for why it may be important that public relations is a management function: How an organization presents itself, which publics it chooses to target, which relationships it prioritizes, and the reputation it wants to achieve, are matters of strategic importance. These are also matters of doing as well as communicating, as noted by Aula and Mantere (2008) in their analysis of reputation management: "Reputation management is doing good, communicating good, and 'treating well' or good relations" (p. 211). Hence, the actions cannot be decoupled from the communication, and public relations must be involved in the decision making related to both the doing and the communication.

The options open for an organization partly depends, however, on the organization's environment, including its history, existing relationships and publics, and competitors. Hence, all strategic decisions should be preceded by environmental scanning, broadly defined as the—preferably systematic—gathering of information about an organization's publics and external environment in order to identify potential problems and opportunities (Dozier & Repper, 1992; Witmer, 2006). For the information gained through environmental scanning to be incorporated in strategic decision making, public relations professionals need to be involved in the development of organizations' strategies. As stated by J. Grunig and Repper (1992): "The emphasis that theories of strategic management place on monitoring the external environment and adjusting the organization's mission to it suggests a crucial role for public relations in the process. And the emphasis on organizational mission provides the connection to organizational goals that public relations must have to contribute to organizational effectiveness." Hence, public relations "must be part of the strategic management of the total organization—in surveying the environment and in helping to define the mission, goals, and objectives of the organization" (p. 120).

The key word here is *strategic*. According to Botan (2006), this term subsumes the two overlapping concepts of *grand strategy* and *strategy*. Grand strategy refers to "the policy-level decisions an organization makes about goals, alignments, ethics, and relationship with publics and other forces in its environment"; strategy refers to "the campaign-level decision making involving maneuvering and arranging resources and arguments to carry out organizational grand strategies," and tactics refers to "the specific activities and outputs through which strategies are implemented—the doing or technical aspect of public relations" (Botan, 2006, pp. 225–226). For public relations and strategic communication to be effective, their practitioners must be involved when making decisions on both grand strategy and strategy, and not confined to the role of technicians carrying out the tactics (Botan, 2006; J. Grunig & Repper, 1992; Hallahan, Holtzhausen, van Ruler, Verčič, & Sriramesh, 2007; Pfau & Wan, 2006).

This is equally true in the context of political public relations. In his classic *Professional Public Relations and Political Power*, Kelley (1956) approvingly quoted some political public relations practitioners, saying "to be of any value, the public relations man must sit in on all planning sessions and do his part in the selecting of issues," and "public relations in a campaign is worthless unless the public relations man has at least a voice in selecting, determining, and projecting issues" (pp. 211–212). To this Kelley (1956) added, "To put the public relations man in a policy-making position is to put him where he can affect some of the basic relationships between the public and its government" (p. 213).

Following the literature, for political public relations to be effective, the top practitioners hence have to be part of the strategic decision making in their organizations. Considering the contentious and competitive nature of politics, and the complexity of political environments, environmental scanning, boundary spanning, and the strategic choice of publics and relationships to prioritize may even be more important in the context of political public relations than of corporate public relations. This is particularly true with respect to organizations that are involved in political public relations on a continuous basis. The more visible and deep their involvement in political processes, the greater is the need for organizations to make political public relations a part of the management and strategic decision making.

Due to the public and contentious nature of politics, political organizations are also more likely to find themselves involved in scandals—either real, grounded in ethically questionable behavior, or manufactured by competitors or the media—than many other organizations (Castells, 2009; Thompson, 2000). And as always, to be effective in monitoring the environment, assessing risks, detecting possible crises, and managing crisis and crisis communication, a precondition is that political public relations is part of the management structure (Coombs, 1999; Stacks, 2004; Ulmer, Sellnow, & Seeger, 2007).

An example might further illustrate the importance of perceiving political public relations as a management function. As suggested by theory in the field of political marketing, conceptually a distinction can be made between product-, sales-, and market-oriented parties (Lees-Marshment, 2001, 2009; Lees-Marshment, Strömbäck, & Rudd, 2009; Lilleker & Lees-Marshment, 2005; see also Newman, 1994; Wring, 2005). Briefly, a product-oriented party argues for what it stands for and believes in, and most efforts are oriented toward a development of the political product—the policy commitments, the party image, and the party's candidates and leaders. The members and activists are crucial in the development of the political product, which thus is developed internally based on ideology as interpreted by members and activists. A product-oriented party tends to assume that voters will realize that its ideas and policies are superior and therefore vote for it.

A sales-oriented party is similar to a product-oriented party in the sense that the political product is developed internally and based on the members' and activists' interpretation of the party's core values and ideology, but dissimilar in the sense that it realizes that the party and its product has to be sold and communicated effectively. Thus, a sales-oriented party tries to make people want what the party offers through the effective use of marketing and campaign techniques.

A market-oriented party is fundamentally different from both the product- and sales-oriented party. Instead of developing the political product mainly through internal processes, a market-oriented party uses market intelligence to identify expressed and latent voter needs and demands, and attempts to design a political product to meet voters' wants and needs and hence provide voter satisfaction. In contrast to sales-oriented parties that try to change what people want, market-oriented parties try to provide a product that people already want.

Of course, these party types are ideal types, and in reality no party is fully product-, sales-, or market-oriented. Rather, they tend toward either type of party. The same is true of the distinction in political science between vote seeking, office seeking, and policy seeking parties (Harmel & Janda, 1994; Strom, 1990). What is important in this context, however, is that the role of political public relations will differ significantly between party types. The relationships with different publics or stakeholders, and what is considered as key publics or stakeholders, will also differ significantly. Hence, for political public relations, not to be involved in the process of deciding which orientation or party type—a matter of grand strategy—the party should tend toward, would render political public relations less effective. Hence, to be able to function effectively, political public relations managers need to be involved in the decision making with respect to both grand strategy and strategy.

Political Public Relations and Publics

One of the core concepts in political science, political communication, and public relations is that of *public* or *publics*. It is also one of the fuzziest concepts in these fields of research, which is true also of related concepts such as public opinion (Donsbach & Traugott, 2008; Price, 1992; Splichal, 2001). As Key (1964) once wrote, "To speak with precision of public opinion is a task not unlike coming to grips with the Holy Ghost" (p. 8). Something similar could be said with respect to public and publics.

Still, most conceptualizations of who belongs to, or what constitutes a public range from mass to situational perspectives (Vasquez & Taylor, 2001). Thus, in some cases the term *public* refers to virtually everyone, or everyone entitled to vote in a polity; for example, in discussions about mass opinion. In other cases, the term refers to a much narrower group; for example, in the situational theory of publics.

In the context of political public relations, both the mass public and situational publics are relevant. Most theory and research has been devoted to the mass public, not least as measured in opinion polls. From the perspective of both the media and political actors themselves, public opinion as measured by opinion polls is highly important in virtually all political communication and political campaign processes (Geer, 1996; Lavrakas & Traugott, 2000; Mitchell & Daves, 1999). Due to the rise of "permanent campaigning" (Blumenthal, 1980; Dulio & Towner, 2009), polling has become more prominent also in policymaking and governing processes.

What has largely been neglected in political communication research, however, is the situational theory of publics. According to Dewey (1927), for a group to be considered a public, it should (a) face a similar problem, (b) recognize that the problem exists, and (c) organize to do something about it. Based on this, J. Grunig and colleagues have developed the situational theory of publics, according to which four types of publics can be distinguished. The first is the *nonpublic*. People in this group do not face a similar problem, do not recognize that a problem exists, and do not organize to do something about it. The second is the *latent public*. While people in this group face a similar problem, they do not recognize that it exists or organize to do anything about it. Only when groups of people both face a similar problem and recognize that the problem exists does it become an *aware public*. If they in addition organize to do something about it, it becomes an *active public* (J. Grunig & Hunt, 1984, pp. 145–160; see also J. Grunig & Repper, 1992; Vasquez & Taylor, 2001). The three independent variables are problem recognition, constraint recognition, and level of involvement.

At any moment in time, aside from the mass public, there are thus nonpublics, latent publics, aware publics, and active publics. These can be found within and outside of organizations, and within other organizations as well as within the unorganized parts of the population. Depending on which group a certain individual belongs to, his or her need for orientation (Weaver, 1980), awareness (Zaller, 1992), and motivation (Prior, 2007) will vary, as will the exposure and attention to and processing of information.

For all organizations, it is therefore crucial to monitor the environment and identify the different types of publics, and shape their communications accordingly. What might make political organizations different from corporate and other organizations is that the number of latent as well as aware and active publics is likely to be much higher. This is particularly true of political parties because they are continuously involved in political communication and policymaking processes. The sheer visibility of political parties and their representatives, and their responsibility for solving public issues and problems, increases the likelihood that groups of people will face a similar problem, recognize that it exists, and organize to do something about it. In addition, all kinds of collateral and interest organizations will always try to mobilize people to make them recognize the problem that these organizations have identified, and then mobilize them to take actions.

Comparatively speaking, political organizations may thus face a higher number and a more diversified and complex set of publics than most corporate organizations. What is more, some political organizations—not least political parties—are unusually dependent on their relationships with different publics for their prospects of achieving their goals. This makes their political public relations strategies, tactics, and efforts even more important.

In addition, the environment that political organizations face is more complex than that of many other organizations. It is more heterogeneous, unstable, dispersed, turbulent, and characterized by conflicts and dissensus than that of other types of organizations, further increasing the importance of and challenges facing political public relations.

The Importance of Relationships in Political Public Relations

One of the key characteristics of many definitions of public relations—including our own definition of political public relations—is the importance assigned to relationships with key publics. As noted by Jackson (2010, p. 3), the relational approached has gained currency over the years, and "interprets public relations by inverting the components of the term 'public relations,' so that it is relations with publics." The idea as such is not new, however; Kelley (1956) decades ago stressed the importance of relationships in public relations.

Nevertheless, the relational perspective is closely associated with the cocreational turn in public relations theory and research, and holds that "public relations is a professional practice that helps organizations and publics to under stand each other's interests. Once these interests are understood, efforts can be made to blend them or at least reduce the conflict by helping the publics and the organizations to be less antagonistic toward each other" (Heath, 2001b, p. 3). The rise of the relational perspective helped to move public relations from an emphasis on influencing opinion through propaganda and persuasion toward an emphasis on establishing, building, and maintaining relationships that, purportedly, are mutually beneficial to an organization and its publics (Ledingham, 2006; Ledingham & Bruning, 2000).

This is not to say that persuasion and opinion formation is mutually opposed to relationship management or public relations in general: persuasion as the use of communication in attempts to influence perceptions, affect, cognitions, and behavior is an intrinsic part of all public relations and political communication processes (Pfau & Wan, 2006). It is rather to say that from a relational perspective, public relations success is not measured primarily by communication output or influence on the opinions of various publics, but by the quality of the relationships between an organization and its publics. High quality relationships are those characterized by features such as trust, control mutuality, satisfaction, openness, involvement, investment, and commitment (J. Grunig, 2002; J. Grunig & Huang, 2000; Hon & J. Grunig, 1999; Ledingham, 2006; Ledingham & Bruning, 2000).

While the relational approach is equally valid and applicable in the context of political public relations as in corporate public relations, it is again important to note that the political environment tends to be more contentious and conflictual than the environment of many other organizations (Sellers, 2010). Conflicts, often enduring due to incompatible values and interests, are at the heart of politics. This makes relationship management both more important and more difficult in political contexts, increasing the stakes involved when selecting key publics and finding strategies to approach active and hostile publics. This is particularly the case, as organizations cannot always choose their publics; the publics oftentimes choose them.

Although the goal for organizations is to establish, build, and maintain quality relationships with key publics, oftentimes—and perhaps particularly in political contexts—organizations might find themselves in a situation with a complex set of relationships which range from mutually beneficial to outright hostile (Sellers, 2010). All these relationships have to be managed somehow, however, particularly with aware and active publics.

In this context, the contingency theory of public relations is relevant. This theory has been developed mainly by Cancel and Cameron with colleagues (Cancel, Cameron, Sallot, & Mitrook, 1997; Cancel, Mitrook, & Cameron, 1999; Jin & Cameron, 2007; Mitrook, Parish, & Seltzer, 2008), as an alternative to the excellence theory mainly explicated by J. Grunig and colleagues (J. Grunig, 1992, 2001; J. Grunig & Hunt, 1984; J. Grunig & L. Grunig, 1992).

According to J. Grunig, four different models of public relations can be distinguished: (a) the press agentry/publicity model, (b) the public information model, (c) the two-way asymmetric model, and (d) the two-way symmetric model. The functional purpose of public relations varies across these models. In the press agentry/publicity model, public relations serves a propaganda purpose. The task at hand for public relations practitioners is to maximize positive publicity, minimize negative publicity, and shape public opinion through publicity, propaganda, and persuasion. In the public information model, the purpose of public relations is to disseminate information. Both of these models presuppose one-way communication from organizations to their publics, and there is not much room for or interest in feedback. In the two-way asymmetric model, the purpose of public relations is what J. Grunig and Hunt (1984) describe as "scientific persuasion"; here practitioners "use what is known from social science theory and research about attitudes and behavior to persuade publics to accept the organization's point of view and to behave in a way that supports the organization" (p. 22). Feedback is important, but mainly to provide information that can be used in further activities to persuade publics to accept the organization's point of view. In the two-way symmetrical model, in contrast, the purpose of public relations is to achieve mutual understanding between an organization and its publics. The organization and its publics are perceived as equals, and the balance of power is symmetrical.

According to excellence theory, the two-way symmetrical model is normatively superior to the other models, and it is also the most effective model: As claimed by J. Grunig (2008), "excellent public relations departments use the two-way symmetrical model and that as a result they more often meet the objectives of the communication and make the organization more effective" (p. 44). However, in practice, all models are utilized, with the two-way symmetrical model being one of the least followed models. Instead, the most common model still appears to be the publicity model (J. Grunig & L. Grunig, 1992), although there are differences across sectors in society. For example, in government agencies, the most common model is the public information model (J. Grunig, 2008; Lee, 2008).

There is not much research on these models in the context of political public relations, although it is reasonable to assume that there are differences across political organizations and contexts. For example, during political campaigns, the publicity and two-way asymmetrical models are likely to be more common than the other models, whereas the two-way symmetrical model is more likely to be used in intraparty relationships, negotiations between parties and closely linked collateral organizations, and in actual policymaking processes. The application of game theory offers one tool for explaining situations and circumstances when different models are more dominant (Murphy, 1991).

In either case, according to the contingency theory, which public relations model is most appropriate and normatively appealing cannot be decided out of context. Instead, it depends on the circumstances. As noted by Cancel et al. (1997),

> The practice of public relations is too complex, too fluid, and impinged by far too many variables for the academy to force it into the four boxes known as the four models of public relations. Even worse, to promulgate one of the four boxes as the best and most effective model not only tortures the reality of practicing public relations but has problems, even as a normative theory. It fails to capture the complexity and multiplicity of the public relations environment.

(pp. 23–33)

Instead, the contingency theory posits that the practice of public relations moves on a continuum from total advocacy for an organization to total accommodation of a public (Cancel et al., 1997; Cancel, Mitrook, & Cameron, 1999; Shin, Cameron, & Cropp, 2006). The different degrees of advocacy or accommodation represent many different roles that an organization might assume when dealing with an individual public. In some cases, total advocacy is the most appropriate strategy, whereas in other cases, total accommodation is more appropriate, and none of these positions is inherently superior to the others. Both empirically and normatively, it depends on the situation and the context. Some situational factors that are important are the urgency of the situation, characteristics of the public, potential costs and benefits of different strategies, whether there is a threat toward the organization, general or specific public perceptions of the issue under question, characteristics of the public's claims or actions, and feasibility of accommodation (Cancel et al., 1999).

In the context of political public relations this theory is highly relevant, due to the complexity of the various publics, claims, and actions that political organizations face. In some cases accommodation might be a possible strategy, but in other cases it might be counterproductive and decrease the organization's opportunities to achieve its goals (Sellers, 2010). As the appropriate strategy always "depends," the importance of environmental scanning and the identification and segmentation of publics can hardly be overstated.

What this discussion suggests is that there are a number of theories in public relations that seldom have but could be applied in research on political public relations. Such research could help inform public relations as well as political communication and political science theory and research. To what extent the theories are equally valid in political as in other contexts is an open and ultimately empirical question, which is yet another reason for why it is important to encourage more integrative research on political public relations.

This is not to say that there is no research on the purposeful communication of politics. On the contrary, as noted earlier there is an abundance of research on strategic political communication, political campaigning, political marketing, and news management in political contexts. In the next section, we will discuss some of this research and how it fits into our conceptualization of political public relations.

Strategic Political Communication and Political Public Relations

Aside from political marketing already discussed, there exists an extensive body of research on political campaigning in different countries. While some of this research focuses on the professionalization of political campaigning in general (Negrine, Mancini, Holtz-Bacha, & Papathanassopoulos, 2007; Swanson & Mancini, 1996) or as measured through the use of different campaign techniques (Gibson & Römmele, 2001, 2009; Strömbäck, 2009), other research focuses on the increasing use and management of political consultants—primarily although not exclusively in the United States (Bohne, Prevost, & Thurber, 2009; Johnson, 2009a; Nimmo, 2001; Plasser & Plasser, 2002; Sussman, 2005; Thurber & Nelson, 2000). There is also an extensive literature on different campaign strategies or tactics such as, for example, the use of political advertising (Kaid & Holtz-Bacha, 2006; Kaid & Johnston, 2001), negative campaigning (Buell & Sigelman, 2008; Geer, 2006; Lau & Pomper, 2004), voter segmentation (Shaw, 2006), and the use of wedge issues (Hillygus & Shields, 2008). The literature on Internet and social media in political communication and campaign processes is also growing rapidly (Davis, 2009; Foot & Schneider, 2006; Harfoush, 2009; Perlmutter, 2008; Ward, Owen, Davis, & Taras, 2008).

Moreover, there are a number of books that present a more holistic depiction of election campaigns and characteristics of purposive political communication processes (Kavanagh, 1995; Medvic, 2010; Negrine, 2008; Sanders, 2009; Trent & Friedenberg, 2004). In countries such as the United Kingdom (Kavanagh & Butler, 2005; Norris & Wlezien, 2005) and the United States (Ceaser, Busch, & Pitney, 2009; Johnson, 2009b), a number of books are also usually published after each election, attempting to describe and analyze the election campaigns as such, their dynamics and importance for vote results.

Outside of election campaigns, there is also extensive research on the U.S. presidency from a communication perspective. Included here is research on, for example, "going public" as a strategy for building public support and pressure on lawmakers (Kernell, 2007), the organization of the White House communications operations (Kumar, 2007), and the use of speeches for signaling the president's preferences to other actors in the policy processes (Eshbaugh-Soha, 2006).

All of this research, plus of course the extensive literature on news management and media relations (Davis, 2002; Entman, 2004; Franklin, 2004; Manning, 2001; Skewes, 2007), as well as message and framing strategies in political communication processes (Domke & Coe, 2008; Schaffner & Sellers, 2010; Sellers, 2010; Vavreck, 2009), is relevant in the context of political public relations. The same is true of the extensive literature on attitude formation, persuasion and propaganda (Ajzen, 2005, Albarracin, Johnson, & Zanna, 2005; Eagly & Chaiken, 1993; Jowett & O'Donnell, 1999; Petty & Cacioppo, 1987) and on media effects (Iyengar, 1991; Iyengar & Kinder, 1987; Kinder, 2003; McCombs, 2004; Preiss, Gayle, Burrell, Allen, & Bryant, 2007). In one way or another, all of this research is, *directly* or *indirectly*, linked with or conditions political public relations.

While it is beyond the scope of this book to investigate all the theories, contexts, linkages, and processes that are relevant in the context of political public relations, the ambition has been to include chapters that cover the most important areas and aspects of political public relations. In the next section, we will describe the outline of the book. Before that, we only wish to reiterate one of the central premises of this book; what matters is not in which field of research different theories have originated and been applied. What matters is rather whether different theories can cast further light on and increase our understanding of the management process by which an organization or individual actor for political purposes, through purposeful communication and action, seeks to influence and to establish, build, and maintain beneficial relationships and reputations with its key publics to help support its mission and achieve its goals.

Outline of the Book

In this chapter, we have introduced our definition of political public relations and made an attempt to map this emergent field of research. As already noted, political public relations actually has a long and prominent history, which is reflected in a number of classic works and theories. In chapter 2, "Political Public Relations: Remembering Its Roots and Classics," Diana Knott Martinelli revisits a selected number of classics, and traces the roots of political public relations. After that follow two chapters that focus on the role of the media in political public relations: In chapter 3, "Political Public Relations, News Management and Agenda Indexing," Paul S. Lieber and Guy Golan review theory and research on news management and media relations, and develop the concept of agenda indexing. In chapter 4, "Political Public Relations and Agenda-Building," John C. Tedesco continues by reviewing theory and research on agenda–building processes in the context of political public relations, and the importance and role of information subsidies.

Perhaps the most important and resourceful office involved in political public relations is the U.S. presidency, and in chapter 5, Matthew Eshbaugh-Soha reviews and analyzes theory and research on "Presidential Public Relations." This chapter shows that political public relations is crucial not only in election campaigning, but also as part of governing processes. Nevertheless, there is no doubt that political public relations is an important and intrinsic part of contemporary election campaigning. Therefore in chapter 6, Paul Baines explores "Political Public Relations and Election Campaigning," with a particular focus on the cases of the United Kingdom and the United States.

Public relations in political contexts is often associated with political parties and candidates, but corporations are another highly important set of actors also involved in political public relations. This is the focus of chapter 7, by Robert L. Heath and Damion Waymer, which reviews theory and research on "Corporate Issues Management and Political Public Relations."

A nice illustration of the close linkages between political and corporate or commercial spheres of activities is the development of political marketing, a field of theory and practice closely related to political public relations. The relationship between political public relations and political marketing and their parent disciplines is the focus of chapter 8 by Darren Lilleker and Nigel Jackson: "Political Public Relations and Political Marketing."

One highly important aspect of all political and public relations processes is the framing of messages, events, and processes, and framing theory has become one of the most applied theories in political communication research during the last decade. Against this background, in chapter 9 Kirk Hallahan reviews theory and research on framing and analyzes how framing applies in the context of "Political Public Relations and Strategic Framing."

A ubiquitous and largely unavoidable part of all politics is crises. This is of course true not only of politics, but there are some features that make crisis communication and management in political contexts differ from corporate or commercial contexts. Against this background, chapter 10 by Timothy Coombs, "Political Public Relations and Crisis Communication: A Public Relations Perspective," reviews and analyzes theory and research on crisis communication and management, and how that applies to political public relations.

One crucial aspect of all public relations is the notion of relationships, and relationships are undoubtedly crucial in political as well as in other contexts. Relationship theory has also evolved to become one of the most prominent public relations theories—although too seldom applied to political contexts. To remedy this, chapter 11 by John A. Ledingham reviews and analyzes theory and research on "Political Public Relations and Relationship Management."

Chapter 12 by Karen Sanders focuses on "Political Public Relations and Government Communication." This is another strangely neglected area of theory and research, without even an established definition of government communication, particularly considering the democratic, practical, and normative importance and implications of government communication. Like the other chapters, this one thus fills an important gap in the literature.

Like public relations in general, political public relations is not confined only to domestic contexts. It is also an important part of international public relations and public diplomacy, and aside from governments, transnational corporations may be among the most important international actors involved in global political public relations and public diplomacy. Based on this, chapter 13 by Juan-Carlos Molleda focuses on "Global Political Public Relations, Public Diplomacy, and Corporate Foreign Policy."

This is followed by chapter 14, which focuses on one of the most rapidly evolving fields of both theory and practice in the contexts of political communication and political public relations: "Digital Political Public Relations." In this chapter, Kaye Sweetser explores how digital media have been used in different political public relations contexts, ranging from election campaigns to e-government.

In the final chapter, "Political Public Relations Research in the Future," we identify some of the common themes of the other chapters that can be used to inform future research and to identify some potential domains that call for further attention in political public relations research. In addition, we also develop a conceptualization of political public relations along a continuum of stakeholder engagement, with reputation and relationship quality at each end of the continuum. This conceptualization highlights that political public relations is critical to all stages of stakeholder engagement, that it involves both short-term and long-term interactions between organizations and key stakeholders, and that political public relations is not limited to simple information dissemination of media relations.

To reiterate our definition: Political public relations is the management process by which an organization or individual actor for political purposes, through purposeful communication and action, seeks to influence and to establish, build, and maintain beneficial relationships and reputations with its key publics to help support its mission and achieve its goals. Taken together, the chapters in this volume clearly show the applicability of this definition, across different domains, types of political organizations, contexts, and processes.

References

Ajzen, I. (2005). *Attitudes, personality and behavior* (2nd ed.). London: Open University Press.

Albarracin, D., Johnson, B. T., & Zanna, M. P. (Eds.). (2005). *The handbook of attitudes*. Mahwah, NJ: Erlbaum.

Aula, P., & Mantere, S. (2008). *Strategic reputation management*. New York: Routledge.

Baines, P. R. (1999). Voter segmentation and candidate positioning. In B. I. Newman, (Ed.), *Handbook of political marketing* (pp. 403–420). Thousand Oaks, CA: Sage.

Baines, P., Egan, J., & Jefkins, F. (2004). *Public relations: Contemporary issues and techniques*. Oxford, England: Butterworth-Heinemann.

Bennett, L. W., & Entman, R. M. (Eds.). (2001). *Mediated politics*. New York: Cambridge University Press.

Bernays, E. L. (1923). *Crystallizing public opinion*. New York: Boni & Liveright.

Bernays, E. L. (1952). *Public relations*. Norman: University of Oklahoma Press.

Blumenthal, S. (1980). *The permanent campaign: Inside the world of elite political operatives*. Boston, MA: Beacon Press.

Blumler, J. G., & Gurevitch, M. (1975). Towards a comparative framework for political communication research. In S. H. Chaffee (Ed.), *Political communication: Issues and strategies for research* (pp. 165–193). Beverly Hills, CA: Sage.

Blumler, J. G., & Gurevitch, M. (1995). *The crisis of public communication*. London: Routledge.

Bohne, M., Prevost, A. K., & Thurber, J. A. (2009). Campaign consultants and political parties today. In D. W. Johnson (Ed.), *Routledge handbook of political management* (pp. 497–508). New York: Routledge.

Botan, C. H. (2006). Grand strategy, strategy, and tactics in public relations. In C. H. Botan & V. Hazleton (Eds.), *Public relations theory II* (pp. 223–247). New York: Erlbaum.

Botan, C. H., & Hazleton, V. (Eds.). (2006). *Public relations theory II*. New York: Erlbaum.

Botan, C. H., & Taylor, M. (2004). Public relations: State of the field. *Journal of Communication, 54*(4), 645–661.

Buell, E. H., Jr., & Sigelman, L. (2008). *Attack politics: Negativity in presidential campaigns since 1960*. Lawrence: University Press of Kansas.

Cancel A. E., Cameron, G. T., Sallot, L., & Mitrook, M. A. (1997). It depends: A contingency theory of accommodation in public relations. *Journal of Public Relations Research, 9*(1), 31–63.

Cancel A. E., Mitrook, M. A., & Cameron, G. T. (1999). Testing the contingency theory of accommodation in public relations. *Public Relations Review, 25*(2), 171–197.

Carroll, C., & McCombs, M. (2003). Agenda-setting effects of business news on the public's images and opinions about major corporations. *Corporate Reputation Review, 6,* 36–46.

Castells, M. (2009). *Communication power.* New York: Oxford University Press.

Ceaser, J. W., Busch, A. E., & Pitney Jr., J. J. (2009). *Epic journey: The 2008 elections and American politics.* Lanham, MD: Rowman & Littlefield.

Christopher, M., Payne, A., & Ballantyne, D. (2002). *Relationship marketing: Creating stakeholder value.* Oxford, England: Butterworth-Heinemann.

Coombs, W. T. (1999). *Ongoing crisis communication: Planning, managing, and responding.* Thousand Oaks, CA: Sage.

Coombs, W. T., & Holladay, S. J. (2007). *It's not just PR: Public relations in society.* Malden, MA: Blackwell.

Cutlip, S. M. (1995). *Public relations history: From the 17th to the 20th century.* New York: Routledge.

Cutlip, S. M., Center, A. H., & Broom, G. M. (2000). *Effective public relations* (8th ed.). Upper Saddle River, NJ: Prentice Hall.

Dalton, R. J., & Wattenberg, M. P. (Eds.). (2000). *Parties without partisans: Political change in advanced industrial democracies.* New York: Oxford University Press.

Davis, A. (2002). *Public relations democracy: Public relations, politics and the mass media in Britain.* Manchester, England: Manchester University Press.

Davis, R. (2009). *Typing politics: The role of blogs in American politics.* New York: Oxford University Press.

De Bussy, N. (2008). Applying stakeholder thinking to public relations: An integrated approach to identifying relationships that matter. In B. van Ruler, A. T. Verčič, & D. Verčič (Eds.), *Public relations metrics: Research and evaluation* (pp. 282–300). New York: Routledge.

Dewey, J. (1927). *The public and its problems.* Chicago, IL: Swallow.

Domke, D., & Coe, K. (2008). *The god strategy: How religion became a political weapon in America.* New York: Oxford University Press.

Donsbach, W., & Traugott, M. W. (2008). Introduction. In W. Donsbach & M. W. Traugott (Eds.), *The Sage handbook of public opinion research* (pp. 1–5). London: Sage.

Dozier, D. M. (1992). The organizational roles of communications and public relations practitioners. In J. E. Grunig (Ed.), *Excellence in public relations and communication management* (pp. 327–355). Hillsdale, NJ: Erlbaum.

Dozier, D. M., & Broom, G. M. (2006). The centrality of practitioner roles to public relations theory. In C. H. Botan & V. Hazleton (Eds.), *Public relations theory II* (pp. 137–170). New York: Erlbaum.

Dozier, D. M., & Ehling, W. P. (1992). Evaluation of public relations programs: What the literature tells us about their effects. In J. E. Grunig (Ed.), *Excellence in public relations and communication management* (pp. 159–184). Hillsdale, NJ: Erlbaum.

Dozier, D. M., & Grunig, L. A. (1992). The organization of the public relations function. In J E. Grunig (Ed.), *Excellence in public relations and communication management* (pp. 395–417). Hillsdale, NJ: Erlbaum.

Dozier, D. M., & Repper, F. C. (1992). Research firms and public relations practices. In J. E. Grunig (Ed.), *Excellence in public relations and communication management* (pp. 185–215). Hillsdale, NJ: Erlbaum.

Dulio, D. A., & Towner, T. L. (2009). The permanent campaign. In D. W. Johnson (Ed.), *Routledge handbook of political management* (pp. 83–97). New York: Routledge.

Eagly, A. H., & Chaiken, S. (1993). *The psychology of attitudes.* Belmont, CA: Thomson Wadsworth.

Ehling, W. P., White, J., & Grunig, J. E. (1992). Public relations and marketing practices. In J. E. Grunig (Ed.), *Excellence in public relations and communication management* (pp. 357–393). Hillsdale, NJ: Erlbaum.

Entman, R. M. (2004). *Projections of power: Framing news, public opinion, and U.S. foreign policy.* Chicago, IL: University of Chicago Press.

Eshbaugh-Soha, M. (2006). *The president's speeches: Beyond "going public."* Boulder, CO: Rienner.

Esser, F., & Pfetsch, B. (Eds.). (2004). *Comparing political communication: Theories, cases, and challenges.* New York: Cambridge University Press.

Farnsworth, S. J. (2009). *Spinner in chief: How presidents sell their policies and themselves.* Boulder, CO: Paradigm.

Foot, K. A., & Schneider, S. M. (2006). *Web campaigning.* Cambridge, MA: MIT Press.

Franklin, B. (2004). *Packaging politics: Political communications in Britain's media democracy* (2nd ed.). London: Arnold.

Froehlich, R., & Rüdiger, B. (2006). Framing political public relations: Measuring success of political communication strategies in Germany. *Public Relations Review, 32,* 18–25.

Geer, J. G. (1996). *From tea leaves to opinion polls: A theory of democratic leadership.* New York: Columbia University Press.

Geer, J. G. (2006). *In defense of negativity: Attack ads in presidential campaigns.* Chicago, IL: University of Chicago Press.

Gibson, R. K., & Römmele, A. (2001). Changing campaign communications: A party-centered theory of professionalized campaigning. *Harvard International Journal of Press/Politics, 6*(4), 31–43.

Gibson, R. K., & Römmele, A. (2009). Measuring the professionalization of political campaigning. *Party Politics, 15*(3), 265–293.

Gotsi, M., & Wilson, A. M. (2001). Corporate reputation: Seeking a definition. *Corporate Communications, 6,* 24–30.

Grunig, J. E. (Ed.). (1992). *Excellence in public relations and communication management.* Hillsdale, NJ: Erlbaum.

Grunig, J. E. (2001). Two-way symmetrical public relations: Past, present, future. In R. L. Heath (Ed.), *Handbook of public relations* (pp. 11–30). Thousand Oaks, CA: Sage.

Grunig, J. E. (2002). *Qualitative methods for assessing relationships between organizations and publics.* Gainesville, FL: Institute for Public Relations.

Grunig, J. E. (2008). Public relations management in government and business. In M. Lee (Ed.), *Government public relations: A reader* (pp. 21–64). Boca Raton, FL: CRC Press.

Grunig, J. E., & Grunig, L. A. (1992). Models of public relations and communication. In J. E. Grunig (Ed.), *Excellence in public relations and communication management* (pp. 285–325). Hillsdale, NJ: Erlbaum.

Grunig, J. E., & Huang, Y-H. (2000). From organizational effectiveness to relationship indicators: Antecedents of relationships, public relations strategies, and relationship outcomes. In J. A. Ledingham & S. D. Bruning (Eds.), *Public relations as relationship management: A relational approach to the study and practice of public relations* (pp. 55–69). Mahwah, NJ: Erlbaum.

Grunig, J. E., & Hunt, T. (1984). *Managing public relations.* Belmont, CA: Thomson Wadsworth.

Grunig, J. E., & Repper, F. C. (1992). Strategic management, publics, and issues. In J. E. Grunig (Ed.), *Excellence in public relations and communication management* (pp. 117–157). Hillsdale, NJ: Erlbaum.

Grunig, L. A., Grunig, J. E., & Ehling, W. P. (1992). What is an effective organization. In J. E. Grunig (Ed.), *Excellence in public relations and communication management* (pp. 65–90). Hillsdale, NJ: Erlbaum.

Grönroos, C. (2000). *Service management and marketing: A customer relationship management approach.* Chichester, England: Wiley.

Gummesson, E. (1999). *Total relationship marketing: Marketing management, relationship strategy and CRM approaches for the network economy* (2nd ed.). Oxford, England: Butterworth-Heinemann.

Gunther, R., & Mughan, A. (Eds.). (2000). *Democracy and the media: A comparative perspective.* New York: Cambridge University Press.

Hallahan, K., Holtzhausen, D., van Ruler, B., Verčič, D., & Sriramesh, K. (2007). Defining strategic communication. *International Journal of Strategic Communication, 1*(1), 3–35.

Hallin, D. C., & Mancini, P. (2004). *Comparing media systems: Three models of media and politics.* New York: Cambridge University Press.

Harfoush, R. (2009). *Yes we did: An inside look at how social media built the Obama brand.* Berkeley, CA: New Riders.

Harlow, R. F. (1976). Building a public relations definition. *Public Relations Review, 2*(4), 34–42.

Harmel, R., & Janda, K. (1994). An integrated theory of party goals and party change. *Journal of Theoretical Politics, 6*(3), 259–287.

Harris, P., & Fleisher, C. S. (Eds.). (2005). *The handbook of public affairs.* London: Sage.

Heath, R. L. (Ed.). (2001a). *Handbook of public relations.* Thousand Oaks, CA: Sage.

Heath, R. L. (2001b). Shifting foundations: Public relations as relationship building. In R. L. Heath (Ed.), *Handbook of public relations* (pp. 1–9). Thousand Oaks, CA: Sage.

Heath, R. L. (2006). A rhetorical approach to issues management. In C. H. Botan & V. Hazleton (Eds.), *Public relations theory II* (pp. 63–99). New York: Erlbaum.

Hillygus, D. S., & Shields, T. G. (2008). *The persuadable voter: Wedge issues in presidential campaigns.* Princeton, NJ: Princeton University Press.

Hon, L. C., & Grunig, J. E. (1999). *Guidelines for measuring relationships in public relations.* Gainesville, FL: Institute for Public Relations.

Hutton, J. G., Goodman, M. B., Alexander, J. B., & Genest, C. M. (2001). Reputation management: The new face of corporate public relations? *Public Relations Review, 27*(3), 247.

Iyengar, S. (1991). *Is anyone responsible? How television frames political issues.* Chicago, IL: University of Chicago Press.

Iyengar, S., & Kinder, D. R. (1987). *News that matters: Television and American opinion.* Chicago, IL: University of Chicago Press.

Jackson, N. (2010, April). *Political public relations: Spin, persuasion or reputation building?* Paper presented at the Political Studies Association Annual Conference, Edinburgh, Scotland.

Jacobson, G. C. (2007). *A divider, not a uniter: George W. Bush and the American people.* New York: Pearson Longman.

Jin, Y., & Cameron, G. T. (2007). The effects of threat type and duration on public relations practitioner's cognitive, affective, and conative responses in crisis situations. *Journal of Public Relations Research, 19*(3), 255–281.

Johnson, D. W. (2007). *No place for amateurs. How political consultants are reshaping American democracy* (2nd ed.). New York: Routledge.

Johnson, D. W. (Ed.). (2009a). *Routledge handbook of political management.* New York: Routledge.

Johnson, D. W. (Ed.). (2009b). *Campaigning for president 2008: Strategies and tactics, new voices and new techniques.* New York: Routledge.

Jowett, G. S., & O'Donnell, V. (1999). *Propaganda and persuasion* (3rd ed.). London: Sage.

Kaid, L. L., & Holtz-Bacha, C. (Eds.). (2006). *The Sage handbook of political advertising.* London: Sage.

Kaid, L. L., & Johnston, A. (2001). *Videostyle in presidential campaigns: Style and content of televised political advertising.* Westport, CT: Praeger.

Katz, R. S., & Crotty, W. (2006). Introduction. In R. S. Katz & W. Crotty (Eds.), *Handbook of party politics* (pp. 1–4). London: Sage.

Katz, R. S., & Kolodny, R. (1994). Party organization as an empty vessel: Parties in American politics. In R. S. Katz & P. Mair (Eds.), *How parties organize: Change and adaptation in party organizations in western democracies* (pp. 23–50). London: Sage.

Kavanagh, D. (1995). *Election campaigning: The new marketing of politics.* Oxford, England: Blackwell.

Kavanagh, D., & Butler, D. (2005). *The British general election of 2005.* Basingstoke, England: Palgrave Macmillan.

Kelley, Jr., S. (1956). *Professional public relations and political power.* Baltimore, MD: John Hopkins University Press.

Kernell, S. (2007). *Going public. New strategies of presidential leadership* (4th ed.). Washington, DC: CQ Press.

Key, V. O. (1964). *Politics, parties and pressure groups* (5th ed.). New York: Crowell.

Kinder, D. R. (2003). Communication and politics in the age of information. In D. O. Sears, L. Huddy, & R. Jervis (Eds.), *Oxford handbook of political psychology* (pp. 357–393). New York: Oxford University Press.

Kiousis, S., Popescu, C., & Mitrook, M. (2007). Understanding influence on corporate reputation: An examination of public relations efforts, media coverage, public opinion, and financial performance from an agenda-building and agenda-setting perspective. *Journal of Public Relations Research, 19,* 147–165.

Kiousis, S., & Strömbäck, J. (2010). The White House and public relations: Examining the linkages between presidential communications and public opinion. *Public Relations Review, 36*(1), 7–14.

Kotler, P., & Kotler, N. (1999). Political marketing: Generating effective candidates, campaigns, and causes. In B. I. Newman (Eds.), *Handbook of political marketing* (pp. 3–18). Thousand Oaks, CA: Sage.

Kumar, M. J. (2007). *Managing the president's message: The White House communications operation.* Baltimore, MD: John Hopkins University Press.

Lamme, M. O., & Russell, K. M. (2010). Removing the spin: Toward a new theory of public relations research. *Journalism & Communication Monographs, 11*(4), 281–362.

Lasswell, H. D. (1936). *Politics: Who gets what, when, how.* New York: McGraw-Hill.

Lau, R. R., & Pomper, G. M. (2004). *Negative campaigning: An analysis of U.S. senate elections.* Lanham, MD: Rowman & Littlefield.

Lavrakas, P. J., & Traugott, M. W. (Eds.). (2000), *Election polls, the news media, and democracy.* New York: Chatham House.

Ledingham, J. A. (2006). Relationship management: A general theory of public relations. In C. H. Botan & V. Hazleton (Eds.), *Public relations theory II* (pp. 465–483). New York: Erlbaum.

Ledingham, J. A., & Bruning, S. D. (Eds.). (2000). *Public relations as relationship management: A relational approach to the study and practice of public relations.* Mahwah, NJ: Erlbaum.

Lee, M. (Ed.) (2008). *Government public relations: A reader.* Boca Raton, FL: CRC Press.

Lees-Marshment, J. (2001). *Political marketing and British political parties: The party's just begun.* Manchester, England: Manchester University Press.

Lees-Marshment, J. (2004). *The political marketing revolution: Transforming the government of the UK.* Manchester, England: Manchester University Press.

Lees-Marshment, J. (2009). *Political marketing: Principles and applications.* London: Routledge.

Lees-Marshment, J., Strömbäck, J., & Rudd, C. (Eds.). (2009). *Global political marketing.* London: Routledge.

L'Etang, J. (2008). *Public relations: Concepts, practice and critique.* London: Sage.

Lilleker, D. G., & Lees-Marshment, J. (Eds.). (2005). *Political marketing: A comparative perspective.* Manchester, England: Manchester University Press.

Lippmann, W. (1997). *Public opinion.* New York: Free Press. (Original work published 1922)

Liu, B. F., & Horsley, J. S. (2007). The government communication decision wheel: Toward a public relations model for the public sector. *Journal of Public Relations Research, 19*(4), 377–393.

Manning, P. (2001). *News and news sources: A critical introduction.* London: Sage.

McCombs, M. (2004). *Setting the agenda: The mass media and public opinion.* Cambridge, England: Polity.

McKie, D. (2001). Updating public relations: "New science," research paradigms, and uneven developments. In R. L. Heath (Ed.), *Handbook of public relations* (pp. 75–91). Thousand Oaks, CA: Sage.

McKinnon, L. M., Tedesco, J. C., & Lauder, T. (2001). Political power through public relations. In R. L. Heath (Ed.), *Handbook of public relations* (pp. 557–563). Thousand Oaks, CA: Sage.

McLeod, J. M., Kosicki, G. M., & McLeod, D. M. (1994). The expanding boundaries of political communication effects. In J. Bryant & D. Zillman (Eds.), *Media effects: Advances in theory and research* (pp. 123–162). Hillsdale, NJ: Erlbaum.

McNair, B. (2000). *Journalism and democracy. An evaluation of the political public sphere.* London: Routledge.

McNair, B. (2003). *An introduction to political communication* (3rd ed.). London: Routledge.

McNair, B. (2004). PR must die: Spin, anti-spin and political public relations in the UK, 1997–2004. *Journalism Studies, 5*(3), 325–338.

Medvic, S. K. (2010). *Campaigns and elections: Players and processes.* Boston, MA: Wadsworth.

Mitchell, P., & Daves, R. (1999). Media polls, candidates, and campaigns. In B. I. Newman (Ed.), *Handbook of political marketing* (pp. 177–195). Thousand Oaks, CA: Sage.

Mitrook, M. A., Parish, N. B., & Seltzer, T. (2008). From advocacy to accommodation: A case study of the Orlando Magic's public relations efforts to secure a new arena. *Public Relations Review, 34,* 161–168.

Moloney, K. (2006). *Rethinking public relations* (2nd ed.). London: Routledge.

Montero, J. R., & Gunther, R. (2002). Introduction: Reviewing and reassessing parties. In R. Gunther, J. R. Montero, & J. J. Linz (Eds.), *Political parties: Old concepts and new challenges* (pp. 1–35). New York: Oxford University Press.

Murphy, P. (1991). The limits of symmetry: A game theory approach to symmetric and asymmetric public relations. *Public Relations Research Annual, 3,* 115–133.

Negrine, R. (2008). *The transformation of political communication: Continuities and changes in media and politics.* New York: Palgrave Macmillan.

Negrine, R., Mancini, P., Holtz-Bacha, C., & Papathanassopoulos, S. (Eds.). (2007). *The professionalisation of political communication.* Bristol, England: Intellect.

Newman, B. I. (1994). *The marketing of the president: Political marketing as campaign strategy.* Thousand Oaks, CA: Sage.

Newman, B. I. (1999). Preface. In B. I. Newman (Ed.), *Handbook of political marketing* (pp. xiii–xiv). Thousand Oaks, CA: Sage.

Newman, B. I., & Verčič, D. (Eds.) (2002). *Communication of politics: Cross-cultural theory building in the practice of public relations and political marketing.* New York: Haworth Press.

Newsom, D., Turk, J. V., & Kruckeberg, D. (2010). *This is PR: The realities of public relations* (10th ed.). Boston, MA: Wadsworth.

Newton, K., & van Deth, J. W. (2005). *Foundations of comparative politics.* Cambridge, England: Cambridge University Press.

Nimmo, D. (2001). *Political persuaders: The techniques of modern election campaigns.* New Brunswick, NJ: Transaction.

Nimmo, D., & Combs, J. E. (1983). *Mediated political realities.* New York: Longman.

Norris, P., & Wlezien, C. (Eds.). (2005). *Britain votes 2005.* Oxford, England: Oxford University Press.

O'Cass, A. (1996). Political marketing and the marketing concept. *European Journal of Marketing, 30*(10/11), 37–53.

Ormrod, R. P. (2009). *Understanding political market orientation.* Aarhus, Denmark: Aarhus School of Business, University of Aarhus.

O'Shaughnessy, N. J., & Henneberg, S. C. M. (Eds.). (2002). *The idea of political marketing.* Westport, CT: Praeger.

Palmer, J. (2000). *Spinning into control: News values and source strategies.* London: Leicester University Press.

Perlmutter, D. D. (2008). *Blog wars.* New York: Oxford University Press.

Petersson, O., Djerf-Pierre, M., Holmberg, S., Strömbäck, J., & Weibull, L. (2006). *Media and elections in Sweden.* Stockholm, Sweden: SNS Förlag.

Petrocik, J. R., Benoit, W. L., & Hansen, G. J. (2003). Issue ownership and presidential campaigning, 1952–2000. *Political Science Quarterly, 118*(4), 599–626.

Petty, R. E., & Cacioppo, J. T. (1981). *Attitudes and persuasion: Classic and contemporary approaches.* Boulder, CO: Westview Press.

Pfau, M., & Wan, H-H. (2006). Persuasion: An intrinsic function of public relations. In C. H. Botan & V. Hazleton (Eds.), *Public relations theory II* (pp. 101–136). New York: Erlbaum.

Plasser, F., & Plasser, G. (2002). *Global political campaigning: A worldwide analysis of campaign professionals and their practices.* Westport, CT: Praeger.

Poguntke, T. (2006). Political parties and other organizations. In R. S. Katz & W. Crotty (Eds.), *Handbook of party politics* (pp. 396–405). London: Sage.

Preiss, R. W., Gayle, B. M, Burrell, N., Allen, M., & Bryant, J. (Eds.). (2007). *Mass media effects research: Advances through meta-analysis.* Mahwah, NJ: Erlbaum.

Price, V. (1992). *Public opinion.* Thousand Oaks, CA: Sage.

Prior, M. (2007). *Post-broadcast democracy: How media choice increases inequality in political involvement and polarizes elections.* New York: Cambridge University Press.

Rozell, M. J., Wilcox, C., & Madland, D. (2006). *Interest groups in American campaigns: The new face of electioneering* (2nd ed.). Washington, DC: CQ Press.

Sanders, K. (2009). *Communicating politics in the twenty-first century.* Basingstoke, England: Palgrave Macmillan.

Scammell, M. (1995). *Designer politics: How elections are won.* London: Palgrave.

Schaffner, B. F., & Sellers, P. J. (Eds.). (2010). *Winning with words: The origins and impact of political framing.* New York: Routledge.

Sellers, P. J. (2010). *Cycles of spin: Strategic communication in the U.S. Congress.* New York: Cambridge University Press.

Shaw, D. R. (2006). *The race to 270: The Electoral College and the campaign strategies of 2000 and 2004.* Chicago, IL: University of Chicago Press.

Shin, J-H., Cameron, G. T., & Cropp, F. (2006). Occam's razor in the contingency theory: A national survey on 86 contingent variables. *Public Relations Review, 32,* 282–286.

Skewes, E. A. (2007). *Message control: How news is made on the presidential campaign trail.* Lanham, MD: Rowman & Littlefield.

Splichal, S. (Ed.). (2001). *Public opinion and democracy: Vox populi–Vox dei?* Cresskill, NJ: Hampton Press.

Stacks, D. W. (2004). Crisis management: Toward a multidimensional model of public relations. In D. P. Millar & R. L. Heath (Eds.), *Responding to crisis: A rhetorical approach to crisis communication* (pp. 37–49). Mahwah, NJ: Erlbaum.

Strom, K. (1990). A behavioral theory of competitive political parties. *American Journal of Political Science, 34*(2), 565–598.

Strömbäck, J. (2007). Political marketing and professionalized campaigning: A conceptual analysis. *Journal of Political Marketing, 6*(2/3), 49–67.

Strömbäck, J. (2009). Selective professionalisation of political campaigning: A test of the party-centred theory of professionalised campaigning in the context of the 2006 Swedish election. *Political Studies, 57*(1), 95–116.

Strömbäck, J., & Kaid, L. L. (Eds.). (2008). *Handbook of election news coverage around the world.* New York: Routledge.

Strömbäck, J., Mitrook, M. A., & Kiousis, S. (2010). Bridging two schools of thought: Applications of public relations theory to political marketing. *Journal of Political Marketing, 9*(1/2), 73–92.

Sussman, G. (2005). *Global electioneering: Campaign consulting, communications, and corporate financing.* Lanham, MD: Rowman & Littlefield.

Swanson, D. L., & Mancini, P. (Eds.). (1996). *Politics, media, and modern democracy: An international study of innovations in electoral campaigning and their consequences.* Westport, CA: Praeger.

Thompson, J. B. (2000). *Political scandal: Power and visibility in the media age.* Cambridge, England: Polity.

Thurber, J. A., & Nelson, C. J. (Eds.). (2000). *Campaign warriors: Political consultants in elections.* Washington, DC: Brookings Institution Press.

Toth, E. L. (2006). Building public affairs theory. In C. H. Botan & V. Hazleton (Eds.), *Public relations theory II* (pp. 499–522). New York: Erlbaum.

Trent, J. S., & Friedenberg, R. V. (2004). *Political campaign communication: Principles and practices* (5th ed.). Lanham, MD: Rowman & Littlefield.

Ulmer, R. R., Sellnow, T. L., & Seeger, M. W. (2007). *Effective crisis communication: Moving from crisis to opportunity.* Thousand Oaks, CA: Sage.

Vasquez, G. M., & Taylor, M. (2001). Research perspectives on "the public." In R. L. Heath (Ed.), *Handbook of public relations* (pp. 139–154). Thousand Oaks, CA: Sage.

Vavreck, L. (2009). *The message matters: The economy and presidential campaigns.* Princeton, NJ: Princeton University Press.

Ward, S., Owen, D., Davis, R., & Taras, D. (Eds.). (2008). *Making a difference: A comparative view of the role of the internet in election politics.* Lanham, MD: Lexington Books.

Ware, A. (1996). *Political parties and party systems.* Oxford, England: Oxford University Press.

Wartick, S. (1992). The relationship between intense media exposure and change in corporate reputation. *Business & Society, 31*, 33–49.

Weaver, D. H. (1980). Audience need for orientation and media effects. *Communication Research, 7*(3), 361–376.

Webb, P. (2002). Introduction: Political parties in advanced industrial democracies. In P. Webb, D. Farrell, & I. Holliday (Eds.), *Political parties in advanced industrial democracies* (pp. 1–15). New York: Oxford University Press.

White, J., & Dozier, D. M. (1992). Public relations and management decision making. In J. E. Grunig (Ed.), *Excellence in public relations and communication management* (pp. 91–108). Hillsdale, NJ: Erlbaum.

Wilcox, D. L., & Cameron, G. T. (2006). *Public relations: Strategies and tactics.* New York: Pearson Allyn & Bacon.

Witmer, D. F. (2006). Overcoming system and cultural boundaries: Public relations from a structuration perspective. In C. H. Botan & V. Hazleton (Eds.), *Public relations theory II* (pp. 375–392). New York: Erlbaum.

Wring, D. (2005). *The politics of marketing the labour party.* Basingstoke, England: Palgrave Macmillan.

Xifra, J. (2010). Linkages between public relations models and communication managers' roles in Spanish political parties. *Journal of Political Marketing, 9*(3), 167–185.

Zaller, J. R. (1992). *The nature and origins of mass opinion.* New York: Cambridge University Press.

Zipfel, A. (2008). Public relations, political. In L. L. Kaid & C. Holtz-Bacha (Eds.), *Encyclopedia of political communication* (Vol. 2, pp. 677–680). Thousand Oaks, CA: Sage.

Zoch, L. M., & Molleda, J-C. (2006). Building a theoretical model of media relations using framing, information subsidies, and agenda-building. In C. H. Botan & V. Hazleton (Eds.), *Public relations theory II* (pp. 279–309). New York: Erlbaum.

2

POLITICAL PUBLIC RELATIONS

Remembering Its Roots and Classics

Diana Knott Martinelli

Although many people who hear the term *political public relations* may think it is synonymous with *propaganda*, most public relations scholars today would strongly disagree. The latter term, coined in 1622 by the Catholic Church, was not originally associated with deception or "selective history," but it has become increasingly considered "subversive falsehood" (Miller, 2005). Indeed, propaganda in its negative sense has been part of government communications throughout the ages, and scholars have underscored the differences between it and political PR.

For example, Nelson (1996), who describes propaganda "as American as apple pie" (p. vii), notes that "propagandists often willingly lie" (p. ix), and L'Etang (2006) defines it as "monolithic communication on a grand scale that attempts to encompass all aspects of culture" (p. 24). By contrast, as stated by Strömbäck and Kiousis in chapter 1, modern political public relations aims to *build relationships* with others to help achieve political goals, and certainly long-term positive relationships cannot exist when one party aims to deceive, to overpower, or to isolate the other from the truth.

Taylor (2003) chronicled an early example of propaganda's corrosive influence on relationships, when he described how Caesar intentionally promulgated misleading military information, which came to threaten the aristocracy and ultimately contributed to his assassination. Still, it must be acknowledged that both means of communication—those that are intentionally biased and inaccurate and those that aim to persuade through honest debate and discussion—are used to help further political aims, and both have deep historical roots.

Many scholars have noted that political communication and its emphasis on persuasive messages extend back to at least the third century BCE in ancient

Greece, when Plato and Aristotle taught of the importance of skilled rhetoric. The latter's persuasive speech elements of *ethos, pathos,* and *logos* are still employed in campaigns today via the use of issue experts and emotional and logical appeals to resonate with, persuade, and build the support and loyalty of political audiences.

In fact, Denton (1997) argues that human interaction is the very essence of politics: "Such interaction may be formal or informal, verbal or nonverbal, public or private, but it is always persuasive, forcing us consciously or subconsciously to interpret, to evaluate, and to act" (Denton, 1997, p. xi). Indeed, it is communication that forms the heart of democracy and its free speech protection, which in turn forms the foundation for modern public relations, albeit from a Western perspective. That said, the author of this chapter acknowledges the need for, as T. Bender (2006) describes it: "a history of a nation that is attentive to, perhaps even shaped by, an awareness that a national history is part of a larger history, that it is, so to speak, a province in a larger global human community and history" (p. 277).

As John Milton wrote in *Areopagitica,* in 1644: "Where there is much desire to learn, there of necessity will be much arguing, much writing, many opinions; for opinion in good men is but knowledge in the making" (Project Gutenberg, 2006). His confident directive to "let truth and falsehood grapple" brings to mind 18th century German philosopher Georg Hegel's thesis–antithesis dynamic of reason, in which contradictions or tensions are ultimately synthesized into natural resolution (Shaw, Hamm, & Knott, 2000). British philosopher John Stuart Mill's 1869 work *On Liberty* also is known for its allusion to the marketplace of ideas, in which he argues that people should be allowed to speak and exchange ideas freely (Mill, 1913). M. Taylor (2009) notes simply, "At the heart of civil society is discourse" (p. 88), and continues: "theories of public relations can be complemented" by how society participates in what's been called the "wrangle of the marketplace" (p. 89).

These are but a few of the philosophical underpinnings for political public relations theory. However, before turning to its theoretical foundations, we must first examine the difference between political communication and political public relations scholarship. Although the former has long been recognized as an area of study, with a "self-consciously cross-disciplinary focus" starting in the late 1950s (Denton, 1997, p. xi), the latter has not been as systematically recognized or explored. However, political public relations activity has been documented throughout history.

For example, Watson (2008) describes how British church leaders used public relations tactics and strategies in political communications during the "Dark Ages" of the 10th century. Read (1961) writes of Elizabethan public relations, stating that "one of the characteristic attributes of [16th century] Tudor government was its increasing interest in public relations, that is to say, in the relations between the Crown and its neighbours and the Crown and its subjects, through public channels of communication" (p. 21). L'Etang (1998) found evidence that by the 1930s, there was "an understanding of the importance of good public relations to facilitate smooth administration" within British central and local government and that "achieving 'understanding' between the populace and local government" was considered to help improve democracy (p. 417).

Puchan (2006) writes that public relations in Germany also is tied to its political history and "the development of press and press freedom" (p. 113). She notes that German public relations activities have been traced to the Middle Ages, but that the mid-19th century is when organized "communication efforts of both public and private organizations appeared" (p. 113). In Sweden, PR started in the 1940s "within state authorities and is in line with the development and growth of the governmental sector at different levels," including state-owned railroads and Sweden's National Board of Health (Larsson, 2006, p. 124).

So how then do we untangle the intersections of political communication and political public relations? The previous chapter provided a thorough overview of the definitions and suppositions of each area, but in short, contemporary political public relations scholarship examines purposeful or strategic *communication management* and *relationship building and maintenance* for political ends of all kinds. Such a definition is in concert with J. Grunig's (1992) excellence studies, which "produced a general theory ... focused on the role of public relations in strategic management and the value of relationships" (J. Grunig, 2006, p. 151).

Additionally, the aims of public relations, as its name implies, are typically dependent upon *stakeholder groups*, rather than with *individuals* per se. For example, public affairs, government, or political public relations practice all include communication among government agencies and representatives, as well as among government entities and nongovernmental publics, corporations, or groups. Therefore, political public relations includes communication management and relationship building across groups, and includes ethics, advocacy, diplomacy, public information, evaluation, and electoral campaigns in ways arguably broader than "*the role, processes, and effects of communication* [emphasis aded] within the context of politics" (Denton, 1997, p. xii).

Despite these differences, the established field of political communication presents a good theoretical foundation of which public relations scholars should be aware, as we work to build, extend, and differentiate our own field's specialized political body of knowledge. Therefore, this chapter examines modern political communication theory's social science origins and varied approaches, revisits some of its classic underpinnings, and posits possible extensions of these works for today's political public relations sphere.

Political Communication

Political communication has historically been defined as the "role of communication in the political process" (Chafee, 1975, p. 15) and as "a process intervening between formal governing institutions and citizen voting behavior" (Nimmo & Sanders, 1981). However, within a decade of this latter definition, calls to move the field beyond the "voter persuasion paradigm" were being made (Kaid, 1996, p. 444) and heeded. Today, its study is broad, involving interdisciplinary fields and using various theoretical research perspectives and approaches, including but not limited to rhetorical analysis; attitude change; direct and minimal effects; critical, interpretive, functional, and systems analyses; mass and social media, and interpersonal communication.

Although it is beyond the scope of this chapter to address literature from all of these varied approaches and perspectives, for the student of political public relations, it is good to know that scholarship in all of these areas can be explored. What this chapter will do is to provide early, classic research examples from four common scholarly political communication approaches, as outlined by Kaid (1996), that can be viewed as historical foundations from which more modern, nuanced political public relations study might emanate. These approaches include media effects, agenda setting, uses and gratifications, and rhetorical and critical approaches. In addition, it will include reference to some public relations-related classic political books.

Media Effects and Classic Texts

It is neither a surprise nor a coincidence that political communication has been intertwined with mass media effects research as far back as the 1920s. It was during this era that the magic bullet or hypodermic needle model of communication was posited to explain what was believed to be the direct and uniform influence of propaganda on the public. Born from concerns of the federal government's influence in building support for U.S. involvement in World War I—largely owing to the propaganda techniques used by the federal Committee on Public Information (of which public relations pioneer Edward Bernays and journalist and political commentator Walter Lippmann were both a part)—the direct and uniform effects model reflected the perception of mass media's power to unduly influence and persuade.

A flurry of books appeared during this decade about media, public opinion, propaganda, and public relations. These included *Public Opinion* (1922/1997), in which Lippmann expressed concern about the average citizen's ability to make informed decisions in an increasingly complex age, and thus for traditional democracy to work effectively. The same year, in *Political Parties and Electoral Problems*, author Robert Brooks (1922, cited in Kelley, 1956) argued that research about political communication should be able to help political campaigns be more strategic and efficient. He asserted that modern research methods be used to help evaluate the value of various communication tactics, including advertising, speeches, and publications.

His insights are particularly impressive, given they were published the year before Bernays taught the first U.S. collegiate public relations course and authored the book *Crystallizing Public Opinion,* in which he spoke of the new profession of public relations counselor (cited in Cutlip, Center, & Broom, 2000).

In 1925, Lippmann again expressed concern, this time in *The Phantom Public,* about the public's ability to function intelligently within the modern democratic political process. Two years later, John Dewey published a more optimistic account of modern political society in *The Public and Its Problems.* In this book, Dewey argues that we can empower citizens to contribute intelligently to society and the political process by making scientific and specialized knowledge more readily available to them.

Also in 1927, political scientist and early communication researcher Harold Lasswell wrote his dissertation, *Propaganda Techniques in the World War,* which examined how America, Britain, France, and Germany gained support for their war efforts. It is not surprising that amid this era of concerns about mass effects, the American Society of Newspaper Editors and the Society of Professional Journalists adopted their first national codes of ethics, in 1923 and 1926, respectively (Penning, 2008).

In 1928, Bernays wrote *Propaganda,* seeking to reverse the negative connotations the word had come to possess by providing case studies of his socially beneficial campaigns and arguing that propaganda is necessary to a democracy because it informs public opinion. In the chapter titled "Propaganda and Political Leadership," Bernays writes:

> Political campaigns today are all sideshows, all honors, all bombast, glitter, and speeches. These are for the most part unrelated to the main business of studying the public scientifically, of supplying the public with party, candidate, platform, and performance, and selling the public these ideas and products.... The politician understands the public. He knows what the public wants and what the public will accept. But the politician is not necessarily a general sales manager, a public relations counsel, or a man who knows how to secure mass distribution of ideas.
>
> (pp. 111–112)

Bernays acknowledges that such a process is often criticized as manipulation and that its power can be misused. Yet he maintains that such organization and focus are necessary to bring order to a chaotic world of ideas.

The author of perhaps the first book specifically about PR and politics, *Professional Public Relations and Political Power,* Kelley (1956) no doubt agreed. The book's inside front cover includes the following quote from Leone Baxter, originally published in an issue of the *Public Relations Journal:*

It's because the public relations profession, and its allied professions, know something about presenting abstract ideas, in attractive form, to masses of people who are too occupied with their daily lives to think analytically on their own account, that the average man today is in a position to know more about the trend of human affairs than ever in history.

The book provides details from public relations practitioners, including Baxter, who worked for political campaigns. It documents Dwight Eisenhower's 1952 presidential "Campaign Plan," touted as "the most complete blueprint ever drawn up in advance of a presidential campaign.... Prepared in standard advertising agency format, the plan outlined basic strategy, organization, appeals, types of speeches, literature, advertising, television and radio programs, the relative weight to be given to the various media, the kinds, places, and times of campaign trips and rallies, and the areas in which efforts were to be concentrated" (Kelley, 1956, p. 1).

Kelley's (1956) introduction reads:

> The activities of the public relations man have become a significant influence in processes crucial to democratic government. Any system of government ... owes its life to some kind of support in public opinion.... It is into this fundamental relationship between politician and electorate, between those who seek power and those who bestow authority, that the public relations man inserts himself, seeking to guide the action of the politician toward the people and the people toward the politician.
>
> (p. 3)

Thus, in the mid-1950s, Kelley recognized public relations as essential to the development of relationships within the political process.

It is interesting to observe the writings noted above from the 1920s and 1950s, especially in light of the uproar caused by the classic book, *The Selling of the President* (McGinniss, 1969). During the 1968 U.S. presidential campaign, McGinniss was given access to Richard Nixon's advertising campaign, including its memos, meetings, and production (the book includes an appendix of fascinating advertising strategy memos), and the book chronicles the strategies and tactics used by Nixon's campaign. Nixon's advertising agency used Madison Avenue techniques that had proved successful for selling products. In fact, the original edition showed Nixon's face on a package of cigarettes—linking the President to a controversial product with known detrimental health effects.

As Bernays had acknowledged in *Propaganda* 40 years before, some people were appalled to learn of the strategic communication tactics used in the political campaign. However, its real controversy lay in their lack of authenticity, creating a television persona of the candidate that differed substantially from his previous public image—and, many would argue, his true personality—

by controlling every nuance of communication in television production and limiting actual public debate.

In *Propaganda,* Bernays (1928) suggests that a Secretary of Public Relations be created as part of the President's Cabinet "to interpret America's aims and ideals throughout the world, and to keep the citizens of this country in touch with governmental activities and the reasons which promote them" (p. 127). In *Spin Control,* Maltese (1992/1994) describes the modern White House Office of Communications, created by Nixon in 1969, and its work to control the media and public agenda.

"The White House embrace of public relations techniques has corresponded with an increasing dependence on public support for the implementation of presidential policy," Maltese (1992/1994) writes. "No longer does public support merely elect presidents. Now public support is a president's most visible source of ongoing political power" (pp. 3–4). He notes that starting with Nixon, these public relations techniques included the "tightly regimented line-of-the-day coupled with limited press access and direct appeals to the people. Polling data helped formulate the line, and efforts were made to see that certain stories dominated the news…" (p. 3).

Maltese (1992/1994) examines each U.S. president's communications office from 1969 through 1993 and includes some fascinating organizational charts that illustrate the changes that took place during that period. Hertsgaard (1988) and Kurtz (1998) also write of the strategic political communications of presidents Reagan and Clinton in *On Bended Knee* and *Spin Cycle,* respectively, and Jamieson (1996) takes a historical look at advertising in presidential campaigns, focusing particularly on television.

At least one political science scholar (Sheingate, 2006) points to the Progressive Era (1890 to 1920) as the origin of political communication innovations, including the press release, paid political advertisements, and political public relations campaigns, and argues that these were the seeds for the *business* of U.S. politics and for professional political consultancy. However, Cutlip et al. (2000) chronicle the effectiveness of strategic political public relations counselor Amos Kendall's work for U.S. President Andrew Jackson nearly a century earlier.

Still, the rise of mass media and political communication innovations, coupled with the federal government's demonstrated abilities to sway public opinion, led to wariness, concern, and even respect for political communication power. For example, a 1942 *Saturday Evening Post* editorial, titled "The Nazis Learned How From Us," acknowledges Germany's adept use of war propaganda in World War II and criticizes the U.S. government's lack of it (Stout, 1942).

Inspired by her observations of life in Nazi Germany, Elisabeth Noelle-Neumann used the spiral of silence model (1974) to help explain the notion of a silent political majority. The concept involves people's reluctance to publicly express what they believe to be minority opinions for fear of social or political retribution or isolation. Therefore, the democratic marketplace of ideas is compromised.

Although the spiral of silence model's greatest contribution has perhaps been its fusion of media, individuals, and public opinion research, it is ultimately rooted in the nature of social interaction or relationships, an aspect of the model that has not been systematically explored.

Political PR and Agenda Setting Research

Another rich political communication effects research stream with public relations implications is that of agenda setting. Drawing on Cohen's (1963) belief that media tell us not what to think, but what to think about, the classic McCombs and Shaw (1972) Chapel Hill agenda-setting study, conducted during the 1968 U.S. presidential campaign, demonstrated that media inform and influence people regarding what political issues are important. In other words, they found that the issues covered most extensively by the media became issues deemed most salient to voters.

McCombs, Shaw, and Weaver (1997) noted that "understanding the dynamics of agenda setting is central to understanding the dynamics of contemporary democracy" (p. xiii). Therefore, it is not surprising that since the original study's publication, political agenda-setting studies have been replicated around the world (Davie & Maher, 2006; McCombs & Lopez-Escobar, 2000; Valenzuela & McCombs, 2007). In anticipation of the study's 40th anniversary, McCombs, Shaw, Weaver, and others are working to conduct another agenda-setting study in Chapel Hill, incorporating today's complex traditional and digital media environments (D. L. Shaw, personal communication, January 15, 2010).

From a strategic communication management perspective, political practitioners still know the media are important places to begin to build awareness of issues and to perhaps "seed" receiver relationships through message saliency and conveyed personal attributes. McCombs and others (Balmas & Sheafer, 2009) have also explored the second level of agenda setting, sometimes (albeit not always) equated with framing, which has demonstrated that media communicate not only about issue agendas or political candidates, but also the specific attributes of those agendas or candidates. This second level of agenda setting is consequently sometimes referred to as attribute agenda setting.

Research has shown that media frames tend to be stable over time because they are rooted in culture and particular political ideologies (Gamson & Modigliani, 1989). Message frames are used to define issues and problems, their causes, related moral judgments, and to offer solutions (Entman, 1993), and they involve not just overt message elements but also more subtle ones that can activate intrapersonal cues, including political affiliation, which influence framing effects (Iyengar, 1991). Iyengar identified media's dominant use of episodic issue frames, which focus on specific events or individuals, as opposed to thematic frames, which provide greater societal context, and he showed that the frames used influenced audiences' perceptions of responsibility.

Agenda-setting research has grown to include other types of scholarship as well. Studies have demonstrated intermedia agenda-setting, or how major news outlets serve as agenda setters for other outlets, including international coverage and political blogs (Golan, 2006; Meraz, 2009); intercandidate agenda setting at both the issue and issue attribute levels (Kiousis & Shields, 2008); "agenda building," or how agendas come to be absorbed by or promulgated by media and political publics (Curtin & Gaither, 2003); and how and why agendas are "cut" out by media outlets (Colistra, 2009).

Political agenda-setting effects have also been studied in terms of presidential agenda-setting influence. This type of research commonly explores the power of presidents to set the national agenda in terms of media coverage and related public and congressional support (see, for example, Peake, 2001; Peake & Eshbaugh-Sohha, 2008). All of these areas have rich research potential and practical implications for strategic public relations management.

Another, arguably related, classic effects area of research is that of cultivation analysis. Signorielli and Morgan (1996) explain cultivation research as concerned with "a system of messages, made up of aggregate and repetitive patterns of images and representations to which entire communities are exposed—and which they absorb—over long periods of time" (p. 112). Cultivation research also has its roots in the era of mass media, specifically television. It began in the late 1960s, when the effects of television violence were of great concern, and the research was privately funded through the Cultural Indicators Project, founded by George Gerbner.

This research stream has found that television's unique place in society has cultivated "shared conceptions of reality among otherwise diverse publics" (Signorielli & Morgan, 1996, p. 115), and what is most popular or dominant in a given culture is what tends to be reflected and cultivated, which then can influence viewers' ideas about society, and this chapter's author would argue, their relationships with various members within it.

Rhetorical and Persuasion

As noted previously in this chapter, rhetorical study dates to ancient Greece, where persuasive discourse was prized for its influence in all areas of life (Fisher & O'Leary, 1996). Heath (2009) explains that "public relations and the rhetorical heritage focus attention not narrowly on the self-interest and opinions of the organization but on the persons whose goodwill is needed for the organization to succeed. In this way, public relations and rhetoric are inherently other oriented" (p. 19).

Research in this area includes a wide variety of methods and typically involves message sources, source characteristics, specific language used, and persuasion studies. A study of political public relations by Croft, Hartland, and Skinner (2008) used a case study approach to show how the Crown and Church cooperated in medieval England to use the powerful narratives of rumor, legend, and myth to successfully promote themselves to others.

Politicians continue to seek influential third-party endorsements and testimonials and to engage in local grassroots campaigns, where individual citizens become engaged in and ambassadors for the cause. Even in a highly connected, mediated society, we know that interpersonal communication and the use of homophily, the belief that someone is similar to us, are both highly effective persuasive strategies. On the other side, organizations and companies continue to use grassroots and "grasstops" campaigns as well, where influentials and opinion leaders are mobilized to act to help sway government officials.

It is well documented that the peer-to-peer networking made possible through Internet social media resulted in many individual donations and a strong sense of community among supporters of Barack Obama's presidential campaign. Today, the use of opinion leaders, whether formal or informal, through word of mouth, traditional/legacy, or social media, remains powerful and perhaps of growing importance.

A classic study that first illustrated the power of interpersonal influence is the *People's Choice* study of media influences on voters in Erie County, Ohio, during the 1940 U.S. presidential election campaign (Lazarsfeld, Berelson, & Gaudet, 1944). Its "unanticipated discovery of the role of social relationships in the mass communication process" resulted in the two-step flow model of communication (Lowery & DeFleur, 1988, p. 430). This research documented that some people attended to mediated political messages more than others, and that these people became persuasive opinion leaders when they discussed issues with people who were less interested or informed. Today's multimedia and mediated interpersonal channels of communication hold promise for research in the multiple-step flows of both formal and informal opinion leaders of all kinds.

Such research may be more important than ever. International public relations firm Edelman conducts an annual survey of global opinion leaders, which surveys college-educated people, ages 25 to 64, whose incomes are in the top quartile for their age and country, who report using at least three to four media sources a day, and who follow public policy issues. The latest survey, conducted in fall 2009, included 22 countries on five continents. The results indicate that trust in media has fallen to 45% of adult "informed publics," and subject experts were found to be the most trusted source of information, with NGOs the most trusted institutions (Edelman Trust Barometer, 2010, p. 3). Governments were trusted to do the "right thing" by fewer than half of those surveyed in every country but China (p. 3).

Low political trust was also documented in a 2006 UK report (*Power Inquiry*, cited in Gaber, 2007). It said, in part, there is a "well-ingrained popular view across the country that our political institutions and their politicians are failing, untrustworthy, and disconnected from the great mass of the British people" (p. 28).

Perhaps some of the widespread distrust of government lay within the recognized strategies used to influence the electorate, including politicians' language. Although used across political parties, conservative U.S. political strategists Frank Luntz and Karl Rove have become well-known for their success at "wordsmithing." Deliberate, consistent word choice has been effective at altering public opinion regarding at least some issues. For example, using the terms *death tax* instead of *estate tax* stirred opposition that was ultimately successful in eliminating the tax; the more neutral and less alarming term *climate change* was deliberately and consistently used in place of *global warming*; and the *War on Terror*, which dehumanized the enemy, was used in lieu of the *Iraq War* (Goodman & Dretzin, 2004). Although these terms don't include issue or candidate attributes per se, they do possess affective, semantic power.

In fact, political speeches and great orators have long been studied, as have statements made as a result of political scandals and the words used to describe political candidates and issues. As a result, there are hundreds of content and rhetorical analyses that examine political topics of all kinds.

Of course, persuasion, or attitude change, is the objective behind much, if not most, political communication. But because persuasion research is vast and typically examines individual attitude change, as opposed to larger societal or stakeholder responses, the discussion about it that follows is cursory. However, it is important for political public relations scholars to be aware of major persuasion streams because of their relevance to democratic political activity. We have already discussed the importance of *source* characteristics in persuasive messaging, as well as some of the ways in which *message* elements persuade.

Other classic areas of message persuasion research have included the study of fear appeals and of inoculation, where people are exposed to a message that contains content to refute future counterpersuasive attempts. Early inoculation studies come from psychology (Papageorgis & McGuire, 1961), and the technique has been proven effective when used to discuss many different topics, including political ones (Pfau, Kenski, Nitz, & Sorensen, 1990).

In addition to source and message characteristics, persuasion research has also long focused on the message *receiver*. Hovland and his associates at Yale University in the mid-20th century were among the first to systematically explore communication and attitude change (Hovland, Janis, & Kelley, 1953). Their perspective was one of message learning. Other persuasion research streams include Leon Festinger's (1957) theory of cognitive dissonance, which involves the idea of receiver attitude consistency and efforts to psychologically resolve conflicts.

Dissonance can cause people to seek out messages that reinforce existing beliefs and to avoid those that contradict them, thus resulting in selective message exposure and perception (Knobloch-Westerwick & Meng, 2009). This is a growing area of concern for democracies; both traditional and digital media channels are multiplying and they are narrowing their focus along ideological lines, potentially decreasing people's exposure to varied political viewpoints. A detailed look at this phenomenon in today's conservative media can be found in Jamieson and Cappella (2008). Other classic persuasion research, such as Fishbein and Ajzen's (1975) theory of reasoned action and Petty and Cacioppo's (1986) elaboration likelihood model (ELM), has focused on receivers' *message processing* and attitude change. This research stream has grown increasingly more sophisticated and continues to be an area of both communication and psychological study (Haugtvedt & Kasmer, 2008).

Political public relations practitioners can apply what's been learned about source credibility and characteristics, message elements and techniques, and receiver cognitions and responses to help better develop and plan message content and delivery to reach and influence stakeholder groups. However, from a relationship perspective, it must be noted that an overemphasis on persuasion has been criticized by public relations scholars (L. Grunig, J. Grunig, & Dozier, 2002), who see it as asymmetrical communication and counterproductive to dialogue and relationships.

Culbertson (2007) writes of this asymmetry in the "permanent [political] campaign," citing Sidney Blumental's definition of the concept as "a combination of image making and strategic calculation that turns government into a perpetual campaign..." (p. 36). Heclo (2000) believes the political focus on persuasion tends to indicate an adversarial, rather than a collaborative, perspective that is to be "sold."

Yet other scholars argue that public relations practitioners typically use a combination of communication approaches, ranging from asymmetrical to two-way symmetrical, depending on the situation. Write Pfau and Wan (2006): "Sometimes the best approach involves use of cooperation and dialogue between communicator and receiver, but at other times, especially in dealing with external publics, the optimal approach requires influence" (p. 105).

Critical Approaches and Activist Perspectives

A relatively recent stream from the perspective of this "classics" research chapter, and thus only briefly discussed here, is constituted by critical approaches to political communications and public relations. Critical scholarship examines hegemony and other ideological and sociological factors, including gender, as crucial variables whether studying media, messages, politics, or their resultant relationships.

In a recent study, McKie and Munshi (2009) challenge public relations scholars to give up our focus on the field's management function and instead look at our larger social impact on the world. Weaver, Motion, and Roper

(2006) studied rhetoric through critical discourse theory as a "means of understanding the significance of the public relations contribution to the formation of hegemonic power, constructions of knowledge, truth, and the public interest ... public relations becomes a tool of social power and change for utilization by not only those who hold hegemonic power but also those who seek to challenge and transform that power and reconfigure dominant perceptions of the public interest" (p. 21).

Certainly, societies tend to privilege the voices of those in power, which affects communication management and relationships at all levels, from individual to cultural to societal and, in today's global communications sphere, beyond. Indeed, public relations scholars have begun to explore communications from the perspective of activists and social movement literature (Martinelli, 2010; Stokes & Rubin, 2010).

Social movements have been defined as "the attempt of a challenging group within society to affect change and achieve goals" (Trivedi, 2003, p. 3). They must not only motivate, but mobilize a "significant segment of society under a common cause or identity, often outside traditional electoral channels" (p. 3). Recent literature (Jiang & Ni, 2007) has recognized the dual role of movement activists: as both a public communicator and as a public of its targeted organizations or institutions.

Gamson (1990) argued that after 1945, there were two major changes in American society that created "a radically different environment for challengers" than had existed before (p. 145). The first revolved around the rise of the "the national security state" and its "sophisticated covert action capability"; the second change was television and its use by both "challengers and authorities" (p. 146).

In Gitlin's *The Whole World Is Watching* (1980/2003), he chronicled the actions of the Students for a Democratic Society and discussed the tendency for media to support existing power structures and frames and to marginalize those who differed. In the book's latest edition, he links it to critical scholarship when he writes: "Hegemonic ideology enters into everything people do and think is 'natural'—making a living, loving, playing, believing, knowing, even rebelling. In every sphere of social activity, it meshes with the 'common senses' through which people make the world seem intelligible; it tries to *become* that common sense" (p. 10).

Gitlin also demonstrates the activists' and media representatives' contrary objectives, and reiterates Bernays's point about the usefulness of public relations, when he says, "The media create and relay images of order" (p. 11). Snow and Benford's exploration of social protest frames (1988, 1992; Benford & Snow, 2000) also helped bridge communications and social movement literature, and their work continues to be used by contemporary public relations scholars (Zoch, Collins, Sisco, & Supa, 2008).

Drawn from sociology, notions of micro- and mesomobilization involve the actors involved in movements (Gerhards & Rucht, 1992). Micromobilization actors are defined as pursuing their own goals independently or in loosely structured organizations, while mesomobilization actors coordinate and integrate the micromobilized. Gerhards and Rucht describe how mesomobilization occurred during 1988 protests in Berlin, when activist groups were connected together and achieved "a cultural integration ... by developing a common frame of meaning to interpret the issue at stake" (p. 559).

This joining together of groups is similar to Shaw et al.'s agenda–melding concept, which describes how people join groups by, in effect, joining their issue agendas via both mediated and interpersonal means (Shaw, McCombs, Weaver, & Hamm, 1999). Friedan and McAdam (1992) contend that "collective identity and identity incentives play a distinctive part in furthering or hindering the development of the SMO [social movement organization]" (p. 162), and Tilly (2008) believes that for activists to be successful, they must communicate not only the worthiness of their cause, but also that there is unity on the issue among large numbers of committed supporters.

Uses and Gratifications in Political PR

Uses and gratifications theory is a longstanding area of political communication research, in which media consumers are viewed as active and deliberate in their message consumption. It examines what people derive from different types of political messages and communication activities. For example, people might attend to political communication for general news and information, for excitement or entertainment, to be "in the know" or an expert on particular issues, or to reinforce existing ideas and beliefs and, thus, a sense of identity.

Uses and gratifications research dates back to at least the 1940s, when Lasswell (1948) explored why people use media generally; but its connection to politics was first tested in 1960s British campaigns by Blumler and McQuail (1969). Since then, uses and gratifications research has grown to include all kinds of media, from television to telephones to supermarket tabloids (Rayburn, 1996, p. 147).

In terms of political public relations, researchers might extend uses and gratifications to explore whether message consumers gain a sense of relationship or community from media content. Political talk show listeners, for example, might derive satisfaction from feeling connected to and part of a larger political community. As noted previously, Obama's presidential campaign engaged large numbers of young people through social media. Because most social media activity is used to stay in touch with others (Ellison, Steinfield, & Lampe, 2007), it also seems a natural area of research that can explore political relationship development, networks, and maintenance.

A classic public relations theory that one could argue is related to uses and gratifications is the situational theory of publics (J. Grunig & Hunt, 1984).

This theory includes audiences' problem recognition, level of involvement, and constraint recognition to determine what level of information seeking or processing they engage in on an issue. Therefore, they can be segmented into distinct audience types: nonpublics, inactive publics, latent publics, and active publics. Werder's work (2008) has extended the theory to include goal compatibility as an additional independent audience variable, while Stewart, Settles, and Winter (1998) found that in addition to activists, social movements also include "engaged observers—individuals who are attentive to movement writings and activities, and express moral and even financial support for them, but who take no further action" (p. 63). These engaged observers, therefore, could also be counted as nascent activists, as they could prove critical in terms of political donations or votes.

One might suggest that audiences are thus motivated to become active through the gratifications or outcomes they envision as a result of their activity. Through strategic campaign management and search engine optimization, digital and social media make logical modern agoras for political messaging that could serve to activate—through projected gratification—latent publics.

Moving Forward

Whether viewed from the tradition of media effects, agenda setting, persuasion, rhetorical, critical, activist, uses and gratifications or something else, today's political landscape beckons public relations scholars. Gaber (2007) calls it a "political communications paradox," where voters expect honesty from politicians, who have dual motives for communicating: legitimate information updates and selfish political intentions. "As a result the trust which is a fundamental to the workings of a democratic system is constantly being undermined" (Gaber, 2007, p. 219). Similarly, Culbertson (2007) says, "The permanent campaign—and the underlying emphasis on asymmetric, adversarial thinking—seem to have contributed to a disturbing tendency to 'win battles, but lose wars' in recent American political, foreign-relations, and business history" (p. 38). Indeed, Cappella and Jamieson (1996) found that this focus on the strategic, competitive nature of politics has resulted in increased cynicism about the political process.

Given the potential of digital media, Gaber remains hopeful that political communication and relationships can improve, and he specifically calls on us—academics and journalists—for "increased attention … to the process of political communications" (2007, p. 220). As political public relations scholars, we can help lead the way through our understanding of past political communication research and our desire for new frameworks that help us understand, encourage, and foster a more transparent and accountable age.

In his book *Unbounded Publics,* Gilman-Opalsky (2008) discusses Jürgen Habermas's study of the public sphere, in which "the ideal public fulfilled the intrastate function of democratic legitimization; it served as a conduit of influence between civil society and the state" (p. xii). However, he reports that many theorists today say that such national spheres are inadequate and that transnational communication frameworks are required. He argues that, instead, a *transgressive* public sphere, one that inhabits both the national and transnational simultaneously and in a complementary way, represents a new "potentiality for rethinking and expanding the parameters of political identity, civil society, and citizenship" (p. xii). Such thinking also opens theoretical possibilities for political public relations scholarship.

In addition, presidential communication studies should continue to be explored. How is the "selling" and image maintenance of a president different today? How has the White House Office of Communications changed since the early 1990s? Certainly, an emphasis on mediated interpersonal communication via social media to "meld agendas," "mesomobilize," and grow grassroots support would be part of it. Applying social network analysis to political discourse hubs also is a ripe area for continued political public relations research, as is our growing exposure to and reliance on visuals. Maltese and others (Schaller, 1992) noted President Reagan's adept use of visual images and phrases some 30 years ago, which they contend helped maintain the "Teflon President's" popularity, for nothing negative seemed to stick to him.

Social media's political agenda-setting and agenda-melding also are relationship-driven areas of study that seem to hold vast research potential, including international and transgressive implications, as well as the spiral of silence concept of political self-suppression.

Presidential agenda setting also influences relationships beyond those of the media. Political public relations research might examine its resultant issue–organization relationships—or the implicit undertones surrounding issues that involve related government, corporate, or NGO relationships. For example, a speech by President Obama that supports tougher environmental regulations related to global climate change, by extension indicates positive affect and potential relationships for "green" industries and their supporters and potentially negative ones for the oil and coal supported industries.

Cultivation studies also remain relevant to political public relations scholarship. Although only a few political public relations studies seem to have used cultivation analysis (Maxian, Wise, Siegrist, Nutting, & Bradley, 2008), the theory might be extrapolated to include how groups cultivate and reinforce particular ideologies among their members and how various radio and television talk shows cultivate shared views of the world among splintered audience groups. Findings might allow for better understanding of how such groups initiate, build, and maintain political–public relationships.

Television also remains useful to explore. For instance, we know that issues placement (a form of product placement) occurs as a result of both activists and government employees, who lobby to get such issues as drug abuse and pregnancy prevention written into popular television dramas and soap operas (Wilcox & Cameron, 2010). In a recent study, Mutz and Nir (2010) found that fictional television programming influences viewers' attitudes about public policy issues. Therefore, what kinds of political issues are certain viewers most susceptible to accepting?

How might the growth of citizen-developed Internet series influence others' perceptions about public policy, political candidates, or issues? As evidenced by Al Qaeda's digital recruitment of middle class, Philadelphia-born "Jihad Jane," there is more opportunity than ever before for activist organizations to reach, resonate with, and engage like-minded others, and political public relations scholars have the foundation to explore this flattened media hegemony and its resultant varied activism. In addition, our instantaneous posting of and access to information could test Dewey's 1920s argument that citizens can contribute intelligently to the political process when knowledge is readily available to them.

Amid all of this potential scholarship, one thing is certain: political public relations has been an area of professional discussion and public concern for nearly 100 years. As new and more sophisticated techniques and technologies have appeared, they have been incorporated into the communications mix to help educate, persuade, and build relationships with key political constituents and advocates. Theories that arose in the 20th century continue to be adapted, tested, and expanded to explain these processes in today's fragmented, but highly connected world. It is hoped this chapter about classics helps inspire you to join in the effort.

References

Balmas, M., & Sheafer, T. (2009, May). *Candidate image in election campaigns: Attribute agenda setting, affective priming, and voting intentions.* Presented at the International Communication Association Annual Meeting, Chicago, IL.

Benford, R. D., & Snow, D. A. (2000). Framing processes and social movements: An overview and assessment. *Annual Review of Sociology, 26,* 611–640.

Bender, T. (2006). The boundaries and constituencies of history. *American Literary History, 18,* 267–282.

Bernays, E. (1928). *Propaganda.* New York: Liveright.

Blumler, J. G., & McQuail, D. (1969). *Television and politics.* Chicago, IL: University of Chicago Press.

Cappella, J. N., & Jamieson, K. H. (1996). News frames, political cynicism, and media cynicism. *American Academy of Political and Social Science, 546,* 71–84.

Chafee, S. H. (1975). *Political communication: Enduring issues for research.* Beverly Hills, CA: Sage.

Cohen, B. (1963). *The press and foreign policy.* Princeton, NJ: Princeton University Press.

Colistra, R. (2009, August). *TV reporters' perceptions of organizational influences on news content and coverage decisions.* Paper presented at the Association for Education in Journalism and Mass Communication Convention, Boston.

Croft, R., Hartland, T., & Skinner, H. (2008). And did those feet? Getting medieval England "on-message." *Journal of Communication Management, 12,* 294–304.

Culbertson, H. (2007). Asymmetry in the permanent campaign. *Public Relations Quarterly, 52,* 36–38.

Curtin, P., & Gaither, K. (2003, May). *International agenda-building in cyberspace: A quantitative content analysis.* Paper presented at the International Communication Association Annual Meeting, San Diego, CA.

Cutlip, S. M., Center, A. H., & Broom, G. M. (2000). *Effective public relations* (8th ed.). Upper Saddle River, NJ: Prentice-Hall.

Davie, W. R., & Maher, T. M. (2006). Maxwell McCombs: Agenda-setting explorer. *Journal of Broadcasting & Electronic Media, 50,* 358–364.

Denton, R. E. (1997). Series foreword. In K. S. Johnson-Cartee & G. A. Copland (Eds.), *Inside political campaigns: Theory and practice* (pp. xi–xiii). Westport, CT: Praeger.

Dewey, J. (1927). *The public and its problems.* Chicago: Swallow.

Edelman. (2010). Trust barometer. Retrieved from http://www.scribd.com/full/26268655?access _key=key-1ovbgbpawooot3hnsz3u.

Ellison, N. B., Steinfield, C., & Lampe, C. (2007). The benefits of Facebook "friends": Social capital and college students' use of online social network sites. *Journal of Computer-Mediated Communication, 12,* 1143–1168.

Entman, R. M. (1993). Framing: Toward clarification of a fractured paradigm. *Journal of Communication, 43,* 51–58.

Festinger, L. (1957). *A theory of cognitive dissonance.* Evanston, IL: Row, Peterson.

Fishbein, M., & Ajzen, I. (1975). *Belief, attitude, intention, and behavior: An introduction to theory and research.* Reading, MA: Addison-Wesley.

Fisher, W. R., & O'Leary, S. D. (1996). The rhetorician's quest. In M. B. Salwen & D. W. Stacks (Eds.), *An integrated approach to communication theory and research* (pp. 243–260). Mahwah, NJ: Erlbaum.

Friedman, D., & McAdam, D. (1992). Collective identity and activism: Networks, choices, and the life of a social movement. In A. D. Morris & C. M. Mueller (Eds.), *Frontiers in social movements* (pp. 156–173). New Haven, CT: Yale University Press.

Gaber, I. (2007). Too much of a good thing: The "problem" of political communications in a mass media democracy. *Journal of Public Affairs, 7,* 219–234.

Gamson, W. A. (1990). *The strategy of social protest* (2nd ed.). Belmont, CA: Wadsworth.

Gamson, W. A., & Modigliani, A. (1989). Media discourse and public opinion on nuclear power: A constructionist approach. *The American Journal of Sociology, 95,* 1–37.

Gerhards, J., & Rucht, D. (1992). Organizing and framing in two protest campaigns in West Germany. *The American Journal of Sociology, 98,* 555–596.

Gilman-Opalsky, R. (2008). *Unbounded politics: Transgressive public spheres, Zapatismo, and political theory.* Lanham, MD: Lexington Books.

Gitlin, T. (1980, 2003). *The whole world is watching: Mass media in the making and unmaking of the new left.* Berkeley, CA: University of California Press.

Golan, G. (2006). Inter-media agenda setting and global news coverage. *Journalism Studies, 7,* 323–333.

Goodman, B., & Dretzin, R. (Directors). (2004). The persuaders [Television series episode]. In R. Dretzin, B. Goodman, & M. Soenens (Producers). *Frontline.* Boston, MA: Public Broadcasting Service.

Grunig, J. E. (1992). *Excellence in public relations and communication management.* Hillsdale, NJ: Erlbaum.

Grunig, J. E. (2006). Furnishing the edifice: Ongoing research on public relations as a strategic management function. *Journal of Public Relations Research, 18,* 151–176.

Grunig, J. E., & Hunt, T. (1984). *Managing public relations.* New York: Holt, Rinehart & Winston.

Grunig, L., Grunig, J., & Dozer, D. M. (2002). *Excellent public relations and effective organizations: A study of communication management in three countries.* Mahwah, NJ: Erlbaum.

Haugtvedt, C. P., & Kasmer, J. A. (2008). Attitude change and persuasion. In C. P. Haugtvedt, P. M. Herr, & F. R. Kardes (Eds.), *Handbook of consumer psychology* (pp. 419–435). New York: Erlbaum.

Heath, R. L. (2009). The rhetorical tradition: Wrangle in the marketplace. In R. L. Heath, E. L.

Toth, & D. Waymer (Eds.), *Rhetorical and critical approaches to public relations* (Vol. 2, pp. 17–47). New York: Routledge.

Heclo, J. (2000). Campaigning and governing: A conspectus. In N. J. Ornstein & T. E. Mann (Eds.), *The permanent campaign and its future* (pp. 1–37). Washington, DC: American Enterprise Institute and Brookings Institution.

Hertsgaard, M. (1988). *On bended knee: The press and the Reagan presidency.* New York: Farrar, Straus & Giroux.

Hovland, C. L., Janis, I., & Kelley, H. H. (1953). *Communication and persuasion.* New Haven, CT: Yale University Press.

Iyengar, S. (1991). *Is anyone responsible? How television news frames political issues.* Chicago, IL: University of Chicago Press.

Jamieson, K. H. (1996). *Packaging the presidency. A history and criticism of presidential campaign advertising* (3rd ed.). New York: Oxford University Press.

Jamieson, K. H., & Cappella, J. N. (2008). *Echo chamber: Rush Limbaugh and the conservative media establishment.* Oxford, England: Oxford University Press.

Jiang, H., & Ni, L. (2007, May). *Activists playing a dual role: Identities, organizational goals, and public relations practices.* Paper presented at the International Communication Association Annual Meeting, San Francisco, CA.

Kaid, L. L. (1996). Political communication. In M. B. Salwen & D. W. Stacks (Eds.), *An integrated approach to communication theory and research* (pp. 443–457). Mahwah, NJ: Erlbaum.

Kelley, S. (1956). *Professional public relations and political power.* Baltimore, MD: Johns Hopkins Press.

Kiousis, S., & Shields, A. (2008). Intercandidate agenda-setting in presidential elections: Issue and attribute agendas in the 2004 campaign. *Public Relations Review, 34,* 325–330.

Knobloch-Westerwick, S., & Meng, J. (2009). Looking the other way: Selective exposure to attitude-consistent and counterattitudinal political information. *Communication Research, 36,* 426–448.

Kurtz, H. (1998). *Spin cycle: Inside the Clinton propaganda machine.* New York: Free Press.

Larsson, L. (2006). Public relations and democracy. In J. L'Etang & M. Pieczka (Eds.), *Public relations. Critical debates and contemporary practice* (pp. 123–141). Mahwah, NJ: Erlbaum.

Lasswell, H. (1927). *Propaganda techniques in the world war.* New York: Knopf.

Lasswell, H. (1948). The structure and function of communications in society. In L. Bryson (Ed.), *The communication of ideas* (pp. 37–51). New York: Harper and Row.

Lazarsfeld, P. F., Berelson, B., & Gaudet, H. (1944). *The people's choice.* New York: Columbia University Press.

L'Etang, J. (1998). State propaganda and bureaucratic intelligence: The creation of public relations in 20th century Britain. *Public Relations Review, 24,* 413–441.

L'Etang, J. (2006). Public relations and propaganda: Conceptual issues, methodological problems, and public relations discourse. In J. L'Etang & M. Pieczka (Eds.), *Public relations: Critical debates and contemporary practice* (pp. 23–40). Mahwah, NJ: Erlbaum.

Lippmann, W. (1993). *The phantom public.* Piscataway, NJ: Transaction. (Original work published 1925)

Lippmann, W. (1997). *Public opinion.* New York: Free Press. (Original work published 1922)

Lowery, S. A., & DeFleur, M. L. (1988). *Milestones in mass communication research.* White Plains, NY: Longman.

Maltese, J. A. (1994). *Spin control.* Chapel Hill: The University of North Carolina Press. (Original work published 1992)

Martinelli, D. K. (2010, July). *A practical and theoretical look at women's use of public relations to spur early- to mid-20th century U.S. social change.* Presented at the First International Public Relations History Conference, Bournemouth, England.

Maxian, W., Wise, W., Siegrist, E., Nutting, B., & Bradley, S. (2008, May). *Is television's mean world mean only for conservatives? The interactive effects of political affiliation and processing strategy.*

Paper presented at the International Communication Association Annual Meeting, Montreal, Canada.

McCombs, M., & Lopez-Escobar, E. (2000). Setting the agenda of attributes in the 1996 Spanish general election. *Journal of Communication, 50,* 77–92.

McCombs , M. E., & Shaw, D. L. (1972). The agenda-setting function of the mass media. *Public Opinion Quarterly, 36,* 176–187.

McCombs, M. E., Shaw, D. L., & Weaver, D. (Eds.). (1997). *Communication and democracy. Exploring the intellectual frontiers in agenda-setting theory.* Mahwah, NJ: Erlbaum.

McGinniss, J. (1969). *The selling of the president, 1968.* New York: Trident Press.

McKie, D., & Munshi, D. (2009). Theoretical black holes: A partial A to Z of missing critical thought in public relations. In R. L. Heath, E. L. Toth, & D. Waymer (Eds.), *Rhetorical and critical approaches to public relations* (Vol. 2, pp. 61–75). New York: Routledge.

Meraz, S. (2009). Is there an elite hold? Traditional media to social media agenda setting influence in blog networks. *Journal of Computer-Mediated Communication, 14,* 682–707.

Mill, J. S. (1913). *On liberty.* (People's ed.). New York: Longmans, Green.

Miller, M. C. (2005). Introduction. In E. Bernays (1928), *Propaganda* (pp. 9–30). Brooklyn, NY: Ig.

Mutz, D. C., & Nir, L. (2010). Not necessarily the news: Does fictional television influence real-world policy preferences? *Mass Communication & Society, 13,*196–217.

Nelson, R. A. (1996). *A chronology and glossary of propaganda in the United States.* Westport, CT: Greenwood Press.

Nimmo, D. D., & Sanders, K. R. (Eds.). (1981). *Handbook of political communication.* Beverly Hills, CA: Sage.

Noelle-Neumann, E. (1974). The spiral of silence: A theory of public opinion. *Journal of Communication, 24,* 43–51.

Papageorgis, D., & McGuire, W. J. (1961). The generality of immunity to persuasion produced by pre-exposure to weakened counterarguments. *Journal of Abnormal and Social Psychology, 62,* 475–481.

Peake, J. S. (2001). Presidential agenda setting in foreign policy. *Political Research Quarterly, 54,* 69–87.

Peake, J. S., & Eshbaugh-Soha, M. (2008). The agenda-setting impact of major presidential TV addresses. *Political Communication, 25,* 113–137.

Penning, T. (2008). First impressions: US media portrayals of public relations in the 1920s. *Journal of Communication, 12,* 344–358.

Petty, R. E., & Cacioppo, J. T. (1986). *Communication and persuasion: Central and peripheral routes to persuasion.* New York: Springer-Verlag.

Pfau, M., Kenski, H. C., Nitz, M., & Sorenson, J. (1990). Efficacy of inoculation strategies in promoting resistance to political attack messages: Application to direct mail. *Communication Monographs, 57,* 25–43.

Pfau, M., & Wan, H-H. (2006). Persuasion: An intrinsic function of public relations. In C. H. Botan & V. Hazelton (Eds.), *Public relations theory II* (pp. 101–136). New York: Routledge.

Project Gutenberg. (2006). *Areopagitica: A speech for the liberty of unlicensed printing to the parliament of England,* by J. Milton. Retrieved from http://www.gutenberg.org/files/608/608.txt.

Puchan, H. (2006). An intellectual history of German public relations. In J. L'Etang & M. Pieczka (Eds.), *Public relations: Critical debates and contemporary practice* (pp. 111–112). Mahwah, NJ: Erlbaum.

Rayburn, J. D. (1996). Uses and gratifications. In M. B. Salwen & D. W. Stacks (Eds.), *An integrated approach to communication theory and research* (pp. 145–163). Mahwah, NJ: Erlbaum.

Read, C. (1961). William Cecil and Elizabethan public relations. In S. T. Bindoff, J. Hurstfield, & C. H. Williams (Eds.), *Elizabethan government and society* (pp. 21–55). London: Athlone Press.

Schaller, M. (1992). *Reckoning with Reagan.* New York: Oxford University Press.

Shaw, D. L., Hamm, B. J., & Knott, D. L. (2000). Technological change agenda challenge and social melding: Mass media studies and the four ages of place, class, mass and space. *Journalism Studies, 1,* 57–79.

Shaw, D. L., McCombs, M. E., Weaver, D. H., & Hamm, B. (1999). Individuals, groups, and agenda melding: A theory of social dissonance. *International Journal of Public Opinion Research, 11,* 2–24.

Sheingate, A. (2006, August). *Artful politics and the origins of political consulting.* Paper presented at the American Political Science Association Annual Meeting, Philadelphia, PA.

Signorielli, N., & Morgan, M. (1996). Cultivation analysis: Research and practice. In M. B. Salwen & D. W. Stacks (Eds.), *An integrated approach to communication theory and research* (pp. 111–126). Mahwah, NJ: Erlbaum.

Snow, D. A., & Benford, R. D. (1988). Ideology, frame resonance, and participant mobilization. *International Social Movement Research, 1,* 197–217.

Snow, D. A., & Benford, R. D. (1992). Master frames and cycles of protest. In A. D. Morris & C. M. Mueller (Eds.), *Frontiers in social movements* (pp. 133–155). New Haven, CT: Yale University Press.

Stewart, A. J., Settles, I. H., & Winter, N. J. G. (1998). Women and the social movements of the 1960s: Activists, engaged observers, and nonparticipants. *Political Psychology, 19,* 63–94.

Stokes, A., & Rubin, D. (2010). Activism and the limits of symmetry: The public relations battle between Colorado GASP and Philip Morris. *Journal of Public Relations Research, 22,* 26–48.

Stout, W. W. (1942, April 11). The Nazis learned how from us. *The Saturday Evening Post,* p. 30.

Taylor, M. (2009). Civil society as a rhetorical process. In R. L. Heath, E. L. Toth, & D. Waymer (Eds.), *Rhetorical and critical approaches to public relations* (Vol. 2, pp. 76–91). New York: Routledge.

Taylor, P. M. (2003). *Munitions of the mind: A history of propaganda from the ancient world to the present day* (3rd ed.). Manchester, England: Manchester University Press.

Tilly, C. (2008). *Contentious performances.* New York: Cambridge University Press.

Trivedi, R. (2003, July). *Marketing ideology: The role of framing and opportunity in the American woman suffrage movement, 1850–1919.* Paper presented at the American Political Science Association Annual Meeting, Philadelphia.

Valenzuela, S., & McCombs, M. (2007, May). *Agenda-setting effects on vote choice: evidence from the 2006 Mexican election.* Paper presented at the International Communication Association Annual Meeting, San Francisco, CA.

Watson, T. (2008). Creating the cult of a saint: Communication strategies in 10th century England. *Public Relations Review, 34,* 19–24.

Weaver, K., Motion, J., & Roper, J. (2006). From propaganda to discourse (and back again): Truth, power, the public interest and public relations. In J. L'Etang & M. Pieczka (Eds.), *Public relations: Critical debates and contemporary practice* (pp. 7–21). Mahwah, NJ: Erlbaum.

Werder, K. (2008, May). *Communicating for social change: An experimental analysis of activist message strategy effect on receiver variables.* Paper presented at the International Communication Association Annual Meeting, Montreal, Canada.

Wilcox, D. L., & Cameron, G. T. (2010). *Public relations strategies and tactics* (9th ed.). Boston, MA: Allyn & Bacon.

Zoch, L. M., Collins, E. L., Sisco, H. F., & Supa, D. H. (2008). Empowering the activist: Using framing devices on activist organizations' web sites. *Public Relations Review, 34,* 351–358.

3

POLITICAL PUBLIC RELATIONS, NEWS MANAGEMENT, AND AGENDA INDEXING

Paul S. Lieber and Guy J. Golan

Introduction

Throughout history, political messages have been formulated and disseminated for the purpose of persuasion. From biblical times to the present day, the court of public opinion has consistently been influenced by individuals or groups with a stake in its outcome. In so doing, political communicators have always tried to make the best use of the media available to them.

Media relations and news management strategies and tactics thus constitute an essential part of all strategic communication. However, while dozens of studies have examined how organizations attempt to build and maintain relationships with various publics, influence the media agenda, and manage crisis communications, only a limited number of studies have directly related public relations and political communication scholarship to each other, and to news management and media relations strategies and tactics.

The current book breaks new grounds in its exploration and definition of political public relations. As defined by Strömbäck and Kiousis in the introductory chapter,

> Political public relations is the management process by which an organization or individual for political purposes, through purposeful communication and action, seeks to influence and to establish, build, and maintain beneficial relationships and reputations with its key publics to help support its mission and achieve its goals.

Unlike most public relations research, which is almost exclusively focused on corporate and not-for-profit contexts, political public relations focuses on political parties, candidates, office-holders, political campaigns, and special interest groups such as lobbying firms (Strömbäck, Mitrook, & Kiousis, 2010), their interrelationships, and their relationships with various key publics, including the mass public. In all these contexts, media relations and news management strategies and tactics are crucial.

Against this background, the purpose of this chapter is to synthesize theories from the fields of public relations and political communication that have a bearing on media relations and news management in the context of political public relations. In doing so, it will identify key information subsidies used in political public relations, ranging from traditional tactics such as news releases to social media such as blogs. It will also introduce the concept of agenda indexing, which we believe offers a promising venue for research on political public relations, media relations, and news management.

Tactical versus Strategic Media Relations

Any discussion of political public relations theory should arguably begin within the greater public relations context. Considering the importance of media relations for both political communication and its public relations umbrella, a somewhat surprising scholarly divide persists in providing a steadfast definition for this critical communication function.

To elaborate, a fair amount of studies sport an exclusive, media-centric emphasis solely on the strategic aspects of media relations. Among others, these include topics such as creating strategic communication plans or responding to changes in the media environment (Brody, 1989; Colby, 2005; Goldstein, 2004; Howard, 2000); building long-term relationships with the media (Howard, 2004); and media relations planning and evaluation as part of the overall public relations process (Bollinger, 2001; Dyer, 1996; Kelleher, 2001; Tilson, 2005).

On the flip side is an almost exclusively tactical approach to the public and media relations' combination. Research on this aspect of media relations has explored areas such as increasing media attention for products or services (Brooks, 1999; Cantelmo, 1994), the use of media relations with respect to the Internet (Duke, 2001; Fitzgerald-Sparks & Spagnolia, 1999; Howard, 2000; Kent & Taylor, 2003), and how to use the media during crises (Adams, 2000).

The problem with many of the predominantly tactical approaches is that they do not situate media relations and news management in a proper theoretical and strategic context. To remedy this, we will next discuss media relations and news management in the context of some of the most important theoretical contexts, starting with the situational theory of publics.

Situational Theory of Publics

Public relations—both within and outside the context of politics—is ultimately about relationships formed through communication with different publics.

Hence, the concept of publics is key for understanding all public relations strategies and tactics, and for enabling a strategic use of news management and media relations.

The most basic definition of a public comes from Dewey (1927), who first defined a public as a collection of individuals who were (a) facing a similar problem, (b) that recognizes said problem exists, and (c) organizes to do something about it. Dewey's notion of publics has since been extended (J. Grunig & Hunt, 1984; J. Grunig & Repper, 1992; Vasquez & Taylor, 2001) to include four types of publics, which combine to describe situational versus mass publics:

1. The *nonpublic*—individuals who fail to meet all three of Dewey's above criteria;
2. The *latent public*—individuals who acknowledge that the problem exists (point a), yet fail to either acknowledge the problem (point b) or act on it (point c);
3. The *aware public*—those who are aware of the problem facing them (points a and b are present) yet fail to act on it;
4. The *active public* (comprised of points a, b, and c)—individuals that are aware of their problem, and subsequently organize to address it.

It is important to recognize that all four types can exist simultaneously, and that they should not be perceived as mutually exclusive categories. What this means is that individuals classified as *latent* members of one particular public might be *active* in a second, and so on. Also important is that people's need for orientation (Weaver, 1980), awareness (Zaller, 1992), and motivation (Prior, 2007) will differ among publics, also accompanying exposure or access to information subsidies across issues.

Although the distinction between different types of publics is crucial, it may be the case that the line between them will become increasingly blurred through the increasing importance of social media that can serve as viable mechanisms for reaching individuals across types of publics. If trends persist, segmentation of situational publics and the media to service them can be expected to become both more sophisticated and more precise. The adage that organizations do not necessarily choose their publics may to some extent be turned on its head by this.

Powered by the Internet and flash polling, political communicators have become increasingly sophisticated and interested in continuous analyses of public attitudes, opinions, and sentiments, and public opinion analyses continue their march toward relevancy in almost every aspect of political communication and the campaigns that drive it (Geer, 1996; Lavrakas & Traugott, 2000; Mitchell & Daves, 1999). This forms part of the phenomenon of permanent campaigning (Blumenthal, 1980; Dulio & Towner, 2009), where public opinion polling is no longer relegated to isolated election cycles. This trend is furthered by global television and media conglomerates—insatiably looking for new and fresh content—that turn toward sophisticated, situational public opinion analyses to drive and supplement the 24/7 news cycles.

Despite all this, most research on political publics remains outdated, and echoes Lippmann (1922/1997) on its mass versus situational emphasis—specifically on opinion polling dynamics. This preference for mass versus situational public opinion not only fails to ignore the realities of first and second level agenda setting processes (Golan & Wanta, 2001; Lopez-Escobar, Llamas, McCombs, & Rey, 1998), it also overlooks faction-driven, groundswell norms of Internet-powered political communication.

What may be even more important in this context, however, is that the implications for media relations and news management strategies and tactics have not been sufficiently explored. For example, different publics (nonpublics, latent publics, aware publics, and active publics) may not only be reached through different media; they may also seek out and, not least important, be influenced differently by different media. Strategic news management and media relations hence need to take into consideration the different kinds of publics that choose different types of media both when choosing media and the messages to promote.

Relational Approaches to Public Relations

Also important, but insufficiently theorized in the context of political public relations, news management, and media relations, is the relational approach to public relations. Although Kelley already in 1956 espoused the importance of relationships in public relations, it is only during the last couple of decades that the relational approach has been developed and implemented in public relations research—including political public relations research.

Jackson (2010), for instance, highlighted the increased value of the relational approach to explain public opinion, while Strömbäck et al. (2010) highlighted relationship theory as crucial for political marketing and political public relations. This coincided with a key theoretical adjustment in explaining the strategic communication process at large. In place of influence through propaganda and persuasion, there emerged a paradigm of establishing, building, and maintaining mutually beneficial relationships between an organization and its publics (Ledingham, 2006; Ledingham & Bruning, 2000).

Aspects of measurement reflected this shift toward emphasizing a more advanced, relational understanding of information subsidies and their purpose. For instance, L. Grunig, J. Grunig, and Ehling (1992) offered a mix of attributes as barometers of success or failure in the relational approach to public relations—reciprocity, trust, credibility, mutual legitimacy, openness, mutual satisfaction, and mutual understanding. Relatedly, Huang (1997) labeled trust, control mutuality, relational commitment, and relational satisfaction as indicators of positive relationship management. Lastly and during times of crisis, Coombs (2000) posited that a relational approach may both avert and mitigate communication calamities and their effects.

Pfau and Wan (2006) deemed persuasion a central and natural component to relationship building, without which the process would likely falter. In political communication, for instance, constituents—the situational public(s)—are inherently aware of a persuasive means toward desired ends, such as a vote, policy, or related political capital exchange. Constituents, of course, simultaneously negotiate persuasion channels toward achieving matching ends most beneficial for their needs. Thus, relational exchange is an equal dance partner to that of relational outcomes, as both political communicator and communicated are simultaneously aware of a pending influence or action exchange with tangible consequences.

The persuasion process, however, does not occur in isolation. An active, situational political public can be met by one or more hostile ones, groups of individuals with opposing viewpoints seeking to maximize relational exchange toward their own wants/needs. This same reality holds true for those attempting to communicate, as competing voices will vie for similar influence or action among situational publics, albeit toward different opinion outcomes.

In the context of political public relations, news management and media relations, the problem is compounded by the fact that the media themselves may be targets for relationship building efforts, while at the same time they are crucial arenas for building relationships with other publics. In addition, the media's penchant for political conflicts and negative news as well as their professional identity as independent from political organizations (Patterson, 1993) may make it highly difficult for political actors and organizations both to build relationships with the media and to use them in their efforts to build relationships with other key publics that rely on the media for information.

Unfortunately, there is not much research that attempts to theorize or investigate the role of the media as targets or arenas for relationship building efforts by political actors; differences across media or political actors; or the factors that hinder or help efforts to build relationships with or through various media for different political actors.

Contingency Theory of Public Relations

Contingency theory is also important to the public relations area (Cancel, Cameron, Sallot, & Mitrook, 1997; Cancel, Mitrook & Cameron, 1999; Jin & Cameron, 2007; Mitrook, Parish, & Seltzer, 2008). Contingency theory was intended to advance Grunig and others' excellence theory of public relations, which segments the field into four specific models: (a) press agentry/publicity, (b) public information, (c) two-way asymmetric, and (d) two-way symmetric (J. Grunig 1992; J. Grunig & L. Grunig, 1992; J. Grunig & Hunt,

1984). Models (a) and (b) assume one-way communication for the purposes of information dissemination, sans feedback. Model (c) is described as "scientific persuasion" (J. Grunig & Hunt, 1984). The final model is a normative approach with particular emphasis on feedback loops. J. Grunig (2008) and Lee (2008) identified public information as the most common model within political communication settings.

While excellence theory proved useful in providing benchmarks for good practice, it did not produce comprehensive measurement attempts or experimental approaches to validate its models or extend them further. Being normative, these models also reasoned for mutual exclusivity between them, ignoring the complexities of particular sectors or the audiences they serve. As noted by Cancel et al. (1997), "The practice of public relations is too complex, too fluid, and impinged by far too many variables for the academy to force it into the four boxes known as the four models of public relations.... It fails to capture the complexity and multiplicity of the public relations environment" (p. 32).

As an alternative, contingency theory, as its name suggests, sees public relations on a fluid persuasion continuum akin to Coombs's (2000) designation of crisis communication responses—ranging from total advocacy to complete accommodation (Cancel et al., 1997, 1999; Shin, Cameron, & Cropp, 2006).

A continuum approach theorizes a natural movement across different degrees and stages of a relational context. Hypothetically and among the same situational public, a targeted, persuasive response to one particular problem might be illogical when applied to a different problem or timeframe regarding these same individuals. This is especially true within political communication, where the delicate practice of relational exchange is essential to achieving public consensus. The challenge is compounded by the presence of an array of hostile publics and communicators—including the media themselves—all seeking to maximize relational exchange.

Perhaps nowhere is this more evident than with respect to the media. On the one hand, political actors are dependent on the news media for reaching their mass audiences, which calls for accommodation of the media's wants and needs. On the other hand, the interests of the media and of political actors are usually not the same, which rather calls for advocacy toward the media on the part of political actors. At the same time, political actors cannot afford to alienate the media, which again calls for accommodation. Hence, the choice of strategy toward the media on the continuum ranging from total advocacy to total accommodation in news management and media relations is both crucial and highly complex.

The same is basically true in Web-based media environments, where an abundance of political interests and interaction options combine for a dynamic communication space. Blogs, for example, have redefined the political space and opened it up for more dialogic communication (Kent & Taylor, 1998).

Blogs and microblogs also allow candidates greater opportunities to strategically communicate via different topics and styles than more static Web pages. More importantly, these mechanisms enable candidates to readjust political communication tactics to match ebbs and flows in news media and constituent sentiment.

On the other hand, blogs have also opened up the space for groups that are highly energized and seeking conflicts with different political actors, which poses new challenges for political actors both in general, and in choosing the proper response on the continuum from total advocacy to total accommodation. Thus, the contingency theory of public relations is relevant with respect to political actors' relationship with and strategies toward traditional and newer media. Media relations and news management theory, research, and practice would do well to take the contingency theory of public relations into greater consideration when developing strategies and tactics.

Information Subsidies

One of the most important concepts with respect to media relations and news management is *information subsidies*, a term coined by Gandy (1982). Basically, information subsidies include all efforts created by public relations practitioners to "reduce the prices faced by others for certain information in order to increase its consumption" (p. 12). In sum, information subsidies are the currency of trade within the marketplace of information.

Direct information subsidies, according to Gandy, become indirect ones once filtered through the media before reaching an intended audience(s). These indirect filters—from a political communication perspective—might include subject matter experts, grassroots lobbying, wire services, and satellite distribution (Zoch & Molleda, 2006).

In a competitive political landscape, information subsidies become the weapon of choice for political communicators to forge relationships with both their constituents and the mass media who service them. Lobbyists, for example, combine subsidized information from clients and their own research-based data to influence policy (Zoch & Molleda, 2006). Moreover, legislators turn to indirect subsidies for guidance in advance of critical decisions. In fact, even mass media reporting of political issues and interchanges may function as invaluable information subsidies. Thus, information subsidies are not only directed toward the media—even if that is one highly important aspect, particularly in the context of media relations and news management—but used by all actors in information exchange processes.

Mirroring its broader public relations counterpart, political communication-centric information subsides are not static; they will increase or decrease in value stemming from a number of factors which combine to explain the legitimacy of the message. Gandy (1982) operationalized these relational, value factors into a number of smaller categories to include: how well disguised the self-interest underlying the message is; source credibility; and the diversity of competing, available information.

While information subsidies are not used only to influence the media, most research on information subsidies has focused on their use this context, Perhaps the most researched area is the usefulness of press releases in shaping media coverage or public opinion. Several of these studies explored political communication problem sets, notably the perceived usefulness of the press release with respect to the media's coverage of, for example, state agencies (Martin & Singletary, 1981; Turk, 1985, 1986, 1991; Turk & Franklin, 1987; L. M. Walters & T. N. Walters, 1996); educational institutions (Bollinger, 1999; Morton & Warren, 1992a, 1992b, 1992c); and interest groups (Griffin & Dunwoody, 1995).

While information subsidies remains underinvestigated from a political public relations perspective, recent research has attempted to close this gap by exploring links between political public relations efforts, media coverage, and public opinion (Carroll & McCombs, 2003; Cho & Benoit, 2005; Kiousis & Strömbäck, 2010; Lancendorfer & Lee, 2003). For example, T. N. Walters, Walters, and Gray (1996) compared press releases in the 1992 U.S. presidential campaigns of Bush and Clinton. This study explored levels of perceived issue salience among voters, and in doing so discovered a more significant statistical association between the issue priorities for Clinton campaign voters versus those of Bush. A secondary analysis of the 2002 Florida gubernatorial election (Kiousis, Mitrook, Wu, & Seltzer, 2006) discovered a similar interchange between news releases and media content, extending this finding into matters of public opinion.

Despite an ever-increasing abundance of information that the Internet provides, it remains a challenge to connect media coverage and public opinion to the very individuals that consume the media and form their opinions, and the Internet remains a work in progress as a viable information subsidy. Tedesco (2004) labeled early campaign Web sites as nothing more than brochurelike content posted on the Web. Taylor and Kent (2004) echoed Tedesco's conclusions, and even later research suggests that many political actors still do not use the Internet as an information subsidy to the extent possible (Sweetser & Lariscy, 2008). Prominent among criticisms is that most Web sites are insufficiently interactive, and that candidates' use of e-mail or newsletters to target key publics is deficient (Sweetser & Lariscy, 2008; Trammell & Williams, 2004; Williams & Trammell, 2005).

Such criticisms notwithstanding, there is no doubt that Web-based media constitute a potentially and increasingly important information subsidy for all involved in political communication processes; political communicators in their efforts to influence the media, the public or each other; the media in their efforts to influence audiences, political communicators, or each other; and citizen groups and interest groups in their efforts to influence the media, political actors, or the public.

One prominent example of the importance of the Internet and social media in political public relations contexts and as information subsidies was provided by the 2008 U.S. presidential election campaigns, that also displayed tangible evidence of the link between traditional and social media subsidies. For example, traditional town hall formats featured dedicated time allocations for preselected, YouTube-hosted questions on key policy issues. Facebook walls inspired traditionally complacent younger citizens to both actively engage these forms and the ballot box on Election Day. Not to be outdone, Twitter and SMS messaging served as their own virtual press release engines.

As the U.S. Congress moved toward a very controversial 2010 universal health care vote, social media once again emerged as a viable information subsidy for the president and the Congress. For Congressional members, delicate use of information subsidies simultaneously sought to justify ideology and action to constituents, as well as to dispel rumors during the prevote period. For President Obama, social media filled time gaps where traditional media could not, a 24/7 relational engine intended to build consensus through less overt mechanisms (Phillips, 2009). At the same time, Drury (2008) has cautioned against the misuse of social media as a media relations or news management tool. More specifically, Drury discovered an excessive emphasis on communicating versus genuine efforts to build relationships. To be effective, "social," must remain the core component of this communication tactic (Paun, 2009).

Agenda Building

Integrated from mass communication scholarship and compatible with new social media phenomena, agenda building is one of the more robust and applicable theoretical frameworks in public relations research. Unlike the original agenda setting hypothesis (McCombs & Shaw, 1972) or the second level of agenda setting (Golan & Wanta, 2001; Lopez-Escobar et al., 1998)—both primarily focused on the transfer of issue or attribute saliency from the media to the public   agenda building explores processes and actions that help shape the media agenda. As such, agenda building provides an excellent theoretical framework for research dealing with media relations and news management. Of course, information subsidies are extremely important in conscious efforts to build the media's agendas.

Akin to information subsidies, initial research on agenda building began via traditional media analyses. Ohl, Pincus, Rimmer, and Harrison (1995) examined the agenda building influence of press releases regarding a hostile corporate takeover. Results of their content analysis suggested that press releases are an effective tool for agenda building as story leads, salient issues, and organizational points of view were successfully transferred from press releases to matching news articles.

Curtin and Rhodenbaugh (2001) examined the influence of public relations packets and of online tip sheet briefs on environmental journalism. The authors found both public relations tactics effective in shaping the media agenda, especially when reflecting news values such as "conflict" and "impact." Harmon and White (2001) examined the influence of video news releases (VNRs) on television news programs. Results of their analysis highlight a strong agenda building function of video news releases in both small and large television markets. Moreover, these findings hold additional significance with the prominence of YouTube as a social medium alternative tactic to VNRs. Finally, Kiousis, Popescu, and Mitrook (2007) examined the agenda building function of public relations publications (mostly news releases) on the agenda of financial news publications. Their findings show that issues and attributes that were salient in public relations publications were also salient on the media agenda. These authors also advanced research on agenda building by examining the influence of public relations releases on the tone of coverage. In particular, they posited that this second level of agenda building goes beyond the cognitive dimension of the communication effect and into the affective dimension. One could imagine that robust media environments (i.e., Facebook, MySpace, etc.), featuring mixed modalities (audio, video, text) for inputs/outputs are ripe for additional research to validate this thesis.

Agenda building is particularly valuable for research on political public relations, as public relations tactics and information subsidies are commonly taken and produced by government officials, lobbying and special interest groups, and even by foreign governments in an attempt to shape and influence the media agenda. As noted by Perloff (1998), agenda building illustrates that "a policymaker tries to move an issue to the top of the policy agenda by using the media to move public opinion, which, it is hoped, will influence the policy agenda" (p. 234).

Mirroring information subsidies, agenda building research examines how news management tactics are used by a variety of policy makers and political organizations in an attempt to shape the media agenda. Research has, for example, investigated agenda building efforts by the President of the United States (Johnson, Wanta, & Boudreau, 2004; Lang & Lang, 1983; Wanta & Foote, 1994; Wanta & Kalyango, 2007); political campaigns (Sheafer &Weimann, 2005; Walters, Walters, & Gray, 1996), issue advocacy groups (Huckins, 1999; Miller, 2010); and foreign governments (Kiousis & Wu, 2008). Although most of agenda building research has focused on the manner in which political campaigns attempt to influence the media agenda, largely ignoring such attempts after the candidate becomes a public official (Kiousis & Strömbäck, 2010), it has provided ample empirical support for the transfer of saliency of both issues and attributes between organizations and the media.

However, while much attention has been paid to different information subsidies and their potential impact on the media agenda, scholars have largely fallen short of providing an in-depth explanation for the mechanisms underlying agenda building processes. In response, the current chapter offers a theoretical explanation that accounts for the agenda building processes in the context of political public relations, building on a merger of indexing theory and agenda building theory.

Indexing

Perhaps not surprisingly, most agenda building research dealing directly with those in power has focused on the President of the United States. While some studies point to a largely reciprocal relationship between the president, the mass media, and the public (Lang & Lang, 1983), others identified a largely linear one in which the president is a dominant force in shaping the mass media agenda (Johnson, Wanta, & Boudreau, 2004). As noted by Kingdon (1995), "the President can single-handedly set the agendas, not only of people in the executive branch, but also of people in Congress and outside government" (p. 23).

Studies have examined different information subsidies used by White House and other government officials in their efforts to shape the mass media agenda, including state of the union addresses (Wanta et al., 1989), presidential public statements and papers (Wanta & Foote, 1994; Edwards & Wood, 1999), press releases (Turk, 1986), and press conferences (Eshbaugh-Soha, 2003; Kumar, 2005). While this research argued for the president serving as a key shaper of the mass media agenda, it stopped short of providing an explanation to account for this phenomenon.

As an alternative, indexing theory can serve as a useful theoretical framework to account for the agenda building function of both the president and other official sources. As one of the leading political communication theories, indexing identifies the underlying dependency of mass media sources on government officials and predicts an influence on the nature of corresponding coverage (Bennett, 1990). Indexing theory predicts that mass media coverage of events is typically constrained by the journalistic practice of limiting media coverage to reflect that of official sources. More specifically, Bennett (1990) argued that: "Mass media news professionals, from the boardroom to the beat, tend to 'index' the range of voices and viewpoints in both news and editorials according to the range of views expressed in mainstream government debate about a given topic" (p. 106).

The indexing hypothesis is both tested and for the most part supported by scholars across a variety of case studies. These include mass media coverage of U.S. policy in Nicaragua (Bennett, 1990), U.S. and Soviet downing of civilian planes (Entman, 1991), Salvadoran death squads (Livingston & Eachus, 1996), the Libyan crisis (Althaus, Edy, Entman, & Phalen, 1996), the Cold War (Zaller & Chiu, 1996), and the War in Iraq (Dimitrova & Strömbäck, 2005). As noted by Livingston and Bennett (2003), "controversy and debate in media content conform to the contours of debate found among political elites whom journalists regard as decisive in the outcomes of the issues in the news" (p. 366). Research also indicates that indexing may limit the range of voices more with respect to some issues, such as military affairs and foreign policy, compared to other issues (Althaus et al. 1996; Bennett, 1990). The bottom line, though, is that the outcome of indexing depends on the range of official voices promoting different issues or frames.

Although media gate-keeping processes remain complex and multifaceted, following Bennett (1990), three underlying mechanism may help explain the indexing processes. First, journalists depend on official and elite sources for access and information. Second, indexing provides a quick guide for framing of complicated news items. Third, indexing issues and frames function as a defense for news organizations against criticism of bias.

Agenda Indexing

Despite the breadth of scholarship on indexing and agenda building, there are few attempts to link these two closely related concepts to one another. This appears a glaring oversight for what should be both in theory and practice a strong theoretical link between the two. While the former predicts a transfer of issue or attribute saliency from information subsidies used in news management efforts to the mass media agenda, the latter provides an explanation as to why this transfer may occur.

To remedy this, the current chapter introduces the concept of agenda indexing, which extends the basic agenda building function of using information subsidies in news management and media relations, and predicts that the range of elite information subsidies will subsequently be reflected in the range of coverage in the mass media.

In other words, agenda indexing adds a third dimension to the agenda building process. In addition to the transfer of issues and attributes, agenda building should also measure the indexing effect of information subsidies produced by elite sources in shaping the range of coverage by the mass media. Indexing scholarship consistently shows that elite sources are able to limit the range of coverage of certain issues. Agenda indexing asserts that political public relations efforts by government insiders may not only influence the transfer of issue and attribute saliency but also its range of coverage. The process is illustrated in Figure 3.1.

To better understand why agenda indexing may occur, one must first consider the notion of the news media as a political institution. Sparrow (1999, 2006), for instance, designated the news media as an institutional actor within the

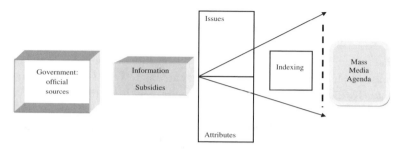

FIGURE 3.1 Agenda indexing in the agenda building process.

U.S. political system, one driven by economic, professional, and informational uncertainties. Borrowing from an organizational perspective, Sparrow (1999) reasoned, "media firms mitigate these three kinds of uncertainty by developing journalistic practices to buffer themselves from volatility on each of these fronts" (p. 147). Recognizing the dependence of political journalists on elite sources for information plus economic and professional needs institutionalized in the news organization, Sparrow perceived political journalists as core components of the greater political establishment. Following Sparrow, agenda indexing may thus follow not from deliberate editorial decisions, but rather from institutional routines meant to address an organization's need for economic, professional, and informational certainties.

Cook (1998, p. 70) likewise argued for an interdependent news media and government, a combined political institution featuring "social patterns of behavior identifiable across the organizations that are generally seen within a society to preside over a particular social sphere" (p. 70). He (1998, 2006) furthermore saw governmental actors as central participants in the news making process, while also highlighting that journalists' dependence on government subsidies—financial aid, use of government facilities such as press rooms in governmental buildings, the governmental public relations infrastructure— combine to create a dependence on the part of the journalists that can ultimately reduce the media's interdependence.

Both Cook (1998, 2006) and Sparrow (1999, 2006) thus perceive the news media as a semi-independent political institution. As such, the news media can (un)intentionally solidify an elite group's agenda through the indexing of its own news agendas and issue framing (Bennett & Livingston, 2003). It is also important to note, however, that an increasing number of Web-based news outlets simultaneously may undermine the notion of a singular, "political media institution." At the same time, continued ownership concentration of mainstream news organizations and their affiliates by a small number of multinational corporations (McChesney, 1997) lend support for Sparrow's (1999) assertion that: "these multilayered news media institutions are, by and large, mutually consistent: they cohere into a single actor for most intents and purposes" (p. 133).

Agenda indexing is not unconditioned, however. Consistent with the indexing literature, it can be assumed that agenda indexing is more likely to occur under some circumstances than under others. For example, the news media may be most apt to index its coverage when dealing with matters of military affairs, macroeconomics, and foreign policy (Althaus et al., 1996; Bennett, 1990). As such, the transfer of saliency from organizational information subsidies to news coverage—and its range of issues and attributes—may be predicted to be a function of how dependent journalists are on a limited range of elite sources.

In recognizing these aspects, it is important to note that agenda indexing is not limited to political public relations, and applies to any paradigm in which the mass media are dependent on a limited number of key sources for their coverage. Agenda indexing may hence be relevant not only with respect to the White House or Congress—or their equivalents in other countries—but also with respect to Fortune 500 companies, sports organizations, or any other entity distinguished by (a) featuring high newsworthiness to the public, and (b) a limited number of key sources for information. More specifically, agenda indexing may not be relevant with respect to all issues, processes, or information subsidies, but mainly to those that are considered highly newsworthy and where there are only a limited number of key sources of information. This has several implications in the context of media relations and news management in political public relations.

Agenda Indexing, News Management, and Media Relations

Ultimately, media relations and news management in the context of political public relations serve to build relationships with or through the media. The more political communicators are dependent on various media for influencing different publics, the more important media relations and news management become. Hence, the strategic use of media relations and news management is contingent on several factors. First, what are the wants and needs of different media; what are the logics of different media, how do the processes of newsgathering and news production look; and under what constraints do they operate? Second, what are the crucial publics, what media do they use, and for what purposes do they use the different media? Third, and related, what publics can be defined by the political communicators themselves, and what publics may be characterized as nonpublics, latent publics, aware publics, and active publics—and how does that shape their media use, information seeking, and information processing? Fourth, and again related, where should different publics be located on a continuum ranging from friendly to hostile, and how does that affect the choice of response on the continuum ranging from total advocacy to total accommodation? Fifth, and perceiving the media as a public, how can long-term relationships be built with media that have different interests and professional roles and identities from those of political communicators? Sixth, and finally, how do the media perceive different groups of political communicators, their importance as providers of information and information subsidies, as well as their power and influence with respect to different issues and processes?

To answer questions such as these and strategically use media relations and news management, a number of theories from the field of public relations are important, as discussed in this chapter. For example, the situational theory of publics can help political actors to strategically identify and locate different publics. The relational approach to public relations can help political actors to establish, evaluate, and maintain relationships with different publics. The contingency theory can help political actors to strategically choose the appropriate strategy toward different publics, ranging from total accommodation to total advocacy. The theories of agenda building and information subsidies can furthermore help political actors to understand how to build media agendas through the use of different information subsidies.

In this context, agenda indexing as outlined in this chapter is also important because it may help political actors to understand the mechanisms through which journalists search for or accept information subsidies from different political actors. This depends on how newsworthy something is, the range of potential sources from the perspective of the media and based on their assessments of who the key sources and providers of information subsidies are, and how limited is the range of key sources and providers of information subsidies.

Based on all this, the merger of research in political communication and public relations into political public relations can serve an important role in identifying not only the tools of media relations, news management, and ultimately persuasion, but also their strategic value and potential impact on the larger political environment. The theoretical intersection between public relations and political communication scholarship may in addition serve as the basis for more macrolevel investigations. For example, it offers an opportunity to extend directional research on either best past practices or isolated information subsidy effectiveness of public relations into a more meaningful examination of the impact of political communication on the greater democratic process. For instance, future studies may examine how different information subsidies are used by political organizations to build and maintain relationships with different publics. Such strategic communications could potentially impact audience trust in institutions, political knowledge, and political involvement and participation.

In this context, we believe agenda indexing might be important, conceptually as well as theoretically and practically. Having said this, we also recognize several limitations of the agenda indexing concept. Most importantly, while the agenda building process—on both its first and second levels—is widely tested and supported through empirical research, agenda indexing is still in its infancy and currently but a theoretical concept that attempts to bridge two areas of scholarship. However, as the field of political public relations continues its evolution into a significant area of scholarship, there is a pressing need to synthesize public relations theory with those of political communication, political science, and political marketing to reach this end (Strömbäck et al., 2010). In all these areas, media relations and news management are crucial, and thus need both to be integrated with and draw from theories within all these fields. Here we have mostly focused on public relations theory, but further research on media relations and news management in political public relations would benefit from a closer integration with theories also from political science, political marketing, and political communication in general.

Much like its greater public relations umbrella, political public relations will continue its theoretical evolution to incorporate new technologies, processes, and audiences. To explain these shifts necessitates a thorough analysis—and occasional expansion—of theories underlying its practice and analysis.

Through its introduction of agenda indexing, this chapter celebrates the legacy of several key scholarly areas in both general and political public relations, including and among others: information subsidies, tactical versus strategic discrepancies, agenda building, and contingency theory. Combined, they provide a glimpse into the potency of revisiting sender and receiver modeling of media relations and news management toward political and democratic gain.

References

Adams, W. C. (2000). Responding to the media during a crisis: It's what you say and when you say it. *Public Relations Quarterly, 45*(1), 26–28.

Althaus, S. L., Edy, J. A., Entman, R. M., & Phalen, P. (1996). Revising the indexing hypothesis: Officials, media, and the Libya crisis. *Political Communication, 13*(4), 407–421.

Bennett, W. L. (1990). Toward a theory of press–state relations. *Journal of Communication, 40*(2), 103–125.

Bennett, W. L., & Livingston, S. (2003). Editors' introduction: A semi-independent press: Government control and journalistic autonomy in the political construction of news. *Political Communication, 20*(4), 359–362.

Blumenthal, S. (1980). *The permanent campaign: Inside the world of elite political operatives*. Boston, MA: Beacon Press.

Bollinger, L. (1999). *Exploring the relationship between the media relations writer and the press: An analysis of the perceptions, goals and climate of communication*. (Unpublished doctoral dissertation). University of South Carolina, Columbia.

Bollinger, L. (2001). A new scoring method for the press release. *Public Relations Quarterly, 46*(1), 31–35.

Brody, E. W. (1989). PR management: Are we facing up to the revolution in media relations? *Public Relations Quarterly, 34*(2), 20.

Brooks, D. S. (1999). The media supply chain: How to increase media coverage for your product or service by understanding and meeting shared responsibilities with the media. *Public Relations Quarterly, 44*(4), 26–30.

Cancel A. E., Cameron, G. T., Sallot, L., & Mitrook, M. A. (1997). It depends: A contingency theory of accommodation in public relations. *Journal of Public Relations Research, 9*(1), 31–63.

Cancel A. E., Mitrook, M. A., & Cameron, G. T. (1999). Testing the contingency theory of accommodation in public relations. *Public Relations Review, 25*(2), 171–197.

Cantelmo, D. (1994). Targeting: Hitting the mark every time with your publicity. *Public Relations Quarterly, 39*(3), 12–14.

Carroll, C., & McCombs, M. (2003). Agenda-setting effects of business news on the public's images and opinions about major corporations. *Corporate Reputation Review, 6*(1), 36–46.

Cho, S., & Benoit, W. (2005). Primary presidential election campaign messages in 2004: A functional analysis of candidates' news releases. *Public Relations Review, 31*(2), 175–183.

Colby, D. (2005). Toward a new media autonomy. *Communication Law & Policy, 10*(4), 433–476.

Cook, T. E. (1998). *Governing with the news: The news media as a political institution.* Chicago, IL: University of Chicago Press.

Cook, T. E. (2006). The news media as a political institution—Looking backward and looking forward. *Political Communication, 23*(2), 159–171.

Coombs, W. T. (2000). Crisis management: Advantages of a relational perspective. In J. Ledingham & S. Bruning (Eds.), *Public relations and relationship management* (pp.73–93). Mahwah, NJ: Erlbaum.

Curtin, P. A., & Rhodenbaugh, E. (2001). Building the news media agenda on the environment: A comparison of public relations and journalistic sources. *Public Relations Review 27*(2), 179–195.

Dewey, J. (1927). *The public and its problems.* Chicago, IL: Swallow.

Dimitrova, D. V., & Strömbäck, J. (2005). Mission accomplished? Framing of the Iraq War in the elite newspapers in Sweden and the United States. *Gazette: The International Journal for Communication Studies, 67*(5), 399–417.

Drury G. (2008). Social media: Should marketers engage and how can it be done effectively? *Journal of Direct, Data and Digital Marketing Practice, 9*(3), 274–277.

Duke, S. (2001). Email: Essential in media relations, but no replacement for face-to-face communication. *Public Relations Quarterly, 46*(4), 19–22.

Dulio, D. A., & Towner, T. L. (2009). The permanent campaign. In D. W. Johnson (Ed.), *Routledge handbook of political management* (pp. 83–97). New York: Routledge.

Dyer, S. C. (1996). Public relations strategies for small business growth. *Public Relations Quarterly, 41*(3), 43–46.

Edwards, G. C., III, & Wood, B. D. (1999). Who influences whom? The president, Congress, and the media. *American Political Science Review, 93,* 327–344.

Entman, R. M. (1991) Framing U.S. coverage of international news: Contrasts in narratives of KAL and Iran Air incidents. *Journal of Communication, 41*(4), 6–27.

Eshbaugh-Soha, M. (2003). Presidential press conferences over time. *American Journal of Political Science, 47*(2), 348–353.

Fitzgerald-Sparks, S., & Spagnolia, N. (1999). Four predictions for PR practitioners in the new millennium. *Public Relations Quarterly, 44*(3), 12–14.

Gandy, O. H., Jr. (1982). *Beyond agenda setting: Information subsidies and public policy.* Norwood, NJ: Ablex.

Geer, J. G. (1996). *From tea leaves to opinion polls: A theory of democratic leadership.* New York: Columbia University Press.

Golan, G., & Wanta, W. (2001). Second-level agenda-setting in the New Hampshire primary: A comparison of coverage in three newspapers and public perceptions of candidates. *Journalism & Mass Communication Quarterly, 78*(2), 247–259.

Goldstein, G. B. (2004). A strategic response to media metamorphoses. *Public Relations Quarterly, 49*(2), 19–22.

Griffin, R. J., & Dunwoody, S. (1995). Impacts of information subsidies and community structure on local press coverage of environmental contamination. *Journalism and Mass Communication Quarterly, 72,* 271–284.

Grunig, J. E. (Ed.). (1992). *Excellence in public relations and communication management.* Hillsdale, NJ: Erlbaum.

Grunig, J. E. (2008). Public relations management in government and business. In M. Lee (Ed.), *Government public relations: A reader* (pp. 21–64). Boca Raton, FL: CRC Press.

Grunig, J. E., & Grunig, L. A. (1992). Models of public relations and communication. In J. E. Grunig, (Ed.), *Excellence in public relations and communication management* (pp. 285–325). Hillsdale, NJ: Erlbaum.

Grunig, J. E., & Hunt, T. (1984). *Managing public relations.* Belmont, CA: Thomson Wadsworth.

Grunig, J. E., & Repper, F. C. (1992). Strategic management, publics, and issues. In J. E. Grunig (Ed.), *Excellence in public relations and communication management* (pp. 117–157). Hillsdale, NJ: Erlbaum.

Grunig, L. A., Grunig, J. E., & Ehling, W. P. (1992). What is an effective organization? In J. E. Grunig (Ed.), *Excellence in public relations and communication management: contributions to effective organizations* (pp. 483–501). Hillsdale, NJ: Erlbaum.

Harmon, M. D., & White, C. (2001). How television news programs use video news releases. *Public Relations Review, 27,* 213–222.

Howard, C. M. (2000). Technology and tabloids: How the new media world is changing our jobs. *Public Relations Quarterly, 45*(1), 8–12.

Howard, C. M. (2004). Working with reporters: Mastering the fundamentals to build long term relationships. *Public Relations Quarterly, 49*(1), 36–39.

Huang, Y. H. (1997). *Public relations strategies, relational outcomes, and conflict management strategies* (Unpublished doctoral dissertation). University of Maryland, College Park.

Huckins, K. (1999). Interest-group influence on the media agenda: A case study. *Journalism & Mass Communication Quarterly, 76*(1), 76–86.

Jackson, N. (2010, April). *Political public relations: Spin, persuasion or reputation building?* Paper presented at the Political Studies Association annual conference, Edinburgh.

Jin, Y., & Cameron, G. T. (2007). The effects of threat type and duration on public relations practitioners' cognitive, affective, and conative responses in crisis situations. *Journal of Public Relations Research, 19*(3), 255–281.

Johnson, T. J., Wanta, W., & Boudreau, T. (2004). Drug peddlers: How four presidents attempted to influence media and public concern on the drug issue. *Atlantic Journal of Communication, 12*(4), 177–199.

Kelleher, T. (2001). Public relations roles and media choice. *Journal of Public Relations Research, 13*(4), 303–320.

Kelley, Jr., S. (1956). *Professional public relations and political power.* Baltimore, MD: John Hopkins University Press.

Kent, M., & Taylor, M. (1998). Building dialogic relationships through the World Wide Web. *Public Relations Review, 24*(3), 321–334.

Kent, M. L., & Taylor, M. (2003). Maximizing media relations: A Web site checklist. *Public Relations Quarterly, 48*(1), 14–18.

Kingdon, J. (1995). *Agendas, alternatives, and public policies* (2nd ed.). New York: HarperCollins.

Kiousis, S., Mitrook, M., Wu, X., & Seltzer, T. (2006). First- and second-level agenda-building and agenda-setting effects: Exploring the linkages among candidate news releases, media coverage, and public opinion during the 2002 Florida gubernatorial election. *Journal of Public Relations Research, 18*(3), 265–285.

Kiousis, S., Popescu, C., & Mitrook, M. A. (2007). Understanding influence on corporate reputation: An examination of public relations efforts, media coverage, public opinion, and financial performance from an agenda-building and agenda-setting perspective. *Journal of Public Relations Research, 19*(2), 147–165.

Kiousis, S. & Strömbäck, J. (2010). The White House and public relations: Examining the linkages between presidential communications and public opinion. *Public Relations Review, 36*(1), 7–14.

Kiousis, S., & Wu, X. (2008). International agenda-building and agenda-setting: Exploring the influence of public relations counsel on US news media and public perceptions of foreign nations. *International Communication Gazette, 70*(1), 58–75.

Kumar, M. J. (2005). Presidential press conferences: The importance and evolution of an enduring forum. *Presidential Studies Quarterly, 35*(1), 166–192.

Lancendorfer, K. M., & Lee, B. (2003, August). *Agenda building and the media: A content analysis of the relationships between the media in the 2002 Michigan Governor's race.* Paper presented at the annual meeting of the Association for Education in Journalism and Mass Communication, Kansas City, MO.

Lang, G. E., & Lang, K. (1983). *The battle for public opinion: The president, the press, and public opinion.* New York: Columbia University Press.

Lavrakas, P. J., & Traugott, M. W. (Eds.). (2000), *Election polls, the news media, and democracy.* New York: Chatham House.

Ledingham, J. A. (2006). Relationship management: A general theory of public relations. In C. H. Botan & V. Hazleton (Eds.), *Public relations theory II* (pp. 465–483). New York: Erlbaum.

Ledingham, J. A., & Bruning, S. D. (Eds.). (2000). *Public relations as relationship management: A relational approach to the study and practice of public relations.* Mahwah, NJ: Erlbaum.

Lee, M. (Ed.). (2008). *Government public relations: A reader.* Boca Raton, FL: CRC Press.

Lippmann, W. (1997). *Public opinion.* New York: Free Press. (Original work published 1922)

Livingston, S., & Bennett, W. L. (2003). Gatekeeping, indexing, and live event news: Is technology altering the construction of news? *Political Communication, 20*(4), 363–380.

Livingston, S., & Eachus, T. (1996). Indexing news after the Cold War: Reporting U.S. ties to Latin American paramilitary organizations. *Political Communication, 13*(4), 423–436.

Lopez–Escobar, E., Llamas, J. P., McCombs, M., & Rey, F. (1998). Two levels of agenda setting among advertising and news in the 1995 Spanish elections. *Political Communication, 15*(2), 225–238.

Martin, W. P., & Singletary, M. W. (1981). Newspaper treatment of state government releases. *Journalism Quarterly, 58*(1), 93–96.

McChesney, R. W. (1997). *Corporate media and the threat to democracy.* New York: Seven Stories Press.

McCombs, M. E., & Shaw, D. L. (1972). Agenda-setting function of mass media. *Public Opinion Quarterly, 36*(2), 176–184.

Miller, B. (2010). Community stakeholders and marketplace advocacy: A model of advocacy, agenda building, and industry approval. *Journal of Public Relations Research, 22*(1), 85–112.

Mitchell, P., & Daves, R. (1999). Media polls, candidates, and campaigns. In B. I. Newman (Ed.), *Handbook of political marketing* (pp. 177–195). Thousand Oaks, CA: Sage.

Mitrook, M. A., Parish, N. B., & Seltzer, T. (2008). From advocacy to accommodation: A case study of the Orlando Magic's public relations efforts to secure a new arena. *Public Relations Review, 34*(2), 161–168.

Morton, L. P., & Warren J. (1992a). Acceptance characteristics of hometown press releases. *Public Relations Review, 18*(4), 385–390.

Morton, L. P., & Warren J. (1992b). News elements and editors' choices. *Public Relations Review, 18*(1), 47–52.

Morton, L. P. & Warren J. (1992c). Proximity: Localization vs. distance in PR news releases. *Journalism Quarterly, 69*(4), 1023–1028.

Ohl, C. M., Pincus, J. D., Rimmer, T., & Harrison, D. (1995). Agenda building role of news releases in corporate takeovers. *Public Relations Review, 21*(2), 89–101.

Patterson, T. E. (1993). *Out of order: How the decline of the political parties and the growing power of the mass media undermine the American way of electing presidents.* New York: Knopf.

Paun, M. (2009). Perceptions on the effectiveness of communication between public institutions and journalists through social media. *Styles of Communication, 1*(1), 1–14.

Perloff, R. M. (1998). *Political communication: Politics, press, and public in America.* Mahwah, NJ: Erlbaum.

Pfau, M., & Wan, H-H. (2006). Persuasion: An intrinsic function of public relations. In C. H. Botan & V. Hazleton (Eds.), *Public relations theory II* (pp. 101–136). New York: Erlbaum.

Phillips, M. (2009). *A national discussion on health care reform.* The White House—President Barack Obama. Retrieved from http://www.whitehouse.gov/blog/A-National-Discussion-on-Health-Care-RefoRM/

Prior, M. (2007). *Post-broadcast democracy: How media choice increases inequality in political involvement and polarizes elections.* New York: Cambridge University Press.

Sheafer, T., & Weimann, G. (2005). Agenda-building, agenda-setting, priming, individual voting intentions and the aggregate results: An analysis of four Israeli elections. *Journal of Communication, 55*(2), 347–365.

Shin, J-H., Cameron, G. T., & Cropp, F. (2006). Occam's razor in the contingency theory: A national survey on 86 contingent variables. *Public Relations Review, 32*(3), 282–286.

Sparrow, B. H. (1999). *Uncertain guardians: The news media as a political institution.* Baltimore, MD: Johns Hopkins University Press.

Sparrow, B. H. (2006). A research agenda for an institutional media. *Political Communication, 32*(2), 145–157.

Strömbäck, J., Mitrook, M. A., & Kiousis, S. (2010). Bridging two schools of thought: Applications of public relations theory to political marketing. *Journal of Political Marketing, 9*(1/2), 73–92.

Sweetser, K. D., & Lariscy, R. W. (2008). Candidates make good friends: An analysis of candidates' use of Facebook. *International Journal of Strategic Communication, 2*(3), 175–198.

Taylor, M., & Kent, M. L. (2004). Congressional web sites and their potential for public dialogues. *Atlantic Journal of Communication, 12*(2), 59–76.

Tedesco, J. C. (2004). Changing the channel: Use of the Internet for communicating about politics. In L. L. Kaid (Ed.), *Handbook of political communication research* (pp. 507–532). Mahwah, NJ: Erlbaum.

Tilson, D. J. (2005). Religious-spiritual tourism and promotional campaiging: A church state partnership for St. James and Spain. *Journal of Hospitality & Leisure Marketing, 12*(1/2), 9–40.

Trammell, K. D., & Williams, A. P. (2004). Beyond direct mail: Evaluating candidate e-mail messages in the 2002 Florida gubernatorial campaign. *Journal of eGovernment, 1*(1), 105–122.

Turk, J. V. (1985). Information subsidies and influence. *Public Relations Review, 11*(3), 10–25.

Turk, J. V. (1986). Information subsidies and media content: A study of public relations influence on the news. *Journalism Monographs, 100,* 1–29.

Turk, J. V. (1991). Public relations' influence on the news. In D. L. Protess & M. McCombs (Eds.), *Agenda-setting: Readings on media, public opinion and policymaking* (pp. 211–222). Hillsdale, NJ: Erlbaum.

Turk, J. V., & Franklin, B. (1987). Information subsidies: Agenda-setting traditions. *Public Relations Review, 13*(4), 29–41.

Vasquez, G. M., & Taylor, M. (2001). Research perspectives on "the public." In R. L. Heath (Ed.), *Handbook of public relations* (pp. 139–154). Thousand Oaks, CA: Sage.

Walters, L. M., & Walters, T. N. (1996). It loses something in the translation: Syntax and survival of key words in science and nonscience press releases. *Science Communication, 18,* 165–180.

Walters, T. N., Walters, L. M., & Gray, R. (1996). Agenda-building in the 1992 presidential campaign. *Public Relations Review, 22*(1), 9–24.

Wanta, W., & Foote, J. (1994). The president–news media relationship: A time series analysis of agenda setting. *Journal of Broadcasting & Electronic Media, 38,* 437–448.

Wanta, W., & Kalyango, Y. J (2007). Terrorism and Africa: A study of agenda building in the United States. *International Journal of Public Opinion Research, 19*(4), 434–450.

Wanta, W., Stephenson, M. A., Turk, J. V., & McCombs, M. E. (1989). How presidents' State of the Union talk influences news media agendas. *Journalism Quarterly, 66,* 537–541.

Weaver, D. H. (1980). Audience need for orientation and media effects. *Communication Research, 7*(3), 361–376.

Williams, A. P., & Trammell, K. D. (2005). Candidate campaign e-mail messages in the presidential election 2004. *American Behavioral Scientist, 49*(4), 560–574.

Zaller, J. R. (1992). *The nature and origins of mass opinion*. New York: Cambridge University Press.

Zaller, J., & Chiu, D. (1996). Government's little helper: U.S. press coverage of foreign policy crises, 1945–1991. *Political Communication, 13*(4), 385–405.

Zoch, L. M., & Molleda J-C. (2006). Building a theoretical model of media relations using framing, information subsidies and agenda building. In C. Botan & V. Hazleton (Eds.), *Public relations theory II* (pp. 279–309). Mahwah, NJ: Erlbaum.

4

POLITICAL PUBLIC RELATIONS AND AGENDA BUILDING

John C. Tedesco

Introduction

Without doubt, public relations and politics have been intertwined in American politics since the American Revolution and the fight for independence from England. In fact, "No taxation without representation" was one of the first political slogans widely used to emphasize British colonists' fight for independence from England and its monarchy (McKinnon, Tedesco, & Lauder, 2001). The slogan is associated with the Boston Tea Party, which was one of the ensuing nation's first significant political events. The Boston Tea Party was a staged event aimed to earn media attention and to emphasize the American colonists' disagreement with the Tea Act passed by the British Parliament in 1773 to impose taxes on tea shipped to America (McKinnon et al., 2001). The slogan emphasized American colonists' objection to taxes going back to the British monarchy when colonists were without direct representation in the British Parliament. In current-day, Washington, DC residents use the campaign slogan to emphasize their desire for direct representation in the U.S. Congress.

The Boston Tea Party remains an important part of political history in the United States. The fact that "Tea Party" references are still used in American politics demonstrates not only the poignant power and legacy of the pivotal political event but also an enduring national concern among its people for representation and accountability in politics. A modern "Tea Party" movement rose to the national media agenda through a series of organized local and national protests throughout the country in 2009 and 2010. The protests were organized to raise public awareness about sweeping federal laws enacted by President Barack Obama and his administration, specifically laws that required significant economic spending. Supporters of the modern Tea

Party movement were upset with the government spending associated with the economic stimulus and recovery packages and the costs associated with, and the idea behind the mandatory aspects of, the healthcare reform bill. Protesters behind the Tea Party movement earned valuable media attention through their events and were successful at getting their message on the mainstream media agenda mostly by the way of political protests and rallies.

During the 2010 U.S. midterm primary election season, several candidates backed by supporters of the modern Tea Party movement were successful at earning their party's nomination and some were elected to the U.S. Congress. Perhaps the most pivotal role of the Tea Party movement developed in the 2010 special election held to replace the U.S. Senate seat made vacant through the death of the long-standing, revered Democratic Senator Ted Kennedy of Massachusetts. Aided in part by fund-raising support, advertising buys, and endorsements from Tea Party groups and in part by the media attention surrounding the unique Tea Party groups, Republican Scott Brown won the special election and the legendary Democratic seat held by Kennedy since 1962 and Democrats since 1953 (Powell, 2010).

As McKinnon et al. (2001) acknowledge in their *Handbook of Public Relations* chapter on political public relations, others have specified Thomas Paine's *Common Sense*, James Madison's draft of the Bill of Rights, and Alexander Hamilton, Madison, and John Jay's *The Federalist Papers* as persuasive political public relations documents used to influence media and to persuade and mobilize colonists in support of the U.S. Constitution and its first set of amendments (Cutlip, Center, & Broom, 1994; Seitel, 1995).

Although these examples are illustrative of political public relations generally, they may also be viewed as specific instances of events and documents that influenced, or set, the political agenda of their day. Against this background, this chapter aims to define agenda building within the context of political communication and public relations, review political public relations and agenda building theory and research, and offer suggestions for future research in this area.

Political Public Relations

In "Political Power through Public Relations," McKinnon et al. (2001) acknowledge that throughout history public relations strategies and tactics have witnessed widespread application in political contexts. From staging political events (protests, rallies, whistle-stop tours, speeches) to developing or disseminating promotional materials or information subsidies (advertisements, posters, fliers, press releases, campaign brochures, and leaflets), and from creating campaign logos and slogans (for example, Eisenhower's 1952, "I Like Ike"; Reagan's 1984, "Morning Again in America"; Obama's 2008, "Change We Can Believe In" and "Hope") to packaging, promoting, and spinning political information for media, public relations strategies and strategists are so widespread in politics that it is impossible to list all the various ways public relations tactics are strategically employed in political contexts.

Despite this, political public relations is a relatively new research area within both the political communication and public relations academic communities. As Strömbäck and Kiousis acknowledge in the opening chapter of this volume, the role of media is central to both political communication and public relations research and theory. In fact, Strömbäck and Kiousis define political public relations as follows:

> Political public relations is the management process by which an organization or individual for political purposes, through purposeful communication and action, seeks to influence and to establish, build, and maintain beneficial relationships and reputations with its key publics to help support its mission and achieve its goals.

While the chapters in this edited volume collectively span much of the terrain within this comprehensive definition of political public relations, this chapter will focus more specifically on the ways that political actors and political organizations, political audiences (publics), and media influence and shape the political agenda.

Perhaps part of the increased scholarly attention to political public relations stems from the trend whereby political public relations strategies and tactics have become increasingly influential in political processes (Esser, Reinemann, & Fan, 2001; Tedesco, 2005a). In fact, Esser et al. (2001) assert that there are three historical stages that characterize campaign news coverage in the United States. The first stage, which they identify as news coverage prior to 1972, is characterized by media focus on campaign issues. Stage 2, which spans 1972 to 1988, saw a shift away from issues and an increased focus on candidate and campaign strategies. From 1988 onwards, metacommunication, or media coverage of the campaign strategies and the role of media in reporting those strategies, came to dominate election coverage. While this observation alone is interesting, Esser et al. (2001) also assert that the shifts in election news reporting styles have been accompanied by shifts in sources informing the political news content. For example, in the first stage, candidates and official campaign statements about issue positions represented the primary sources of election news content. In the metacommunication stage, campaign spin doctors, or the campaign's sophisticated and calculating message strategists, have emerged as both sources of the news content and objects of its analysis by journalists.

Increased journalistic use of and reliance on the campaigns' professional and strategic public relations efforts suggests a more influential and prominent role for political public relations in the current media environment. Since campaigns disseminate a massive amount of information aimed to favorably influence interpretation of polling figures, current events, political outcomes, and policies to ensure their campaign is featured in the best possible light, the metacommunication phase also suggests that the campaign's public relations efforts have greater potential to shape news and public opinion than they used to. Also contributing to this might be the fact that the need for information subsidies has become greater as most newspapers and broadcast media are facing ever-tighter budgets.

Agenda Building: Theoretical Foundations

Agenda building is an aspect of agenda setting research (McCombs, 2004), although Cobb and Elder (1971) first used the term *agenda building* to question why some issues get attention from decision makers while others fail to do so. While the original agenda setting effect explores relationships between issue salience within mass media content and issue salience among the mass audience, agenda building explores the sources that make up news content and influence the mass media agenda. In fact, the idea behind agenda setting has roots in observations made by Walter Lippmann in *Public Opinion* (1922/1997), published almost a century ago. Lippmann observed the power of the media in their ability to signal, or to select and present, information and events worthy of public attention. By signaling and channeling attention through editorial gate keeping, he theorized that media have the power not only to draw attention to issues but also to present information in ways that shape public opinion. Another important origin for agenda setting research stems from Cohen's (1963) classic assertion that the press "may not be successful much of the time in telling people what to think, but it is stunningly successful in telling its readers what to think about" (p. 13). Lippmann's observation and Cohen's assertion served as important foundational building blocks for McCombs and Shaw's initial investigations of the agenda setting hypothesis (1972; see also Shaw & McCombs, 1977). Their pioneering work clearly demonstrated the ability of the press to influence and shape public opinion regarding the salience of issues.

Now more than 11 presidential elections and more than 40 years removed from McCombs and Shaw's first empirical evidence for agenda setting, the theory has expanded and evolved considerably, as evidenced by the more than 400 scholarly publications spanning some feature of agenda setting (McCombs, 2004).

In a review of the agenda setting tradition, McCombs (2004) acknowledges five stages of agenda setting research as follows: basic agenda setting effects, attribute agenda setting effects, contingent conditions for agenda setting effects, sources of the media agenda, and consequences of agenda setting effects. What McCombs identifies as the fourth stage, or the stage that questions the sources of the media agenda, has become known as agenda building (Berkowitz & Adams, 1990; Lang & Lang, 1981, 1983).

Agenda building takes the agenda setting hypothesis—that media influence or shape the public agenda—one step backward to questions related to which sources, if any, influence the media agenda. More specifically, scholars define agenda building as the process of influence sources hold over the media agenda (Salwen, 1985) or the "overall process of creating mass media agendas" (Berkowitz & Adams, 1990, p. 723). Others have described agenda building in the public relations setting as a process of "sources' interactions with gatekeepers, a give-and-take process in which sources seek to get their information published and the press seeks to get that information from independent sources" (Ohl, Pincus, Rimmer, & Harrison, 1995, p. 90). Yet others describe the source–journalist relationship as a tug-of-war: "While sources attempt to 'manage' the news, putting the best light on themselves, journalists concurrently 'manage' the sources in order to extract the information they want" (Gans, 1979, p. 116). Also employing the metaphor of a dance, Gans depicted a relationship in which the "sources do the leading" (p. 116).

Exploring public relations is essential to the study of agenda building because public relations information and activities, mostly in the way of information subsidies, are purposefully created to influence the media agenda (Curtin, 1999; Gandy, 1982; Turk, 1986). In fact, estimates from various sources indicate that upwards of 25% (to as much as 80%) of news content is generated by public relations efforts (Cameron, Sallot, & Curtin, 1997; Curtin, 1999; Kaid, 1976; Sallot & Johnson, 2006), with journalists responding to a survey estimating the influence at the rate of 44% (Sallot & Johnson, 2006). While this reliance on public relations materials may seem high, many journalists indicate a reluctance to use public relations information subsidies due to a lack of trust between the journalism and public relations fields (Cameron et al., 1997; Supa & Zoch, 2009).

Agenda building research received increased scholarly attention following Gandy's (1982) appeal for researchers "to go beyond agenda setting constructs to determine who sets the media agenda, how and for what purpose it is set, and with what impact on the distribution of power and values in society" (p. 7). Gandy's call prompted researchers to expand the agenda setting hypothesis to include exploration of sources of the news agenda (Berkowitz, 1987; Cobb & Elder, 1983, Weaver & Elliott, 1985). Nevertheless, compared to traditional agenda setting research, agenda building research has been much less explored (Rogers, Dearing, & Bregman, 1993).

In addition to exploring the sources of the media agenda, scholars interested in agenda building have begun to explore the possibility that public relations materials, mostly in the way of information subsidies, can influence not only the salience of issues presented in media but also the substance or tone in which media report an issue. In order to distinguish these types of agenda setting effects, the scholarly community has distinguished between "first-level" and "second-level" agenda setting. First-level agenda setting is what is traditionally referred to as the agenda setting effect whereby the salience of objects on the media agenda (for example, issues or candidates) are compared with the salience of these same objects on the public agenda. As agenda setting theory expanded, scholars began questioning whether the media, in addition to influencing the salience of objects, also could influence the salience of the object attributes (for example, issue or candidate attributes).

Typically, researchers explore two types of attributes in studies of second-level agenda setting: substantive and affective (Kiousis, Mitrook, Wu, & Seltzer, 2006; McCombs, Lopez-Escobar, & Llamas, 2000). For example, when describing candidate characteristics or candidate image, McCombs et al. (2000) demonstrated that a substantive image appeal may include references to such things as a candidate's qualifications, biographical information, personality traits, or past performances. Measures of affective attributes are more likely to focus on favorable, unfavorable, or neutral descriptions provided to describe the substantive attributes. In fact, McCombs and Shaw (1993) began to assert the possibility that object attributes could be included as part of the agenda setting hypothesis and acknowledge:

> Both the selection of objects for attention and the selection of frames for thinking about these objects are powerful agenda-setting roles. Central to the news agenda and its daily set of objects—issues, personality, events, etc.—are the perspectives that journalists and, subsequently, members of the public employ. These perspectives direct attention toward certain attributes and away from others.
>
> (p. 62)

Similarly, McCombs and Evatt (1995) argue that when journalists, just like members of the public, describe issues or individuals, some attributes are emphasized, some are deemphasized or simply mentioned in passing, and others are ignored completely.

Attributes of an agenda object have been conceived as being similar to framing and its effects, but the scholarly community continues to debate whether framing and second-level agenda setting are the same theoretical phenomenon. More on the scholarly debate about framing and second-level agenda setting can be found elsewhere (Ghanem, 1997; Kosicki, 1993; McCombs, Llamas, Lopez-Escobar, & Rey, 1997; Price & Tewksbury, 1995; Scheufele, 2000)

Information Subsidies

Because much of the agenda building research focuses on information subsidies, investigations of agenda building typically require researchers to explore a range of information subsidies stemming from the nonprofit, corporate, government, and media sources that typically are found in the media. Berkowitz and Adams (1990), citing the work of Gandy (1982) and Turk (1986), indicate that information subsidies concern "the efforts of news sources to intentionally shape the news agenda by reducing journalists' costs of gathering information" (p. 723). As Gandy (1982) explains, information may be viewed like other commodities in that it is also subject to periods of high and low supply or demand. Thus, if sources ensure their information is available to journalists in times of high demand, it is more likely the source will influence the media agenda. Sources influencing the media agenda range from the president, politicians and political candidates, interest groups, and nonprofit organizations (Berkowitz & Adams, 1990), and include a relatively narrow group of government and corporate elites (Reese, Grant, & Danielian, 1994).

Although mostly within political communication, but increasingly expanding into public relations domains, researchers have explored the influence of advertising, special events, and even the role of other media in influencing the media agenda. The section of the chapter on intermedia agenda setting explores the role of media in agenda building for other media, but typically political advertising and political public relations materials represent much of the communication sources explored in agenda building research. For example, one of the earliest agenda building studies investigated the sources used by journalists in Watergate coverage and demonstrated that the shifts in coverage were reflected by the dominant sources that comprised much of the coverage (Lang & Lang, 1983).

Perhaps best known as one of the first studies to employ agenda building explicitly, Lang and Lang (1981) proposed a four-step model of agenda building in which media first spotlight or signal specific issues, events, individuals, or groups. The second step involves consolidating information into a single frame or a clear description of a problem. The third step involves the strategic alignment of the information subsidy to a recognizable feature in the political landscape in order to help propel it and legitimize the issue. The final step requires spokespersons or spin doctors to ensure the media understand the relevance of the issue and its importance to the political environment.

Typically, information subsidies take the form of press releases, advertisements, direct mail, Web pages, press conference, speeches, rallies, or protests (Gandy, 1982; Turk, 1986; Turk & Franklin, 1987). In the Internet age, Web sites in particular have emerged as important information subsidies both for current news and information and as repositories for previous information. As Tedesco and McKinnon (1998) observed, ease of transfer of electronic information available online could advantage political public relations professionals as providing the information in a format easily transferable to news should increase the likelihood of use by media. While the large majority of research on agenda building has explored sources of the media agenda, there is also the possibility that the Internet has enabled organizations to bypass media and directly communicate with the public, making agenda setting effects possible directly on the public agenda. However, television, in particular, remains a significant source for voters and a more likely agenda influencer. While the depiction of an influential media able to select, interpret, and frame news through the gatekeeping process endures (Entman, 1989, 1993), Turk acknowledged that "sources of the raw material of information upon which journalists rely may ultimately have as much to do with the media's agenda as the selection process of journalists themselves" (1986, p. 15).

Considering that the news helps inform the public and that information appearing in news helps lend credibility and legitimacy to messages (Walters, Walters, & Gray, 1996), corporations, governments, nonprofit organizations, political campaigns, and the like spend millions on information subsidies with the goal of earning free media coverage or to influence journalistic interpretation and analysis of information. In political campaigns, influencing the media agenda is about both getting the campaign's top agenda items in the news and influencing the tone and interpretation of coverage. While first- and second-level agenda setting effects will be explored briefly later in the chapter, it is important to note that the struggle for "interpretive dominance" is also an important consideration for agenda building. For example, several scholars refer to the source–journalist relationship and the struggle by sources to have their voice and opinions presented as a battle for interpretive dominance (C. Smith, 1995; Stuckey & Antczak, 1995). Attempts to influence the way an issue is reported would fall within the second-level of agenda setting, which focuses not only on the issue items on the agenda but also the attributes or features of those issues. In fact, in line with the argument about interpretive dominance, Kanervo and Kanervo (1989) argue that when sources are successful at getting their information presented within the news, it represents a victory for the source and a defeat for all the other sources competing for that same spot to have their viewpoint expressed in the news.

Relevant in this context is the theoretical model for influencing the media agenda through the use of framing and information subsidies offered by Zoch and Molleda (2006). Their model offers practitioners a step-by-step guide to influence the media agenda. They argue that the first step is to understand the need to generate an information subsidy. This is followed by producing or implementing the information subsidy; verifying information contained in the subsidy; and preparing talking points in the event of media scrutiny or attention. The media are then contacted and the subsidy is distributed. Media coverage or public response is monitored or surveyed, a follow-up is issued if necessary, and the effectiveness or success of the strategy is evaluated. As with any public relations effort at influencing media, knowledge of media routines and structures, relevance of information to audience, timeliness, and news values will increase public relations success.

When it comes to agenda building, the media relations aspect of public relations takes center stage. Media relations is not a particularly complex notion, as demonstrated by the formula for success provided by Zoch and Molleda

(2006), However, successful media relations require a professional skilled at relationships because public relations is a "people-to-people business" requiring media relations professionals to "deal with writers, editors, producers and photographers—not with newspapers, television stations, radio microphones and Web sites" (p. 70). Managing relationships with media professionals is crucial to public relations success because reporters and sources mutually evaluate each other's credibility, openness, and trust.

Against this background, the following sections will review agenda building research in several areas where it has clustered: president–press relationship, election and political campaigns, intermedia agenda building, and international agenda building.

President–Press Relationship

In an analysis of the president and public relations, Tedesco (2003) asserts that consideration of the president as the chief public relations officer in the United States is not too much of a stretch, especially taking into account that the president is charged with forging mutually beneficial relationships between his administration and the other branches of government, foreign governments, and the U.S. and international media and citizens. As with any other high profile public relations position, president–press relations are a critical dynamic in the success of the presidency. In this context, the president's platform as one of the most influential leaders in the world provides him with a critical advantage for influencing the media agenda. In fact, scholars argue that no other "figure dominates the news like the president of the United States" (Johnson, Wanta, & Boudreau, 2004, p. 178).

In one of the initial investigations of presidential power to influence the media agenda, Iyengar and Kinder (1987) demonstrated that a presidential speech delivered on energy increased the public concern about energy by more than 4%. However, for other issues, the president was not as successful at shifting the public agenda, but instead the public agenda shifted after the media agenda shifted. Yet other researchers suggest that presidential personality may be an intervening factor in the president's ability to set the media agenda (Wanta, Stephenson, VanSlyke Turk, & McCombs, 1989). Along this line, Wanta (1991) found that the president–press–public relationship was interdependent, but that the president was more likely to influence the media and public agendas in times of favorable public approval or high popularity.

Delli Carpini (1994) examined the president–press relationship in the electronic age and identified three prominent relational shifts. The first period, which spans the 1920s up to the 1960s, was characterized by supportive relationships between presidents and the press as a relatively "neutral conduit for White House news" (Delli Carpini, 1994, p. 172). Tumultuous times at home in the United States with the Civil Rights struggles, the assassination of John F. Kennedy, and Watergate, combined with the unpopular Vietnam War, increased media scrutiny of presidential administrations. This resulted in the media uncovering various forms of manipulation and deceit. Delli Carpini characterized the president–press relationship as "adversarial rather than cooperative" (1994, p. 193) during the 1960s and 1970s. As Delli Carpini explains, "public relations and media specialists in Jimmy Carter's administration were often frustrated by the president's unwillingness to recognize the importance of courting the press and managing the information environment effectively" (1994, p. 193). Reagan's presidency was successful at creating a new presidential–press dynamic since Reagan had a "unique blend of personal qualities, media savvy and top-flight advisers" (Delli Carpini, 1994, p. 194). As a result, Reagan was able to demonstrate the potential ability of a president to dominate the president–media relationship.

Despite the president's vantage point and the advantage it provides to "gather the nation to its feet" (Broder, 1987, p. 4), research does not show the president as having an unconditional ability to influence the political agenda. In most cases, researchers exploring the president–press–public relationship conclude that there is a reciprocal relationship among the three (Dalton, Beck, Huckfeldt, & Koetzle, 1998; Gonzenbach, 1992; Lang & Lang, 1983; Tedesco, 2001, 2005a, 2005b). Various studies, conducted with different presidents under different circumstances, have demonstrated that at various times media (Gonzenbach, 1992) or the president (Johnson, Wanta, & Boudreau, 2004) were able to exert more influence on the agenda. In their analysis of the way four presidents attempted to influence media coverage of drugs, Johnson, Wanta, and Boudreau (2004) found that the president was a very influential agenda builder. While at least one study found that the president exerted little influence on the agenda building process (Johnson, Wanta, Boudreau, Blank-Libra, Schaffer, & Turner, 1996), most studies conclude that a president's characteristics, personality, approval rating, and the political circumstances dictate whether agenda building is likely (Wanta et al., 1989). Interestingly, even in times of national crises like the immediate aftermath of the September 11, 2001 terrorist attacks on the United States, the president did not demonstrate the ability to build the media agenda. Instead, research demonstrates a reciprocal relationship between first- and second-level agendas from the Bush administration and media (Mitrook, Seltzer, Kiousis, Popescu, & Shields, 2006).

In an exploration of how single political events may shape the media agenda, Kaid, Hale, and Williams (1977) explored President Ford's campaign visit to Oklahoma City and its resulting impact on media. In this case, Kaid et al. (1977) concluded that the visit did not significantly influence agenda rankings of issues on radio, television, or newspaper outlets. Furthermore, Kaid reported that the issues stressed by media coverage of the visit did not correlate significantly with public recollection of issues discussed. While the recent "Tea Party" protests represent cases where specific events appeared to capture the media attention, research regarding social movements indicates that public demonstrations rarely receive much media attention in Washington, DC—particularly if they do not fit within the news agenda already established by the media (J. Smith, McCarthy, McPhail, & Augustyn, 2001).

Several scholars have focused on the State of the Union address as a single event with great potential to set the media agenda. The State of the Union is presented before members of both houses of Congress, the Supreme Court, military leaders, and the heads of the president's cabinet, and is televised on most major television channels. The television audience for most State of the Union addresses typically approaches 50 million on the evening of the address and millions more in secondary exposure. In one of the first analyses of the State of the Union and the press agenda, Gilberg, Eyal, McCombs, and Nicholas (1980) found that issues prominent in the media prior to the address influenced the content of the State of the Union. Miller and Wanta (1996) also indicate that the single State of the Union address may not be enough to set the media agenda. They assert that the "president needs the cumulative effect of the daily repetition of news media coverage to advance the agenda of issues that he deems important" (p. 400).

While not the president, the Speaker of the House has the advantage of being able to use the office as a bully pulpit. Kiousis, Laskin, and Kim (2009) examined the Speaker's ability to influence the media agenda and found significant first- and second-level agenda building links between Congressional communication and media coverage. In another political setting below the presidential level, Weaver and Elliott (1985) concluded that the Bloomington, Indiana city council agenda appeared to build the media agenda when reporting on local issues.

Candidates and Election Campaigns

Turning to election campaigns, several studies have investigated if, and to what extent, candidates are able to build the media agenda. One of the earliest studies was done by Kaid who, in an investigation of press release content distributed by a 1972 state senate campaign, found that the majority (30 of 50) of "stories printed were verbatim from the candidate's release or verbatim with a few omissions" (1976, p. 137). Kaid (1976) also found that personal information and campaign announcement were more likely than issue content to get picked up by the press.

The variability of candidates to influence the media agenda was the result in three related studies of press releases and their influence on both media and opposing candidates' agendas. Using official press releases appearing on presidential primary candidate and presidential candidate Web sites, Tedesco (2001, 2005a, 2005b) explored the ability of a candidate's agenda to influence not only the media agenda but also his or her political opponent's agenda.

Results from these studies demonstrate reciprocal or mutual influence between candidates and media for policy issues during political campaigns. However, when measuring strategy agenda items, Tedesco demonstrated that the reciprocal relationship existed only for McCain during the 2000 presidential primaries, suggesting that McCain may have enjoyed a more favorable relationship with media than the other presidential contenders. The studies also demonstrated that the candidates are likely to influence each other's campaign agenda, or even set the agenda for their opponent, at various times throughout the election campaign (Tedesco, 2005a, 2005b). Tedesco labeled this "intercandidate agenda setting."

Intermedia Agenda Building

The media agenda may be influenced not only by external sources, but also by other media. Known as intermedia agenda setting, this process is a form of agenda building in which one media source shapes the agenda for another media source (Lopez-Escobar, Llamas, McCombs, & Lennon, 1998; Reese & Danielian, 1989). In a comprehensive analysis of media coverage of the cocaine war, Danielian and Reese demonstrated the ability of the *New York Times* to establish the agenda on this issue for the major broadcast networks. In fact, *The New York Times* (Gilberg et al., 1980) and other elite press rather consistently appear to shape the agenda for other media, particularly local newspapers and television (Golan, 2006; Protess & McCombs, 1991).

During a study of the 1990 Texas gubernatorial campaign advertising, Roberts and McCombs (1994) demonstrated the ability of political advertising to exert influence on the print media agenda. Perhaps it might be considered an information subsidy because it stemmed from a political campaign, but perhaps it could also be viewed as a form of media within the intermedia agenda setting tradition. With multiple levels of agendas under analysis, the authors first demonstrated the ability of the newspaper agenda to influence the television agenda, but political advertising's ability to influence both sets of media agendas. Roberts and McCombs (1994) concluded that the "influence found here of the newspaper agenda on local television news is not surprising, but the evidence from this study adds political advertising as an agenda setter for both television news and newspaper coverage of the issues" (p. 260). Roberts and McCombs's (1994) research on political advertising, a candidate-controlled medium, inspired researchers to study other forms of campaign media—controlled and uncontrolled—with the goal of exploring the ability of campaigns to influence the media agenda. For example, in an investigation of political advertising and its agenda setting abilities, Boyle (2001) reported that controlled campaign media from Republican challenger Senator Bob Dole (R-KA) during the 1996 presidential campaign appeared to influence media coverage of news late in the campaign, but the same result was not found for incumbent President Bill

Clinton. While Boyle concluded that Dole's advertising content was a strong predictor of issues discussed by media, findings for Clinton indicated that the more he emphasized particular issues in his advertisements, the "less the major daily newspapers covered the issues late in the campaign" (p. 39).

Scholars are also exploring the role of the Internet in agenda building processes. Roberts, Wanta, and Dzwo (2002) found that online news media set the agenda for electronic bulletin board discussions, while Lee, Lancendorfer, and Lee (2005) found a reciprocal influence of issue agendas and their attributes between Korean Internet bulletin boards and newspapers. Ku, Kaid, and Pfau (2003) argued for a potential agenda setting effect based on voter exposure to campaign Web sites during the 2000 U.S. presidential election. In a study of intermedia agenda setting that examined television, advertising, and blogs during the 2004 U.S. presidential election, Sweetser, Golan, and Wanta (2008) furthermore explored whether candidate-controlled public relations tools, in the form of political ads and official campaign blogs, were successful at influencing the news agenda for the major television networks. Although there was a strong correlation between issues covered by candidates on their blogs and issues presented in the other media, the authors conclude that the media actually set the candidates' agenda. There was no correlation between issues presented in candidate ads and media, thus no evidence of agenda building through political advertising.

Scholars have already begun to investigate the role of online social media in the agenda building process. For example, Lariscy, Avery, Sweetser, and Howes (2009) conducted interviews with business journalists throughout the country to investigate the influence of social media on journalists. Although this initial look at the influence of social media showed that journalists do not consider social media important to their daily work, with even fewer indicating consulting social media (less than 3%) such as Twitter or Facebook for news, the fact that social media have become almost ubiquitous makes this scholarly line of investigation worthy of additional exploration.

International Agenda Building

A developing area of scholarship, and one that promises great hope for the future given the global nature of contemporary media, looks at agenda building on the international stage. For example, Wanta and Kalyango, Jr. (2007) studied a variety of U.S. government sources and *The New York Times* coverage of 20 African countries. The authors explored multiple agendas (the president, real-world events, amount of coverage in *The New York Times*, and antiterrorism aid the countries receive) and found that the more President Bush mentioned a specific country in his public statements, the more coverage the country received. They conclude that "President Bush was able to influence *The New York Times* coverage patterns for the 20 African nations through his public statements" (p. 446). Wanta and Kalyango, Jr. (2007) were also able to demonstrate that the countries that received the most coverage linking them to terrorism were also the ones that received the most aid to combat terrorism.

In yet another pioneering work, Sheafer and Gabay (2009) explored international agenda building and frame building through an analysis of the Israeli–Palestinian conflict by exploring how these two rivals influenced international media coverage of their conflict. Results demonstrated that Israel was more successful in presenting its agenda in the U.S. media, while the Palestinian Authority was more successful in the British media. Sheafer and Gabay also stress that news values and event characteristics play a significant role in garnering attention. However, Zhang and Cameron (2002) demonstrate that public relations efforts by international governments were only conditionally successful. While a campaign by the Chinese government was waged to improve its image in the United States, evidence of the campaign's ability to reduce the negative tone in coverage was only moderately successful in *The New York Times*. In a similar study, Kiousis and Wu (2008) found that public relations strategies were successful at the affective attribute level by decreasing the negative coverage and increasing the positive coverage for foreign nations registered with U.S. State Department. In contrast, Sweetser and Brown's exploration (2008) of military public affairs surrounding the 2006 Israeli–Lebanon conflict demonstrates that the military was successful at influencing coverage. Their study points to open-access and on-scene personnel as critical components to increasing media influence.

Conclusion and Future Directions

As this chapter should make clear, there is much vitality in the research on political public relations and agenda building. Since Gandy (1982) first urged scholars to go beyond agenda setting to explore the sources of the media agenda, much territory has been covered. Despite the ground covered in the research community, there remain great opportunities to explore agenda building by studying a wider range of public relations strategies and tactics, more information subsidies, broader or narrower issues and attributes, and more political actors, organizations, and media spanning local to international contexts. There are many opportunities for researchers to carve out research agendas focused on agenda building and political public relations, especially considering the field of political public relations is just now being defined despite years of public relations influence in politics.

As several scholars note, there is an increase in the volume of information subsidies aimed at media with the goal to influence coverage of their issue and the way it gets reported. The increase in information subsidies comes at a time when at least some scholars argue that political public relations is more influential than at any time in our recent past (Esser et al., 2001). Yet, simply because the media environment might be conducive to influence does not mean the public relations effort will exert influence on media. Scholars continue to spotlight the general mistrust and suspicion that has characterized the relationship between media and public relations professions (Cameron et al., 1997; Sallot & Johnson, 2006; Supa & Zoch, 2009; Zoch & Molleda, 2006).

As Howard (2004) stressed, the source–media relationship is one built on interpersonal relationships—and research appears to suggest that favorable relationships with media are an important consideration in the agenda building process (Delli Carpini, 1994; Wanta, 1991; Wanta et al., 1989). Despite the generally contentious relations between media and public relations professionals, research on agenda building shows that sources can be successful at building an agenda for the media. This may be particularly true for routine and official sources (Berkowitz, 1987).

Nevertheless, research indicates that presidents as well as other high-ranking political actors and sources are not uniformly able to influence the media agenda. Instead, research suggests that agenda building may be contingent on the president's personality, approval ratings, or specific issues and attributes of those issues stressed (Gonzenbach, 1992; Iyengar & Kinder, 1987; Johnson et al., 2004; Kiousis et al., 2009; Lang & Lang, 1983; Wanta et al., 1989). Research also demonstrates that political candidates have been inconsistently successful at building the media agenda or influencing agenda attributes (Kaid, 1976; Kiousis, Bartimaroudis, & Han, 1999; Tedesco 2001); that agenda is built over time; and that singular events, such as protests or demonstrations, are not particularly effective in terms of shaping the media agenda (Kaid et al., 1977; J. Smith et al., 2001).

It is the research on intermedia agenda setting that provides the strongest evidence for agenda building. In particular, *The New York Times* stands out as having the most powerful influence on other media (Danielian & Reese, 1989; Gilberg et al., 1980; Golan, 2006; Protess & McCombs, 1991).

Looking ahead, much remains to be done to increase our knowledge and understanding of how media agendas are built; relative effectiveness of different types of agenda builders and information subsidies; and the contingent conditions for agenda building success involving different types of agenda builders and information subsidies. For example, while the president receives a great deal of attention as a potential agenda builder, the contingent conditions for which the president is successful at influencing the media agenda remains to be comprehensively established. Researchers could continue to explore the president through the use of specific events to determine the characteristics of an event that help it shape the media agenda. Furthermore, including the president's public opinion polling data, length of time in office, and the types of issues and their attributes may help researchers make more definitive claims about the president's influence. Additionally, there is a great opportunity to study offices below the presidency as Kiousis et al. (2009) have demonstrated;

for example, governors and military and defense leaders. Foreign heads of state offer researchers some additional sources worthy of exploration in research on agenda building. The fact that researchers have only recently included second-level (attribute) agendas in the agenda building process means that this area is also rich with opportunities.

Additional investigations of intermedia agenda setting/agenda building may offer the most promise for researchers considering that only a handful of studies have looked at agenda building from online sources. While researchers will be challenged by the methodological obstacles of identifying agendas in social media, the fact the news on social media can be distributed across social networks, tagged, and rated indicate that there are abundant possibilities to explore contingent considerations for agenda building through online sources in general and social media in particular. The initial investigations by Lariscy et al. (2009) suggest that continued exploration of online social media will be fruitful for agenda building.

Because the findings on political advertising suggest that it can be a powerful agenda building tool (Boyle, 2001; Roberts & McCombs, 1994), researchers should also include advocacy advertising in agenda building research. Since U.S. advocacy advertising expenditures increased from $50 million in 1994 to more than $1 billion during 2004 (Tedesco, 2007), it is clear that corporate and political organization advertising expenditures beg researchers to explore whether the advertising is influencing the issue agenda, the ways issues are presented in the media, and potential policy impact behind the advertising influence.

References

Berkowitz, D. (1987). TV news sources and news channels: A study in agenda building. *Journalism Quarterly, 64*, 508–513.

Berkowitz, D., & Adams, D. B. (1990). Information subsidy and agenda-building in local television news. *Journalism Quarterly, 67*(4), 723–731.

Boyle, T. P. (2001). Intermedia agenda setting in the 1996 presidential election. *Journalism and Mass Communication Quarterly, 78*(1), 26–44.

Broder, D. S. (1987). *Behind the front page: A candid look at how the news is made.* New York: Simon & Schuster.

Cameron, G. T., Sallot, L. M., & Curtin, P. A. (1997). Public relations and the production of news: A critical review and a theoretical framework. In B. R. Burleson (Ed.), *Communication yearbook, 20* (pp. 111–155). Thousand Oaks, CA: Sage.

Cobb, R. W., & Elder, C. D. (1971). The politics of agenda-building: An alternative perspective for modern democratic theory. *Journal of Politics, 33*, 892–915.

Cobb, R. W., & Elder, C. D. (1983). *Participation in American politics: The dynamics of agenda-building* (2nd ed.). Baltimore, MD: Johns Hopkins University Press.

Cohen, B. (1963). *The press and foreign policy.* Princeton, NJ: Princeton University Press.

Curtin, P. A. (1999). Reevaluating public relations information subsidies: Market-driven journalism and agenda-building theory and practice. *Journal of Public Relations Research, 11*(1), 53–90.

Cutlip, S. M., Center, A. H., & Broom, G. M. (1994). *Effective public relations* (7th ed.). Englewood Cliffs, NJ: Prentice-Hall.

Dalton, R. J., Beck, P. A., Huckfeldt, R., & Koetzle, W. (1998). A test of media-centered agenda setting: Newspaper content and public interests in a presidential election. *Political Communication, 15,* 463–481.

Danielian, L. H., & Reese, S. D. (1989). A closer look at intermedia influences on agenda setting: The cocaine issue of 1986. In P. Shoemaker (Ed.), *Communication campaigns about drugs, government, media and the public* (pp. 47–66). Hillsdale, NJ: Erlbaum.

Delli Carpini, M. X. (1994). Critical symbiosis: Three themes on president–press relations. *Media Studies Journal, 8*(2), 185–197.

Entman, R. M. (1989). *Democracy without citizens: Media and the decay of American politics.* New York: Oxford University Press.

Entman, R. M. (1993). Framing: Toward clarification of a fractured paradigm. *Journal of Communication, 43*(4), 51–58.

Esser, F., Reinemann, C., & Fan, D. (2001). Spin doctors in the United States, Great Britain, and Germany. *Harvard International Journal of Press/Politics, 6,* 16–45.

Gandy, O. H., Jr. (1982). *Beyond agenda setting: Information subsidies and public policy.* Norwood, NJ: Ablex.

Gans, H. (1979). *Deciding what's news.* New York: Random House/Vintage Books.

Ghanem, S. (1997). Filling in the tapestry: The second level of agenda setting. In M. E. McCombs, D. Shaw, & D. Weaver (Eds.), *Communication and democracy: Exploring the intellectual frontiers in agenda setting theory* (pp. 3–14). Mahwah, NJ: Erlbaum.

Gilberg, S., Eyal, C., McCombs, M. E., & Nicholas, D. (1980). The state of the union address and press agenda. *Journalism Quarterly, 57*(4), 584–588.

Golan, G. (2006). Inter-media agenda setting and global news coverage: Assessing the influence of the New York Times on three network television evening news programs. *Journalism Studies, 7*(2), 323–334.

Gonzenbach, W. J. (1992). Time-series analysis of the drug issue, 1985–1990: The press, the president, and public opinion. *International Journal of Public Opinion Research, 4,* 126–147.

Howard, C. M. (2004). Working with reporters: Mastering the fundamentals to build long-term relationships. *Public Relations Quarterly, 49*(1), 36–39.

Iyengar, S., & Kinder, D. (1987). *News that matters: Television and American opinion.* Chicago, IL: University of Chicago Press.

Johnson, T. J., Wanta, W., & Boudreau, T. (2004). Drug peddlers: How four presidents attempted to influence media and public concern on the drug issue. *Atlantic Journal of Communication, 12*(4), 177–199.

Johnson, T. J., Wanta, W., Boudreau, T., Blank-Libra, J., Schaffer, K., & Turner, S. (1996). Influence dealers: A path analysis model of agenda building during Richard Nixon's War on Drugs. *Journalism and Mass Communication Quarterly, 73*(1), 181–194.

Kaid, L. L. (1976). Newspaper treatment of a candidate's news releases. *Journalism Quarterly, 53*(1), 135–157.

Kaid, L. L., Hale, K., & Williams, J. (1977). Media agenda-setting of a specific political event. *Journalism Quarterly, 54,* 584–587.

Kanervo, E. W., & Kanervo, D. (1989). Attempts at agenda controlling in the community press. *Journalism Quarterly, 66,* 308–315.

Kiousis, S., Bartimaroudis, P., & Ban, H. (1999). Candidate image attributes: Experiments on the substantive dimension of second-level agenda setting. *Communication Research, 26,* 414–428.

Kiousis, S., Laskin, A., & Kim, J. K. (2009). *Congressional agenda-building: Examining the influence of Congressional communications from the Speaker of the House.* Paper presented at the International Communication Association convention, Chicago, IL.

Kiousis, S., Mitrook, M., Wu, X., & Seltzer, T. (2006). First- and second-level agenda-building and agenda-setting effects: Exploring the linkages among candidate news releases, media coverage, and public opinion during the 2002 Florida gubernatorial election. *Journal of Public Relations Research, 18*(3), 265–285.

Kiousis, S., & Wu, X. (2008). International agenda building and agenda setting: Exploring the influence of public relations counsel on US news media and public perceptions of foreign nations. *International Communication Gazette, 70*(1), 58–75.

Kosicki, G. M. (1993). Problems and opportunities in agenda-setting research. *Journal of Communication, 43*(2), 100–123.

Ku, G., Kaid, L. L., & Pfau, M. (2003). The impact of Web campaigning on traditional news media and public information processing. *Journalism & Mass Communication Quarterly, 80,* 528–547.

Lang, G. E., & Lang, K. (1981). Watergate: An exploration of the agenda-building process. In G. C. Wilhoit & H. de Bock (Eds.), *Mass communication review yearbook 2* (pp. 447–468). Newbury Park, CA: Sage.

Lang, G. E., & Lang, K. (1983). *The battle for public opinion: The president, the press and the polls during Watergate.* New York: Columbia University Press.

Lariscy, R. W., Avery, E. J., Sweetser, K. D., & Howes, P. (2009). An examination of the role of online social media in journalists' source mix. *Public Relations Review, 35,* 314–316.

Lee, B., Lancendorfer, K., & Lee, J. (2005). Agenda-setting and the Internet: The intermedia influence of Internet bulletin boards on newspaper coverage of the 2000 general election in South Korea. *Asian Journal of Communication, 15,* 57–71.

Lippmann, W. (1997). *Public opinion.* New York: Free Press. (Original work published 1922)

Lopez-Escobar, E., Llamas, J. P., McCombs, M. E., & Lennon, F. R. (1998). Two levels of agenda setting among advertising and news in the 1995 Spanish elections. *Political Communication, 15,* 225–238.

McCombs, M. (2004). *The evolution of agenda-setting theory.* Paper presented to the National Communication Association Convention, Chicago.

McCombs, M., & Evatt, D. (1995). Los temas y los aspectos: Explorando una nueva dimension de la agenda setting [Objects and attributes: Exploring a new dimension of agenda setting]. *Comunicacion y Sociedad, 8*(1), 7–32.

McCombs, M., Llamas, J. P., Lopez-Escobar, E., & Rey, F. (1997). Candidate images in Spanish elections: Second-level agenda-setting effects. *Journalism and Mass Communication Quarterly, 74,* 703–717.

McCombs, M., Lopez-Escobar, E., & Llamas, J. P. (2000). Setting the agenda of attributes in the 1996 Spanish general election. *Journal of Communication, 50,* 77–92.

McCombs, M., & Shaw, D. L. (1972). The agenda setting function of mass media. *Public Opinion Quarterly, 36,* 176–187.

McCombs, M., & Shaw, D. L. (1993). The evolution of agenda setting research: Twenty-five years in the marketplace of ideas. *Journal of Communication, 43*(2), 58–67.

McKinnon, L. M., Tedesco, J. C., & Lauder, T. (2001). Political power through public relations. In R. L. Heath & G. M. Vasquez (Eds.), *Handbook of public relations* (pp. 557–564). Boston, MA: Sage.

Miller, R. A., & Wanta, W. (1996). Sources of the public agenda: The president–press–public relationship. *International Journal of Public Opinion Research, 8*(4), 390–402.

Mitrook, M., Seltzer, T., Klousis, S., Popescu, C., & Shields, A. (2006). *First- and second-level agenda building and agenda setting: Terrorism, the president, and the media.* Paper presented at the International Communication Association convention, Dresden, Germany.

Ohl, C. M., Pincus, J. D., Rimmer, T., & Harrison, D. (1995). Agenda-building role of news releases in corporate takeovers. *Public Relations Review, 21,* 89–101.

Powell, S. S. (Jan. 19, 2010). Scott Brown: The tea party's first electoral victory. *Christian Science Monitor* online. Retrieved from http://www.csmonitor.com/Commentary/Opinion/.

Price, V., & Tewksbury, D. (1995). News values and public opinion: A process: How political advertising and TV news prime viewers to think about issues and candidates. In F. Biocca (Ed.), *Television and political advertising* (pp. 265–309). Hillsdale, NJ: Erlbaum.

Protess, D., & McCombs, M. E. (1991). *Agenda setting: Readings on media, public opinion, and policymaking.* Hillsdale, NJ: Erlbaum.

Reese, S. D., & Danielian, L. H. (1989). Intermedia influence and the drug issue: Converging on cocaine. In P. Shoemaker (Ed.), *Communication campaigns about drugs: Government, media and the public* (pp. 29–46). Hillsdale, NJ: Erlbaum.

Reese, S. D., Grant, A., & Danielian, L. H. (1994). The structure of news sources on television: A network analysis of "CBS News," "Nightline," "MacNeil/Lehrer," and "This Week with David Brinkley." *Journal of Communication, 44*(2), 84–107.

Roberts, M., & McCombs, M. (1994). Agenda-setting and political advertising: Origins of the news agenda. *Political Communication, 11*, 249–262.

Roberts, M., Wanta, W., & Dzwo, T. (2002). Agenda setting and issue salience online. *Communication Research, 29*, 452–465.

Rogers, E. M., Dearing, J. W., & Bregman, D. (1993). The anatomy of agenda-setting research. *Journal of Communication, 43*, 68–84.

Sallot, L., & Johnson, E. A. (2006). Investigating relationships between journalists and public relations practitioners: Working together to set, frame, and build the public agenda, 1991–2004. *Public Relations Review, 32*, 151–159.

Salwen, M. B. (1995). News of Hurricane Andrew: The agenda of sources and the sources' agenda. *Journalism and Mass Communication Quarterly, 72*(4), 826–840.

Scheufele, D. A. (2000). Agenda-setting, priming, and framing revisited: Another look at cognitive effects of political communication. *Mass Communication & Society, 3*(2&3), 297–316.

Seitel, F. S. (1995). *The practice of public relations.* Englewood Cliffs, NJ: Prentice-Hall.

Shaw, D., & McCombs, M. (Eds.). (1977). *The emergence of American political issues: The agenda-setting function of the press.* St. Paul, MN: West.

Sheafer, T., & Gabay, I. (2009). Mediated public diplomacy: A strategic contest over international agenda building and frame building. *Political Communication, 26*, 447–467.

Smith, C. A. (1995). The struggle for interpretive dominance. In K. E. Kendall (Ed.), *Presidential campaign discourse* (pp. 293–303). Albany, NY: SUNY Press.

Smith, J., McCarthy, J. D., McPhail, C., & Augustyn, B. (2001). From protest to agenda building: Description bias in media coverage of protest events in Washington, D.C. *Social Forces, 79*(4), 1397–1423.

Stuckey, M. E., & Antczak, F. J. (1995). The battle of issues and images: Establishing interpretive dominance. In K. E. Kendall (Ed.), *Presidential campaign discourse* (pp. 117–134). Albany, NY: SUNY.

Supa, D. W., & Zoch, L. M. (2009). Maximizing media relations through a better understanding of the public relations–journalist relationship: A quantitative analysis of changes over the past 23 years. *Public Relations Journal, 3*(4), 1–28.

Sweetser, K. D., & Brown, C. W. (2008). Information subsidies and agenda-building during the Israel–Lebanon crisis. *Public Relations Review, 34*, 359–366.

Sweetser, K. D., Golan, G. J., & Wanta, W. (2008). Intermedia agenda setting in television advertising, and blogs during the 2004 election. *Mass Communication & Society, 11*, 197–216.

Tedesco, J. C. (2001). Issue and strategy agenda-setting in the 2000 presidential primaries. *American Behavioral Scientist, 44*(10), 2048–2067.

Tedesco, J. C. (2003). Clinton's public relations nightmares begin. In R. E. Denton & R. L. Holloway (Eds.), *Images, scandal, and communication strategies of the Clinton presidency* (pp. 39–59). Westport, CT: Praeger.

Tedesco, J. C. (2005a). Intercandidate agenda-setting in the 2004 Democratic primary. *American Behavioral Scientist, 49*(1), 92–113.

Tedesco, J. C. (2005b). Issue and strategy agenda-setting in the 2004 presidential election: Exploring the candidate–journalist relationship. *Journalism Studies, 6*(2), 187–201.

Tedesco, J. C. (2007). Advocacy advertising. In L. L. Kaid & C. Holtz-Bacha (Eds.), *Encyclopedia of political communication* (pp. 4–8). Thousand Oaks, CA: Sage.

Tedesco, J. C., & McKinnon, L. M. (1998). *Agenda-setting comparisons of mainstream and on-line publications: The case of presidential press releases.* Paper presented at the National Communication Association convention, New York.

Turk, J. V. (1986). Information subsidies and media content: A study of public relations influence on the news. *Journalism Monographs*, No. 100.

Turk, J. V., & Franklin, B. (1987) Information subsidies: Agenda-setting traditions. *Public Relations Review, 13,* 29–41.

Walters, T. N., Walters, L. M., & Gray, R. (1996). Agenda building in the 1992 presidential campaign. *Public Relations Review, 22*(1), 9–24.

Wanta, W. (1991). Presidential approval ratings as a variable in the agenda building process. *Journalism Quarterly, 68*(4), 672–679.

Wanta, W., & Kalyango, Jr., Y. (2007). Terrorism and Africa: A study of agenda building in the United States. *International Journal of Public Opinion Research, 19*(4), 434–450.

Wanta, W., Stephenson, M. A., VanSlyke Turk, J., & McCombs, M. E. (1989). How president's State of Union talk influenced news media agendas. *Journalism Quarterly, 66,* 537–541.

Weaver, D., & Elliott, S. N. (1985). Who sets the agenda for the media? A study of local agenda-building. *Journalism Quarterly, 62*(1), 87–94.

Zhang, J., & Cameron, G. T. (2003). China's agenda building and image polishing in the US: Assessing an international public relations campaign. *Public Relations Review, 29,* 13–28.

Zoch, L. M., & Molleda, J. C. (2006). Building a theoretical model of media relations using framing, information subsidies, and agenda building. In C. H. Botan & V. Hazleton (Eds.), *Public Relations Theory II* (pp. 279–310). Mahwah, NJ: Erlbaum.

5

PRESIDENTIAL PUBLIC RELATIONS

Matthew Eshbaugh-Soha

Public relations is paramount to political power in American democracy (McKinnon, Tedesco, & Lauder, 2001). And no office in the U.S. government better exemplifies political public relations than the office of the presidency. Presidential power is the power to persuade (Neustadt, 1990), just as public relations is geared fundamentally toward persuasion (Miller, 1989). In the contemporary age, moreover, presidents do not bargain with legislators as Neustadt observed years ago, but presidential persuasion now involves communicating through public speaking and engaging in media relations to reach various target audiences to achieve their policy agendas (Kernell, 1997). In many ways, this is a strategic enterprise; presidents and their staff target policies and publics so as to maximize their opportunities for influence (Edwards, 2009).

No other local, state, or federal institution engages in as much communication or persuasion, has as many resources to cultivate and maintain quality relationships with the media and public, or does so as effectively as the presidency. Although the face of presidential public relations is the president himself, it is not the individual alone who promotes the office and its mission. It is also the president's extensive organizational apparatus that does so. And it is the interaction between the individual and institution that is vital to explaining individual performance and behavior. As Moe (1985) writes, "the distinctive behavioral structures that define an institution derive from the choices of individuals, while the choices of individuals derive from incentives and resources that are shaped by the institutional context itself, as well as the surrounding environment" (p. 236). This is no different from the presidency, its communications operations, and effectiveness.

This chapter will examine the recent development and effectiveness of presidential public relations in an organizational context. In other words, how has the contemporary White House communications organization affected the president's ability to "establish, build, and maintain quality relationships and reputations with its target publics through communication and action to help support its mission," to quote the definition of political public relations in chapter 1? How does the White House hope to reach its target publics? How effective is the presidency in reaching them? And how do these publics influence the White House? It is, of course, through the president's public speeches that he most forcefully and clearly communicates his message of public outreach—rhetoric being central to effective public relations (see Heath, 2001)—just as these organizations facilitate and buttress the president's efforts to do so.

The President's Speeches

The best way for presidents to communicate their message, to maintain and build a relationship with their ultimate target public, the American people, is through public speeches. Presidents deliver several kinds of speeches, not solely in terms of audience and outreach, but also in terms of the president's goals. Presidents deliver few minor, policy-specific speeches (averaging about 13 per year) to communicate and build support for policies pertinent to their agendas. Increasingly, presidents have targeted specific constituencies or interest groups with these speeches, a strategy some have labeled "going narrow." The president's reelection incentive and role as party leader fuel about 50 yearly political speeches to target voters and raise campaign funds for him and members of his political party running for Congress or governor.

The bulk of the president's speeches are generally symbolic or ceremonial speeches without specific policy content. These speeches, delivered anywhere in the domestic United States, amount to a yearly average of 206 and give presidents the opportunity to appear presidential, to play head of state without providing a clear angle for opponents to criticize policy or undermine the office. Some obvious examples include congratulating successful sports teams in the Rose Garden or pardoning a turkey on Thanksgiving, a tradition begun only recently by President George H. W. Bush. Even when symbolism is pronounced, such as during an Obama visit to Home Depot to promote do-it-yourself home weatherization, it is still difficult for presidents to disassociate from their policy record or desire for reelection. Nationally televised addresses allow presidents to blend a policy message while appearing presidential, an important symbolic goal of any speech.

As Figure 5.1 shows, presidents engage frequently in public discourse, with an average of 266 speeches per year since 1953, or about four speeches every 5 days (Ragsdale, 2009). Although the number of speeches declines during the 1950s, there exists a clear upward trend over the remainder of the time

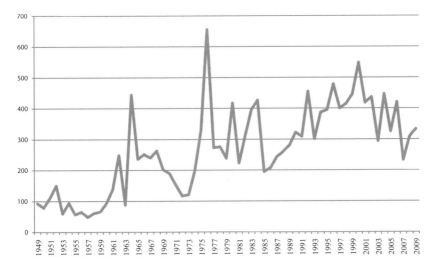

FIGURE 5. 1 Total number of yearly non-major president speeches, 1949–2009. Note: Data compiled from Ragsdale (2009). It is an additive measure of public appearances in Washington, DC and the United States, minor speeches, and political appearances. 2008 and 2009 estimated by the author from The American Presidency project database.

series, with presidents delivering over 400 speeches per year throughout much of the 1980s and 1990s. Closer inspection reveals two eras of presidential speechmaking since 1953. The first period, which runs until 1972, shows an average annual number of speeches of 154. The more recent time period, from 1974 to 2009, produces a 351-speech yearly average.

The increase in speeches is attributable to a number of factors. Technological advances have provided presidents with the basic means to communicate frequently with the American people (Hager & Sullivan, 1994; Lammers, 1982; Powell, 1999). With each technological development, the presidency has not only delivered more speeches, it has also adjusted his communications strategy. With radio, President Franklin Roosevelt communicated directly with the American people through fireside chats, and answered questions from the news media in radio press conferences. With television, John F. Kennedy fostered an enduring image of being presidential, and cultivated the news media and public through televised press conferences and national addresses from the Oval Office. Even advances in presidential travel, from the railways to the airways, have fostered new means of public relations. New media provide additional complications to presidential speaking, but have not deterred presidents from doing so (Cohen, 2008).

Political conditions may have advanced a need to "go public" more frequently. Kernell (1997) argues that institutional changes in Congress encouraged presidents to speak more and enlist the public as an ally in their quest for legislative victories. With the decentralization of congressional decisions—

from committee chairs and party leaders to subcommittees and individual legislators—and increasing instances of divided and gridlocked legislatures, presidents could not rely on bargaining privately with the legislative leadership as they once had. Instead, presidents had to speak to the public to break the logjam in Congress, to raise the stakes, and encourage Congress to act in response to public pressure.

Although some reject the claim that presidential speeches have increased in response to institutional changes in Congress (Powell, 1999), others show that divided government increases presidential speeches (Hart, 1987). Still others show that the state of the economy and the president's approval ratings encourage fewer speeches, although this relationship has lessened in recent years (Eshbaugh-Soha, 2010). Further, a change in approval leads to more national addresses (Ragsdale, 1984), just as each major address translates into a 6% increase in presidential approval ratings (Brace & Hinckley, 1992, p. 56). Higher approval ratings, conversely, and a poor economy encourage fewer political activities (Hager & Sullivan, 1994). One explanation missing from these studies concerns the impact of the presidential communications organizations on the tendency for the president to target the public and media with speeches.

Presidential Communications Organizations and Public Relations

Just as presidential speeches are numerous and vital to public outreach in the contemporary White House, so too does the president rely extensively upon the institutions that organize and coordinate these efforts. This institutionalization of the presidency demands more and specialized offices to facilitate increasing presidential responsibilities (Burke, 2000; Dickinson, 1996; Ragsdale & Theis, 1997), without diverging substantially from the president's own priorities and overall mission of the White House (Kessel, 1974; Kumar, 2007). The White House is an institution, according to Ragsdale and Theis (1997), because it is autonomous, complex, coherent, and adaptable. Concerning public relations and presidential communications, we find three primary offices: The Office of Communications, Press Office, and Office of Public Liaison.

The Office of Communications

Prior to the 1970s, efforts to control the news, through press conferences, speeches, or other coordination efforts were decided upon and organized in an individual and ad hoc fashion (Maltese, 1994, p. 7). Lacking sufficient formal structures for presidential communications, presidents used various means of communication to influence the news. Kennedy initiated live televised press conferences to embellish his public appeal, while Johnson attempted to control all media contacts through the White House Press Office (Maltese, 1994, p. 10). Thus, there was no consistent and enduring organizational structure to cultivate and perpetuate relations between the White House, media, and the public, aside from the Press Office, which still only structured public relations in an ad hoc manner (Walcott & Hult, 1995, p. 52), and was seldom consistent or effective (Maltese, 1994).

It was not until 1969 when President Nixon sought to manage formally the media and their growing importance to the presidency, that we see the creation of the Office of Communications (OOC). The OOC equipped the presidency with an institutional mechanism to organize communications strategies and respond to public expectations through public outreach and speechmaking. It altered the president's basic approach to communicating with the media and public, which includes myriad speeches, of course, but also other efforts to control the president's messages, such as disseminating information about the president's priorities in a timely and strategic fashion. Although its initial use was inconsistent, with some presidents after Watergate resistant to institutionalizing a communications operation (early Carter), the OOC has become an indispensable part of the presidency's public strategy (Kumar, 2007; Maltese, 1994). Now, the OOC includes speechwriting and media affairs operations, along with housing research and strategic planning efforts (Kumar, 2007, chapter 4).[1]

The OOC has managed three functions: as a liaison with non-Washington-based media, coordinator of information flows from the White House, and "political tool for generating public support for administration initiatives" (Maltese, 1994, p. 118). It has the following goals: "to set the public agenda, to make sure that all parts of the presidential team ... are adhering to that public agenda, and to aggressively promote that agenda through a form of mass marketing" (Maltese, 1994, p. 2). As liaison, the OOC specifically cultivates relationships with local and regional reporters and columnists, inviting them to White House events, providing coveted information, and granting interviews. Its staff engages in advocating for the president, defending his actions, coordinating publicity, and explaining the president's many decisions (Kumar, 2007, pp. 6–32). The organization is charged with highlighting characteristics of the president (e.g., leadership, conviction, or flexibility) that the public approves of, known through both private and public polling (Hult & Walcott, 2004, chapter 4). It then coordinates to emphasize these qualities in the president's own speeches and through public outreach to the media to present the best possible face of the presidency (Jacobs & Shapiro, 1995). Ultimately, the communications organization helps presidents manage public expectations, enhance the effectiveness of presidencies, and build support for the president.

With its primary responsibility to help the president set the public and media agendas—to engage in "merchandising" the presidency (Hult & Walcott, 2004, p. 63)—the OOC attempts to influence what about the president the media will cover in the news and what the public thinks about the president and his policies. These efforts include "barnstorming" regional media and distributing fact sheets to editors and other "opinion leaders" to build public support for the president's policies. Recent efforts by presidents to "go local" (Cohen, 2010), to target local news organizations and local publics with their policy messages are a foray by the OOC as well, with one of the best known and most extensive efforts to do this occurring in the George W. Bush administration, and his "60 stops in 60 days" Social Security Reform tour (Eshbaugh-Soha & Peake, 2006). Presidents frequently hold symbolic events, such as Rose Garden bill signings or hosting the Super Bowl victors, to play head of state and foster a favorable public image.

The president's message—expressed mostly through speeches—is crucial to the success presidents may have in the legislative, public, or reelection arenas. It is not lost on presidents that their successes, whether signing legislation or avoiding an impeachment conviction, rise and fall with their communications operations (Edwards, 2003, p. 6). As Kumar (2007) notes, when the president is unpopular or is struggling politically, the problem is usually a communications problem. New staff members are methodically hired to enhance a communications operation that is failing, or to refocus a message from domestic or foreign policy to reelection campaigns, for example. We have seen this not only in terms of the White House during a number of administrations hiring more individuals with previous communications experience, but also in terms of the number of staffers who work exclusively in the OOC. Aside from a brief leveling of staff size during Clinton's the second term, in which the Office of Media Affairs was a part of the Press Office (Kumar, 2007, p. 88), OOC staff has remained in the neighborhood of 50 individuals (see Figure 5.2).

Press Office

The Press Office plays a vital role in presidential communication, and thus in public relations. In fact, it was this office that has shaped much of the communications operations of modern presidents, with the OOC entering the foray only recently. According to Walcott and Hult (1995), President Hoover employed the first press secretary, and Eisenhower, consistent with his own preferences for institutional structures, formalized many of the procedures and responsibilities of the press secretary. Although less formal and structured than during the Eisenhower years, both Kennedy and Johnson, who governed during the beginning of serious television exposure of the presidency, altered the office to address the growing importance television would play on presidential public relations and communications.

Whereas the larger communications operation that is housed primarily within the OOC (or its equivalent) has the broad task of communicating the president's message, the press secretary provides the official record of the president, and is geared toward influencing (or at least communicating with) the

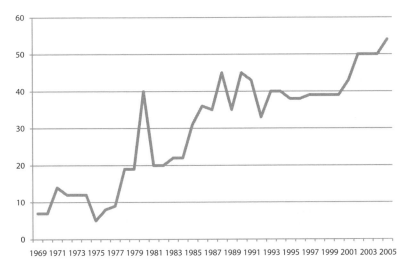

FIGURE 5. 2 Approximate staff size for the Office of Communications, 1969–2005.

Washington press corps. Kumar (2007, p. 199) identifies three roles for the press secretary: information conduit, constituencies' representative, and manager of the Press Office. Obviously, representing the president's views credibly is vital to a successful press secretary. Yet, providing information to the news media— conveying the president's agenda to the media—through gaggles and daily briefings provides an additional voice for the president's agenda and another opportunity for the president's policy positions to be expressed through news broadcasts and, perhaps, affect the public's agenda. This relationship between the press secretary and Washington press is one of give-and-take, whereby the president needs the press corps to filter his message to the public and the media need the president as a reliable political news source (Grossman & Kumar, 1981). That news coverage of the presidency tends to be primarily negative (Cohen, 2008) raises questions about the press office's ability to cultivate its relationship with the news media in a way that maximizes the president's policy success and his personal image.

The Office of Public Liaison

All modern presidents have attempted to maintain contact with interest groups and mobilize their support. But much like with the Office of Communications, concerted and institutionalized efforts to reach out to interest groups did not begin until the Nixon administration (Hult & Walcott, 2004). The goal of this outreach is clear: to maintain relationships with key external groups while in office and use institutional resources to mobilize external supporters for both policy and electoral ends. Reaching out to other interest groups to expand the president's coalition of support is important as well. Interest groups, in turn, can help presidents influence the press or even legislation before Congress. Groups may be an especially important source of support given the inevitable rocky and contentious relationships presidents develop with the news media (Grossman & Kumar, 1981) and typically have with Congress. Whether or not these outreach efforts have proven successful or not, "the notion that diverse constituencies should have channels into the White House has come to be accepted" (Hult & Walcott, 2004, p. 103). Certainly, the institutionalization of this office allows presidential administrations to accommodate a wide range of organized interests (Pika, 1999). The importance of public liaison remains important and has become a relatively stable part of all recent administrations, even though its tasks often extend beyond the confines of one organizational entity (Peterson, 1992).

Organizational Influences on Public Relations

The White House communications organization offers the president many opportunities to reach the public, media, and interest groups. Whether George W. Bush's successful first term communications operation that set priorities and planned ahead or Clinton's strong defensive operation, effective at dealing with numerous scandals and distractions, including impeachment, there are examples aplenty that the White House organization matters in terms of effective public relations. But the literature has not uncovered whether White House communications essential to presidential public relations have affected presidential speechmaking. Two components of organizational theory, such as organizational capacity and learning, may help us determine whether the Office of Communications (OOC) has facilitated an increase in the president's public outreach efforts over time.

Organizational Capacity

Capacity to achieve goals and implement a mission is crucial to an organization's activity (Selznick, 1948). Capacity tends to develop and affect organizations dynamically, given that an organization first establishes a mission, goals, and determines budgetary needs and then, as it evolves and develops either achieves its goals or fails in trying to fulfill them. If it achieves its initial goals, an organization may also increase its capacity and become better equipped to achieve existing and future goals (Yuchtman & Seashore, 1967). Simply put, an organization needs capacity to function, achieve its goals, and be successful, just as capacity allows an organization to do more of what it does, so that more capacity also contributes to more activity. An organization without sufficient capacity to operate, however, may have a mission and a plan to achieve its goals but is unlikely to be able to act on its mission adequately. Capacity is defined as the organization's ability to use institutional arrangements effectively to achieve a desired outcome, operationalized as an organization's staff or budgetary inertia.

Hypothetically, organizational capacity provides the resources needed to engage in greater public relations activity, so as staff resources of the OOC increase, *the number of speeches will also increase.*[2] Table 5.1 presents mixed results for our capacity hypothesis on the number of yearly speeches (Ragsdale, 2009). First, the univariate model shows that the creation of the OOC had a strong, positive impact on the increase in the number of yearly speeches over time, leading to nearly 115 additional speeches delivered by the president over the remainder of the time series. Operationalizing organizational capacity as the number of staff working in the Office, however, results in a negative although statistically insignificant impact on speeches. Inertial effects are present, nevertheless, because there is a strong, first-order autoregressive impact on the

TABLE 5. 1 Determinants of Yearly Presidential Speeches, 1953–2005

	Full Model	*Univariate Model*
OOC Staff	−0.80	
	(2.79)	
OOC (step variable)		114.73*
		(64.48)
Presidential Approval	−2.25*	
	(1.20)	
Divided Government	−45.34	
	(29.99)	
Cable Households (%)	3.76*	
	(1.86)	
Misery Index	4.27	
	(4.46)	
Election Year	161.02*	
	(16.24)	
Constant	269.71*	
	(99.81)	
AR1	0.41*	0.46*
	(0.15)	(0.13)
MA|4|	−0.55*	0.23
	(0.15)	(0.14)
R-square	.74	.46
Box-Ljung Q ($\chi2$)	14.34	15.48
Park Test	1.90*	1.77*
Mean of Dependent Variable	278.58	278.58
N	53	53

* p < .05 (one-tailed)

number of speeches, such that speeches in the previous year affect speeches in the current year at a regularly recurring rate. Staff resources are also inertial, as OOC staff size in the previous year strongly predicts OOC staff size in the current year,[3] which suggests the importance of organizational capacity to presidential public relations over time. It is also worth noting effects by several political or contextual variables. The percentage of households with cable television and presidential reelection years, especially, lead to more speeches.

Organizational Learning

Just as capacity helps an organization do more of what it can to achieve its goals, an organization that learns from its mistakes should improve its ability to handle its responsibilities and engage in effective task management. Learning permits an organization to "maintain and accumulate" routine "lessons of experience" (Levitt & March, 1990, p. 22; see also Feldman, 1993), while organizations learn by "encoding inferences from history into routines that guide behavior" (Levitt & March, 1990, pp. 15–16). As organizations understand the role of constraints and patterned fluctuations in their environment, furthermore, organizational uncertainty declines (Thompson, 1967, chapter 2). Organizations that learn from past experiences may improve their ability to achieve future goals, as most active and successful organizations—those that survive—tend to be learning organizations (Levitt & March, 1990). Learning, therefore, prepares an organization to respond more effectively, efficiently, and with greater certainty to its environment. Moreover, even organizations with enough capacity to function must also learn about what works and what does not work over time if they are to succeed (Wilson, 1989).

Organizational learning also relates to organizational effectiveness. The OOC's goal is to improve the president's public standing in part through presidential speeches. Arguably, its mission has persisted over time and, despite constant turnover, developed and retained successful formulas and discarded failures.[4] Indeed, because organizational learning should allow the OOC to maintain and accumulate knowledge about presidential speeches, mistakes made by past presidents should be reflected in successors' decisions on public speeches. Surely, subsequent members of the OOC recognized earlier staff failures during Watergate, and guided Reagan away from similar gaffes during the Iran–Contra scandal,[5] just as presidents may not always learn what is best (Moe, 1985) and suffer defeats. The communication successes of the George W. Bush's first term as president are often attributed to a communications organization comparable with Ronald Reagan's successful first term (Kumar, 2007), clearly an example of Bush's staff learning from successful strategies of previous administrations. Maltese (1994) even shows how the OOC has evolved over time, culminating in the Reagan administration's effective use of the office to limit presidential mistakes, control information flows, and pitch policies for public support.

Ultimately, learning should reduce uncertainty about speeches and increase the organization's understanding of which public outreach strategies may be most successful. If learning occurs over time, then speeches adhere to routine "lessons of experience" and are less ad hoc, so we would expect less variation in the number of speeches as an organization learns, controlling for the appropriate political context, of course. Thus, *less variance after the creation of the OOC means that the OOC has affected speechmaking and is therefore learning about presidential speeches and their potential effectiveness.* A Park test for heteroskedasticity, which takes the logged squared residuals of each model regressed on the log of time, is one way to test this hypothesis. A negative coefficient shows that variance has decreased over time, which implies that speechmaking has become less ad hoc over time and provides evidence that organizational learning has occurred as part of the OOC. Yet, the Park test in Table 5.1 is positive (1.89) and significant, indicating that variance has increased over time and despite the institutionalization of presidential speechmaking, there exists a great deal of variation in how individual administrations conduct public relations. In other words, presidential public relations is still a highly individualized process, even within the institutionalized presidency.

Communications Effectiveness

Having explored the White House communications organization and its impact on the president's primary vehicle for public outreach, his speeches, I turn now to the effectiveness of speeches in reaching their target publics. We begin with theories of political communication to assess whether the media may accept the president's overtures and respond to them, according to the literature. Next, I review theories of public receptivity to evaluate whether the public may be aware of or even respond to the White House's public relations efforts and review the literature that examines whether these outreach efforts are effective. That is, the president's communications efforts are organized and coordinated by the White House, but do they help the president reach the intended targets, the public, media, and interest groups? And do they help these targets reach the president and his agenda?

Presidential Public Relations and the News Media

The president's ability to affect news coverage of his administration is at the core of the White House public relations operation, and there is much reason to expect presidential influence. At base, the president devotes substantial resources to engaging the news media, whether through his myriad public speeches, the press secretary's daily press briefings and gaggles with the Washington press corps, or outreach to interest groups. The White House, as already discussed, goes to great lengths to reach the media, by orchestrating news events that are easily accessible to reporters. Presidents clearly generate news coverage, much more than any other single individual or political institution. In many ways, this is not a surprise. The public is very interested in presidential news, after all, and the news media, being a business driven heavily by ratings, readers, and profits, want to give the public what they want by way of political news coverage (Eshbaugh-Soha & Peake, 2011).

Much of the political communications literature theorizes that presidents are able to influence news coverage and do so frequently. Bennett's (2003) theory of indexing speaks directly to this. Reporters are likely to index—or report the official line—especially when it comes to the presidency. After all, the president (especially as it concerns foreign affair) has: "the greatest perceived power to affect the situation or issue; greatest institutional capacity to engage government news; and the best communications operations" (Bennett, Lawrence, & Livingston, 2007, p. 63). Much of research that examines the lead-up to the war in Iraq contends that indexing did indeed take place, and that presidents affected news coverage of the war in a favorable direction (Bennett, Lawrence, & Livingston, 2007; Howell & Pevehouse, 2007). Effective communications undoubtedly contributed to the public's initial support on Iraq.

Despite these expectations, the evidence that the White House consistently affects news coverage is mixed. In one of the most comprehensive studies of presidential agenda setting, Edwards and Wood (1999) show that presidential attention to foreign policy issues does not influence the news media's coverage of those same issues. Although presidents appear to have some impact on the media's domestic policy agenda (such as health care and education), the authors conclude that these are rare instances fostered by strategic action (see Eshbaugh-Soha & Peake, 2005) concerning economic issues). That is, if presidents act entrepreneurially and prioritize an issue not previously in the news, then they are best situated to lead the media. Policy innovation, not necessarily effective communication, may thus be vital to generating news coverage (Graber, 2006). At least in the instance of health care reform, Clinton was effective in setting the agenda, despite having benefited most from his organization's defensive posture (Kumar, 2007). Other research raises additional questions about the president's ability to lead the news media by the use of a nationally televised address (Peake & Eshbaugh-Soha, 2006) or even parlay their public speeches into coverage of national, prestige newspapers, leading Barrett (2007) to conclude that even when the president speaks, he may not necessarily make a sound.

The general profit motive that encourages news coverage of the presidency summarily undercuts it, too. Although the presidency is the best source of political news, a decreasing percentage of the population watches network television news or reads newspapers. Viewers are drawn to soft rather than policy-related hard news, encouraging news organizations to promote these, not stories on the president's policy agenda (Bennett, 2009; Cohen, 2008). In the main, the media lack "staying power" to maintain their focus on policy issues over time (Downs, 1972; Kingdon, 1995, p. 62), and presidents have difficulty affecting what the media cover in part because issues compete for limited agenda space (Jones & Baumgartner, 2005, pp. 20, 237; Wood & Peake, 1998). When the media cover issues that do not portray the president favorably, this primes the public to lower their evaluation of the president's job performance (Krosnick & Kinder, 1990). When the media do not cover the president at all, then the president has virtually no chance to communicate with the public given the paucity of national addresses and the few Americans who might seek out presidential speeches independently on the Internet.

Presidents prefer to be out in front of news coverage, but given the difficulties outlined above, the White House must be prepared to respond to news stories. As world events—often outside of the president's control—drive myriad news stories, presidents tend to respond to, rather than lead news coverage, even in the area of foreign policy (Wood & Peake, 1998). Of greater political concern for the White House are times of crisis for the president and his administration. The White House has to be prepared to play defense when the media air stories that are critical of the president or his policies. The Clinton Administration's ability to respond effectively to impeachment proceedings illustrates how the White House public relations operation can succeed in response to negative circumstances. The Bush Administration's failed response to Katrina is often blamed on the White House's ineffectiveness in anticipating the public outcry and responding aptly and quickly with an effective communications response. In short, the effectiveness of the White House public relations operation in responding appropriately to critical news coverage, as these two examples help illustrate, may be even more important to a presidential administration than leading news coverage of their policy agendas.

Presidential Public Relations and the Public

According to much of the literature, the president *should* be able to lead the public, and especially its policy agenda (see Baumgartner & Jones, 1993; Kingdon, 1995). Through the State of the Union address, presidents have at least a short-term agenda setting impact on the public (Cohen, 1995; see also Iyengar & Kinder, 1987). This impact, however, tends to be primarily symbolic, not substantive. Others find modest evidence of presidential leadership over public opinion, again in the short-term, through nationally televised addresses (Rottinghaus, 2009). Wood (2007) also shows a strong link between the tone of presidential rhetoric and public perceptions of the economy, just as Brace and Hinckley (1992) illustrate that presidential approval ratings increase after a national address. Kiousis and Strömbäck (2010) show that press conferences and major speeches correlate positively with the president's overall job approval rating and the public's approval of his handling of foreign policy. Theoretically, presidential speeches increase the public's access to political information in a relatively cost-free manner (Zaller, 1992). Because the presidency has the organizational resources and means to reach out to the public regularly—and because the public's most accessible source of political information is often from the president—it makes sense that the president would be effective in cultivating public opinion to the administration's own ends.

Other theories of public perception suggest much difficulty for public relations, however. Even if the president can regularly reach the public, political predispositions make it difficult for presidents to ensure that the public takes the president's priorities as its own. Individuals actively select and filter the information that they receive (e.g., Bennett, 2009), or as Edwards (2003) suggests, individuals actively screen political messages and discard those that do not fit or are inconsistent with their predispositions (Zaller, 1992, p. 44). Given that much of the public is predisposed to disagree with the president, whether due to partisanship or lack of approval of the president, the prospects for successful public outreach are diminished. What may hurt the president even more, however, is the public's general disinterest in politics (Neuman, 1986), meaning that even the best-orchestrated and coordinated efforts at public outreach may simply fall on "deaf ears" (Edwards, 2003).

Indeed, much research calls into question the president's ability to convince the public to support his policy goals, even with a massive communications operation intent on doing so. Edwards's (2003) study may be the most comprehensive, noting that whether through national addresses or other speeches, presidents typically do not move public opinion, even on their top policy priorities to which they devote the most political capital, personal interest, and organizational tools. Presidents are similarly unable to increase their job approval ratings or the public's approval of their handling of most issue areas. Even though this research does not target the effectiveness of the internal workings of the White House communications offices, it certainly speaks to the difficulties even a well-staffed and equipped organization may have in engaging successfully in public relations.

What is more striking is that the effectiveness of presidential public relations appears to have diminished as organizational tools to cultivate relationships have expanded. Simply put, presidents were most effective setting the public's agenda during the golden age of presidential television, prior to 1986, that is, but not since then (Young & Perkins, 2005). The effectiveness of public opinion leadership through national addresses also appears to have waned, as national addresses delivered by Presidents Carter through Clinton have had no positive impact on public opinion (Rottinghaus, 2009). In addition, although Brace and Hinckley (1992) show that national addresses increase presidential approval ratings from Eisenhower through Reagan's second term, Edwards (2003) illustrates no such relationship for presidents Reagan, George H. W. Bush, and Clinton.

If presidents fail to lead the public through public relations efforts, the president may still listen to public concerns and respond to them through these strategies. Indeed, the president's willingness to listen to public concerns and express them as part of his policy agenda is increasingly important. But it is by no means pandering to public opinion. Instead, presidents respond to public opinion in a relatively strategic manner. As Canes-Wrone (2006) illustrates, presidents are more likely to speak publicly about policies that are already popular with the public and are even more likely to take popular positions. Jacobs and Shapiro (2000) show, as well, how the White House communications operation is adept at polling the public to figure out not which policies to promote in public, but how to "craft" their message in a way that will play to popular support. Presidents also incorporate policy issues as part of their policy agendas when public concern is high enough (Eshbaugh-Soha & Peake, n.d.).

Presidential Public Relations and Interest Groups

Evidence concerning the effectiveness of presidential outreach to interest groups is limited, at best. Peterson (1992) shows a partisan angle to this office, with the Reagan administration's liaison strategy being driven extensively by groups that demonstrated Republican partisanship. The president's own speeches illustrate the extent of this outreach, as presidents increasingly "go narrow" (Cohen, 2008), targeting not the mass public, but more specialized groups in their outreach efforts. Unfortunately, the actual impact of these efforts in terms of increased lobbying efforts, voter mobilization, or membership expansion, remains an unanswered question in the literature. We can conclude, nevertheless, that the "interest group liaison capabilities of the White House, supplementing the president's...command of public attention, add to the instruments available for exercising presidential leadership in the modern age" (Peterson, 1992, p. 624).

Presidents regularly work with interest groups which have expertise in the president's policy priorities. Not only is working with interest groups helpful in formulating a policy, it also helps presidents secure legislative victory by tapping the interest group's lobbyists to influence members of Congress. Cultivating positive relationships with interest groups may not guarantee that the president achieves his policy goals in Congress, but it certainly cannot hurt. In his failed attempt to reform health care, President Clinton failed to include the health insurance and pharmaceutical lobbies in the formulation of his health care bill. Perhaps learning from this mistake, the Obama Administration worked out agreements with these key groups prior to pushing legislation in Congress. All in all, it is logical that the Office of Public Liaison would work to respond to core pressure groups and bring their concerns to the attention of the president— incorporating the ideas of interest groups into their communications strategy— especially over policies central to the president's domestic policy agenda.

Discussion and Conclusion

The White House communications organization is designed to facilitate presidential communication with target publics—primarily, the public and news media—and build support, prestige, and foster a positive reputation to help presidents achieve their larger goals. Although the president has an institutional machine to cultivate these relationships, the evidence is mixed that it has advanced the president's relationships substantially with either the public or the media.[6] Much of the evidence points to a weak correlation between public relations efforts and influence over target publics, a correlation that has also decreased over time. The president appears most successful, nevertheless, using the symbolic rather than substantive aspects of his office to communicate.

Part of the reason for this is that the media, the entity that the presidency is really trying to engage to reach the public, has become increasingly decentralized and fragmented in the new media age. With each new administration comes new technology for presidents to utilize, but which the administration struggles to master. Just as the Reagan administration governed as the 24-hour news cycle began, so too did the Clinton administration contend with expanded cable news coverage (MSNBC and Fox News), and the Bush administrations grappled with Internet news programming and the continued decline of traditional media (network news broadcasts and newspapers). These technological advances summarily complicate the ability of the presidency to maintain and focus a consistent message to not only lead but also listen to and respond to target publics. Once an administration learns about how to navigate one new medium, another arises, presenting additional possibilities and complications. This alone may help explain why the institutionalization of the presidential communications operation has not reduced variability in the president's primary means for public outreach, his speeches.

Even the most comprehensive treatment of the contemporary White House communications operation (Kumar, 2007) recognizes the obstacle that changing media present for presidential public relations, without providing a clear prescription for how to navigate these unknown waters. So even though institutionalization was vital to coordinating and exploiting television as a resource in the 1970s, the ability to reach the public and engage effectively in public relations has become much more complicated with more variation on cable news and the Internet, which does not substantially enhance political engagement (Boulianne, 2009).

Undoubtedly, presidents will continue to use their organizational resources to cultivate relationships with its target publics. But can it continue to adapt quickly enough to take advantage of new technology in such a way that it can continue to maximize its goal achievement? Surely, candidate Obama used the Internet, text messages, and e-mail effectively to marshal support during the 2008 presidential election campaign. But questions remain as to whether those campaign successes can be translated into effective governance and whether the White House is even equipped to cultivate relationships through new social media technology. Perhaps the strategy that near-future presidencies may undertake is to target interested and organized groups through their outreach efforts, to "go narrow" (Cohen, 2008). Presidents can target groups to mobilize their own members and use their own resources to communicate the president's goals to the mass public, media, and even Congress. This may require presidents to give up a good deal of control over their message, or at least expand the role of public liaison in the White House. But given the difficulties of reaching the mass public through a fragmented and decentralized news media, this may be exactly what the president needs to do to manage a successful public relations operation in the future.

Notes

1 The Office of Communications has gone by different names. For George W. Bush, communications operations were centralized by the Counselor to the President. Although slightly different organizationally, the goals remain similar across administrations (see Kumar, 2007).

2 Although not a perfect measure of capacity, staff size is the most available quantitative indicator of OOC capacity. I found most staff numbers at Whitehouse2001.org. I tallied OOC staff (1969–1977) with data provided by John Maltese, who collected them from the Nixon, Ford, and Carter libraries. I estimated some years from organizational charts and the previous year's staff size. Other charts are available in Kumar (2007). The OOC data are available only through 2005, thereby restricting the length of the time series.

3 These results are available from the author.

4 White House staff structure that may even be unrelated to the communications operation is much like this. All recent presidents know that a chief of staff is necessary for successful operations, for example, despite regular turnover.

5 Organizational learning helps presidents meet expectations that they communicate with the public. It does not allow them to exclude speeches from their governing strategy. Even if Richard Nixon wanted to avoid all press conferences, for example, he could not have done so.

6 Vanessa Beasley (2010) argues, in fact, that the institutionalization of the presidency actually constrains the president, limiting the incentives for presidents to use the bully pulpit or engage in public relations to build public support for their policy initiatives. My results suggest that individual presidents still have much discretion in their public relations strategies despite the institutionalization of the presidency.

References

Barrett, A. (2007). Press coverage of legislative appeals by the president. *Political Research Quarterly, 60*(4), 655–668.

Baumgartner, F., & Jones, B. D. (1993). *Agendas and instability in American politics.* Chicago, IL: University of Chicago Press.

Beasley, V. B. (2010, March). *Overcome: President Obama and the constraints of race talk.* Paper presented at the Rhetoric, Politics, and Obama Phenomenon Conference in Bryan, TX.

Bennett, W. L. (2003). The burglar alarm that just keeps ringing: A response to Zaller. *Political Communication, 20*(2), 131–138.

Bennett, W. L. (2009). *News: The politics of illusion* (8th ed.). New York: Pearson, Longman.

Bennett, W. L., Lawrence, R. G., & Livingston, S. (2007). *When the press fails: Political power and the news media from Iraq to Katrina.* Chicago, IL: University of Chicago Press.

Boulianne, S. (2009). Does Internet use affect engagement? A meta-analysis of research. *Political Communication, 26*(2), 193–211.

Brace, P., & Hinckley, B. (1992). *Follow the leader: Opinion polls and the modern presidents.* New York: Basic Books.

Burke, J. P. (2000). *The institutional presidency* (2nd ed.). Baltimore, MD: Johns Hopkins University Press.

Canes-Wrone, B. (2006). *Who leads whom? Presidents, policy, and the public.* Chicago, IL: University of Chicago Press.

Cohen, J. E. (1995). Presidential rhetoric and the public agenda. *American Journal of Political Science, 39*(1), 87–107.

Cohen, J. E. (2008). *The presidency in an era of 24-hour news.* Princeton, NJ: Princeton University Press.

Cohen, J. E. (2010). *Going local: Presidential leadership in the post-broadcast age.* New York: Cambridge University Press.

Dickinson, M. J. (1996). *Bitter harvest: FDR, presidential power, and the growth of the presidential branch.* Cambridge, MA: Cambridge University Press.

Downs, A. (1972). Up and down with ecology: The issue-attention cycle. *Public Interest, 28*(1), 38–50.

Edwards, G. C., III. (2003). *On deaf ears: The limits of the bully pulpit.* New Haven, CT: Yale University Press.

Edwards, G. C., III. (2009). *The strategic president: Persuasion and opportunity in presidential leadership.* Princeton, NJ: Princeton University Press.

Edwards, G. C., III, & Wood, B. D. (1999). Who influences whom? The president and the public agenda. *American Political Science Review, 93*, 327–344.

Eshbaugh-Soha, M. (2006). *The president's speeches: Beyond "going public."* Boulder, CO: Rienner.

Eshbaugh-Soha, M. (2010). The politics of presidential speeches. *Congress and the Presidency, 37*(1), 1–21.

Eshbaugh-Soha, M., & Peake, J. S. (2005). Presidents and the economic agenda. *Political Research Quarterly, 58*(1), 127–138.

Eshbaugh-Soha, M., & Peake, J. S. (2006). "Going local" to reform social security. *Presidential Studies Quarterly, 36*(4), 689–704.

Eshbaugh-Soha, M., & Peake, J. S. (2011). *Breaking through the noise: Presidential leadership, public opinion, and the news media.* Palo Alto, CA: Stanford University Press.

Feldman, M. (1993). Organization theory and the presidency. In G. Edwards, J. Kessel, & B. Rockman (Eds.), *Researching the presidency* (pp. 267–288). Pittsburgh, PA: University of Pittsburgh Press.

Graber, D. A. (2006). *Mass media and American politics* (7th ed.). Washington, DC: CQ Press

Grossman, M. B., & Kumar, M. J. (1981). *Portraying the president: The White House and the news media.* Baltimore, MD: Johns Hopkins University Press.

Hager, G. L., & Sullivan, T. (1994). President-centered and presidency-centered explanations of presidential public activity. *American Journal of Political Science, 38*(4), 1079–1103.

Hart, R. (1987). *The sound of leadership: Political communication in the modern age.* Chicago, IL: University of Chicago Press.

Heath, R. L. (2001). A rhetorical enactment rationale for public relations: The good organization communicating well. In R. L. Heath (Ed.), *Handbook of public relations* (pp. 31–50). Thousand Oaks, CA: Sage.

Howell, W. G., & Pevehouse, J. C. (2007). *When dangers gather: Congressional checks on presidential war powers.* Princeton, NJ: Princeton University Press.

Hult, K. M., & Walcott, C. E. (2004). *Empowering the White House: Governance under Nixon, Ford, and Carter.* Lawrence: University Press of Kansas.

Iyengar, S., & Kinder, D. R. (1987). *News that matters: Television and American opinion.* Chicago, IL: University of Chicago Press.

Jacobs, L. R., & Shapiro, R. Y. (1995). The rise of presidential polling: The Nixon White House in historical perspective. *Public Opinion Quarterly, 59*(2), 163–195.

Jacobs, L. R., & Shapiro, R. Y. (2000). *Politicians don't pander: Political manipulation and the loss of democratic responsiveness.* Chicago, IL: University of Chicago Press.

Jones, B. D., & Baumgartner, F. (2005). *The politics of attention: How government prioritizes problems.* Chicago, IL: University of Chicago Press.

Kernell, S. (1997). *Going public: New strategies of presidential leadership* (3rd ed.). Washington, DC: CQ Press.

Kessel, J. H. (1974). *The domestic presidency.* North Scituate, MA: Duxbury Press.

Kingdon, J. W. (1995). *Agendas, alternatives, and public policies.* Boston, MA: Little, Brown.

Kiousis, S., & Strömbäck, J. (2010). The White House and public relations: Examining the linkages between presidential communications and public opinion. *Public Relations Review, 36*(1), 7–14.

Krosnick, J. A., & Kinder, D. R. (1990). Altering the foundations of support for the president through priming. *American Political Science Review, 84*(2), 497–512.

Kumar, M. J. (2007). *Managing the president's message: The White House communications operation.* Baltimore, MD: Johns Hopkins University Press.

Lammers, W. (1982). Presidential attention-focusing activities. In D. Graber (Ed.), *The president and the public* (pp. 145–171). Philadelphia, PA: Institute for the Study of Human Issues.

Levitt, B., & March, J. G. (1990). Chester I. Barnard and the intelligence of learning. In O. E. Williamson (Ed.), *Organization theory* (pp. 11–39). New York: Oxford University Press.

Maltese, J. A. (1994). *Spin control: The White House office of communications and the management of presidential news.* Chapel Hill: University of North Carolina Press.

McKinnon, L. M., Tedesco, J. C., & Lauder, T. (2001). Political power through public relations. In R. L. Heath (Ed.), *Handbook of public relations* (pp. 557–664). Thousand Oaks, CA: Sage.

Miller, G. R. (1989). Persuasion and public relations: Two "Ps" in a pod. In C. H. Botan & V. Hazleton, Jr. (Eds.), *Public relations theory* (pp. 45–66). Hillsdale, NJ: Erlbaum.

Moe, T. M. (1985). The politicized presidency. In J. E. Chubb & P. E. Peterson, (Eds.), *New directions in American politics* (pp. 235–269). Washington, DC: Brookings Institution.

Neuman, W. R. (1986). *The paradox of mass politics: Knowledge and opinion in the American electorate.* Cambridge, MA: Harvard University Press.

Neustadt, R. E. (1990). *Presidential power and the modern presidents.* New York: Free Press.

Peake, J. S., & Eshbaugh-Soha, M. (2008). The agenda-setting impact of major presidential TV addresses. *Political Communication, 25*(2), 113–137.

Peterson, M. A. (1992). The presidency and organized interests: White House patterns of interest group liaison. *American Political Science Review, 86*(2), 612–625.

Pika, J. A. (1999). Interest groups: A doubly dynamic relationship. In S. A. Shull (Ed.), *Presidential policymaking: An end-of-century assessment* (pp. 59–78). Armonk, NY: M. E. Sharpe.

Powell, R. J. (1999). "Going public" revisited: Presidential speechmaking and the bargaining setting in Congress. *Congress and the Presidency, 26*(2), 153–170.

Ragsdale, L. (1984). The politics of presidential speechmaking, 1949–1980. *American Political Science Review, 78*(4), 971–984.

Ragsdale, L. (2009). *Vital statistics on the presidency: George Washington to George W. Bush.* Washington, DC: CQ Press.

Ragsdale, L., & Theis, J. J., III. (1997). The institutionalization of the American presidency, 1924–92. *American Journal of Political Science, 41*(4), 1280–1318.

Rottinghaus, B. (2009). Strategic leaders: Determining successful presidential opinion leadership tactics through public appeals. *Political Communication, 26*(3), 296–316.

Selznick, P. (1948). Foundations of the theory of organization. *American Sociological Review, 13*(1), 25–35.

Thompson, J. D. (1967). *Organizations in action.* New York: McGraw-Hill.

Walcott, C. E., & Hult, K. M. (1995). *Governing the White House.* Lawrence: University Press of Kansas.

Wilson, J. Q. (1989). *Bureaucracy.* Basic Books.

Wood, B. D. (2007). *The politics of economic leadership.* Princeton, NJ: Princeton University Press.

Wood, B. D., & Peake, J. S. (1998). The dynamics of foreign policy agenda setting. *American Political Science Review, 92*(1), 173–184.

Young, G., & Perkins, W. B. (2005). Presidential rhetoric, the public agenda, and the end of presidential television's "golden age." *Journal of Politics, 67*(4), 1190–1205.

Yuchtman, E., & Seashore, S. (1967). A systems resource approach to organizational effectiveness. *American Sociological Review, 32*(6), 891–903.

Zaller, J. (1992). *The nature and origins of mass opinion.* New York: Cambridge University Press.

6

POLITICAL PUBLIC RELATIONS AND ELECTION CAMPAIGNING

Paul Baines

This chapter outlines the ways in which political public relations is used as a technique in election campaigning in the United Kingdom and the United States. While differences across media systems and political systems are highly important and impact both the use of political public relations and how parties campaign and market themselves in elections (Lees-Marshment, Strömbäck, & Rudd, 2010; Plasser & Plasser, 2002), many of the strategies and tactics outlined here are highly similar across democratic political systems. Thus, while acknowledging that political and media systems matter and that the United Kingdom and the United States are not representative cases of all Western democracies, the aim of the chapter is to outline how political public relations is used in election campaigns in a way that is valid beyond those two countries.

Specific attention is paid to the *role* and *process* of public relations and how this compares across the two countries, including consideration of rapid rebuttal, opposition research, election debates, and party election broadcasting and, more recently, the burgeoning use of the Internet. We will also examine the various publics a political party serves; how parties and candidates segment and target voters; and position their candidates. Finally, the chapter outlines how PR research might be developed in the future to ensure parties and academic researchers understand the changing communication environment.

What is Political PR?

According to O'Shaughnessy (1990), the activity indulged in by modern Western political parties and governments is a political marketing–propaganda hybrid. Sometimes parties seek to persuade people to believe in their policies using a unidirectional, manipulative communication process, and sometimes using a two-way dyadic communication process. But political public relations is also a legitimate form of communication activity used to explain policy and inform voters, citizens, and other stakeholder groups and to make a political party and its candidates understood in terms of their positions on the issues. In modern times, in the United Kingdom, particularly under former Labour Prime Minister Blair, political PR came under serious scrutiny. There was a feeling that the 1997 to 2010 Labour government overused PR and *spin doctors*—the pejorative term given to practitioners of political PR—which led to Labour operating a symbolic government, one more interested in its image than its policies and practices (Ingham, 2003; O'Shaughnessy, 2003).

If political PR is about building beneficial relationships and managing reputations with key publics for political purposes, as Strömbäck and Kiousis outline in the opening chapter, political PR in election campaigns is about winning electoral support by influencing public opinion and voting behavior, partly by outlining one's own parties' policies and leadership team and partly by damaging the credibility of the opponents' policy platform and leadership aspirations.

Illustrating the Link between PR and Election Campaigning

Political parties and candidates seek to represent voters' and citizens' views and opinions both in order to get elected and while acting as governing parties or officials. The underlying process in elections is the exchange of promises on policies and future performance in government for votes and this process occurs through the communication of programs, policies, and ideas in return for information from voters relating to these policies, ideas, and programs from the electorate. This communication process is represented in Figure 6.1.

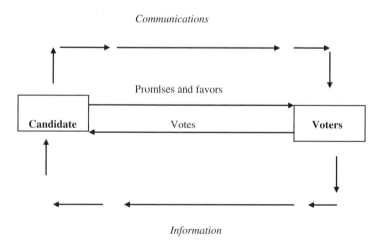

FIGURE 6.1 The political PR communication cycle with voters. Source: Kotler (1982).

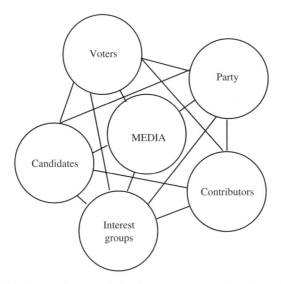

FIGURE 6.2 Political marketing publics. Source: Kotler and Kotler (1981).

Political parties and candidates, however, need to transact with various publics/stakeholders in order to become market oriented, including voters, competitors, internal party stakeholders, and those in the external environment (Ormrod, 2005; Strömbäck, 2007). Kotler and Kotler (1981) have previously argued that the political strategist must communicate with six key publics, including voters, the party, the candidate, interest groups, contributors, and the media. It is worth noting however, that the role of the media—hence the role of PR—is critical to communicating with the other five markets (Figure 6.2). However, media relations is not the only tool of political PR, parties have the opportunity to speak directly to voters in a variety of paid-for media. Sweeney (1995) has argued that political candidates have primary and secondary audiences where the primary audience is the voter and the secondary audiences are campaign staff and volunteers, organizations, opinion leaders, political party, contributors, allies and friends, and the media. Perhaps, the only other group missing from Kotler and Kotler (1981), Sweeney (1995), and Ormrod (2005) are other parties. However, in first-past-the-post systems like those in both the United States and the United Kingdom, it is seldom necessary to create formal alliances with other parties in order to govern. When the Conservatives and Liberal-Democrats formed a coalition government after the 2010 election, it was the first time in 36 years.

In communicating with voters and citizens during elections, parties need to provide policy information on how they would govern the country if they are elected, provide an illustration of how fit they are to govern (either through explanation and argument in relation to what they would do in government or by outlining past good deeds in government—local, regional, or national) and make commitments which are credible (Bauer, Huber, & Herrmann, 1996).

The Professionalization of Election Campaigning

Election campaigning has professionalized rapidly in recent decades. Smith and Saunders (1990) outline four eras of British politics: (a) the unsophisticated selling era (where candidates promoted themselves to different social classes in the 19th century); (b) the selling era (in the early part of the 20th century when politicians used the mass media to disseminate their messages; (c) the sophisticated selling/nascent marketing era (after private polls were developed to provide voter information); and the final stage, which was identified as the development of the strategic marketing era. Wring (1996) subsumes these eras into three phases—the propaganda era, the media era, and the political marketing era—arguing that each developed as a result of significant electoral setbacks at the polls for one of the major parties.

Much of this professionalization has occurred through the contracting of specialist marketing/PR agencies on an ad hoc basis. These agencies take the form of pollsters and advertising agencies in Britain and the rest of Europe. In America, by contrast, political consultants have a much wider remit in campaigns, taking roles such as polling, petition management, fund-raising, strategy, media buying, advertising, law, donor list maintenance, and campaign software consulting among many others. In the United States, the presidential election marketing campaign and the political campaign are fought semi-independently by different teams with the candidate linking the two (Newman, 1994).

The UK Labour Party developed its election campaigning techniques to a high degree, particularly during the period from 1992 to 1997, making extensive use of market research, particularly as a means by which the modernizers in the party (e.g., Gould, 1999; Mandelson, 1988) could fuel their internal campaign for policy and style changes within the party. This change in campaigning approach helped the Labour party to defeat the Conservatives after 17 years in office. But what they learned was at least partly influenced by the embedding of senior Labour Party practitioners in the Clinton campaign organization in 1992 (Braggins, McDonagh, & Barnard, 1993).

A Model of British/U.S. Political Campaigning

Figure 6.3 illustrates that the process of research, in principle, is largely the same as in the United States. Research tends to provide parties and campaign organizations with information on the existing vote-share and information for message and policy development. In both the United States and the United Kingdom, research is subcontracted. However, the party and constituency

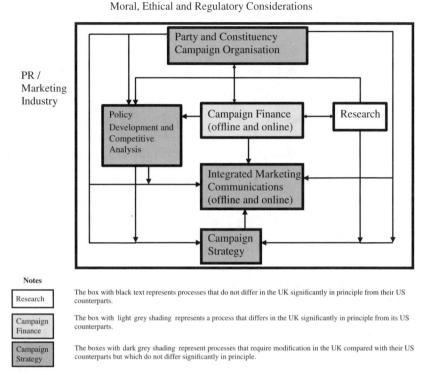

Moral, Ethical and Regulatory Considerations

PR /
Marketing
Industry

Notes

| Research | The box with black text represents processes that do not differ in the UK significantly in principle from their US counterparts. |

| Campaign Finance | The box with light grey shading represents a process that differs in the UK significantly in principle from its US counterparts. |

| Campaign Strategy | The boxes with dark grey shading represent processes that require modification in the UK compared with their US counterparts but which do not differ significantly in principle. |

FIGURE 6.3 Model depicting UK/US political campaign management process.

campaign organization, policy and message development process, an integrated marketing communications strategy, and campaign strategy development processes (targeting, segmentation, and positioning) are all areas that are not the same in the United Kingdom, compared to their U.S. counterparts. In the United Kingdom, because political constituency candidates are essentially franchised to their party, unlike in the United States where the relationship is better described by using a licensing analogy, there is a need to consider the organization of the constituency campaign. While the process of message development in the United Kingdom is somewhat similar to the United States, it is based more on party ideology and is developed largely by politicians rather than a team of political consultants. The communication of the message and policy also requires modification because of the different media structure and legislation associated with political communication in the United Kingdom (where political broadcast advertising is illegal). The process of developing campaign strategy in the United Kingdom, because of the different message and policy development processes and the relationship between local and national campaigning, also requires adaptation from the American model.

In the United Kingdom, the process of financing election campaigns is substantially different from the United States. Constituency expenditure and national expenditure ceilings rule out the conduct of sophisticated research and communication strategies within individual seats. Regulation on national expenditure ceilings also rules out expensive subcontracted communication and research at the national level. This contrasts sharply with the United States where no such ceilings exist. This regulation impacts upon British campaigning culture significantly in the following ways: (a) Foreign donations are banned and declaration of all donations of £5,000 or above are mandatory, and (b) a limit has been placed on expenditure by national parties (excluding that spent at the constituency level) of approximately £20m for a Westminster general election, with other limits applying to European elections.

Such legislation may ensure that political campaign activity remains in-house and any outside marketing expertise is seconded rather than hired out to consultants from external agencies. The disclosure of donations at or above £5,000 may also bring about fewer large donations, thereby placing a premium on generating more and smaller donations. This may have significant impact upon the demand for the use of direct marketing expertise by UK parties. In this area, British parties may borrow heavily from the expertise of their American counterparts, in terms of the process of effectively and efficiently producing and sending direct mail and conducting telemarketing and Internet campaigning operations. However, it is unlikely that they will adopt the same tone, in terms of content, as their American counterparts, principally because the message development process is different (e.g., American campaigns tend to have more negative advertising attacking opponents personally and in terms of their policies). British electoral law on campaign finance thus detracts from the use of some American political campaigning techniques.

There is currently also a major difference in the way that UK parties research their oppositions compared to in the United States. Because the focus in British politics is more on policy development than in the United States, opposition research tends to focus more on researching the opposition's policies than their personalities. UK parties also have a much greater input into the development of their policy (and message) than U.S. parties, and so the UK campaign management process is more producer (politician) oriented than voter oriented (as it is in the U.S.). In the United Kingdom, parties are also affected by different regulatory, cultural, and moral considerations. The campaign infrastructure associated with political campaigning is largely underdeveloped and borrows extensively from the marketing industry, despite its lack of experience in the application of marketing/PR techniques to political campaigning.

Campaign Strategy and Objective Setting

Political campaigns need an overall theme (using a broadcast message) that targets specialized groups (using narrowcast messages) (Baer, 1995). Election strategy is therefore critically concerned with message development and its dissemination among target groups.

The first stage of the campaign strategy process requires the political consultant and candidate or party to determine what they wish to achieve with the campaign. This stage involves the setting of objectives and the definition of an overall campaign theme. Most political parties' objectives are short-term and based upon the premise of gaining more representation in the national parliament or winning office. However, simply winning office is not a raison d'être. Parties and candidates have to provide a convincing story of why they should be elected, especially when an existing government is operating in reasonably strong economic circumstances. The former Labour Party leader, Neil Kinnock, simply did not convince the electorate, who marginally voted in Conservative Prime Minister John Major in 1992. Equally, even though the 2000 presidential election was close between the Republicans and the Democrats, and even though he was very unpopular, the Americans voted in George W. Bush again in 2004, because Senator John Kerry failed to convince the electorate.

The importance of campaign strategy in message terms was outlined in the United Kingdom for the Labour Party by the then Director of Communications, Peter Mandelson (1988), after the 1987 general election defeat, in which he stated that the main objectives in future campaigns were fivefold as follows:

1. To encapsulate the party's message in memorable phrases (sound bites);
2. To dispatch campaign materials and statements quickly and efficiently;
3. To extend press and broadcasting contacts beyond [Parliamentary] "lobby" journalists (and not just to political editors);
4. To target "priority" seats for maximum, national impact; and,
5. To project the party leadership as united and able.

The single-minded focus with which Mandelson and other modernizers in the Labour Party developed a professional communication approach bore dividends in the 1997 election, ushering in New Labour, which stayed in power until 2010.

Campaign strategy can be seen to be based on four notions according to Bradshaw (1995), including: (1) the division of the electorate into three groups, (a) your voters, (b) your opponents' voters, and (c) "floating" voters; (2) the use of public opinion research to identify what voters think and where they are located; (3) the solicitation of votes from the entire electorate; and (4) once the voters have been targeted, the organization's resources should be targeted to these segments accordingly.

However, a critical element of the process is developing a suitable message with which to persuade different groups of voters. Baines, Lewis, and Ingham (1999) devised a model (see Table 6.1) which illustrates how parties and candidates might position themselves in countries where policies are a key criterion in determining voting behavior.

Parties can use the model to evaluate whether or not their policies are popular and if they should hold a position of strength within a party's manifesto. The extent to which those policies should be communicated depends on the strength of importance that voters attach to them and how central these policies are to the party or candidate's ethos or mission. The latter is important because parties cannot credibly reposition themselves using stances that are completely at odds with their previous positions. The need for the policy to be relatively central to the party's ethos takes into account the fact that parties and candidates tend to be ideologically driven in the United Kingdom and Europe more generally. In the United States, this axis might be replaced with one based on "perceived policy strength" or "degree of issue ownership."

In the case where the electorate feels an issue is important but is of low centrality to party ethos (such as the environment was in 2005), the party needs to build up the environment agenda and hold communications constant until its agenda sufficiently represents the electorate's (or target segment's) considerations. Communications can be increased at a later date, depending upon the changing state of the electorate's (or target segment's) feelings—as determined by tracking polls. This is particularly important since issue positions in the policy positioning model will change as agendas and communications are modified.

In many countries, however, policies are not the only criteria for determining the voter's choice on Election Day. As a result, the policy model is useful in illustrating which issues the party or candidate should focus on, but this should not be considered as the total positioning strategy. The party or candidate may still need to consider the development and dissemination of the theme of the party or candidate and personality- or style-based, components that may also constitute the way in which the voter makes his or her electoral choice. In the

TABLE 6.1 Policy Positioning Model

Electorate's viewpoint of importance	Centrality to party ethos		
	High	*Mid*	*Low*
High	Decision: - Build agenda - Build communications		Decision: - Build agenda - Hold communications
Mid		Decision: - Hold agenda - Hold communications	
Low	Decision: - Reduce agenda - Build communications		Decision: - Reduce or terminate policy

Source: Adapted from Baines, Lewis, and Ingham (1999).

2010 British general election, leader image was regarded as just as important a voting criterion as policies and way ahead of party image (Mortimore, 2010), when in most elections over the last 30 years, policies have been more important than leader image and party image in helping voters make up their minds who to vote for.

The use of Table 6.1 will, however, only indicate which policies a party should focus on rather than the exact nature of what that policy should be. In order to reach a determination, a party has to reconcile the results of their private public opinion polls with the desires of their political leaders and policy staff. This inevitably involves difficult trade-offs, especially around the question of how voter-oriented a party ought to be. It also involves questions of the extent to which a party should position itself on an issue it feels that it owns; for example, the UK Conservative Party on defense or the U.S. Republican Party on gun control. In some cases, a party may own an issue by being perceived to be the best party on that issue, but the issue is of low salience to the electorate. In this case, the party can either try to raise the salience of the issue on which it has a lead, or it can campaign on other issues that are more important to the electorate and try to convince them that they hold the better position than another party. In the 2005 British general election, the Liberal Democrats owned the issue of the Iraq war. Most voters agreed with their policy. Unfortunately, despite a valiant attempt by the Liberals to raise the salience of the issue, ultimately, it was simply not perceived as important enough to the voters to influence the election outcome.

Organizational Development in Political Campaigning

The organizations that run political campaigns in the United Kingdom, and Europe more generally, are derived from members of the party executive and members of the parliamentary party with functions such as polling and advertising subcontracted to external agencies. In the United States, campaign committees are built up of external political consultants, the candidate, and a campaign manager. To maintain loyalty and morale, there is a need for political parties and candidates' campaign teams to conduct internal PR exercises. The extent to which political organizations decentralize their campaign operations is also an important strategic issue. Farrell (1996) argues that this is a result of the extent to which television has penetrated households within a particular country. Where television penetration is high, political campaigning is capital-intensive. Wherever it is low or not permitted, political campaigning is likely to be somewhat more labor-intensive. With the advent of the Internet, this argument may change entirely; Internet campaigning is relatively low cost yet can be used to motivate large online communities across an entire country.

The subcontracting of the marketing function, based on the American experience, is likely to lead to the loss of party power (Bowler, Donovan, &

Fernandez, 1996). Baines, Scheucher, and Plasser (2001) have argued that the use of American (and indeed other) political consultants in Western European campaigns could also lead to the erosion of the parties' centralized campaigning structure, although this has yet to happen.

Financing the Political Campaign

In America, large sums of money are required to finance campaigning for office, and fund-raising has become a major component of the campaign planning function, usually requiring candidates to hire professional fund-raising consultants (McDevitt, 1996). Political fund-raising in Britain is very different from that in America. Pattie and Johnston (1997) outline that in the annual fund-raising process, the national party sets fund-raising quotas for financial remittances from all local associations to the centre party on the basis of the size, wealth and electoral strength of that constituency association. Some money is also raised from companies through lobbying activity (and this income has been increasing over the last 13 years as party conferences take in more exhibitors), and in the case of the UK Labour Party through trade union organizations. However, business donations to the Labour Party have increased considerably with, in some cases, controversial consequences. Both the Conservative Party and the Labour Party's links with lobbyists were under media scrutiny in the 1990s as the links among commercial companies, the lobbyists, and government ministers were uncovered in the "cash for questions" (where MPs were asking questions in the House of Commons in return for cash payments from companies) and "cash for access" scandals (where parties accepted donations in return for providing access to government ministers) respectively.

In America, fund-raising has tended to occur through the medium of direct marketing in the past and more recently through the Internet. The principal reason for this is because federal law limits the size of an individual donor's contribution, although in the 2010 *Citizens United v. Federal Election Commission* Supreme Court case it was ruled that corporate funding of independent political broadcasts cannot be limited under the first amendment (Supreme Court, 2010). In addition to lobbying, direct marketing also allows candidates to personalize each message as if they were actually asking the voter for the money themselves. According to Shea (1996), fund-raising in the United States occurs through various mechanisms including: personal solicitation, political action committees (PACs), and interest group solicitation, direct mail, big and small events, and telemarketing. In the United Kingdom, political action committees do not exist, so a culture of single issue political campaigning and giving donations to support political causes is not so developed as it is in America. However, this may well change as the Labour Party, fairly early on in its first term, received a £1m donation from an antihunting organization that was part of the International Fund for Animal Welfare (IFAW). Lobbying, as a source of fund-raising, makes a significant contribution to the campaign funds of political parties, although the process is highly secretive and little researched.

The Volunteer Program and Internal PR

The maintenance and development of a volunteer network is an important component in the process of grassroots campaigning. Because of the scale and nature of the get-out-the-vote effort, it is important for a party or candidate to mobilize grassroots support since this can contribute to the winning of an election. In Britain, it is forbidden to pay for canvassing. As a result, parties must use volunteers. This has considerable ramifications for the political strategist. Essentially, volunteers will resent reproaches for their failures because they are contributing, not for material gain, but for either their desire for the party to win or for future political gain in terms of selection for local or national office. According to Beaudry and Schaeffer (1986), the key to building a successful grassroots organization is:

- Developing a compelling campaign message that encourages people to get involved;
- Undertaking constant efforts to recruit workers integrated into *all* campaign activities;
- Ensuring good management that uses volunteers effectively.

According to Niffenegger (1989), a volunteer program (for party activists as they are referred to in the United Kingdom) is important to extend the candidate personally into local markets, through canvassing, putting up signs, and soliciting funds. From a PR perspective, it is absolutely imperative that activists are enthused about supporting the campaign. This is often done through special rallying events, through party election broadcasts and the development of manifestos, and through direct marketing, e-mail, and the party's Web site. Parties must undertake internal PR activities to strengthen activists' belief in the message that they intend to deliver to the electorate.

Coordinated Constituency Campaigning

Although Figure 6.3 outlines the general functions inherent in political campaigning, it does not indicate exactly how national parties coordinate with local parties when campaigning. Baines, Lewis, and Harris (2002) have, however, devised just such a model (see Figure 6.4). They argue that, before parties decide on whom they should target and what issues they should campaign on, local parties should conduct research within the constituency and use canvassing to consolidate this process. The model outlines that national parties should coordinate their constituency campaigns by determining which constituencies are most in need of aid. Once this has been determined, national parties need to provide local constituency parties with the finance to conduct constituency research so that the local party can determine who their main political opposition is and, from these data, determine which voters they need to target. Research is further needed to determine how to position the party and to select and place advertising or other promotional material in the relevant media.

Baines, Lewis, and Harris's (2002) model suggests those components that comprise the local campaign. Certain tasks, outlined in bold, can be undertaken by the national political organization. Thus, the national political organization ranks the constituencies in terms of those most in need of resources, provides the local party with historical data, polling data, and constituency research, and provides software to aid the local party in conducting an effective voter segmentation exercise. The national organization should also provide the local party with statements with which they can tie in their own messages. This approach has sometimes been criticized when national parties micromanage what can and cannot be said in a bid to keep local parties "on message." Once the voter has been targeted, the national party should conduct a postelection analysis exercise to determine why events unfolded in the way that they did. The model in Figure 6.4 could not be used in the United States since the idea of a Senate candidate tying in his or her message with that of the party would be less well received. However, a presidential candidate who seeks to target specific states and position him- or herself according to the issues in each state could also use the model. The extent to which parties in the United States coordinate the campaigns of their candidates for either Senate or Congress is limited, however, and does not stem much beyond the provision of funding, media training, and provision of research data.

Measuring the Effectiveness of PR: Research and Polling

Measuring the effectiveness of PR can be delineated into measurements of inputs (for example, of message presentation quality, channel preference, information requirements), outputs (for example the number of messages sent, received, understood), and outcomes (for example, the number who change behavior or attitudes) (Tench & Yeomans, 2006). Most PR research aims to measure the effectiveness of PR at the input and output level. Seldom do parties measure changes in voter behavior but they do often, using polling, try to measure attitudinal shifts.

The extent to which the pollster is integrated into strategy formulation is important. As suggested by Kavanagh (1995), when discussing the relationship between polling consultants and politicians in the United Kingdom, pollsters are rarely part of the party's strategy team, as they are in the United States. Polling along with other sources of information is therefore an input to the

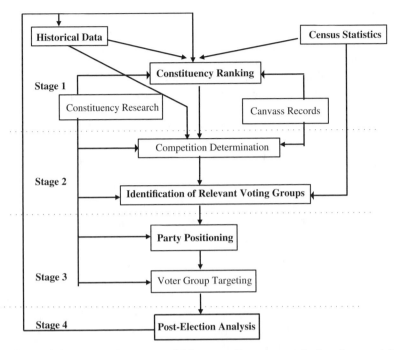

FIGURE 6.4 Political planning model for co-ordinated campaigning. Source: Adapted from Baines, Lewis, and Harris (2002).

communication group. Robert Worcester of MORI—a former advisor to Labour premiers Harold Wilson and Jim Callaghan—complained after the 1979 and 1983 elections about his lack of access to Labour's campaign decision makers compared with the access he had previously enjoyed under Harold Wilson, a former statistician, who really understood the importance of market research.[1] Polling organizations provide information for the candidate and party that enable them to make more educated decisions with regard to the strategy team's deliberations. Kavanagh (1995) states that polling organizations can provide information on the following:

- Election timing—but only in countries where the government determines when to have an election. This is likely to change in the United Kingdom in the next election, currently planned for 2015.
- Image building—polls provide parties with an understanding of how voters perceive them and how they are positioned with the electorate and, therefore, provide parties with the necessary ammunition to reposition themselves, as Labour did in 1997, the Conservatives have partly done under David Cameron (now Prime Minister), and Bill Clinton did in 1996. In America, pollsters conduct benchmark surveys to determine a candidate's

name recognition levels—since the personal vote is more important there—and their electoral strength in relation to their opponent's and citizens' evaluations of an incumbent officeholder's performance (Asher, 1995).

- Policy—opinion polls in Britain have tended to be used for the presentation of policy rather than for policy formulation per se (Kavanagh, 1995). In America, by contrast, opinion polls can and do affect a candidate's policy stance.
- Tracking—political parties use opinion polls to evaluate their own weaknesses and strengths. For this process to be effective, it must be undertaken regularly to allow parties to identify meaningful changes in public opinion. But while parties track opinion, they do not currently track the effectiveness of their communications in real-time (see below).
- Targeting voters—in addition to asking questions about issues, pollsters include questions to determine the characteristics and profile of voters for particular parties and candidates for segmentation purposes.

Candidates and parties also conduct extensive qualitative research into individuals' thoughts and values using focus groups of typically between four to eight people, moderated by a specialist facilitator. Focus groups were thought to have been particularly effective in the 1988 American presidential election; they were used to identify "hot button" issues that the Bush campaign wielded with devastating effect against Dukakis. Philip Gould similarly conducted extensive focus group discussions in marginal constituencies around the United Kingdom, reporting the research results directly to Tony Blair (Gould, 1999). Managers, political or otherwise, sometimes forget that conclusions from focus groups cannot, however, be applied to a broader group of people (Mitofsky, 1996).

In the United States, campaign committees commission research into their own candidate and the opposition campaign's candidate—this is termed opposition research. Bayer and Rodota (1989) suggest opposition research involves compiling details of an opposing candidate's public record and statements while Varoga and Rice (1999) suggest it involves comprehensive analysis of public records for both your own candidate and their opponents. Opposition research is vital in order to topple incumbents (Shea & Brooks, 1995) and can be likened to competitive analysis and intelligence (Varoga & Rice, 1999). According to Shea (1996), opposition research provides five types of data that can be used against an opponent. These are: (a) public service information, (b) media-derived data, (c) prior campaign details, (d) business and career data, and (e) personal information.

The extent to which the parties in the United Kingdom use these data is not well known. The parties could argue that business and career data are more likely to be covered by the investigative press in the United Kingdom and other countries with a strong critical press, although such details may be leaked anonymously to them, perhaps by the parties themselves.

Integrated Marketing Communication: Message Development in the U.S. and Britain

Political advertising is the primary means of political communication in the United States. In America, party and candidate promotion tends to occur through advertising spots on television and cable networks. Subject to finance and availability, American candidates are free to buy unlimited amounts of advertising time on television (Kaid, 1999). In Britain, by contrast, party promotion mainly occurs through billboard and press advertising, but the principal means by which voters are influenced is through the publicity generated via news management activities, because of the regulations placed upon broadcast media advertising. Public relations has an important role in U.S. elections *supporting* TV advertising, but in the United Kingdom, it has a critical role, *supported by* advertising rather than vice versa. What is clear, however, is that party communications in Britain are far from integrated. There is a strong need not only to ensure the main themes of the election are consistent and used in all forms of promotion, but also that the same execution is used in all media so that voters can instantly recognize the message.

A major difference between PR and election campaigning in the United States and the United Kingdom relates to the development and dissemination of the campaign message. While UK political campaign messages tend to be more substantive and ideological, U.S. political consultants tend to research their messages more to ensure the electorate will be more receptive to them. Message testing is undertaken to a much greater degree. Another major difference is the extent to which U.S. politicians hire subcontracted professional political consultancies for determining media strategy, conducting research, organizing direct mail, Internet campaigning, and developing the PR strategy.

In the United States, key consultants develop the political message between them in strategy groups, whereas in the United Kingdom, the message or policy is largely determined by committees of senior politicians (incorporating some marketing and PR personnel) who consider themselves more capable of its creation and development. They then use the party's central office staff to perform the various activities associated with its dissemination.

Figure 6.5 illustrates the inputs to policy development in the United Kingdom and the process of its dissemination. It can be seen that opposition research, fund-raising, production of party election broadcasts, TV debate preparation, and news management are functions that are generally conducted in-house by the parties in the United Kingdom. Direct marketing, because of its link to fund-raising, is generally also conducted in-house although the parties, with limited success, have flirted with subcontracted agencies. The functions that have tended to be subcontracted are research and communications. UK parties have adopted the U.S. practice of people-metering[2] for the purpose of news management, and have also taken on the U.S. practice of using opposition research taken from political information systems (databases) to inform their

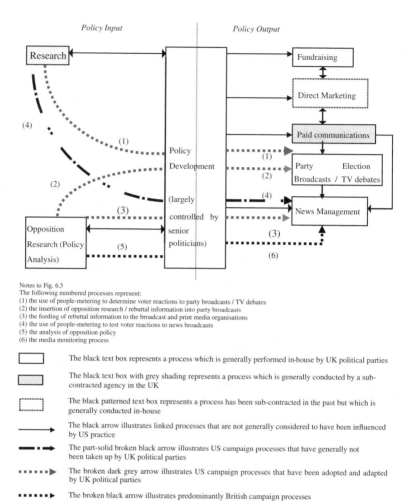

Policy Input   *Policy Output*

Notes to Fig. 6.5
The following numbered processes represent:
(1) the use of people-metering to determine voter reactions to party broadcasts / TV debates
(2) the insertion of opposition research / rebuttal information into party broadcasts
(3) the feeding of rebuttal information to the broadcast and print media organisations
(4) the use of people-metering to test voter reactions to news broadcasts
(5) the analysis of opposition policy
(6) the media monitoring process

The black text box represents a process which is generally performed in-house by UK political parties

The black text box with grey shading represents a process which is generally conducted by a sub-contracted agency in the UK

The black patterned text box represents a process has been sub-contracted in the past but which is generally conducted in-house

The black arrow illustrates linked processes that are not generally considered to have been influenced by US practice

The part-solid broken black arrow illustrates US campaign processes that have generally not been taken up by UK political parties

The broken dark grey arrow illustrates US campaign processes that have been adopted and adapted by UK political parties

The broken black arrow illustrates predominantly British campaign processes

FIGURE 6.5 The policy development and dissemination process.

press releases and respond to their opponents' charges (rebuttal). These trends look set to continue and could certainly continue to be conducted in-house. UK parties are also tending to use opposition research material to inform and design their party election broadcast material and to prepare for the TV debates, although they have tended not to use dial groups to test their content and effectiveness, preferring instead to use focus groups to test billboard and press advertising content.

Figure 6.5 also illustrates a number of processes (denoted by the dark gray broken arrows) that have been influenced by U.S. practice, which includes opposition research. In the UK context, however, political information systems are used more for providing information on opposition policy rather than opposition personalities, although this is developing. Use of opposition research in the United Kingdom includes inserting opposition research and policy analysis material into party broadcasts, feeding rebuttal information to the print and broadcast press, and the use of people-metering to test voter reactions to news items. This contrasts with its application in America where it is used to test reactions to broadcast advertisements. British party executives have been less likely to adopt the use of people-metering expertise to test voter reactions to party election broadcasts, although they could. British parties have always analyzed the policies rather than the personalities of their opponents, and this process has a strategic input to the process of policy development and party positioning, although this might change given the rising importance of leader image in the 2010 British general election. British parties tend to monitor news output to ensure that broadcasters are providing fair coverage, as they are required to do by law. This practice is peculiarly British since Americans can rely much more on their broadcast advertisements for message dissemination and TV news broadcasters do not necessarily feel the same compunction to maintain impartiality (cf. Fox News). In dividing the various functions of UK policy development into input and output, Figure 6.4 illustrates that it is from the inputs into policy development (message development) that British parties can borrow most from their American counterparts. This gives the parties' research departments a pivotal role in aiding the determination of campaign strategy.

The Changing Nature of Internet Campaigning

The 2008 U.S. presidential election was arguably an election like no other, being the longest, most expensive contest in living memory (Johnson, 2009). George W. Bush had become deeply unpopular due to foreign policy hitches in Iraq and Afghanistan. Barack Obama, an inexperienced senator from Illinois, was elected President of the United States of America with 365 electoral college votes (52.9% of the vote) to the Republican challenger John McCain's 173 electorate college votes (45.7% of the vote), partly because the latter was seen by many as someone who would extend the Bush doctrine.

How much does it cost to become President of the United States of America? Barack Obama's campaign raised $246.1 million during the campaign to get him elected as the Democratic nominee for president during the primary campaigns between January 1 and June 30, 2008 (Faucheux, 2009, p. 57). He raised $453.9m up to August 31 for his presidential campaign (Corrado & Corbett, 2009, p. 135). In total, Obama raised around $744.9m by December 31, 2008 to ensure his path into the Oval Office (Federal Election Commission [FEC], 2009). But the 2008 presidential elections were different for another reason; in this election the main candidates' campaign committees substantially invested in social networking strategies as a means to both increase voter support and increase online fundraising. Obama's team, which included Facebook

founder Chris Hughes, developed MyBarackObama.com, a social networking site, to target voters, and to organize its get-out-the-vote effort allowing
members to meet, attend, and organize local meetings and events. More than 1
million online members had been recruited by August 2008, organizing nearly
75,000 events offline (Germany, 2009). The viral marketing undertaken by
the Obama campaign was a particular strength, with the campaign uploading
104,454 videos, viewed 889 million times (Aun, 2008). The *Yes We Can* video
by will.i.am and MoveOn.org's CNNBC video drew views of over 13 million
and over 20 million respectively (Fenn, 2009). With unprecedented numbers
of young people voting in the 2008 election compared with 2004, particularly
after a strong voter registration campaign by Rock the Vote and other voter
registration campaigns, future elections look set to be fought and won on the
Internet, in America at least.

By comparison, Internet campaigning has yet to really take off in the United
Kingdom. In the 2005 British general election, only 2% of the electorate said
that the Internet influenced how they decided to vote. However, this figure
rose to 9% among those aged 18 to 24 years of age, so this approach to campaigning is likely to increase in importance as the next political generation ages
(Worcester, Mortimore, & Baines, 2005).

Postelection Analysis

In devising their model of coordinated campaigning, Baines, Lewis, and Harris
(2002) included postelection analysis as a strategic component. Such analysis
allows election strategists to determine why their campaign progressed in the
way it did. Postelection analysis aims to determine whether or not the correct
voter segments were targeted successfully and if the message used was correctly
positioned. In addition, the election results are a useful indicator as to whether
or not the private opinion polling was accurate, and monitoring of the media,
in terms of positive and negative evaluations of stories and uptake of key themes
helps to indicate the effectiveness of the message development process. The
postelection analysis phase usually also takes into account how the opposition
responded during the campaigns.

The political science and political marketing literature are remarkably silent
on the issue of postelection analysis. This may be because political organizations do not want the media or their opposition to know what lessons they have
learned.

A New Political PR and Election Campaigning Research Agenda?

Despite the substantive research in communication and journalism studies on
the nature of public opinion and its dissemination, there is much we do not
know about political PR, especially from the supply perspective, rather than

from the consumer psychology perspective. Understanding how political organizations develop their PR activities will help us understand how effective PR actually is from the organizational perspective. Such insights should help governments and parties communicate better with citizen and voter groups. However, given public relations concern with reputation, we know surprisingly little about how voters select parties based on their reputation and issue ownership. We also have a very limited understanding of the nature of long-term effects on reputation, particularly in relation to policy development. How do alliances with other parties affect the long-term reputation of the parties involved, for example? This is a particularly pertinent question for the Liberal Democrats in the United Kingdom in 2010 as many Liberal Democrat supporters were disappointed that the party linked up in a coalition with the Conservatives rather than with Labour. Because most election campaigning research covers a single election, often only a single campaign, we fail to take into account that reputation is built up over time. Lynch, Baines, and Egan (2006) have outlined how parties should develop long-term competitive performance by developing their reputation, policy development capacity, leadership, and marketing activities, but further research is needed in this important area.

At present in the United Kingdom, the PR evaluation activities of political parties tend to focus on postelection analysis reports, particularly based on an evaluation of their private polling, media monitoring, and qualitative research programs. One approach that might benefit parties in the future is to track voter sentiment through a real-time experience tracking research program amongst floating voters such as that developed in the United Kingdom by MESH planning. This can be done by asking a panel of floating voters to inform a research company whenever they "experience" a party and its messaging. This could include promotional material from a party, direct mail, an Internet ad, a news or radio broadcast, billboards, posters on front lawns, and even word-of-mouth. Figure 6.6 outlines how the positive and negative persuasiveness of the three main British parties' messages were measured during the 2010 election campaign. The graph indicates how the first and last TV debates in the 2010 British general election were particularly important in persuading floating voters to vote for the Liberal Democrats and Conservatives respectively.

When Labour Prime Minister Gordon Brown publicly called a voter a "bigoted woman" on live TV in an unguarded moment, floating voters felt less inclined to vote Labour since the lady was only voicing moderate immigration concerns that many other voters shared. Only a real-time experience tracking approach can pick up the impact of such events.

A Short Note on the Ethics of Political PR

Public relations is sometimes seen as manipulative, raising the question as to whether or not its application to the political process is ethical. However, ultimately, it is the job of the voter to determine whether or not the politicians

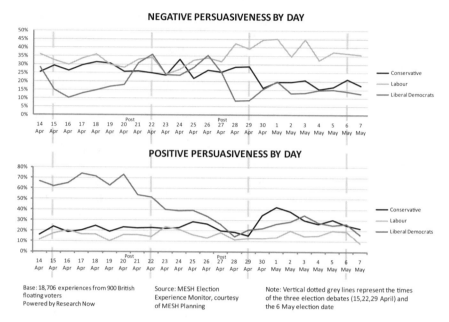

Base: 18,706 experiences from 900 British floating voters
Powered by Research Now

Source: MESH Election Experience Monitor, courtesy of MESH Planning

Note: Vertical dotted grey lines represent the times of the three election debates (15,22,29 April) and the 6 May election date

FIGURE 6.6 Persuasiveness of party messaging in the UK 2010 British General Election.

and their consultants are unethical in their practices and they can and do often unseat governments on this basis (consider Nixon in the United States in the 1970s and the Conservative Party in Britain in the mid-1990s). Goldstein (1995) suggests this process occurs through media scrutiny first. Fowler (1995) argues that citizens must therefore devise their own rules for judging a politician's conduct. Ideally, the ethical mechanism in politics therefore becomes self-righting; if a party or politician steps out of line and damages their own reputation, the electorate can cease to vote for him or her, vote for the opposition, or not vote at all. Unfortunately, it seems that in many Western polities, voters are taking the third option. The question is, is this because or despite the increase in the use of political PR and marketing techniques? This question certainly deserves greater scrutiny.

Conclusion

The role and process of the political PR function differs depending on the context and culture in which it is used. Political PR practitioners have to determine the relative importance of their publics, including party activists, financial contributors, interest groups, PACs and think tanks, candidates, voters, and the group that connects them all, the media. The political PR function does not operate in a strategy vacuum. In the United Kingdom and in European countries more generally, it is a central function, supported by advertising, in developing and disseminating the policy and message of a political party. In the United States, it is a supporting function to advertising, the principal form of communication in a country that allows paid-for broadcast communication. There are numerous techniques such as opposition research which are used widely in the United States but which are little used in the United Kingdom and in other European countries, although these techniques may become ubiquitous over time. While the Internet has also made a significant contribution to political campaigning in the United States, it has not yet to made its mark in the United Kingdom.

Political parties, particularly in the United Kingdom, have not yet undertaken to any great extent a sophisticated evaluation of their campaigns by tracking the effectiveness of their campaigning. Yet, they could very cheaply and effectively analyze their communications' effect on voter groups by tracking voters' experiences and determining whether or not those experiences were influencing voters positively or negatively. Ultimately, political parties' use of political public relations oftentimes aims to win electoral support and develop political reputations, but as a function its proponents sometimes tread a fine line, because building political reputation may involve building that reputation at some other party or candidate's expense. When parties overstep the mark, by damaging the trust they have with their electorate or the media, or by unfairly and viciously attacking their opponents, they risk damage to their own reputations.

Given the nature of representative democracy and the power of the electorate to decide their rulers, this can mean long spells in opposition for parties that fail to use wisely the tools and techniques of political PR. However, the opposite is also true. The best means to rehabilitate a failed party is to make the best use possible of the strategies and tactics of political PR. It seems then that there is a fine balance between no use, use, and overuse. When political parties do not use political PR, they are doomed to failure. When they use PR that is so slick that its use becomes obvious rather than subtle, and the style of politics becomes the content, they can also be doomed to failure. The devil is in the details.

Notes

1   Mentioned in a private conversation with the author.
2   "Dial groups" are where groups of up to 50 people rate various forms of advertising, usually using rating scales and electronic equipment (referred to as people-meters).

References

Asher, H. (1995). *Polling and the public—What every citizen should know* (3rd ed.). Washington, DC: Congressional Quarterly Press.
Aun, F. (2008, November 7). Over long campaign, Obama videos drew nearly a billion views. *ClickZ.*. Retrieved from http://www.clickz.com/3631604.

Baer, D. (1995). Contemporary strategy and agenda setting. In J. A. Thurber & C. Nelson (Eds.), *Campaigns and elections American style* (pp. 47–61). Oxford, England: Westview Press.

Baines, P., Lewis, B. R., & Harris, P. (2002). The political marketing planning process: Improving image and message in strategic target areas. *Marketing Intelligence and Planning, 20*(1), 6–14.

Baines, P., Lewis, B., & Ingham, B. (1999). Exploring the positioning process in political campaigning. *Journal of Communication Management, 3*(4), 325–336.

Baines, P. R., Scheucher, C., & Plasser, F. (2001). The "Americanisation" myth in European political markets: A focus on the United Kingdom. *European Journal of Marketing, 35*(9/10), 1099–1116.

Bauer, H. H., Huber, F., & Herrmann, A. (1996). Political marketing: An information- economic analysis. *European Journal of Marketing, 30*(10/11), 159–172.

Bayer, M. J., & Rodota, J. (1989). Computerised opposition research: The instant parry. In L. J. Sabato (Ed.), *Campaigns and elections: A reader in modern American politics* (pp. 19–25). London: Scott, Foresman.

Beaudry, A., & Schaeffer, B. (1986). *Winning local and state elections: The guide to organizing your campaign.* New York: Free Press.

Bowler, S., Donovan, T., & Fernandez, K. (1996). The growth of the political marketing industry and the California initiative process. *European Journal of Marketing, 30*(10/11), 173–185.

Bradshaw, J. (1995). Who will vote for you and why: Designing strategy and theme. In J. A. Thurber & C. Nelson (Eds.), *Campaigns and elections American style* (pp. 30–46). Oxford, England: Westview.

Braggins, J., McDonagh, M., & Barnard, A. (1993). *The American presidential election 1992—What can Labour learn?* (Internal report). London: The Labour Party.

Corrado, A., & Corbett, M. (2009). Rewriting the playbook on presidential campaign financing. In D. W. Johnson (Ed.), *Campaigning for president 2008* (pp. 126–146). New York: Routledge.

Farrell, D. M. (2006). Political parties in a changing campaign environment. In R. D. Katz & W. Crotty (Eds.), *Handbook of party politics* (pp. 122–133). London: Sage.

Faucheux, R. A. (2009). Why Clinton lost. In D. W. Johnson (Ed.), *Campaigning for president 2008* (pp. 44–59). New York: Routledge.

Federal Election Committee (FEC). (2009). Presidential campaign finance. Retrieved from http://www.fec.gov/DisclosureSearch/mapApp.do?cand_id=P80003338&searchType=&se archSQLType=&searchKeyword=

Fenn, P. (2009). Communication wars: Television and new media. In D. W. Johnson (Ed.), *Campaigning for president 2008* (pp. 210–221). New York: Routledge.

Fowler, L. L. (1995). Campaign ethics and political trust. In J. A. Thurber & C. Nelson (Eds.), *Campaigns and elections American style* (pp. 200–212). Oxford, England: Westview Press.

Germany, J. B. (2009). The online revolution. In D. W. Johnson (Ed.), *Campaigning for president 2008* (pp. 147–159). New York: Routledge.

Goldstein, W. (1995). The ethics of political campaigns. In J. A. Thurber & C. Nelson (Eds.), *Campaigns and elections American style* (pp. 192–199). Oxford, England: Westview Press.

Gould, P. (1999). *The unfinished revolution: How the modernisers saved the Labour party.* London: Abacus.

Ingham, B. I. (2003). *The wages of spin.* London: John Murray.

Johnson, D. W. (Ed.). (2009). *Campaigning for president 2008.* New York: Routledge.

Kaid, L. L. (1999). Political advertising: A summary of research findings. In B. I. Newman (Ed.), *Handbook of political marketing* (pp. 423–438). Thousand Oaks, CA: Sage.

Kavanagh, D. (1995). *Election campaigning: The new marketing of politics.* Oxford, England: Blackwell.

Kotler, P., & Kotler, N. (1981). Business marketing for political candidates. *Campaigns and Elections, 2*(2), 24–33.

Lees-Marshment, J., Strömbäck, J., & Rudd, C. (Eds.). (2010). *Global political marketing.* London: Routledge.

Lynch, R., Baines, P. R., & Egan, J. (2006). Long-term performance of political parties: Towards a competitive resource-based perspective. *Journal of Political Marketing, 5*(3), 71–92.

Mandelson, P. (1988). Marketing Labour: Personal reflections and experience. *Contemporary Record*, 1(4), 11–13.

McDevitt, B. (1996). Fund-raising: Quick tips for candidates. *Campaigns and Elections*, 17(9), 50–52.

Mitofsky, W. (1996). Focus groups: Uses, abuses, and misuses. *The Harvard International Journal of Press/Politics*, 1(2), 111–115.

Mortimore, R. (2010, May 12). *The election in figures*. Presentation to the Coventry Conversation, London.

Newman, B. I. (1994). *The marketing of the president: Political marketing as campaign strategy*. London: Sage.

Niffenegger, P.B. (1989). Strategies for success from the political marketers. *Journal of Consumer Marketing*, 6(1), 45–51.

O'Shaughnessy, N. (1990). *The phenomenon of political marketing*. London: Macmillan.

Ormrod, R. P. (2005). A conceptual model of political market orientation. *Journal of Nonprofit and Public Sector Marketing*, 14(1/2), 47–64.

O'Shaughnessy, N. (2003). The symbolic state: A British experience. *Journal of Public Affairs*, 3(4), 297–312.

Pattie, C., & Johnston, R. (1997). Funding the national party: Changing geographies for the British Conservative Party 1984/85 to 1993/94. *Political Geography*, 16(5), 387–406.

Plasser, F., & Plasser, G. (2002). *Global political campaigning: A worldwide analysis of campaign professionals and their practices*. Westport, CT: Praeger.

Shea, D. M. (1996). Opposition research: Let's look at the record. In D. M. Shea (Ed.), *Campaign craft: The strategies, tactics and art of political campaign management* (pp. 91–118). Westport, CT.: Praeger.

Shea, D. M., & Brooks, S. C. (1995). How to topple an incumbent: Advice from experts who have done it. *Campaigns and Elections*, 16(6), 21–25.

Smith, G., & Saunders, J. (1990). The application of marketing to British politics. *Journal of Marketing Management*, 5(3), 295–306.

Strömbäck, J. (2007). Political marketing and professionalized campaigning: A conceptual analysis. *Journal of Political Marketing*, 6(2), 49–67.

Supreme Court of the United Stated. (2010). *Citizens United v. Federal Election Commission*, retrieved December 20, 2010, from: http://www.supremecourt.gov/opinions/09pdf/08-205.pdf

Sweeney, W. R. (1995). The principles of planning. In J. A. Thurber & C. Nelson (Eds.), *Campaigns and elections American style* (pp. 14–29). Oxford, England: Westview.

Tench, R., & Yeomans, L. (2006). *Exploring public relations*. Harlow, England: FT Prentice Hall.

Varoga, C., & Rice, M. (1999). Only the facts: Professional research and message development. In B. I. Newman (Ed.), *Handbook of political marketing* (pp. 243–256). Thousand Oaks, CA: Sage.

Worcester, R., Mortimore, R., & Baines, P. (2005). *Explaining Labour's landslip*. London: Politicos.

Wring, D. (1996). Political marketing and party development in Britain: A 'secret history'. *European Journal of Marketing*, 30(10/11), 100–111.

7

CORPORATE ISSUES MANAGEMENT AND POLITICAL PUBLIC RELATIONS

Robert L. Heath and Damion Waymer

Politics, however broadly or narrowly defined, regulates activities of individuals, businesses, government agencies, and other types of organizations—including labor unions, nonprofits, and NGOs. Because the stakes of such influence can be high, organizations engage in policy debate as issue communication, however cordial and collaborative or strident and competitive, to seek operating advantage whether narrow or broad. Discussion of such regulatory guidelines centers on implementation through rewards, threats, and punishments to the extent that organizational actions conform to or violate "public" standards. In that regard, politics is the societally created parent that directs, scolds, punishes, encourages, and rewards individual behavior, power resources and their management, and collective behavior, often as the collective management of risk. Thus, organizations for motives that are variously self-interested or altruistically other oriented participate in this political process.

In this sense, politics is not only the playing field, but the umpire, referee, and coach. This chapter addresses one aspect of that participation: Strategic issues management (SIM). It is often seen as a tool used by business, but if we feature issue outcomes as the centerpiece of political controversies and rule making, we argue that issues management is more than only a business strategy. It features organizational citizenship and becomes strategic options for nonprofit and governmental organizations as well as the private sector. As such, a relevant intellectual framework for understanding issues management is to examine the role of organizations in priming and framing political communication. As a voice of organizations, this engagement in dialogue comes under organizational titles such as public affairs and public relations. It is a serious point of engagement between the limits of organizational autonomy and contextual constraint.

As we focus on issues management and politics, this chapter examines the public affairs discourse role of complex organizations in issue debate in politics. As important as that topic is, it ultimately begins with a discussion of the creation and evolution of issues management, its role in society, particularly as a sociopolitical player in the shaping of the playing field for business policies, planning, and operations. Too much emphasis in that regard, on the role of business in society, can incorrectly suggest that issues management is a function only for the selfish and self-interested good of business enterprise. Even though improper, we can assume that issues management is a tool for bending society to the will of business. Although that is a threat, it is not a certainty. One of the best cautions in that regard is stated by Jaques (2010) this way: "*Issue management is not about how to manage an issue, but how to manage because of an issue* [italics in original]" (p. xx).

This framing of the topic of this chapter fits comfortably with the opening comments by Strömbäck and Kiousis in chapter 1 of the present work, who quoted Lasswell as reasoning that politics is about who gets what, when, and how. This fits with the thoughts of another icon on the matter of society, George Herbert Mead (1934), who attributed the development and enactment of society as a place where self-interests collide and then the fun begins:

> Our society is built up out of our social interests. Our social relations go to constitute the self. But when the immediate interests come in conflict with others we had not recognized, we tend to ignore the others and take into account only those which are immediate. The difficulty is to make ourselves recognize the other and wider interests, and then to bring them into some sort of rational relationship with the more immediate ones.
>
> (pp. 388–389)

As such, the problem facing public relations, in a political context, is helping to make society more fully functioning (Heath, 2006) by working for mutual benefit and alignment of interests.

To develop these themes, in keeping with the larger challenge of understanding political public relations, the chapter starts with a definition and discussion of the development of issues management as a field. It has come to rest upon four pillars central to how any or all organizations achieve legitimacy in society—what they do, how they do it, the ends for which they do it, and the constraints on such conduct. Broadly, such a notion, based on rhetorical enactment theory (Heath, 2001), features discourse (statement and counterstatement, action, reaction, and the lesson learned) that leads to the definition and implementation of standards of corporate social responsibility. These are brought into place to justify and advance organizations', especially businesses', strategic business plans as the enactment of mission/vision statements. In all, the question is what of this will society politically support, sanction, and constrain. Several rhetorical problems are at play in this effort of power resource management, including those we discuss in this chapter: The rhetorical problems that discussants face, the paradoxes that confound such dialogue, including the battle over precaution, and the issues, risk, and crises that tug at the cape of legitimacy. In such battles, the wrangle, the question is whose interests prevail, those of one advocate or the collectivity. These themes can be primed for discussion and debate by various types of organizations. Such is the nature of strategic issues management, political public relations, and politics writ large and small.

Strategic Issues Management: Definition and Political Context

Issue(s) management as a working concept of communication and management practice acquired its name in the 1970s. (For more detail on this moment in history, see Jaques, 2010). This discipline joins communication (easily characterized as political communication) with strategic business planning and operation—the rationale for the political voice. It engages in debates over standards of corporate social responsibility and serves as a discipline by which senior managements monitor and analyze political issues with the incentive of addressing some and adapting to others—adopting them for planning and operations.

It was coined and developed, largely out of public affairs departments in large corporations, as a response to a turbulent policy arena. After the angst of the Great Depression, economic recovery and World War II brought a strong sense of self-confidence to American corporate enterprise. Executives widely believed that corporations had rescued the United States and world from economic ruin and political tyranny. If politics favorable to interests is necessary for the development and implementation of management policies and practices, CEOs across the nation were confident that they had shaped reality to their interests. Power and power resource management were clearly, executives thought, on their side as they were using language (vocabulary) to bend political reality defined by public policy to their interests—the era of modernity as the rationale for peace and prosperity (Heath, Motion, & Leitch, 2010). By socially constructing a probusiness reality, their efforts had demonstrably benefited society. After chaos, the nation was seemingly enjoying a period of peace and prosperity.

Even though the practice of issues management was a century old (see for instance, Heath & Palenchar, 2009), what we would call issues management had been used to create the politics, or used current politics, to craft a public policy environment that allowed, fostered, supported, and rewarded big business and the barons that ran them. That sort of politics and political arrangement ran into foes who opposed trusts; these foes created and pressed governmental agencies to implement antitrust legislation and product (consumer) protection legislation in the public interest. Large and small businesses had been engaged in political debate and candidate support. By the end of World War II, they believed that their effort had paid off and businesses enjoyed a climate of universal applause.

That positive feeling collided with new and progressive definitions of the good society starting in the 1950s, raging in the 1960s, and maturing in the following decades of policy politics. Loud voices opposed nuclear weaponry, nuclear generation, environmental damage, denial of civil and human rights, the military–industrial complex including the war in Vietnam. On and on, critics enthusiastically scrutinized every aspect of society, including business enterprise, and found them wanting. This doubt fueled the political priming of business opponents. Executives were caught off guard. Thus, they turned to public affairs and public relations to rescue the reputation of free enterprise.

Out of this fray, and because the public policy wheels were no longer smoothly rolling beneath the corporate cart, issues management was developed. At first it was primarily designed to be advertising, with a public affairs response to this chaotic situation. As it evolved through private and public discourse, academic, industry, and activist, by 1990 it came to rest on four pillars (Heath & Cousino, 1990): (a) strategic business planning/management through budgeting for mission/vision, (b) issue monitoring, (c) achieving corporate social responsibility, and (d) engaging in issue communication. The latter was "heavily political" since it dealt with contestable matters of fact, value/evaluation, policy, and identification.

Since the early years of the modern version of the discipline, it has been anchored around what S. Prakash Sethi (1977) called the legitimacy gap (see also Heath & Palenchar, 2009). Sethi (1977) couched this innovation in political terms:

> The business complaint notwithstanding, it must strive to reduce the gap, real or alleged,[between] societal expectations and performance. One of the ways in which business institutions, especially large corporations, have been attempting to accomplish this is through publicity campaigns called advocacy advertising, in which they take public positions on issues in which they are involved, directly or indirectly, to explain their points of view, and often criticize those of their opponents.

(p. xi)

Any interpretation of this discipline that ignores political efforts and public policy wrangles misses the origins and purposes of issues management as a child of the political hostility and corporate angst of the 1970s. It signaled an effort to regain control over the legislative, regulatory, and judicial/legal environment in which big business preferred to operate.

One of the icons of issue management (here used in the singular as was his preference), W. Howard Chase (1984) in the first book written specifically on SIM observed: "The fourth revolution is the growing recognition that management of policy is as important as the management of people and profit, that it requires new and teachable skills, and that the disciplines of issue/policy management are vital to corporate and institutional survival in a politicized age" (p. xiii). These ideas fleshed out the scope of his ideas presented 2 years earlier: Issue management requires "the capacity to understand, mobilize, coordinate and direct all strategic and policy planning functions, and all public affairs/public relations skills, toward achievement of one objective; meaningful participation in creation of public policy that affects personal and organizational destiny" (Chase, 1982, p 1). Every era is politicized in its own way. Certainly that was true of the latter part of the 19th century, the time during which America led in the development of mass production and consumption, and first part of the 20th century. In the 1970s, corporate public affairs/public relations observed that politicization was swinging (or had swung) against the preferences of big business.

Books by senior practitioners that addressed these themes were flying into print. The senior public affairs guru for Mobil Oil, Schmertz (1986), saw the challenge as saying good-bye to the low profile and hello to the art of creative political and media confrontation, especially against ill-informed and agenda driven media. He was a political foot soldier defending the citadel of American enterprise against infidels in activist media and other activist voices. No stranger to Democrat and labor politics, Schmertz acknowledged, "Fortunately, two or three years ago I suddenly realized what all of my various responsibilities added up to: I am, in effect, the manager of an ongoing political campaign" (p. 17).

Joining the chorus of corporate public affairs executives who were etching out the profile of issues management, Ewing (1987) reasoned: "Issues management is about power. It is about the power that controls the new bottom line of all American corporations—optimal profits and public acceptance" (p. 1). It would be reasonable to read that sentence with "policy and political" intervening between public and acceptance.

> It is about management of the legitimate power a corporation has over its total environment, when it is willing to use it. And it is about the power others have over the same environment and future of the corporation— power that can be shared through foresight and informed planning.
>
> (p. 1)

Not understanding this political nexus, he reasoned, was the worst of management failures. "The ignorance in question is management's lack of knowledge of what is going on in all the corporation's relevant environments, the social and political as well as the economic" (p. 2).

Thus, issues management was born and raised to be a political animal, to help make business management more political and less merely administrative. The challenge in the 1980s and today is to see the political arena as a place of power resource management and politics. The most important theme in succeeding in this gladiatorial arena is to appreciate the role of collaborative politics and every effort to make society more fully functional through the handshake of the business and public policy arenas (Heath, 1988). As such, issues management is a discipline that unites the tensions and struggles of the marketplace with the wrangle of the public policy arena. Politics is part of the business agenda, as the business agenda is part of politics. The theme of this engagement is the dialectic of legitimacy.

Pillars of SIM: Onward toward Legitimacy

As is often the case, strands of a rope need to be wound into one strong strand. Such is the case of issues management; by 1990, through voices specifically from management theory (academic and professional), discussions of corporate social responsibility, futures/issues monitoring, and communication, the discipline slowly evolved based on four pillars.

Strategic business planning is strategic, interactive, and variously sensitive to internal and external conditions, the prevailing political economy. Savvy management works to create the political ideology and operating premises that allow it to achieve its mission and vision through strategic budgeting and operational management. Political ideology sets the standards for this effort through legislation, regulation, and litigation. These political dimensions become the playing field. As such, not only does the organization work to create a favorable playing field, but it also yields to the definitions and dimensions of the field where it plays. Internal control of any organization's destiny is never separate from external efforts to shape its destiny and the means by which it is achieved.

Standards of operation are defined, constrained, and rewarded according to principles of *corporate social responsibility* (CSR). This line of discussion, recently a matter of more general interest among public relations scholars and practitioners, was originally developed and debated by economists and management theorists. Many who labored early in this discussion realized that the essence of issues debate was the contest of CSR standards that translated into external support or opposition. Activists typically alleged in compelling ways that companies, and even governmental agencies as enablers, did not hold sufficiently high CSR standards to reduce risks and serve the public interest regarding matters of fairness, safety/security, equality, and environmental quality. Contentions that products are not safe, for instance, actually are "issues driven" CSR contests. Thus, political battles addressed topics such as environmental quality and regulation.

At first the playground of futurists looking for emergent issues, *issue monitoring* became a SIM pillar through efforts to apply research to learn, listen, and respect the opinions of others as substance of the prevailing and evolving political economy. Such was the case within the risk management philosophy of effective management, of trying to know standards, perceive and appreciate issue arguments, and know the players of the dialogue early enough to engage politically before it became ossified. Issue development is like the charts used for navigation. The captain might know the destination but needs to be able to chart a course and avoid troubled waters and hidden rocks.

Finally, and quite relevant to this discussion, we have the fourth pillar: *Issue communication*. It centers on issues as contestable matters of fact, value/ evaluation, policy, and identity/identification. Here is the nexus of SIM and political public relations. Organizations, individually and collectively, are expected to be voices regarding policy development and refinement. However, the expectation is that this will be a debate, at its best, among responsible citizens. Here we might imagine a triangle of interests: Business, government, and stakeholder/activist/public. This dialogue occurs in all of the available channels. It centers on how well each voice recognizes and responds to rhetorical problems. As political discourse it can emerge through candidates' platforms (and financial contribution), but it is more likely to occur in the established contexts of government: Legislation, regulation, and judicial hearing. Thus, beyond political campaigns, the dialogue also occurs in venues such as lobbying, court litigation, and legislative hearings.

At the best, parties seek to know and judge facts openly and fairly. They develop and apply evaluations of facts and judge actions on merit. They advocate for and challenge anything less than policy positions that collaboratively are in the interest of society, making it an even better place to live. It entails appeals to identify by organization, interest, and goal. Having set this as the ideal, the eternal role of the citizen would say, the reality is that it is corruptible when interests are advanced and championed narrowly rather than defined by the dialogue. As such, we are interested in political discourse as power resource management.

SIM, Rhetoric, and Political Discourse: Power Resource Management

Politics, priming, power, and pressure. These four Ps are the centerpieces of organizational engagement in politics. However well or badly, organizations struggle and strive to control conditions that are relevant to their survival and advancement of their interests. They contest issues as part of that struggle, and do so with the larger sense of achieving their missions and vision, the rationale of the organization and its justification as a contributing participant in society. As Heath (2008) reasoned:

> The prevailing paradigm is that power and control are best handled when they are approached symmetrically rather than asymmetrically, bilaterally rather than unilaterally, and treated as a community resource rather

than privileges to serve a narrow interest. Simply put, even though all players in this tussle do not seek mutually beneficial ends, one can argue that ultimately the best situation, one that does not demand constant power battles, features mutually defined solutions to shared problems and interests as the best way to exert power and control.

(p. 2)

Here is the rationale for power resource management, and the political role of large organizations in the future of society as means for shaping how it thinks (mind), identifying players and their identification (self/identity), and policy, the protocols of actions, sanctions, rewards, and punishments as power and control implementation.

Substance: Platforms of Fact, Value (Evaluation), Policy, and Identity/Identification

Courts and legislatures have officially recognized corporate entities as "persons"; as such, these entities are granted the rights, privileges, and responsibilities of being able to speak responsibly to the public. Speech can take several forms including paid advertising, making financial contributions, or spending money "for or against public policy positions or political candidates" (Heath, 1997, p. 236). In short, corporations can speak to defend themselves or their practices in times of crisis; they can speak to sell, market, or promote their products and services, but more importantly, they can speak to influence and shape public opinion.

When these entities speak to influence and shape public opinion they are engaged in issues communication. In short, since organizations can speak on matters of public interest, often times corporations via issues communication attempt to (and often do) inject values into the public dialogue in hopes that publics will use these values to judge current and subsequent issues. For years, political communication scholars have studied *priming* and its effects. Priming research explores the ways in which increased attention and exposure given to an issue "increases the prominence of these issues in the judgments that people form about public officials" (Holbrook & Hill, 2005, p. 278). Although researchers have begun to devote scholarly attention to the concept of priming in the context of corporate public relations (Wang, 2007), there exists a ripe opportunity to use existing priming research as one means to bridge the gaps between public relations and political communication. In short, the priming effect states that by making certain issues more salient than others a prime can influence the standards by which a particular issue is judged (Iyengar & Simon, 1993). Issue management, however, is not only concerned about the standards by which issues are judged but the discipline is also concerned about the various platforms of argumentation used to both articulate and judge issues.

At the heart of corporate issues management and political public relations are contestable questions of fact, value (evaluation), policy, and identity/identification. Issues are "contestable" and therefore they can be considered unsettled matters. In the wrangle in the marketplace of ideas corporations, government, and publics (including activists) use issue communication to create, shape, influence, or even challenge public policy based on these aforementioned platforms.

To illustrate the first platform, contestable questions of fact, we highlight the recent battle facing the Corn Refiners Association (CRA), which is a national trade association that represents the corn refining industry (and its interests) of the United States. One major issue that the CRA has been faced with is defending high fructose corn syrup. High fructose corn syrup can be found in nearly every processed product consumed in the United States. This product, however, has been the subject of much criticism and scrutiny. In response, the Corn Refiners Association (CRA) has gone to great lengths to use advertisements and public relations campaigns to contest a question of fact—that high fructose corn syrup is an unhealthy product. Critics of this product reason that consumers are being flooded with empty calories from high fructose corn syrup and link consumption of this product and obesity. Critics also suggest that the body processes the fructose in high fructose corn syrup differently than it does traditional cane or beet sugar. This in turn alters the way our bodies' metabolic-regulating hormones function. The way our bodies metabolize the fructose also forces the liver to kick more fat out into the bloodstream. The argument suggests that in the end our bodies are essentially tricked into wanting to eat more while simultaneously storing more fat.

Thus, the CRA has used a series of public relations issue communications to challenge questions of fact. These issue advertisements challenge critics by asserting three facts: (a) fructose is made from corn, (b) has the same calories as sugar or is nutritionally similar to sugar, and (c) is fine to consume in moderation. This truncated version of the argument shows how politicized interests are battling, via issue communication, to establish a platform by which publics judge (evaluate) issues (in this case the nutritional viability of high fructose corn syrup).

When publics judge issues, they debate platforms of value — matters considered bad, moral or immoral, just or unjust. Activists challenge businesses by contesting platforms of value: "it is not responsible to misuse and abuse the environment"; "steroid use in baseball is bad and brings into question the integrity of the game"; "discrimination in the workplace is immoral." These platforms of value (evaluation) often play a major role in political issue communication. Heath (1997) summed it up best with his description of the Activist Public Policy Logic: Corporations are doing Y (facts) which violates X set of societal expectations (and values). Therefore, they should be regulated in Z ways (policy).

Platforms of policy show the interconnectedness of corporate strategic issues management and politics via political communication. Corporations, government, and activists argue from the platforms of policy addressing what should be done in the policy arena; what procedures should be followed to either take advantage of an opportunity or to comply with political pressure; what policies should or must be followed; what laws should be changed.

Earlier we mentioned that organizations are challenged based on those platforms of value (evaluation) because the demands for policy changes are often the result of the platforms of fact being established and the evaluation of those facts that have triggered some sort of emotional, collective, response. Thus, through discussion of platforms of value, activist publics challenge corporations in the following political ways: "We at the Sierra Club have started our Beyond Coal Campaign because coal mining is shown to cause asthma and other health related problems, destroys mountains, and releases toxic mercury into our communities." Similarly, one might find corporations trying to set the public policy platform via issue communication. For the past few years Chevron, a major petrochemical company, uses its "Will You Join Us" campaign to talk about the increasing global use and possible complete exhaustion of the world crude oil supply. In this campaign, Chevron asks the willing people and agencies to join the company's efforts to discover better ways to conserve this resource. What is important to note is that Chevron talks about many energy saving tips. The other exemplars to correspond with the previously mentioned platforms of value might look similar to these: "As a Major League Baseball Hall of Fame voter, I want to pressure the MLB into enacting harsher suspensions to athletes found to be using steroids and other illegal performance enhancing drugs"; "Texaco management must be fired and penalized for their comments and unjust differential treatment toward racial and ethnic minorities in the place of employment."

Publics tend to identify with organizations, policies, and products/services they value and hold dear. As such, one might see publics battle when identities are threatened or challenged. The platform of identity/identification is an interesting concept because it highlights reasons why people come together, how they come together, and why they might choose to come together to support or challenge policy initiatives. Also, as it suggests merger, it also implies division: Us versus them.

For example, Boyd and Waymer (in press) discuss the notion of what "counts" as an American automaker. The authors discussed the leading automobile manufacturers, Toyota and BMW, in their home states (Kentucky and South Carolina) that are not typically considered "American" automakers. But why aren't they considered American automakers? The cars are made in the United States. The companies employ U.S. workers. The companies pay taxes in the United States, and they support U.S. communities; however, in terms of federal stimulus money, government bailouts, and patriotic appeals to support and purchase American cars, these companies do not count as U.S. automakers. These companies could challenge the government and ask why they are not considered American companies; however, we suspect many U.S. citizens would agree that neither Toyota nor BMW is an "American," "domestic" automaker. Questions of identity can be seen in a political public relations context such as nation building, public diplomacy, and the civil society (Taylor, 2000a, 2000b), as well as critiques and challenges to nation building and a civil society (Dutta-Bergman, 2005).

As evidenced above, questions of fact, value, policy, and identity are at play in any discussion of power resource management. Next we explore various rhetorical problems that often are manifested via the advocacy challenging these four contestable questions (fact, value, policy, identification).

Problematic 1: Rhetoric and Rhetorical Problems

Rhetoric as viewed in the Western heritage is the rationale and means of suasory discourse. As Brummett (1990) reasoned, rhetoric "has always been seen as a way of managing contingent human affairs through symbols. Rhetoric is a way of manipulating meanings to secure cooperation" (pp. 89–90). The term *manipulating* can put off various people who long for pure objectivity or pure evaluation. Such terms, however, feature the role of framing and priming as issues communication in political discourse. Modern rhetorical theory reasons that the challenge to those who enter into discourse is to understand and respond to questions which they frame or as framed by others. Each question, as framed can prime competing perspectives.

Rhetorical problems arise from needs that can be solved by strategically meaningful actions and discourse (Bitzer, 1968, 1987; see Ihlen, 2010). At least two general kinds of rhetorical problems (Bitzer, 1968) are worth mentioning relevant to issues management and politics: (a) a challenge raised by one party that requires one or more spokespersons to make a statement or engage in extended discourse, (b) problems that arise from conditions, such as a naturally caused crisis—a disaster of the magnitude of Katrina.

An entity can raise a rhetorical problem that requires response by other voices. It can respond to a problem posed by one or more voices. Or it can be expected to respond to some event. Such response may in fact start the process of framing and debating the event as a rhetorical problem.

Identity, and identification, can also pose rhetorical problems. Such conceptualization helps define the challenges organizations face as they decide why, how, and what to communicate in each rhetorical situation (Bitzer, 1968, 1987). Sillince (2006) addressed the strategic balance between the organization's persona (character, reputation, and identity) and that of audiences in the marketplace (by a logic similar to the concept of a second persona). He reasoned, "When multiple identities exist, the organization can privilege one identity as the salient identity and suppress or disguise the other identities as nonsalient identities. These nonsalient identities then become the salient resources that support the salient identity" (p. 186). As organizations and individuals have multiple identities, the challenge is to assure that they are mutually supportive rather than situationally available for narrow, short-term advantage.

Such challenges, paradoxes, and problematics are contexts that offer opportunities and constraints regarding what can, should, and must be said to address and respond to issues: Challenges of framing and priming. Standard taxonomies of such problems are especially relevant to legitimacy—the gap between expectation and experienced reality or organizational performance.

Vaara, Tienari, and Laurila (2006) distinguished five "legitimation strategies: (1) normalization, (2) authorization, (3) rationalization, (4) moralization, and (5) narrativization" (p. 789). Insights can be achieved that help us decide which and when discursive strategies are effectively and ethically used when legitimating industrial restructuring in the media. "Legitimacy is a prerequisite for institutionalization and institutionalization is key to understanding the resources of legitimacy" (p. 791). The key to understanding this problem rests with language and shared meaning. "From this perspective, *legitimacy means a discursively created sense of acceptance in specific discourses or orders of discourse* [emphasis in original]" (p. 793). Legitimacy by normalization "seeks to render something legitimate by exemplarity" (p. 798); "Authorization is legitimation by reference to authority" (p. 799). This discourse authorizes claims and establishes recurring authorizations and authorities. "Rationalization is legitimation by reference to the utility or function of specific actions or practices" (p. 800); "Moralization is legitimation that refers to specific values" (p. 801). Narrativization is legitimation that occurs when "telling a story provides evidence of acceptable, appropriate, or preferential behavior" (p. 802). The potency of narrativization results from dramatic structures that make some matter concrete and dramatic. And, thus the power bases of legitimacy become the result of and the playing out of narratives that define the norms of influence and shape interpretations (Heath, 1994) used as the rationale for enlightened choice.

Rhetoric presumes that no one necessarily has the best thoughts, makes the best decisions, and offers infallible advice. It presumes that the purpose of discourse, however Pollyannaish it may be, is to help several voices achieve enlightened choices. In this process, every statement should suffer counterstatement. It believes, perhaps naively, that humans are capable of engaging in discourse that brings out the best in them and their efforts to live and work together. However naïve that may seem, it presumes that all voices deserve to be heard, and regarded. At heart, political discourse framed around rhetorical problems has political implications relevant to the legitimacy, or not, of various policies, organizations, and issue responses.

Along these lines of thought, Hallahan (1999) offered framing theory as rationale for issues communication. Framing theory offers a comprehensive foundation for explaining public relations political processes and consequences. Thus, Hallahan helped us understand the framing of situations, attributes (characteristics, and by implication identities), choices (largely as loss or gain), actions (intended to achieve gain and avoid loss), issues (vying for preferred solutions), responsibility (as aspects of stability and control through policies and actions), and news (as culture reflecting and shaping).

By these logics, we find reason to believe that problems and their consideration, along with the legitimacy and identity of voices, constitutes the issues-oriented approach by organizations, including businesses, to politics in a wide array of contexts.

Problematic 2: Paradoxes of Positive and Negative Framing and Priming

According to Heath and Waymer (2009), "by its nature and the consequent roles it plays in society—especially when practiced on behalf of businesses—public relations is a professional practice typically devoted to making positive claims" (p. 200); that tendency to frame positive claims has led to the notion that the discipline and practice is nothing but spin, puffery, and fluff. There are consequences, however, that are more grave than just the reputation of a profession, discipline, and practice. This hegemony is exposed in our articulation of the paradoxes of the positive and the negative.

In contemporary U.S. society, corporate interests, voiced by boosterish developers work diligently to frame and prime public officials to encourage and subsidize urban renewal initiatives. Programs launched for the public good often conceal detrimental side effects to at least some populations. Hence, the paradox of the positive is an imperfection in discourse that is most evident when people in positions of power make public, upbeat announcements of actions they are taking or policies and programs they are implementing that are supposed to produce good and favorable outcomes for the publics who they represent (both those in powerful positions and the actions, policies, and programs). On the surface, represented publics are expected to desire and welcome these announcements. Announcements of good news seem to show that leaders are framing discourse and priming themes that actively seek to advance or improve various publics' quality of life in some way. Digging deeper into these frames reveals that seemingly favorable statements prime plans that can be harmful and damaging to at least some of the publics they are purported to help.

To elucidate this point, we explain how boosterish developers frame issues by proudly announcing (un)pleasant outcomes of urban renewal or gentrification to legitimize strategic business planning through political communication. Gentrification "refers to the rehabilitation of working–class and derelict housing and the consequent transformation of an area into a middle–class neighborhood" (Smith & Williams, 1986, p. 1); a hot topic of political debate over the past decade, "the controversy and publicity surrounding gentrification reflect its importance to almost all those who are concerned about the future of older distressed cities and their poorer residents" (Nelson, 1988, p. 11).

No one desires to live in or near a desolate area; however, one major source of marginalization and alienation is the hegemony that occurs as optimistic claims are made, in this case, about the goals and processes of urban renewal. The initiatives highlight all of the good that will come with renewal while ignoring the marginalization that attends such change. Such priming fails to critically highlight that by implication the frames championing the need for renewal indirectly point to the community denizens as the cause of the blight. Though officials may speak of "community," their community is one of real estate only—not people.

Without a doubt, the paradox of the positive grants the city planners and boosters a major advantage over their muted opposition because by the dynamics of the political and legitimacy terminology of urban development, the critics and victims can easily be deemed as antipositive and antiprogress.

The paradox of the negative can be highlighted using the same example of urban renewal, only this time we shift the pendulum and highlight how a corporate entity may use the rhetorical strategy of identification (Burke, 1969)—uniting against a common enemy—to demonize opponents of urban development in such a negative light that any challenge against the corporate interests seems both nonsensical and ludicrous. The frame often is that opposing change is opposing progress, a theme that primes the paradox of the positive.

Thus, while it is important that businesses have been granted personhood, protected speech, and the right and privilege to speak, we caution against the political power that can leverage their interests to the detriment of less powerful publics (Boyd & Waymer, in press). Whether business voices employ the paradox of the positive or negative, neither yields to the call for responsible advocacy on the parts of the corporate entities seeking legitimacy in the public policy arena. Political public relations is most ethical when it does not violate the paradoxes of the positive or negative, helps people to make informed choices, and does not violate the central assumptions of responsible advocacy.

Public decisions, that support or constrain business, result not only in discussions of fact, value, policy, and identification, but also frame and prime premises that help or hinder decisions preferred by various voices. This wrangle is well-discussed in the development and application of the precautionary principle.

Problematic 3: The Precautionary Principle

In business and political decision making, key premises drive conclusions in light of information. That claim emphasizes the idea that information is relatively unimportant for decision making until it is framed, interpreted based on shared or competing premises, and used for policy formation. If that logic is sound, we can explore a related complication: By what premise is information interpreted, evaluated, and policy formulated? One answer to that question rests with the discussion of the precautionary principle.

Politics and political discourse is a (or the) means by which society collectively manages risks. A risk, traditionally defined, is a probabilistic event that can have predictable consequences of varying magnitudes on risk bearers. One of the political realities of the issues management of politics is that organizations, especially businesses, tend to use politics as a means for framing, assigning, and controlling risk. Specifically, it is a tradition that businesses prime political discourse to maximize gains through risk management while externalizing the costs of doing business. This political stance tends to frame risk as the bending of reality to favor the interest of the advocate. Such stances pit interests against each other and can lead to conflict and misalignment of interests.

As a rationale, philosophy, and even protocol of risk communication as political discourse, advocates are engaged in political policy debates regarding acceptable levels of risk, and as means for imposing control over unacceptable levels they have developed what has become called the precautionary principle. For an excellent discussion of this principle, its current status in regulation, as well as public policy debates, see Maguire and Ellis (2009). Maguire and Ellis (2009) synthesized a vast body of discussion, policy formulation, and paradoxes of decision making as they discuss this concept as relevant to political framing and priming.

To simplify the concept and its application, discussants feature it as "ordinary best practices of decision making" framed as ordinary logics: "look before you leap," "better safe than sorry," or "an ounce of prevention is worth a pound of cure." These are precautionary principles advocated by those who believe, primarily, that insufficient information is known to make sound decisions that avoid unforeseen negative consequences. One of the primary policy contexts for such decisions occurs in the European Community debates over the safety of biotechnology innovation.

Businesses advocating such innovation reply that caution actually can produce more harm than that which is foreseen. For instance, delays in the development of certain agricultural biotechnologies can lead to starvation and malnourishment. These advocates in political policy formation contests advocate the following ordinary logics: "He who hesitates is lost," and "the early bird catches the worm." Caution, however, is often challenged by business if they focus on a return on investment logic. They (not collectively, but generically) argue for a conservative application of precaution if the development and sale of a product is slowed by the discussion. In contrast, they turn the table and argue for more caution in the event that the dialogue and decision might lead to business constraints: Such is the contest over the human (industrial) contribution to climate change.

Internally and externally, organizations are confronted with making decisions and formulating purposeful plans relevant to each political economy. Here is the strategic planning part of SIM and issue monitoring which asks what arguments are being made, what information is being put into play, and what are the sociopolitical implications of that dialogue given the discussants and their political relationships. In this political context, we find dialogues about issues, risks, and crisis.

Problematic 4: Issues, Risks, and Crises

For at least two decades, a case has been made that issues, risks, and crises are interconnected (Heath, 1997; Heath & Palenchar, 2009). As contestable matters of fact, value, policy, and identification, issues form the centerpiece in such analysis.

As risk management is the crux of issues management and political public relations, it often centers on issues such as what is the risk, what is its probability of occurrence, and who is likely to bear the risk? What premises prevail regarding the fairness and equity (likelihood and magnitude of impact on the risk bearer) of this relationship (which is a political matter)? Analysis addresses how well the issues of such analysis are understood and how well they withstand public debate. Are the consequences of the risk ethically worth the risk to one or more risk bearers? What is the corporate social responsibility of the risk creator in such matters? Are the risk arbiters and risk bearer advocates rhetorically competent to voice the needed concerns to achieve and implement appropriate policy to protect risk bearers (see Palmlund, 1992, 2009)? Political questions flow from the concern that risks as probabilistic events have negative consequences that can be detected (issue monitoring) and preventative measures can be developed (probably through politics) to reduce the likelihood that the risk will manifest and if so to mitigate the impact of the event on risk bearers.

The third piece of this puzzle is crisis, which can be defined as a risk manifested. Automobile design and manufacturing, for instance, is not perfect. Defect in either can result in the risk (probabilistic event/magnitude of impact) of failure leading to a safety required recall. Thus, a risk manifests into a crisis. In or during the crisis, one or more issues can be debated? Was the company sufficiently cautious and vigilant in the design and manufacturing? Was it callous and indifferent in these matters? Did it respond and demonstrate that lessons were learned to prevent or reduce subsequent risks? In this dialogue, we can find issues of risk leading to crisis (such as the debate over the health impact of smoking and the punitive consequences of such politics). We can find crisis of risk manifestation leading to issues: Mining deaths and injuries prompt legislation and regulation.

Issues, risks, and crises are three dimensions that combine business policy making and politics. How well these are managed (as issues management) reflects and results from the extent to which society is fully functioning (Heath, 2006).

Conclusion: Whose Society and How Fully Functioning?

As we end this chapter, we feature one final point. Without doubt, any discussion of the role of large organizations in politics is fraught with challenges. In a sense, we as a society cannot live without large organizations, but the critical perspective is to develop a constructive rationale for living with them: Getting the best from them with the least harm. This paradox features the legitimacy gap challenge of issues management. The balancing act is for corporate and other organizational voices to advance society through the collaborative alignment of interests through political discourse.

Heath (2006) argued that the essential question facing the theory, research, and practice of public relations—and issues management—is how organizations of all types make society more fully functioning. This challenge asks researchers and practitioners to address the processes (structures and functions of power) and the social construction of reality through sociopolitical, critical, and rhetorical discourse. Organizations, especially businesses, must start with reflective management (see Holmstrom, 2001). Reflective management guides organizations such as businesses to avoid assuming only their needs and engaging in political communication exclusively to assure those needs can be maximized by achieving stakeholder concurrence. The more ethical, and probably more successful view is for organizations, especially businesses to consider external opinion and look to see how the organization can adapt to that. Thus, we revise the classic assumption that what is good for General Motors is good for society, to this metaphoric restatement: What is good for society is good for General Motors.

A society is more fully functioning if multiple voices can be heard and processes are in place to judge the merits of these voices and work in collaborative and reflective ways to maximize the frame and prime the alignment of interests. Such tensions are not only relevant to the pillars of issues management but the ways those pillars support and foster society

The central theme of this chapter corresponds to the logic of the public sphere (Heath & Frandsen, 2008) by which community is created, fostered, maintained, and damaged. To the extent that the private sector attempts to dominate the political discourse of the public sphere, it is likely to meet opposition. How that opposition serves society and business interests is the challenge of a fully functioning society. Such a position presumes collaboration, reflection, the fostering of community, and listening and respecting as well as advocating and accommodating. Through infrastructures of power and the cocreation of meaning, public policy guides and empowers businesses, nonprofits, and governmental agencies.

References

Bitzer, L. (1968). The rhetorical situation. *Philosophy and Rhetoric, 1,* 1–15.

Bitzer, L. (1987). Rhetorical public communication. *Critical Studies in Mass Communication, 4,* 425–428.

Boyd, J., & Waymer, D. (in press). Organizational rhetoric: A subject of interest(s). *Management Communication Quarterly.*

Brummett, B. (1990). Relativism and rhetoric. In R. A. Cherwitz (Ed.), *Rhetoric and philosophy* (pp. 79–103). Hillsdale, NJ: Erlbaum.

Burke, K. (1969). *A rhetoric of motives.* Berkeley: University of California Press.

Chase W. H. (1982). Issue Management Conference: A special report. *Corporate Public Issues and their Management, 7*(3), 1–2.

Chase, W. H. (1984). *Issue management: Origins of the future.* Stamford, CT: Issue Action.

Dutta-Bergman, M. J. (2005). Civil society and public relations: Not so civil after all. *Journal of Public Relations Research, 17,* 267–289.

Ewing, R. P. (1987). *Managing the new bottom line: Issues management for senior executives.* Homewood, IL: Dow Jones-Irwin.

Hallahan, K. (1999). Seven models of framing: Implications for public relations. *Journal of Public Relations Research, 11,* 205–242.

Heath, R. L. (Ed.). (1988). *Strategic issues management: How organizations influence and respond to public interests and policies.* San Francisco, CA: Jossey-Bass.

Heath, R. L. (1994). *Management of corporate communication: From interpersonal contacts to external affairs.* Hillsdale, NJ: Erlbaum.

Heath, R. L. (1997). *Strategic issues management: Organizations and public policy challenges.* Thousand Oaks, CA: Sage.

Heath, R. L. (2001). A rhetorical enactment rationale for public relations: The good organization communicating well. In R. L. Heath (Ed.), *Handbook of public relations* (pp. 31–50). Thousand Oaks, CA: Sage.

Heath, R. L. (2006). Onward into more fog: Thoughts on public relations' research directions. *Journal of Public Relations Research, 18,* 93–114.

Heath, R. L. (2008). Power resource management: Pushing buttons and building cases. In T. L. Hansen-Horn & B. D. Neff (Eds.), *Public relations: From theory to practice* (pp. 2–19). Boston, MA: Pearson.

Heath, R. L., & Cousino, K. R. (1990). Issues management: End of first decade progress report. *Public Relations Review, 17*(1), 6–18.

Heath, R. L., & Frandsen, F. (2008). Rhetorical perspective and public relations: Meaning matters. In A. Zerfass, B. van Ruler, & K. Sriramesh (Eds.), *Public relations research: European and international perspectives and innovations* (pp. 349–364). Wiesbaden, Germany: VS Verlag.

Heath, R. L., & Palenchar, M. J. (2009). *Strategic issues management: Organizations and public policy challenges* (2nd ed.). Thousand Oaks, CA: Sage.

Heath, R. L., & Waymer, D. (2009). Activist public relations: A case study of Frederick Douglass' "Fourth of July Address." In R. L. Heath, E. L. Toth, & D. Waymer (Eds.), *Rhetorical and critical approaches to public relations II* (pp. 195–215). New York: Routledge,

Heath, R. L., Motion, J., & Leitch, S. (2010). Power and public relations: Paradoxes and programmatic thoughts. In R. L. Heath (Ed.), *SAGE handbook of public relations* (pp. 191–204). Thousand Oaks, CA: Sage.

Holbrook, R. A., & Hill, T. G. (2005). Agenda-setting and priming in prime time television: Crime dramas as political cues. *Political Communication, 22,* 277–295.

Holmstrom, S. (2010). Reflective management: Seeing the organization as if from outside. In R. L. Heath (Ed.), *SAGE handbook of public relations* (pp. 261–276). Thousand Oaks, CA: Sage.

Ihlen, O. (2010). The curses sisters: Public relations and rhetoric. In R. L. Heath (Ed.), *SAGE handbook of public relations* (pp. 59–70). Thousand Oaks, CA. Sage.

Iyengar, S., & Simon, A. (1993). News coverage of the Gulf crisis and public opinion: A study of agenda-setting, priming, and framing. *Communication Research, 20,* 365–383.

Jaques, T. (2010). Embedding issue management: From process to policy. In R. L. Heath (Ed.), *SAGE handbook of public relations* (pp. 435–446). Thousand Oaks, CA. Sage.

Maguire, S., & Ellis, J. (2009). The precautionary principle and risk communication. In R. L. Heath & H. D. O'Hair (Eds.), *Handbook of risk and crisis communication* (pp. 119–137). New York: Routledge.

Mead, G. H. (1934). *Mind, self, and society.* Chicago, IL: University of Chicago Press.

Nelson, K. P. (1988). *Gentrification and distressed cities: An assessment of trends in intrametropolitan migration.* Madison: University of Wisconsin Press.

Palmlund, I. (1992). Social drama and risk evaluation. In S. Krimsky & D. Golding (Eds.), *Social theories of risk* (pp. 197–212). Westport, CT: Praeger.

Palmlund, I. (2009). Risk and social dramaturgy. In R. L. Heath & H. D. O'Hair (Eds.), *Handbook of risk and crisis communication* (pp. 192–204). New York: Routledge.

Schmertz, H. (1986). *Good-bye to the low profile: The art of creative confrontation.* Boston: Little, Brown.

Sethi, S. P. (1977). *Advocacy advertising and large corporations: Social conflict, big business image, the news media, and public policy.* Lexington, MA: D. C. Heath.

Sillince, J. A. A. (2006). Resources and organizational identities: The role of rhetoric in the creation of competitive advantage. *Management Communication Quarterly, 20,* 186–212.

Smith, N., & Williams, P. (1986). Alternatives to orthodoxy: Invitation to debate. In N. Smith & P. Williams (Eds.), *Gentrification of the city* (pp. 1–12). Boston, MA: Unwin Hyman.

Taylor, M. (2000a). Media relations in Bosnia: A role for public relations in building civil society. *Journal of Public Relations Research, 26,* 1–14.

Taylor, M. (2000b). Toward a public relations approach to nation building. *Journal of Public Relations Research, 12,* 179–210.

Vaara, E., Tienari, J., & Laurila, J. (2006). Pulp and paper fiction: On the discursive legitimation of global industrial restructuring. *Organizational Studies, 27*(6), 789–810.

Wang, A. (2007). Priming, framing, and position on corporate social responsibility. *Journal of Public Relations Research, 19,* 123–145.

8

POLITICAL PUBLIC RELATIONS AND POLITICAL MARKETING

Darren G. Lilleker and Nigel Jackson

Political marketing and political public relations have much in common, but their roots can be traced to different academic disciplines: marketing and public relations. This is reflected both in theory and practice, although much may be gained by a closer integration of political marketing and political public relations theory and research. In this chapter we will review theory and research in both fields, suggest similarities and differences, and argue for the need to both integrate and view these fields of theory, research, and practice as complementary rather than as mutually exclusive.

The Concepts of Political Marketing and Political Public Relations

Political marketing emerged as a concept, within academic study at least, in the late 1960s. Yet, Philip Kotler (1975) argued that marketing had always been a feature of political campaigning, a point reinforced in Wring's (2001) historical study of the British Labour Party. In practical terms, political marketing is viewed as the strategic importation of theories, concepts, and tools by political organizations in response to a range of social trends. Marketing, it can be argued, provides the tools that may fill the engagement and loyalty gap left by the weakening of ideological attachments to parties. Political marketing is underpinned by a theoretical conceptualization of the voter as a consumer; an individualistic and rational entity that makes voter choices based on economic equations (Downs, 1957; Heath, Jowell, & Curtice, 2001). A phenomenon referred to in the United States as pocketbook voting, the voter as consumer paradigm holds that voters will decide which candidate or party is best for them personally based on the impact on their standard of living. However, parallel to this theoretical understanding of the voter is a discussion embedded within the practice of political campaigning by parties and candidates. Marketing theorists Philip Kotler and Sidney Levy noted as early as 1969 that political candidates were marketed in similar ways to fast moving consumer goods; their famous analogy being with soap. Kotler went further in 1975 when he suggested: "The very essence of a candidate's interface with the voters is a marketing one, and always has been" (p. 761). These early observations inform much later work on marketing within political contexts, as well as critiques of political marketing as reducing politics to being a product that is consumed.

Early works initially focused on the role of marketing within the field of political public relations, with marketing being the junior discipline that informed public relations strategies (Kelley, 1956). However, as the field expanded, studies focused at both the macrolevel encompassing all areas of politics (Henneberg, 2004a; Johnson 2008; Kavanagh, 1995; Newman, 1999a; O'Shaughnessy, 1990; Scammell, 1997) as well as microlevel studies of areas such as segmentation (Rothschild, 1978), branding (Lilleker, 2005; Smith, 2001), as well as a range of studies of communicative action. Equally, theoretical development has seen a range of marketing concepts applied to politics (Butler & Harris, 2009; O'Cass, 1996). The development of political marketing as an academic field has thus seen marketing become the dominant paradigm for studying postmodern party behavior.

Modeling of party behavior first emerged in the 1970s. Abrahim Shama (1976) conceptualized political parties as production, sales, or market oriented and linked to each of these models different modes of communication. Production oriented candidates and parties would seek exposure through persuasive communication; for Shama this resulted in a propaganda communicational style. Sales oriented candidates and parties would employ more media management and would use the tools of advertising and public relations to convince voters, and communication would be targeted and underpinned by rigorous market research. If a market orientation were adopted, a more expansive communication mode would be adopted. Market research would inform product design as well as the design of all communication. Internal communication among members, loyal supporters, affiliates, and donors would refine policy and allow for strategic positioning vis-à-vis key market segments. While this may appear as contiguous with traditional perspectives of political campaigning, it represents a paradigm shift. As Newman (1999b) notes: "Our electoral system was set up to give candidates the opportunity to let voters know who they are and what they stand for ... candidates now use marketing research to do just the opposite, that is, to find out who the voters are and what they want the candidates to stand for. Candidates then feed back to the voters the ideas that they know will sell" (p. 16). Such a strategy automatically subsumes public relations within a mass media and direct mail strategy for disseminating messages. While some studies place communication prior to marketing, making this the means rather than the starting point (Maarek, 1997), political marketing has developed into a strategic guide for political behavior (Henneberg & Ormrod, 2006). But, due to its roots in marketing theory, political marketing compartmentalizes public relations as a tactical communication function only.

The Shama tripartite model for explaining party and candidate behavior remains a key feature of the field of political marketing, though refined by Lees-Marshment (2001, 2009) and applied in comparative studies (Lees-Marshment, Rudd, & Strömbäck, 2010; Lilleker & Lees-Marshment, 2005). The model is not without significant criticism, however. Conceptually it demands a centralized party structure which focuses mainly on the development of an offering, a program of outcomes, determined from current voter wants and needs. Its links are to the short-term marketing orientation, as opposed to a more long-term market orientation within which an organization anticipates future desires and thereby leads the market (Kohli, Jaworski, & Kumar, 1993). Some argue that this limits the model's power to inform political strategy (Ormrod, 2004). Furthermore, the explicit disavowal of ideology in favor of a neoliberal market-oriented model of understanding voter consumption leads others to suggest that the model reduces politics to offering images of, and encouraging, a consumer culture; this is juxtaposed with the more civic attitude linked with citizenship (Savigny, 2006; Scullion, 2008).

While these critiques stand, political marketing is more conventionally used to explain and model the behavior of parties and candidates in the process of striving to win elections. The short-term nature of brand building as a route to the White House or Westminster is as clear a feature of the work of Newman (1994, 1999b) and Baines, Harris, and Lewis (2002), for example, as with Lees-Marshment's conceptualization of product design. The academic work within the field of political marketing seems to describe the strategic use of tools to achieve either electoral success or the management of political campaigns in order to retain public support (Farrell & Wortmann, 1987).

This literature can be criticized for transplanting marketing into politics and thereby creating what Henneberg (2004b) describes as a dialectic tension. Because marketing is applied reactively as opposed to proscriptively, research describes the political marketing process rather than developing theories to understand the interlocutions between the disciplines of politics and marketing. Synergies in practice between political campaigning and marketing are recognized and highlighted (Baines, Harris, & Lewis, 2002), but equally criticized for reducing political marketing to poll-driven politics (Scammell, 1999). Yet many theoretical expositions of political marketing link back to notions of data gathering and the consequent design and management of behavior and communication to appeal to target groups (Lees-Marshment, 2001; Ormrod, 2004). Thus, what is often referred to as a market or marketing orientation within politics could, when applied empirically, be described as a consumption orientation: that all aspects of party or candidate communication, which would include core messages about policy (the product or offering) are designed with consumption in mind.

What is lacking from the vast majority of work, however, is a call for parties or candidates to go beyond this consumption orientation to focus on the more long-term aspects of politics. Perspectives from relationship marketing, which discuss long-term loyalty building strategies (Gronroos, 1997; Gummesson, 2002; Johansen, 2005, 2009), are positioned as rather idealistic accounts though there have been attempts to apply relationship marketing to politics. In a period of voter volatility, Bannon (2005) suggests that political parties should be applying a longer-term relationship marketing approach. There is also evidence that political actors have particularly utilized the Internet within a relationship marketing approach (Bowers-Brown, 2003; Dean & Croft, 2001; Jackson, 2006). Whilst not universally accepted, relational marketing approaches have been applied to election campaigns in general, and to specific communications channels.

From the public relations literature we can identify some common themes to the study and practice of public relations. The target audience of public relations is considered to be publics, which has been defined as *"any group whose members have a common interest or common values in a particular situation"* (emphasis added; Guth & Marsh, 2006, p. 93; see also Grunig & Hunt, 1984). The concept of publics is in essence concerned with how an organization can use finite resources to reach the right people at the right time. Moreover, such publics are usually identified by being actively involved or interested in an issue; passive publics should not concern the public relations practitioner (Grunig, 1997). The concept of publics highlights a key difference with marketing. An organization is able to choose which markets it wishes to target with a product; however, when communicating, using the tools of public relations, it is not necessarily able to choose its publics. The public relations practitioner may well have to deal with critics such as pressure groups, or those in a position to make something happen or not happen that influences the organization, and not just consumers. It is for this reason that the public relations practitioner plays a boundary spanning role, where he or she interprets the views of external audiences about an organization, and advises the organization how to respond. Thus, the public relations practitioner needs to be able to change not just what an organization says, but also what it does. It is for this reason that the Excellence model suggests that it is only the PR function that can change the culture of an organization (Grunig & Grunig, 1992). In order to help the public relations practitioner build relationships with key audiences, and enhance the reputation of an organization, they can utilize up to 13 different channels and techniques (Newsom, Turk, & Kruckeberg, 2000). Thus, public relations has a clear and distinct meaning, role, and range of techniques that should not be confused with or subsumed by marketing.

Having said this, like relationship marketing, the core concepts of public relations often tend to remain subsumed beneath political marketing; a part of the product design rather than informing that process and how the party or candidate relate to their various publics. As a result, research in political marketing, political science, and electoral studies tends to conflate public relations to essentially media relations. Strömbäck, Mitrook, and Kiousis (2010) consequently suggest that political marketing suffers from a lack of detailed understanding of PR. Moreover, by referring to "spin" (Jones 2001; Scammell 2001a), political PR is given a slight sense of the sinister, and Scammell (2003) suggests it has been viewed as "ugly."

This essentially negative view of public relations implies that it is a process by which the message that voters receive becomes "packaged" for consumption (Franklin, 1994; Lock & Harris, 1996). Political marketing reinforces this negative perspective, due to its conflation with consumption and communication. Aspects of marketing theory that explicitly discuss the relations with market segments are sidelined, due to the short-term nature of political actors dependent upon the electoral cycle and its demands. Perhaps it is to this area that political public relations can most contribute.

However, before we assess the impact of political PR on political marketing, we must first explore the meaning of political PR. While there are many textbooks and articles on the meaning of PR, as noted by Jackson (2010) finding a definition of political PR is highly complex. Some texts use the term *political PR*, but appear to assume that its meaning is fully understood by the reader (Davis, 2000; Esser, Reinemann, & Fan, 2001; Trammell 2006). Where definitions of political PR have been offered, they tend to reflect the primacy of media relations, so Froehlich and Ruddier (2006) note that political actors use political PR through media channels as a means of ultimately persuading the wider public. Brissenden and Moloney (2005) suggest that political PR is not just about using the media as a persuasive tool, but also acts as a trellis behind which an organization can hide from the media, and hence the wider public, those things they do not want them to know. This adds to the negativity implied by commentary on political media relations and spin. However, while the focus of political PR definitions has been on the tactical, and so dominated by media relations and events management, it has also been recognized that it has a strategic role in gaining voter attention (Moloney & Colmer, 2001).

In the opening chapter of this book, Strömbäck and Kiousis provide a strategic definition, which shapes our discussion of the link between political marketing and political PR.

> Political public relations is the management process by which an organization or individual actor for political purposes, through purposeful communication and action, seeks to influence and establish, build and maintain beneficial relationships and reputations with its key publics to help support its mission and achieve its goals.

This definition highlights three interrelated streams of thought within PR. First, the Grunigian paradigm stresses the importance of communication enhancing mutual benefit for both an organization and its publics (Grunig & Grunig, 1992; Grunig & Hunt, 1984). The use of two-way symmetrical communication plays the key role in encouraging understanding, and subsequently mutual benefit. Second, the relational approach goes a stage further and focuses on the building of strong relationships with a limited number of key stakeholders (Bruning, Dials, & Shirka, 2008; Ferguson, 1984; Ledingham & Bruning, 2000). The third stream, closely related to the relational approach, is that the aim of such PR is reputation management. Here the focus is on identifying, managing, and changing the reputation of an organization (Cornelissen, 2008; Fombrun, 1995; Griffin, 2008). All three of these components of the definition of political PR suggest that relying on media relations alone is not enough, and that a much wider range of communication tools is required. Thus, while political marketing may appear as the current dominant paradigm for guiding and understanding party behavior, public relations theory may be better placed to design best practices within a political context.

The Meaning and Practice of Political Marketing

While there is no accepted or scientific definition of political marketing, it has been used to explain a shift in the behavior of parties and candidates seeking election, as well as a range of other institutions which hold offices of power or are adjuncts of government. For example, Lees-Marshment (2005) applied her model beyond UK political parties to include the monarchy, universities, media organizations, and charities. We would argue this broadening of the concept can lead to concept stretching and conflate political marketing with not-for-profit and public sector responses to changes in their audiences and publics, and will thus focus on the context of electoral politics in this chapter. For these purposes, it is useful to reaffirm some basic definitions. Politics, as both a practice and an academic discipline, is concerned with the allocation of power and resources; politics thus focuses on how power is won, the operation of various forms of representation and the social impact of decision making (Crick, 2001). Politics implies both conflict and consensus (Tansey & Jackson, 2008), which requires balancing out, or choosing between, competing interests; reconciling incompatible demands and imposing a collective will (Stoker, 2006). While politics does not have to be democratic, liberal democratic politics presents politics at its most complex, where competition is strongest both between those seeking to wield power and those seeking to have influence.

Marketing may often be conflated with sales and pursuing profit, but equally important, it is a managerial process concerned with understanding and predicting the needs and wants of key audiences and locating mutually satisfactory solutions (Kotler & Levy, 1969). While there may be connotations that evoke images of snake-oil salesmen, modern marketing talks of engendering commitment and trust (Morgan & Hunt, 1994), building relationships between brands and consumers (Gronroos, 1989, 1997) and the existence of social contracts (Firat, Dholakia, & Venkatesh, 1995). Thus, perhaps it is worth drawing these two definitions together to describe political marketing as a managerial process, which apportions power and resources within a society based on understandings and predictions of the needs and wants of that society in order to satisfy the public and meet the aims of the organization. The idea of mutual understanding need not necessarily suggest political marketing is only applicable within liberal democracies; but it is within pluralist systems that demands need careful reconciliation. Within this context, such a definition may be neat, but is not without some significant points of contention born out through study of theory and practice.

Prevalent in studies of the impact of introducing marketing to politics is the notion of managerialism supplanting ideology and doctrine (Savigny, 2006; Savigny & Temple, 2010). While it is questionable whether many parties existed (beyond Communist parties) that had strict codified doctrines that determined policy, ideology played a key role in defining party brands within most democracies throughout the course of the 20th century (Arblaster, 2002). The decline of ideological metanarratives, in particular, linked to the collapse of the Soviet bloc and redefining of socialism, is argued to have been replaced with a more managerial perspective of organizing the state (Lilleker, 2005). The repositioning of parties such as New Democrats and New Labour and the rise of third way political ideas that suggest moving beyond the right–left spectrum (Giddens, 1992), all contribute to a neoliberalization of politics (Savigny, 2006) and the rise of catch-all (Kircheimer, 1966) electoral-professional (Panebianco, 1988) parties and candidates. These candidates, and the leaders of parties, present themselves as managers, or heads of managerial teams, who would be the best to oversee the running of the economic, political, and social relations of the state; in turn they present themselves in ways that appeal to a managerialist political consumer. This term is important here, it does not suggest the demise of the citizen voter, but an evolution of voting behavior that blends the cognition of the consumer with that of the citizen and voter (Scammell, 2001b). The collision of cognition processes, and resulting elision of compartmentalized thinking appropriate for consumer choice making and voter choice making, is argued to now decide elections; though economic theories of voting are by no means new phenomena (Downs, 1957; Heath, Jowell, & Curtice, 2001; for discussion see Lilleker & Scullion, 2009). However there are questions regarding whether the managerial practice of political marketing not only reflects social trends, but can have a role in exacerbating the trend toward processing political communication with a consumerist mindset.

Equally controversial is the notion of resource allocation and how satisfaction within the political marketplace compares to the context of commercial marketing. To simplify core concepts of marketing theory, the exchange of money for a product needs to result in a perception of value for money. Perceived value for money equates to satisfaction, and long-term satisfaction can lead to a relationship of commitment on the part of the consumer and so repeat purchasing and brand loyalty (Kotler & Keller, 2006). Exchange within a political context can be reduced to simply the vote, but this has no intrinsic value in itself. Dermody and Scullion (2000) discussed this exchange process in terms of hope; an investment of our hope in a party or candidate to implement a political agenda that meets personal desires or, more negatively, to keep their own promises.

While entirely logical, practice counters many notions of exchange and satisfaction. In Britain and the United States, where much research on political marketing has been carried out, as well as being the locations for considerable innovation, the two-party winner-takes-all systems mean that elections are fought on a competing logic. The major parties will target voters with varying strengths of loyalty, from absolute to none at all. Equally, the parties fight most intensely over geographic regions where support is most evenly distributed and so the contest is close and results unpredictable (Denver & Hands, 1997). The logic is to target voters with the lowest level of loyalty, but still the highest propensity to vote, within areas that will matter most to the outcome. Reflecting on the 2005 UK election, Heather Savigny (2006) calculated that this meant that floating voters in battleground seats, a maximum of 2% of the electorate, was the key target market for the two major parties.

If it is only the satisfaction of these voters that is promised entirely, while the overall party policy is sufficiently utilitarian to not deter voters with emotional attachments to the party, it reduces the scope of people that parties or candidates seek to form a connection with. Political marketing strategies based on a wide range of marketing communication channels might reach a wide range of people, but the real intended target may only be a very small number of key floating voters.

The aim of the strategy is then the major problem when applying theories and concepts of commercial marketing to the context to politics. Elections, in essence, have become events that have one overall outcome: victory or defeat—particularly so in countries with winner-takes-all electoral systems. While there may be a range of aims across the spectrum for parties and candidates that participate in elections, and of course potential coalition partners may have a more complex market that may include their potential partners, ultimately elections are about gaining democratic power. In a comprehensive analysis of the use of marketing during the 2005 UK general election, consistent with models offered by Baines, Harris, and Lewis (2002) in particular, it was found that the majority of tools imported from marketing were employed to persuade voters as opposed to informing the product design (Lilleker, Jackson, & Scullion, 2006). The editors of one collection of empirical studies likened the parties to magpies, due to the practice of using tools to gain a competitive edge over opponents, as opposed to embedding marketing concepts within their organizations in order to better understand the electorate or build stronger relationships with them (Lilleker, Jackson, & Scullion, 2006, p. 259). This short-term view aims at one single big sell and is a courtship process that may be closer to seeking a one-night stand rather than a marriage (Bannon, 2005). This may be a reflection of the nature of the behavior and strategic thinking of parties and candidates seeking election, or of a political trend to borrow concepts and tools from commercial practice which are inconsistent with the context of politics (Moloney, 2006). While these are big questions that are beyond the remit of this chapter, they are nonetheless worth posing and locating within the context of our discussion.

While political marketing theorists (Lees-Marshment, 2001) have indicated that, if embedded correctly, marketing can reduce disconnections between electors and elected, enhance public interest and engagement, and encourage participation, practice suggests the reverse is the case. The market-oriented party model is a chimera which may be observed using some simplistic behavioral indicators, such as synergy between publicly expressed most important issues and the priority given to those areas by parties and candidates in their election communication (Henneberg & Ormrod, 2006; Lilleker & Negrine, 2006), but seems to be unrecognized by the voter. In many countries trust in politics is low, party membership in decline, and turnout in elections unstable (Stoker, 2006), which suggests that politics itself needs marketing (Mortimore, 2003). The question is whether such a project could compete with the activities of those who seek election. Some studies find a direct connection between the marketing strategy and nonvoting and loyalty, though only among once loyal voters of a party that had rebranded (Lilleker, 2005). At the same time, marketing cannot be held to blame for all the ills of politics, as there are social drivers of the decline in engagement that marketing is a response to and is used to militate against. Whether public relations theory offers a better skill set for application within politics is a moot point, but one worthy of further exploration.

Prior to assessing the links between marketing and public relations, however, it is worth elaborating on the fact that marketing is not a single approach or philosophy. Rather, there are at least three different ways that political marketing can operate: transactional, relational, and experiential.

Political marketing has traditionally been viewed as transactional, whereby the focus is on gaining the vote for a particular election (Lees-Marshment, 2001; Mauser, 1983; Wring, 2001). Messages are broadcast through mass communication media such as television, so the emphasis is on media management and advertising. The focus of such messages is on the political product (policies, leaders, and activities), and once the voter has been persuaded to vote in the election, the process starts all over again at the next contest. The process is akin to Kotler and Levy's (1969) analogy of selling soap powder.

The relationship marketing approach views politics as a service industry, so that influencing voters and others is akin to selling a financial service (Jackson, 2006). The focus is on customer retention (Reichheld & Sasser, 1990) of existing supporters, rather than customer recruitment in the form of chasing undecided voters. To maintain customer loyalty (Berry, 1983) and trust (McKenna, 1985), political actors seek to engage in conversation with citizen voters over a longer period of time (Bannon, 2005). Indeed, Jackson (2008) suggests that such a strategy can actually persuade floating voters. A relationship marketing approach attempts to get a voter to align with the party once, and then move the individual up the rungs of the "loyalty ladder" (Christopher, Payne, & Ballantyne, 1992) so that they become strong identifiers with that party, then members, and finally activists and possibly even stand for election. The emphasis on dialogue and two-way symmetrical communication highlights a link with the Grunigian element of the definition of political PR guiding this book, which also stresses the importance of mutual understanding. Traditionally, political marketing has been viewed either as a one-shot attempt to "buy" votes, or an attempt to build a longer-term relationship that will have an effect over several elections.

A more recent philosophical approach to marketing is experiential marketing (Pine & Gilmore, 1998), where the consumer is not just interested in the tangible components of a product, but also has an emotional attachment to it (Schmitt, 1999). In theory, the consumer personally connects to a product or brand through an experience (Holbrook, 1999). Political parties, therefore, will also seek to offer voters a memorable experience. Experiential marketing emphasizes the six senses (McCole, 2004), and so the political actors' message should not just focus on themselves, but also on how the interaction affects the receiver. This approach to marketing is particularly applicable to events, such as elections, where the product is an experience (Getz, 2008). As well as buying into a party or candidate's policies and image, the voter is also buying into the experience of a general election campaign. This could be in the form of attending a public meeting, but it can also be reflected in the messages they receive. "Time for a change," a slogan often used by oppositions challenging an incumbent government, is actually a suggestion that the recipient can make a difference and will be part of something new. An experiential marketing approach seeks to change the relationship between the voter and those seeking election in two key ways. First, political persuasion is based not just on the tangible aspects of the product offer from the party or candidate, but also intangibles such as how the voter enjoys the experience of the interface with political actors. Second, an election becomes an event of which the voter feels a part. In its own right an election is an event that the voter experiences, and so creates emotional and not just rational responses. Such concepts go beyond current theories and practices developed within the field of political marketing, and suggest a blurring of the boundaries between marketing and public relations and a strengthening of relational ties both between the disciplines and attendant practice.

The Relationship between Political PR and Political Marketing

Before we can explore the relationship between public relations and marketing within the political sphere, we need to understand the relationship between the two disciplines in general. At a practical level the functions of PR and marketing can be seen to work side by side on a daily basis, and both are outward facing, persuasive, and rely on communications. However, there can be some tension between the two disciplines. In the practical world this tends to manifest itself in turf wars over who has control of structures, lines of responsibility, and budgets. For academics the debate is often over the nature and role of each, and which is dominant. Whereas the target audience of marketing is essentially groups of customers within markets (Fill, 2009), public relations, it has been argued, has a wider audience, namely publics (L'Etang, 2008). While public relations may include customers, publics also include anyone who is influenced by or might influence an organization, such as pressure groups. This has led Theaker (2008, to suggest: "All organizations have a need for PR, but not all are involved in marketing" (p. 305). Grunig (1992) argues that the wider focus of PR beyond markets means that whereas marketing spends money, PR saves it. His argument is that the issues management capability of PR identifies potential problems and opportunities in advance, so that an organization can save money by responding in a timely fashion. Transferred to politics, the political marketer hence focuses on political consumers (citizen-voters) while the political PR practitioner considers a wider range of stakeholders and publics.

Probably the best known attempt to conceptualize the relationship between marketing and PR was made by Kotler and Mindak (1978). They identified that there were potentially five different models that could explain how public relations and marketing operated together within an organization: separate but equal functions; equal but overlapping functions; marketing as the dominant function; public relations as the dominant function; and public relations and marketing as the same function. They suggest that no single model will be appropriate for all organizations, but that the two functions will have to evolve due to external pressures, and that eventually they will converge. Pickton and Broderick (2001) revised these five models and added one variant. They suggested that under the conditions of the first model where the functions are separate, that the structure of PR could differ. In some organizations the PR function was integrated into decision making and strategy at the corporate level and so a single function, but that in others PR activities were fragmented across departments and individuals and related mostly to the deployment of tactics. The public relations function might be, as implied by Kotler and Mindak (1978), one unified department or contain a series of autonomous departments such as press office, public affairs, and community relations all located within the overall remit of public relations.

Within a political context, the consumer/market approach is often perceived to be dominant at the expense of approaches that focus on other publics or stakeholders. One reason for this is that political marketing is most often studied within the context of elections, so when describing political marketing as the analysis of wants and needs, it is those belonging to "voters and citizens" (Newman, 1999b, p. 3) that matter. Within the process of rebranding New Labour, Labour strategist Philip Gould (1998) talks of targeting voter segments that the party had lost to the Conservatives, but who were ripe for conversion. Such tactics were informed by Clinton's strategies in the United States, where the New Democrats were created as a catch-all party to win back the center ground. The problem with identifying uses of data, and the source, is that political marketing research is conducted privately and the link that is required to "identify the stages that … political parties have now arrived at in anticipation of the next general election" (Lees-Marshment, 2001, pp. 30–41) is virtually impossible to identify (Lilleker & Negrine, 2006, p. 38). While Lees-Marshment (2001) explicitly talks of adjustment of the product following research among MPs and members, key stakeholders for a political brand, this is not seen as a priority within parties and there is no consideration of wider publics or stakeholders within most of political marketing research.

Hence, within a political context, marketing is often perceived as the dominant function with public relations marginalized to a communication role only. This may suggest a convergence of public relations and marketing, or simply public relations serving marketing strategy; though one may well argue that there is a lack of marketing strategy at the heart of many parties despite there being a use of some marketing tools and concepts.

Kotler and Mindak's view about the inevitability of convergence between PR and marketing is contested. While Hutton (1996) supports this idea and suggests that marketing is dominating, adherents of the Grunigian approach reject that there are clear differences between the two disciplines (Grunig, 1992; Grunig & Hunt, 1984). More recently, New York advertising executive Al Ries (Ries & Ries, 2002) suggests that it may well be PR managers who are in the ascendancy because of their ability to be more creative, to sell and to lead a brand. One argument to support the rise of political marketing has been the growth of professionalism in political communications, encouraging political actors to employ the skills of commercial communicators (Negrine, Mancini, Holtz-Bacha, & Papathanassopoulos, 2007). To confirm this, and so support the dominance of political marketing over political communication, we suggest requires an assessment of both the disciplines of such professionals, and the reporting structure within the political organization. If the preponderance of political communicators, especially the senior staff, come from a marketing background and are involved mostly in direct marketing, product design, and supply chain management then political marketing dominates. However, if such political communicators originate primarily from media relations, events management, and corporate reputation then political PR is more likely to dominate.

This battle over who dominates was transferred to two concepts with each discipline championing a separate approach: integrated marketing communication (IMC) and integrated communication. IMC has been defined by Kotler (1991) as:

> The concept under which a company carefully integrates and co-ordinates its many communication channels to deliver a clear, consistent and compelling message about the organization and its products.
>
> (p. 781)

IMC seeks to present potential and actual customers and suppliers with a consistent brand image (Fill, 2009). As such it focuses on marketing goals, customers, and markets, and hence implies the dominance of marketing over PR within the communication function of an organization. In the political sphere IMC means that the focus is on individual voters or citizens, and not other interested audiences. In party–centered systems the brand is the party, and individual candidates are largely subsumed within the overall party brand. In candidate–centered systems the situation is the opposite. However, it is worth noting that countries such as the UK, largely considered party-centric, are gradually moving toward a middle ground where individual candidates are having more of an impact, with, for example, the election of some Independent candidates. Moreover, the Internet provides candidates/representatives the opportunity of bypassing both the media and their own party hierarchies (Jackson & Lilleker, 2009). By focusing on the achievement of marketing goals, political IMC implies that activities such as lobbying, issues management, and crisis management are largely ignored, and media and events management's role is to attract publicity for the overall marketing strategy.

The public relations alternative to IMC is integrated communication (IC), where the key difference is the purpose and audience of communication. Wightman (1999) suggests that IC stresses a much wider audience than IMC, namely all of an organization's stakeholders (or publics), not just its customers. In the political sphere, therefore, IC seeks to reach not just citizen-voters, but also others who may influence or be influenced by the party/candidate, such as party members, other politicians, pressure groups, different levels of government, and sources of economic or political power such as trade associations. IC, by integrating the communication functions, which communicate to all of an organization's stakeholders, implies that all communication to external audiences is the preserve of the public relations and not the marketing function. Therefore, as Hunter (1999) notes, marketing communications is removed from the marketing function, and placed within the remit of the public relations function. The citizen voter is, therefore, merely one of several stakeholders that the party or candidate communication function seeks to target. This perspective is supported by theorizing that political parties are active on four main arenas, namely an internal arena, a parliamentary arena, a media arena, and, of course, a voter arena. On each arena there are primary and secondary publics, and thus a need to manage the relationships with the publics on all these arenas (Strömbäck, 2007)—not just citizen voters.

How Political PR Can Help Political Marketing

As noted earlier, the evidence suggests that political marketing literature largely views PR within a narrow field, primarily through media and events management. Hence, the role of PR is erroneously limited to gaining publicity for political ideas, policies, and actors. This perfectly legitimate use of PR can best be described as marketing public relations (MPR). Here the public relations function supports marketing by creating visibility and attention primarily through publicity (Harris & Whalen, 2006; Haywood, 2002; Shimp, 1993). Shimp (2010) goes further and suggests that MPR's strength is as a credible source, so it is particularly useful at educating a new market, building up interest, and launching a product (Kotler & Keller, 2006). In the models of the relationship between the two disciplines (Kotler & Mindak, 1978; Pickton & Broderick, 2001), MPR is integrated in the third model where the separate functions overlap, and in the final model where marketing and PR are within one integrated approach where they also overlap. It has been suggested that about 70% of organizational communications spending is allocated to MPR activities (Kitchen & Papasaloumou, 1997). MPR describes a political marketing approach to PR, namely to gain public attention by gaining visibility.

We suggest that political MPR represents a primarily tactical and short-term use of public relations. There is nothing wrong with political actors utilizing MPR, and indeed it is quite likely that the bulk of their activity is within this sphere. However, there are limitations with MPR, which suggest political actors should not rely exclusively on it for their marketing communications. As Moloney (2006) notes, MPR is a one-way top-down communication process and while a purchaser of soap powder might not expect dialogue, this is inherently implied within representative democracy. Consistently treating citizen voters as merely the passive recipients of a message is likely, in the long term, to fuel a sense of alienation or democratic deficit. Though not all citizen voters all of the time expect to be asked their opinion or to engage with political actors, enough do to suggest that political communication should be two-way. Encouraging a conversation is inherently implied in the Grunigian aspect of Strömbäck and Kiousis's definition of political PR, where they refer to mutually beneficial relationships. Another danger of relying exclusively on MPR in a political context is that other important publics in other arenas are neglected, which may have negative consequences at least in the longer-run.

A more sophisticated approach to political PR would recognize not just the relevance of MPR, but supplement this by applying a corporate public relations (CPR) model whose driving philosophy is reputation management (Hutton, Goodman, Alexander, & Genest, 2001). Where political marketing has traditionally used MPR, we suggest that using a CPR approach as well would enhance the role of political public relations. Political MPR is limited to a range of communication tools such as media relations, stunts, events management, and exhibitions, yet PR includes many more techniques than this. For example, Newsom, Turk, and Kruckeberg (2000) identify 14 different activities suggesting that there are 9 or 10 that political MPR is not using, such as issues management, community relations, and public affairs.

Many, but not all of these activities are within CPR, such as corporate image, community relations, issues management, crisis management, corporate social responsibility, investor relations, and lobbying. Ultimately, CPR focuses not on promoting a specific individual campaign, but the overall reputation of an organization (Cornelissen, 2008; Fombrun, 1995; Grifffin, 2008). Where the focus of MPR is very narrow on getting a specific message to a specific audience, CPR is generally much wider in scope. The purpose of CPR is to assess all the factors that might favorably or adversely impact upon the reputation of a political actor. The lesson New Labour learned from electoral losses was that they had to make fundamental changes in their policies, organization, and key personnel (Lees-Marshment, 2001). The Conservatives came to a similar conclusion when they introduced organizational reforms designed to persuade the public that they were electable (Bale, 2006). A political CPR approach requires political actors to take a more strategic and long-term use of public relations.

Conclusion

Political marketing has conflated the need for gaining visibility through public relations activities, and as a consequence political marketing approaches focus on media management and gaining hype by being "loud." This reflects a transactional approach to marketing, which requires "loudness" in marketing communications to gain attention. The volume may be targeted at key voters, but is more akin to short-term persuasion to commit to a single action than creating long-term relationships; Bannon's metaphor (2005) of the one-night stand as opposed to a courtship seems to describe the predominating political strategy.

In contrast, we suggest that two alternative approaches to marketing exist, the relational and experiential, which imply a subtler and potentially softer approach to marketing communications. Relationship marketing implies a longer-term contact using both indirect and more importantly direct communication channels, and with a strategy designed to encourage longer-term support as opposed to winning votes at one moment in time. Experiential marketing focuses on how the citizen voter doesn't just buy into a political product, but interacts with a party, government, as well as an election or political campaign. Therefore, viewing political public relations merely as a means of gaining media coverage is a partial and erroneous approach.

We suggest that political public relations, rather than being "ugly" as Scammell (2003) suggests, is potentially actually "handsome." The key factor for determining if it is ugly or handsome is whether public relations is used in a narrow and tactical media management sense, or as a much wider strategic tool following the definition suggested by Strömbäck and Kiousis. Political marketing's reliance on marketing public relations (MPR) is what makes it ugly, the application of corporate public relations (CPR) adds significantly to a political marketing communication perspective.

What public relations adds to political marketing is a wider consideration of the overall reputation of politics. Hence, political public relations that incorporates both marketing public relations and corporate public relations, and hence is both tactical and strategic, represents an alternative model to those imbued in the marketing management discipline for understanding political activity. Within a political public relations perspective, communication is used as a long-term tool that seeks to engage with citizens and other publics using a variety of channels. Political public relations does not supplant political marketing as either an analytical or practical tool, but it complements it by focusing on different audiences, tools, and, importantly, outcomes.

References

Arblaster, A. (2002) *Democracy* (3rd ed,). Milton Keynes, England: Open University Press.

Baines, P. R., Harris, P., & Lewis, B. (2002). The political marketing planning process: Improving image and message in strategic target areas. *Marketing Intelligence & Planning, 20*(1), 6–14.

Bale, T. (2006). PR man? Cameron's Conservatives and the symbolic politics of electoral reform. *Political Quarterly, 77*(1), 28–34.

Bannon, D. (2005). Relationship marketing and the political process. *Journal of Political Marketing, 4*(2/3), 73–90.

Berry, L. (1983). Relationship marketing. In L. Berry, G. Shostack, & G. Upah (Eds.), *Perspectives on services marketing* (pp. 25–28). New York: American Marketing Association.

Bowers-Brown, J. (2003). A marriage made in cyberspace? Political marketing and UK party websites. In R. Gibson, S. Ward, & P. Nixon (Eds.), *Political parties and the Internet: Net gain?* (pp. 98–119). London: Routledge.

Brissenden, J., & Moloney, K. (2005). Political PR in the 2005 UK General Election: Winning and losing with a little help from spin. *Journal of Marketing Management, 21*(9/10), 1005–1020.

Bruning, S., Dials, M., & Shirka, A. (2008). Using dialogue to build organization–public relationship, engage publics and positively affect organizational outcomes. *Public Relations Review, 34*(1), 25–31.

Butler, P., & Harris, P. (2009). Considerations on the evolution of political marketing theory. *Marketing Theory, 9*(2), 149–164.

Christopher, M. G., Payne, A. F. T., & Ballantyne, D. (1992). *Relationship marketing*. London: Heinemann.

Cornelissen, J. (2008). *Corporate communication: A guide to theory and practice* (2nd ed.). London: Sage.

Crick, B. (2001). *In defense of politics* (5th ed.). London: Continuum.

Davis, A. (2000). Public relations, news production and changing patterns of source access in the British national media. *Media Culture & Society, 22*(1), 39–59.

Dean, D., & Croft, R. (2001). Friends and relations: Long term approaches to political campaigning. *European Journal of Marketing, 35*(11/12), 1197–1216.

Denver, D., & Hands, G. (1997). *Modern constituency elections* London: Frank Cass.

Dermody, J., & Scullion, R. (2000). Perceptions of negative political advertising: Meaningful or menacing? An empirical study of the 1997 British General Election campaign. *International Journal of Advertising, 19*(2), 201–225.

Downs, A. (1957). *An economic theory of democracy.* New York: Harper & Row.

Esser, F., Reinemann, C., & Fan, D. (2001). Spin doctors in the United States, Great Britain and Germany: Metacommunication about media manipulation. *Harvard International Journal of Press/Politics, 6*(1), 16–45.

Farrell, D., & Wortmann, M. (1987). Party strategies in the electoral market: Political marketing in West Germany, Britain and Ireland. *European Journal of Political Research, 15*(3), 297–318.

Franklin, B. (1994). *Packaging politics: Political communications in Britain's media democracy.* London: Edward Arnold.

Ferguson, M. (1984, August). *Building theory in public relations: Inter-organizational relationship.* Paper presented to the Association for Education in Journalism & Mass Communication, Gainesville, FL.

Fill, C. (2009). *Marketing communications: Interactivity, communities and content.* Harlow, England: Prentice Hall.

Firat, A. F., Dholakia, N., & Venkatesh, A. (1995). Marketing in a postmodern world. *European Journal of Marketing, 29*(1), 40–56.

Fombrun, C. (1995). *Reputation: Realizing value from the corporate image.* Boston, MA: Harvard Business School Press.

Froehlich, R., & Rüdiger, B. (2006). Framing political public relations: Measuring success of political communications strategies in Germany. *Public Relations Review, 32*(1), 18–25.

Getz, D. (2008). *Event Studies: Theory, research and policy for planned events.* Oxford: Butterworth-Heinemann.

Giddens, A. (1992). *Beyond left and right — the future of radical politics.* Cambridge, England: Polity.

Gould, P. (1998). *The unfinished revolution.* London: Lawrence Black.

Gronroos, C. (1989). Relationship approach to marketing in service contexts: The marketing and organisational behaviour interface *Journal of Business Research, 20,* 3–11.

Gronroos, C. (1997). From marketing mix to relationship marketing – towards a paradigm shift in marketing, *Management Decision, 35*(4), 322–339.

Griffin, A. (2008). *New strategies for reputation management.* London: Kogan Page.

Grunig, J. (1992). *Excellence in public relations and communication management.* Hillsdale, NJ: Erlbaum.

Grunig, J. (1997). A situational theory of publics: Conceptual history, recent challenges and new research. In D. Moss, T. MacManus, & D. Verčič (Eds.), *Public relations research: An international perspective* (pp. 3–48). London: International Thomson Business.

Grunig, J., & Grunig, L. (1992). Models of public relations and communication. In J. Grunig (Ed.), *Excellence in public relations and communication management* (pp. 285–326). Mahwah, NJ: Erlbaum.

Grunig, J., & Hunt, T. (1984). *Managing public relations.* New York: Holt, Rinehart & Winston.

Gummesson, E. (2002). *Total relationship marketing.* Oxford, England: Butterworth-Heinemann.

Guth, D., & Marsh, C. (2006). *Public relations: A values-driven approach* (3rd ed.). London: Pearson.

Harris, T., & Whalen, P. (2006). *The marketer's guide to public relations in the 21st Century.* Mason, Ohio: Thomson.

Haywood, R. (2002). *All about public relations.* Maidenhead, England: McGraw-Hill.

Heath, A. F., Jowell, R. M., & Curtice, J. K. (2001). *The rise of New Labour: Party policies and voter choices.* Oxford, England: Oxford University Press.

Henneberg, S. (2004a). The views of an advocatus dei: Political marketing and its critics. *Journal of Public Affairs, 4*(3), 136–151.

Henneberg, S. (2004b). Political marketing theory: Hendiadyoin or oxymoron? University of Bath (Working Paper Series 2004.01).

Henneberg, S., & Ormrod, R. (2006). "Are you thinking what we're thinking"? Or "Are we thinking what you're thinking"? An exploratory analysis of the market orientation of the UK parties. In D. Lilleker, N. Jackson, & R. Scullion (Eds.), *The marketing of political parties: Political marketing at the 2005 British general election* (pp. 31–58). Manchester, England: Manchester University Press.

Holbrook, M. (1999). *Consumer value: A framework for analysis and research.* London: Routledge.

Hunter, T. (1999). *The relationship of public relations and marketing against the background of integrated communications: A theoretical and analysis and empirical study at US-American corporations* (Unpublished master's thesis). University of Salzburg, Austria.

Hutton, J. G. (1996). Integrated marketing communications and the evolution of marketing thought. *Journal of Business Research, 37*(3), 155–163.

Hutton, J., Goodman, M., Alexander, J., & Genest, C. (2001). Reputation management: The new face of corporate public relations? *Public Relations Review, 27*(3), 247–261.

Jackson, N. (2006). Banking online: The use of the Internet by political parties to build relationships with voters. In D. Lilleker, N. Jackson, & R. Scullion (Eds.), *The marketing of political parties: Political marketing at the 2005 British general election* (pp. 157–184). Manchester, England: Manchester University Press.

Jackson, N. (2008). MPs and their e-newsletters: Winning votes by promoting constituency service. *Journal of Legislative Studies, 14*(4), 488–499.

Jackson, N. (2010). *Political public relations: Spin, persuasion or reputation building?* Paper presented at the Political Studies Association annual conference, Edinburgh.

Jackson, N., & Lilleker, D. (2009). MPs and E-representation: Me, MySpace and I. *British Politics, 4*(2), 236–264.

Johansen, H. P. M. (2005). Political marketing: More than persuasive techniques. An organisational perspective. *Journal of Political Marketing, 4*(4), 85–105.

Johansen, H. P. M. (2009). *Re-conceptualising party-centred politics in terms of "market": A relationship marketing approach* (Unpublished doctoral dissertation). London School of Economics.

Johnson, D. (Ed.). (2008). *The handbook of political management.* London: Routledge.

Jones, N. (2001). *The control freaks: How New Labour gets its own way.* London: Politicos.

Kavanagh, D. (1995). *Election campaigning: The new marketing of politics.* Oxford, England: Blackwell.

Kelley, S., Jr. (1956). *Professional public relations and political power.* Baltimore, MD: John Hopkins University Press.

Kirchheimer, O. (1966). The transformation of the Western European party systems. In M. Weiner & J. LaPalombara (Eds.), *Political parties and political development* (pp. 177–191). Princeton, NJ: Princeton University Press.

Kitchen, P., & Papasalomou, I. (1997). Marketing public relations: Conceptual legitimacy or window dressing? *Marketing Intelligence & Planning, 15*(2), 71–84.

Kohli, A K., Jaworski, B. J., & Kumar. A (1993, November). MARKOR: A measure of market orientation. *Journal of Marketing Research, 30,* 467–477.

Kotler, P. (1975). Overview of political candidate marketing. In M. J. Schlinger (Ed.), *Advances in consumer research* (Vol. 2, pp. 761–70) Duluth, MN: Association of Consumer Research.

Kotler, P. (1991). *Marketing management: Analysis, planning, implementation and control* (7th ed.). Harlow, England: Prentice-Hall.

Kotler, P., & Keller, K. (2006). *Marketing management* (12th ed.). Upper Saddle River, NJ: Prentice-Hall.

Kotler, P., & Levy, S. (1969). Broadening the concept of marketing. *Journal of Marketing, 33*(1), 10–15.

Kotler, P., & Mindak, W. (1978). Marketing and public relations, should they be partners or rivals? *Journal of Marketing, 42*(10), 13–20.

Ledingham, J., & Bruning, S. (Eds.). (2000). *Public relations as relationship management: A relational approach to the study and practice of public relations.* London: Erlbaum.

Lees-Marshment, J. (2001). *Political marketing and British political parties: The party's just begun.* Manchester, England: Manchester University Press.

Lees-Marshment, J. (2005). *The political marketing revolution.* Manchester, England: Manchester University Press.

Lees-Marshment, J. (2009). *Political marketing: Principles and applications.* London: Routledge.

Lees-Marshment, J., Rudd, C., & Strömbäck, J. (Eds.). (2010). *Global political marketing.* London: Routledge.

L'Etang, J. (2008). *Public relations: concepts, practice and critique.* London: Sage.

Lilleker, D. G. (2005). Political marketing: The cause of an emergent democratic deficit in Britain? *Journal of Nonprofit and Public Sector Marketing, 14*(1/2), 5–26.

Lilleker, D. G., Jackson, N. A., & Scullion, R. (2006). *The marketing of political parties: Political marketing at the 2005 UK general election.* Manchester, England: Manchester University Press.

Lilleker, D. G., & Lees-Marshment, J. (Eds.). (2005). *Political marketing — A comparative perspective.* Manchester, England: Manchester University Press.

Lilleker, D. G., & Negrine, R. M. (2006). Mapping a market-orientation: Can we only detect political marketing through the lens of hindsight? In P. J. Davies & B. I. Newman (Eds.), *Winning elections with political marketing* (pp. 33–56). New York: Haworth Press.

Lilleker, D. G., & Scullion, R. (2009). Political advertising. In H. Powell, J. Hardy, S., Hawkin, & I. MacRury (Eds.), *The advertising handbook* (pp. 187–197). London: Routledge.

Lock, A., & Harris, P. (1996). Political marketing — Vive la difference! *European Journal of Marketing, 20*(10/11), 14–24.

Maarek, P. (1997). *Political marketing and communication.* London: John Libbey.

Mauser, G. (1983). *Political marketing: An approach to campaign strategy.* New York: Praeger.

McCole, P. (2004). The changing role of marketing for business. *Marketing Intelligence and Planning, 22*(5), 531–539.

McKenna, R. (1985). *The regis touch.* Reading, MA: Addison-Wesley.

Moloney, K. (2006). *Rethinking public relations.* London: Routledge.

Moloney, K., & Colmer, R. (2001). Does political PR enhance or trivialise democracy? The UK general election 2001 as a contest between presentation and substance. *Journal of Marketing Management, 17*(9–10), 957–968.

Morgan, R. M., & Hunt, S. D. (1994). The commitment-trust theory of relationship marketing. *Journal of Marketing, 58*(3), 20–38.

Mortimore, R. (2003). Why politics needs marketing. *International Journal of Nonprofit and Voluntary Sector Marketing, 8*(2), 107–121.

Negrine, R., Mancini, P., Holtz-Bacha, C., & Papathanassopoulos, S. (Eds.). (2007). *The professionalization of political communication.* Bristol, England: Intellect Books.

Newman, B. I. (1994).*The marketing of the president.* Thousand Oaks, CA: Sage.

Newman, B. I. (Ed.). (1999a). *The handbook of political marketing.* London: Sage.

Newman, B. I. (1999b). *The mass marketing of politics: Democracy in an age of manufactured images.* New York: Sage.

Newson, D., Turk, J., & Kruckeberg, D. (2000). *This is PR: The realities of public relations* (7th ed.). London: Thomson Learning.

O'Cass, A. (1996). Political marketing and the marketing concept. *European Journal of Marketing, 35*(9/10), 37–53.

O'Shaughnessy, N. (1990). *The phenomenon of political marketing.* Basingstoke, England: Macmillan.

Ormrod, R. (2004). *Operationalising the conceptual model of political market orientation* (Working paper no. 14). Sundsvall, Sweden: Centre for Political Communication Research.

Panebianco, A. (1988). *Political parties: Organization and power.* Cambridge, England: Cambridge University Press.

Pickton, D., & Broderick, J. (2001). *Integrated marketing communications.* Harlow, England: Financial Times Prentice Hall.

Pine, B., & Gilmore, J. (1998). Welcome to the experience economy. *Harvard Business Review, 76*(4), 97–105.

Reichheld, F., & Sasser, W. (1990). Zero defects: Quality comes to service. *Harvard Business Review, 66*(5), 105–111.

Ries, A., & Ries, L. (2002). *The fall of advertising and rise of PR.* New York: Harper Business.

Rothschild, M. L. (1978). Political advertising: A neglected policy issue in marketing. *Journal of Marketing Research, 15*(1), 59–71.

Savigny, H. (2006). Political marketing and the 2005 election: What's ideology got do with it? In D. Lilleker, N. Jackson, & R. Scullion (Eds.), *The marketing of political parties: Political marketing at the 2005 British general election* (pp. 81–97). Manchester, England: Manchester University Press.

Savigny, H., & Temple, M. (2010). Political marketing models: The curious incident of the dog that doesn't bark. *Political Studies, 58*(5), 1049–1064.

Scammell, M. (1997). *Designer politics: How elections are won.* Basingstoke, England: Macmillan.

Scammell, M. (1999). Political marketing: Lessons for political science. *Political Studies, 47,* 718–739.

Scammell, M. (2001a). The media and media management. In A. Seldon (Ed.), *The Blair effect: The Blair government 1997–2001* (pp. 509–533). London: Little, Brown.

Scammell, M. (2001b). The Internet and civic engagement in the age of the citizen-consumer. *Political Communication, 17*(4), 351–355.

Scullion, R. (2008), The impact of the market on the character of citizenship, and the consequences of this for political engagement. In D. Lilleker & R. Scullion (Eds.), *Voter as consumer: Imagining the contemporary electorate* (pp. 51–72). Cambridge, England: Cambridge Scholars.

Scammell, M. (2003). Citizen consumers: Towards a new marketing of politics? In J. Corner & D. Pels (Eds.), *Media and the restyling of politics* (pp. 117–136). London: Sage.

Schmitt, B. (1999). *Experiential marketing: How to get customers to sense, feel, think, act, relate.* New York: Free Press.

Shama, A. (1976). The marketing of political candidates. *Journal of the Academy of Marketing Science, 4*(4), 764–777.

Shimp, T. (1993). *Promotion management and marketing communications.* New York: Dryden Press.

Shimp, T. (2010). *Advertising promotion, and other aspects of integrated marketing communications* (8th ed.). Mason, OH: South-Western Cengage Learning.

Smith, I. G. (2001). The 2001 General Election: Factors influencing the brand image of political parties and their leaders. *Journal of Marketing Management, 17*(9/10), 1058–1073.

Stoker, G. (2006). *Why politics matters.* Basingstoke, England: Palgrave.

Strömbäck, J. (2007). Professionalized campaigning and political marketing: A conceptual analysis. *Journal of Political Marketing, 6*(2/3), 49 67.

Strömbäck, J., Mitrook, M., & Kiousis, S. (2010). Bridging two schools of thought: Applications of public relations theory to political marketing. *Journal of Political Marketing, 9*(1), 73–92.

Tansey, S., & Jackson, N. (2008). *Politics: The basics.* London: Routledge.

Theaker, A. (2008). *The public relations handbook.* London: Routledge.

Trammell, K. (2006). Blog offensive: An exploratory analysis of attacks published on campaign blog posts from a political public relations perspective. *Public Relations Review, 32*(4), 402–406.

Wightman, B. (1999). Integrated communications: Organization and education. *Public Relations Quarterly, 44*(2), 18–22.

Wring, D. (2001). Labouring the point: Operation victory and the battle for a second term. *Journal of Marketing Management, 17*(9/10), 913–927.

9

POLITICAL PUBLIC RELATIONS AND STRATEGIC FRAMING

Kirk Hallahan

In the run-up to the 2004 U.S. elections an obscure cognitive linguist, George Lakoff, suddenly burst upon the American political scene and became a cult hero. He coached Democrats on how to tell their story, spoke at party meetings across the country, appeared on talk shows, and wrote a widely circulated political primer (Lakoff, 2004). Meanwhile White House political adviser Karl Rove (2010) was guiding President George W. Bush's political agenda by promoting "tax *relief*" and the "*war* on terrorism" in the aftermath of 9/11 as Republican consultant Frank Luntz (2006, 2007) also was honing his "new American lexicon" composed of the phrases that conservatives should avoid. American politics had become engulfed in what the *New York Times* magazine coined "the framing wars" (Bai, 2005). Politicians, the media, and the public had begun to focus serious attention on the importance of words, narratives, and metaphors—how to *frame political messages*.

In *Moral Politics*, Lakoff (2002) argued that conservatives and liberals embraced two fundamentally different grand metaphors to describe the relationship between government and citizens. According to Lakoff, conservatives embraced a "strict father model" where the father (government) disciplined citizens to become self-sufficient adults, but then stayed out of their lives once the children had proven their responsibility. By contrast, liberals envisioned a "nurturant parent model" where government acted as mother and father figure intent on protecting its citizens from corrupting influences such as social injustice and pollution.

Lakoff emphasized that arguments or claims about specific issues were only effective if they reinforced some bigger idea that resonated with voters' fundamental beliefs. Merely taking an impassioned position on a specific issue or attacking an opponent was not sufficient. What had differentiated the two parties and disadvantaged Democrats was that Republicans since Reagan had masterfully learned how to activate favorable emotional responses using words and images. He later described the Democrats' lack of imaginative ideas as "hypocognition."

The Democrats' enthusiasm for Lakoff's insights would inevitably be scorned by conservatives and media critics (Baer, 2005; Cooper, 2005; Green, 2005). Nevertheless, Lakoff and the others had drawn attention to an important strategy that has become a part of everyday American politics (Burnett, 2008; Parrott, 2009).

Political Message Framing: Conceptual Foundations

Simply stated, *framing* involves emphasizing or deemphasizing particular aspects of political or social reality. Framing *facilitates* or *enables* communication by shaping *perceptions* and providing a *context* for processing political or other information. Framing fundamentally *enables* communication, but has often been described as a process that delimits the information considered. In contrast to constructing (framing) a house, framing is generally likened to a picture frame that surrounds a painting and thus draws the eye to particular elements in the scene while excluding the extraneous surroundings (König, 2005; Tuchman, 1978). As noted by Gitlin (1980), framing involves "persistent selection, emphasis and exclusion" (p. 7). Entman (1993) similarly submits that "to frame is to select some aspects of a perceived reality and make them more salient in communicating a text, in such a way as to promote a particular problem definition, causal interpretation, moral evaluation and/or treatment recommendation" (p. 52).

Message framing is readily apparent in political communication and political public relations. Framing is an integral part of every nation's discourse and is used in campaigns by candidates as well as supporters and opponents of ballot initiatives and referenda. Social movements and grassroots organizations as well as interest groups also employ framing in their advocacy activities. In addition, media inevitably use framing to explain events to audiences.

Against this background, the purpose of this chapter is to review and analyze theory and research on framing in the context of political communication and political public relations. Consistent with the theme of the book, the focus will be on political framing rather than media framing, although the latter is an important area of research.

Three Levels of Framing and Analysis

Framing stems from people's need to simplify and telegraph messages in today's highly competitive information environment. The process can be conscious or unconscious. In recent years, increased emphasis has been placed on framing as a purposeful, rather than merely pragmatic activity. Reese (2001) goes beyond original conceptualizations of the concept (Goffman, 1974) to argue that framing is always intentional.

Frames are cognitive tools used by people to construct, convey, interpret, or evaluate information. These include *information sources/sponsors, intermediaries,* and *media,* and *audiences.*

Framing by Sources. Public relations practitioners, political consultants, and various political advocates (candidates, sponsors of initiatives, leaders of social movement groups) use framing to communicate messages. Indeed, public relations and other political consultants fundamentally act as *framing strategists* (Hallahan, 1999a, p. 224) by choosing which aspects of a candidate, issue, or cause to emphasize or deemphasize. This can be the most critical choice made in a political campaign. Political figures (and their consultants) serve as *frame builders* by constructing specific arguments and using rhetorical devices to build a case from their preferred perspectives. Political researchers often refer to promotional frames as *elite frames* or *advocacy frames.*

Framing by Intermediaries. Media and other third-party information sources (including other consultants, online commentators, lower-level officials, party operatives and others) share information created by original sources. Effective framing by these third parties can help information sources communicate their story and create a cascading effect among opinion makers in society (Entman, 2004). Unlike information sources, information intermediaries such as news media sometimes must deal with information from multiple sources with competing frames. In particular, mainstream news media strive for *balance* in how they frame information. Intermediaries can adopt or bolster the original framing from an information source—a process known as *frame extension* (Kuypers, 1997). Media and other information intermediaries can also broaden or *reframe* information to incorporate competing perspectives, or build an entirely new frame.

Framing by Message Recipients/Audiences. Through their messaging, information sources and intermediaries shape how audiences perceive a topic—a process that has been labeled individual *frame setting* (D. Scheufele, 1999, 2008). Because audiences are "cognitive misers" (Fiske & Taylor, 1991), they rely on others to prioritize and preorganize information and to create what Sherif (1967, p. 382) referred to as *frames of reference.* Importantly, audiences do not passively absorb messages—they actively choose, assess, and restate (reframe) information before storing it in memory.

Frame setting by so-called *active audiences* is facilitated by a psychological process known as cognitive *priming,* where message recipients determine during the *preattention phase* of message processing the *type* of message, the *topic* of the message, the *relevant knowledge* stored in memory required to process the message, and which cognitive processing and evaluation *rules* should be applied (Baptista,

2003; Cappella & Jamieson, 1997; Simon, 2001). Brain research provides evidence for how printing works physiologically (De Martino, Kumaran, Seymour, & Dolan, 2006). This categorization process is based on message *cues* (message format, formal features, context, spokesperson, etc.) and occurs *before* the message recipient even devotes *focal attention* to the message content. Thus, people process political information differently than social information because they have identified it as such. They also process a political message differently based on whether it appears in the form of news, advertising, or entertainment (Hallahan, 1999b). Priming involves stimulating particular memory nodes or associative networks in the brain and makes particular knowledge (also known as schemata) more accessible and available as the message recipients process the message. Thus, message framing *biases* processing by including or excluding or making more or less salient particular ideas, themes, phrases, or images. Framing enhances comprehension and the subsequent judgments that are made to the degree that the most appropriate or most applicable schemata are triggered. Framing can be dysfunctional or deceptive to the degree that inappropriate schemata are triggered when making a political or other judgment.

Framing Effects

Framing is a *process* of message production and should be distinguished from its *effects* or outcomes (Scheufele, 1999). Framing outcomes can be measured at corresponding micro- (individual) and macro- (societal) levels of analysis. Framing outcomes also can be examined from cognitive, constructivist, and critical perspectives (Van Gorp, 2007).

Effects on Individuals. Effects on individuals potentially include increased thinking and gains in knowledge about particular topics to the extent provocatively framed, attention-getting messages stimulate people to consider messages. Evidence suggests that messages framed differently from extant knowledge heighten the level of cognitive processing as individuals strive to reconcile knowledge and reduce cognitive dissonance. Framing also can facilitate gains in knowledge about new topics by putting new information in a familiar context.

Many researchers are interested in framing as a tool of persuasion, or how framing influences people's *attitudes* or predispositions toward objects that are the topics of framed messages and how framing influences *behavioral intent*, which is the self-reported likelihood that people will take particular actions. Positively valenced frames are presumed to lead to positive attitudes. Consistent with process models of persuasion (Chaiken & Maheswaran, 1994; Petty & Cacioppo, 1986), evidence suggests that strongly framed messages can particularly affect individuals with low knowledge (Chong & Druckman, 2007a). Thus, framing might provide peripheral or heuristic cues that are separate from the (strong or weak) arguments in the message.

Frame setting or individual effects are moderated by various factors, particularly the ability to generate frame-relevant thoughts in the priming process (Shen, 2004). Many of the factors that affect persuasion in general also influence the outcomes of framing: topic-related motivation and knowledge, personal values, prior attitudes and opinions, frequency of exposure, and source credibility (Chong & Druckman, 2007a, pp. 111–112).

In the political arena, an effect of special interest is political priming, which is different from the cognitive process described above. *Political priming* involves changes in the standards that people use to make political evaluations (Iyengar & Kinder, 1987, p. 63). Robust research suggests that issues made prominent in the media are used as major benchmarks for evaluating the performance of leaders and governments (Kiousis, 2008; Roskos-Ewoldsen, Roskos-Ewoldson, & Dillman Carpentier, 2002).

Political framing is sometimes considered an extension of media agenda setting—the correspondence between the salience of topics in the media and what people say is important to them or that they talk about with others. Framing can contribute to the priming process through its ability to focus attention on particular aspects of a topic, not just the topic itself. McCombs (2004) and his colleagues suggest that framing effects can be evidenced in *second-order agenda setting*, the close correspondence between *how* topics are described in the media and *how* individuals describe them. Framing, priming, and agenda setting are discussed by Kosicki (2002), D. Scheufele (1999, 2000), Tewksbury and Scheufele (2009), and Weaver (2007).

Effects on Society. As a culturally based cognitive process, framing perpetuates and reinforces abstract ideas and more concrete concepts that constitute the system of beliefs, values, norms, customs, traditions, and rites found in society. Frames often link new ideas to familiar ideas through analogies, tropes and figurative language, myths, and narratives. Thus frames are tools of cultural integration.

By facilitating public exposure of political and other ideas, framing can either contribute to or confound *public deliberation* about important topics. Evidence suggests that framing of issues follows a classic pattern of deliberation where framed arguments are raised, considered, and dismissed in succession (Kuypers, 2006; Simon & Xenos, 2000; Zhou & Moy, 2007). Simon and Jerit (2007) observed that public reason emerges from communication involving elites and media and discussions and judgments among individuals. Exposure to information, discussion, and deliberation can enhance the quality of public opinion and social capital by reducing uncertainty and public ambivalence and by increasing public participation (Kinder & Nelson, 2005; Pan & Kosicki, 1993, 2001).

Critical scholars argue that framing fundamentally involves the exercise of power (Carragee & Roefs, 2004; Reese, 2007). Thus, to the degree that elites in society (original sources) and media (intermediaries) control the communication of public issues, framing can serve as a form of hegemonic social control. Indeed, media have been criticized for framing news in ways that overemphasize mainstream viewpoints and exclude alternative perspectives from the political right and left (Gitlin, 1980; Kuypers, 2002).

Seven Applications of Framing in Political Communication

As a communication "theory," framing has been criticized because there is no commonly accepted definition. Entman (1993) referred to framing as a "fractured paradigm," but others have argued that framing's multiple perspectives constitute the concept's strength and thus what make the concept intellectually attractive and pragmatically useful (D'Angelo, 2002). Reese (2007) refers to framing as a *bridging model* that crosses multiple perspectives, disciplines, and methodologies. In the early 21st century, framing continued to be examined in a variety of contexts, including strategic thinking (Sloan, 2006), decision making (Beach & Connolly, 2005), management (Fairhurst & Sarr, 1996), and argumentation (Ensink & Sauer, 2003; Kuypers, 2009; Simon, 2001; Watkins, Edwards, & Thakar, 2001).

This chapter purposefully addresses framing broadly. As information sources or information intermediaries, organizational public relations practitioners, government public information officers, lobbyists, political campaign consultants, ballot initiative/referenda proponents and opponents, and grassroots political organizers become integrally involved in framing messages in the wide variety of contexts summarized here.

Drawing on my previous work (Hallahan, 1999a, 2008), this chapter outlines a typology of framing approaches that might be used by political communicators. These seven applications of framing include the framing of situations; attributes; risks; arguments supporting actions; issues; responsibilities; and stories, including news.

Framing of Situations

Perhaps the simplest example of framing in a political context is the creation of situations or scenes that exemplify a key idea. Politicians and political communicators routinely craft situations where political figures interact with others. These encounters provide voters, constituents, supporters, and opponents with glimpses into complex political topics. Examples include speeches, debates, interviews, meet-and-greets, legislative hearings, and media interviews. These situations (including the words stated, the actions taken, and the atmospherics) shape perceptions and often come to symbolize candidates, causes, or issues—and are the frames that people remember.

Bateson (1972, p. 191) was the first to suggest the picture frame metaphor, and defined a *psychological frame* or *perceptual frame* as a "spatial and temporary bounding of a set of interactive messages." Soon thereafter, Goffman (1974, p. 21) defined a frame as a "[schema] of interpretation" that provides a context for understanding information that enables individuals to "locate, perceive, identify and label." Goffman (1974) spoke of frames being composed of "strips of reality," which he defined as any "arbitrary slice or cut from the stream of ongoing activity" (p. 10).

Implications. Much of political communication involves *self-representation* and *impression management*, which can be created by creating events or other memorable strips of political reality that are conductive to promoting a candidate or cause. These can include spectacles, pseudo-events, or stunts (Hallahan, 2010a). Thus, political communicators (as frame sponsors) make strategic decisions about such things as how to make public announcements, conduct inquiries, debate opponents, or organize protests. Because people's actions are based upon the "pictures inside their heads" (Lippmann, 1922/1961), focusing attention on particular elements is a critical political tactic (Brewer, 2002; Edelman, 1993; Entman, 2004).

Considerable criticism has been lodged against superficial promotion of politicians as well as the relentless *advance work* employed in political campaigns (Bruno & Greenfield, 1971). Yet framing theory suggests that such attention to details—a candidate's wardrobe, the presence of enthusiastic supporters, stirring music, and an inspirational backdrop—are critical to effective communication of messages. These carefully honed cues prime how a message should be interpreted and might be especially important if the audience's only exposure is through a snippet of news that is the audience's social reality.

Beyond elections, political figures use framing to dramatize or manipulate control of various situations. In public diplomacy, world leaders hold summit meetings and then conduct public forums where they report on the status of discussions. Legislative bodies welcome gavel-to-gavel coverage on networks such as C-SPAN where individual legislators can appear on television to show constituents they are working toward the resolution of problems. Similarly the judiciary maintains a sense of authority through ostentatious surroundings and its serious courtroom decorum that relies heavily on referential and condensation symbols such as judges' robes (Edelman, 1967).

Framing of Attributes

As suggested by experts such as Lakoff and Luntz, politicians and political communicators can adroitly use language to focus attention on particular aspects of objects, people, and ideas. Whereas the framing of situations involves creating an overall *context* in which communication occurs, attribute framing involves the use of language in the message itself. Attribute framing has assumed greater significance with recognition of second-order media agenda setting (McCombs, 2004; McCombs & Ghanem, 2001; see also Maher, 2001;

Kiousis, Kim, McDevitt, & Ostrowski, 2009; B. Scheufele, 2004; Strömbäck, Mitrook, & Kiousis, 2010).

Semantic framing involves the characterization of objects, events, and people using labels, analogies, or figurative language such as metaphors (Bosman, 1987; Brewer, 2002). Classic examples include the differentiation between the *taxpayer's money* versus *public funds*, the use of the term *social security* to describe the U.S. public pension program, and the nomenclature foreign *aid* to describe investments to assure peace abroad. Such rhetorical labeling reduces large, complex ideas into a few simple words. The struggle for naming ideas is illustrated with the recent differentiation between *global warming* and *climate change* (Broder, 2009).

Words used in attributions take various forms. *Euphemisms* involve the choice of words that appear to be less harsh than the concepts they represent. Abortion proponents and opponents are described as *pro-choice* or *pro-life*, respectively. Other contemporary political examples include *downsizing, lethal injection, correctional facilities, sanitary landfills, troop surges, weapons of mass destruction, and collateral damage.*

Jargon operates as nuanced language with special meaning known to political insiders: *Blue Dog Democrat, bipartisanship support, compassionate conservatism, corporate welfare, earmark, filibuster, grassroots, hard money/soft money, hawk vs. dove, homeland security, Inside the Beltway, law and order, pork barrel, and red state vs. blue state.*

Politically correct language seeks to be inclusive, unoffending, and respectful of others. Consider, for example, the alternative images conjured up by each of the following terms that successively have been used over time to describe people with a physical condition: *lame → crippled → handicapped → disabled → physically challenged → differently abled.* Genderless job titles similarly eliminate common sexual attributes to describe employees.

Metaphors are figures of speech that compare an unfamiliar idea with a more familiar concept to facilitate meaning. Political communication is replete with metaphors that can also double as jargon: *bandwagon effect, dark horse, gridlock, horse race, landslide, mudslinging, plank, platform, spin/spin doctor, underdog, wedge issue, whip, and political witch hunt.*

Attributes can also be framed using numbers. Take, as an example, the statistics churned out regularly by various government agencies. Whereas production numbers are straightforward, percentages can be interpreted in different ways. For example, the U.S. government reports homeownership rates using a positive frame based on the percentage of people who own versus rent, while occupancy of homes is reported using a negative frame that emphasizes vacancies. In each case, the facts are the same (67% own versus 33% rent; 97.4% owned and occupied versus 2.6% owned but vacant), but each could be framed to emphasize the opposite.

Implications. The importance of attribute framing can best be seen in political campaigns. *Candidate positioning* is an extension of product positioning commonly associated with product marketing (Ries & Trout, 1981). Positioning a product or candidate involves focusing attention on particular personal attributes that differentiate the candidate from all others in the category; for example, the honest candidate, the experienced candidate. Similar to political priming, positioning helps prime and frame the basis upon which voters should make a judgment.

Political consultants routinely recommend focusing on those attributes that will have wide appeal to audiences and to ignore less attractive attributes. To maximize the impact of attribute framing, political communicators can (a) label photos and illustrations in ads and collateral materials with a tagline or caption that underscores the key attribute they want voters to remember, (b) link that attribute to voter satisfaction with the candidate or previous positive experiences, and (c) promote how that attribute will transform the voter's life if the candidate is elected or a policy is adopted.

Promoting a candidate or cause's own positive attributes is valuable—while promoting the negative characteristics of opponents might be useful in hotly contested situations. Indeed, negative attribute framing is the basis for much of the political attacks and negative political advertising used in political contests. A prudent defensive strategy in a campaign begins with assessing one's attribute vulnerabilities and fully anticipating direct or media attacks that will attempt to reframe a candidate or a cause in a bad light. Candidates can choose to respond directly to such attacks or to ignore them and continue to focus attention on their positive attributes.

Separately, politicians and political communicators should seize control over the labeling of political concepts, activities, and issues. One of the best examples of attribute framing was Luntz's (2006, 2007) admonition to Republicans to always attack *Washington* specifically—not *big government*. Luntz's other preferred nomenclature included social security *private accounts* vs. personal accounts, *tax simplification* vs. tax reform, *death taxes* vs. inheritance taxes, *legislatively directed spending* vs. earmarks, *free market economy* vs. global economy, *illegal aliens* vs. undocumented workers, and *law abuse reform* vs. tort reform.

Politicians and their communicators also should consider the framing of numerical attributes. In a period of economic uncertainty, a curious question is how government officials might use framing to allay public concerns without being deceptive. The U.S. Department of Labor reports unemployment rates using a negative frame; for example, reporting that 8% of the people were unemployed in a given month. But this also means that 92% of the people actually were employed—an ostensibly impressive proportion. It's surprising that government communicators haven't opted for the more positive approach—in the same way that grocers promote ground beef as being 80% fat-free versus being only 20% fat.

Framing of Risk

Many political communications address risk taking by government officials, legislators, or voters. Risk implies physical harm to people, moral hazards, or economic, political, or social losses. People are risk-averse generally, and psychologists have devoted considerable attention to decision-making processes that involve risky choices.

Prospect theory focuses on people's responses whenever a gain or a loss will result from a decision (Tversky & Kahneman, 1981). In developing the concept, Kahneman and Tversky (1979) argued the asymmetry between how gains and losses are framed shapes a person's perceptions about the prospect of the outcome. They consequently defined a frame as a decision maker's perception of "the acts, outcomes and contingencies associated with a particular choice" (p. 263).

Prospect theory posits that people tend to avoid risks when a choice is stated in terms of gains but will take greater risks when choices are stated in terms of losses—the opposite of the outcome predicted by expected utility theory found in economics, game theory, and decision theory. Health care decisions were the original context for considering risk-based decision making: Patients and their families are willing to choose greater risks if their decision means saving a life or reducing suffering. Such biases in making judgments are consistent with the psychological notions of *negativity basis*, which suggests negative information is more powerful and processed more thoroughly than positive information (Baumeister, Bratslavsky, Finkenauer, & Vohs, 2001), and of *automatic protective responses* to negative social information (Pratto & John, 1991).

Political scientists have mostly applied prospect theory to decisions by government officials, especially in international relations involving high-stakes diplomatic and security decisions. Evidence suggests that government leaders are more likely to intervene in international or domestic situations to prevent a loss than to merely obtain a political gain (Levy, 2003; McDermott, Fowler, & Smirov, 2008; Mercer, 2005; Weyland, 2002). Moreover, because officials must weigh multiple factors when making political decisions, possible economic, political, social, or reputation losses often outweigh the possible gains from a particular action.

In the legislative arena, evidence suggests that lawmakers are more compelled to enact laws or regulations to prevent future losses, rather than make potential gains. Thus, lawmakers might be cautious in good times, but take risks in bad times. Separately, evidence from court trials, strategic bargaining, and organizational behavior suggests that arguments based on potential losses are more persuasive—and parties more inclined to take action—when issues and complaints are framed in terms of losses rather than gains (Hallahan, 1999a, p. 215).

Implications. In political matters that involve risky choices, considerable evidence suggests that the rules for message framing are opposite to those that stress the positive framing of object attributes. Government officials, candidates, or special interest groups that want to promote changes for the betterment of a society face an uphill battle in overcoming arguments that might be promulgated by opponents in a risky context. Thus, policy makers, candidates, and issue proponents must be cognizant of the issue of gains versus losses in terms of their policies and positions on issues and be prepared to address fears about potential losses that might be raised by opponents (Mercer, 2005).

In most elections, the bias that plays on fear of losses gives an advantage to incumbents who argue that voters should stay with a known quantity and be wary of challengers whose ideas are untested. This generally works, even if the incumbent has been only marginally effective. Challengers are only advantaged when there is widespread discontent, and voters feel compelled to take a chance to avoid a further loss.

Managing people's expectations about potential gains or losses from government actions or about a candidate's performance in an upcoming election is one of the goals of "spin doctoring"—using an official spokesperson to provide supplementary information or commentary about statements made by government officials or candidates. Much of spin doctoring focuses on managing public expectations or, in economic terms, focuses on manipulating the reference point upon which gains or losses are judged (Levy, 2003).

Prospect theory, coupled with the overwhelming power of negative information, helps explain the effectiveness of political attacks and negative political advertising. For example, *attack ads* have been shown to be effective late in election cycles and when targeted to independent or undecided voters (Fridkin & Kenney, 2005a, b; Hughes, 2003; Johnson-Cartee, 2005; P. King & McCombs, 1994; Scheneck-Hamlin, Procter, & Rumsey, 2006). Importantly, uncommitted voters might be unable or unwilling to devote the effort required to fully assess a choice. Thus, loss aversion becomes a convenient heuristic for decision making.

Framing of Arguments Supporting Actions

A closely related application of framing involves the valencing of arguments used to encourage desired actions; that is, whether people are more persuaded by claims that are stated in positive versus negative terms. In contrast to the framing of risky choices, the framing of arguments involves no choice and no risk—only the language varies. The question is simply to determine which alternative is more persuasive. Economists refer to the framing of actions as *pure-valence framing* (Elliott & Hayward, 1998), while psychologists refer to this as *goal framing* (Levin, Schneider, & Gaeth, 1998).

In the political arena, this phenomenon can be evidenced in how people express their political preferences or plans to vote. In the 2008 U.S. elections, a voter might have favored Barack Obama or opposed John McCain. In either case, the voter's position is the same. Yet, evidence suggests that stating opposition to an idea or action is more persuasive in influencing others. Moreover, stating beliefs in negative terms (such as "I oppose John McCain") leads to more resistant attitudes, higher conviction, and higher behavioral intent (Bizer, Larsen, & Petty, 2011; Bizer & Petty, 2005; Žeželj, Šoic, Hristić, & Stokić, 2007).

Framing of arguments also is critical to government agencies when seeking compliance with public policies or encouraging prosocial or safe practices. Examples include police and fire departments concerned with protecting public safety and public health officials seeking to control disease. In each case, different results might be obtained by manipulating the description of the goal to affect the persuasiveness of the communication. Consider a university that wishes to encourage students to pay tuition early in a lump sum instead of paying a slightly higher amount in installments. The university might frame the early payment option as a *discount* or the installment plan as a *penalty*. The explanations are different semantically, but the choices are the same.

Similar to the framing of risky choices, research generally suggests that public information campaigns that stress the negative consequences of inaction have greater impact than those that stress potential positive gains of taking action (Elliott & Hayward, 1998; Haydarov, 2010; Levin, Schneider, & Gaeth, 1998; McClure, White, & Sibley, 2009; Piñon & Gambara, 2005). However, studies suggest that the effect might be moderated by factors such as the political sophistication of the audience, depth of message processing, and self-efficacy and expertise related to performing the task (Hallahan, 1999a, pp. 215–217).

Implications. Similar to framing risky choices, political communicators must carefully consider the value of "going negative." For example, political communicators concerned with encouraging participation in elections might find it less effective to make positive appeals (making society a better place) and instead stress the negative impact on individuals (not letting their voices be heard) or society as whole (democracy could suffer).

Over the past several decades, the U.S. federal government has initiated public awareness programs with cute names to encourage public support. Some were dismal failures—witness Gerald Ford's WIN campaign in 1974 where the federal government distributed buttons with the slogan "Whip Inflation Now." By contrast, and although not spectacular successes, campaigns that stressed urgency, conflict, and the consequences of inaction are more effective: the War on Poverty (1960s), the War on Drugs (1980s), and the War on Terrorism (2000s).

The value of stressing negative consequences of inaction underscores the potential role of fear appeals in public information campaigns. Researchers have recognized the value of using moderate levels of fear in persuasive campaigns for more than 50 years (Ruiter, Abraham, & Kok, 2001). However, recent studies suggest that temporal and others factors beyond the intensity of the fear appeal also might be important (Dillard & Anderson, 2004).

Framing of Issues

Framing plays a critical role in the political debates about social problems. Issues involve disputes between two or more individuals or organizations, and often center on the allocation of political, economic, and social resources. Issues framing goes beyond labeling or the valencing of choices or arguments, and strikes at the very definition of problems (Benford & Snow, 2000).

Table 9.1 recaps the variety of topics that have been addressed since 2000 in major studies that have examined the framing of contemporary social issues. Sociologists and others who adopt a constructionist perspective argue that social problems exist in society because one or more individuals or groups identify a particular condition as problematic and engage in a process of *claims making* to draw public attention to their concern (Best, 1987; Schneider, 1985; Spector & Kitsuse, 1987). These organizers also have been labeled *moral entrepreneurs* (Lowney, 2008).

As a distinct form of political communication, claims making by grassroots advocacy and special interest groups employs *typification,* where issue advocates characterize a problem or condition in society as being of a particular type and give a name to the problem. Thus, claims makers *frame* issues. Snow and Benford (1992) described the components of this process as *diagnostic framing* (identification of the problem), *prognostic framing* (identification of solution), and *motivational framing* (identification of a call to action and involvement of the public). Many new problems are often constructed by *piggybacking* on already existing frames.

Claims and frames are *social constructions* created as activists interact and pursue various *agenda-building* activities such as obtaining publicity (Cobb & Elder, 1972; Manheim, 1987). Agenda building has also been labeled *frame enterprise, frame sponsorship,* and the *social construction of collective action frames* (Klandermans, 1997, p. 45). Sponsoring or promoting a particular frame involves both advocacy and adaptation. *Frame alignment* involves building relationships and creating coalitions among otherwise disparate individuals and groups—a process that occurs through subprocesses such as frame *bridging, amplification, extension,* and *transformation* (Snow & Benford, 1992; Snow, Rochford, Worden, & Benford, 1986).

The task before most advocacy groups is to develop sufficient public concern and discussion so that topics emerge onto the public media agenda and eventually into the public policy agenda (Manheim, 1987). However, this route is not the only option; some issues might actually gain visibility first on the public policy agenda, and only then be covered by the media. For this reason, reaching out and framing issues in ways that resonate with lawmakers can be essential in grassroots politicking and lobbying efforts

Issue frames can be topic-specific or rely upon generic themes or concepts that might apply across issues or topics (Benford, 1997). Examples of common *generic issue frames* include *social justice, fairness, equality, and human rights.* Issue-

TABLE 9.1 Selected Research Since 2000 on Framing of Social Issues

Social Issues	Environmental and Technological Issues
Abortion (Esacove, 2004; Schroedel, 2000; Simon & Jerit, 2007)	Biotechnology (Listerman, 2010; Nisbet & Huge, 2007; Priest & Eyck, 2004)
Addiction (Campbell, 2007)	Bird conservation (Boardman, 2006)
AIDS (Bell, 2006; Stockdill, 2003)	Chemical weapons disposal (Futrell, 2003)
Alcoholism (Golden, 2005; Roizen, 2004; White, 2004)	Ecology/environment (Alexander, 2008; C. A. Miller, 2006; Lewicki, Gray, & Elliott, 2003; Seymour, 2008)
Class/poverty (Kendall, 2005)	
Community health (Loue, Lloyd & O'Shea, 2003; Salovey, Schneider, & Apanovitch, 2002; Wong and McMurray, 2002)	Global warming (Boyles Tucey, 2010; McCright & Dunlap, 2000)
Crime, juvenile (Gilliam & Iyengar, 2005)	Human genomics (Bauer & Gutteling, 2006)
Deafness (Kensicki, 2001)	Hurricane Katrina (Brunsma, Overfelt, & Picou, 2007; Dynes & Rodriguez, 2007)
Death penalty (S.L. Jones, 2010)	
Divorce (Adams & Coultrane, 2007)	Oil drilling (Hansen, 2000; Shen, 2004)
Domestic violence (Berns, 2004)	Stem cell research (Boyles Tucey, 2010; Nisbet, Brossard, & Kropsch, 2003; Shen, 2004)
Gay-lesbian rights/homophobia (Beger, 2004; Burack, 2008; Jenness, 2006; Ott & Aoki, 2002)	
Gender (Squires, 2000)	West Nile virus (Yeo, Park, & Arabi, 2007)
Justice (Besley & McComas, 2005)	
Marriage, same-sex (Tadlock, Gordon, & Popp, 2007; Wiggins, 2001)	
Media self-coverage (Zoch, 2001)	
Parental rights (Williams & Williams, 2003)	
Privacy (Bennett, 2008)	
Race (Clawson, 2008; Kellstedt, 2003, 2005; C. R. Mann, Zatz, & Rodriguez 2006; Patton, 2006; Rhodes, 2007; Swain, 2002)	
Pornography (Thornburgh & Lin, 2002)	
Sexual abuse (Kitzinger, 2004, 2006; Lytton, 2008)	
Social movements (Johnston & Noakes, 2006, Nash & Bell, 2007)	
Social security, U.S. (Robhlinger & Quadagno, 2006)	
Sweatshop labor (Ross, 2004)	
Women's rights (Lorber, 2005 ; Metcalfe, 2004)	

specific framing can best be illustrated using the controversy about abortion. Abortion alternatively can be framed as (a) a *medical procedure,* (b) a *political matter,* or (c) a *moral issue.* In fact, abortion involves all three of these dimensions. But pro-choice and pro-life advocates purposely focus on whatever aspect of the controversy supports their preferred solution. Moreover, factions within each side of the abortion issue disagree over how the issue should be framed (Rohlinger, 2002). Research suggests that the mere choice of the term *baby* versus *fetus* alters support for regulating abortion (Simon & Jerit, 2007), while the use of *partial-birth abortion* versus *late-term abortion* strongly influences public support (Esacove, 2004).

Implications. Modern politics involves persuading the public (including the media) that a candidate or cause's definition of a problem is the proper or only frame within which a problem should be considered. Not surprisingly, framing activities of issue advocates are often met by opponents, who seek to *reframe* the problem consistent with their views about any remedy that is needed (Ryan & Gamson, 2006). Political communicators thus need to be prepared to engage in *frame contests* (Ryan, 1991; Snow, 2004), where competing interests vie for whose alternative definition of an issue will prevail. Importantly, comparatively little research has been conducted when frames operate in competitive environments (Chong & Druckman, 2007b).

An important consideration for a political communicator in a frame fight is to assess the viability of an opponent. Indeed, not all social movements, advocacy groups, or special interests are equally successful in their frame sponsorship activities. Various factors can influence their success: the nature of an issue, and the skill, knowledge, political savvy, strategic alliances, and financial resources of the advocating group (Callaghan & Schnell, 2005; Cobb & Elder, 1972; Hilgartner & Bosk, 1988; Thrall, 2006)

Political communicators who become directly involved in the resolution of public issues also can benefit from examining research that details issue framing in contexts that range from negotiation and bargaining to persuading jurors. In particular, economists have examined the framing of fairness as a particular issue that can influence judgments on matters such as tax and income equity, willingness to pay for public goods, and social conflicts pertaining to environmental and public health risks (Hallahan, 1999a).

Framing of Responsibility

Politics invariably involves taking credit for accomplishments and ascribing blame for failures involving public policy or other occurrences (such natural disasters, accidents, or organizational malfeasance) that require government intervention. As Entman's (1993) definition suggests, to frame inevitably involves defining causes and assessing moral implications.

Attribution theory addresses people's perceptions and explanations for why events occur. Kelley (1967) identified three distinct types of attributions: to an actor, to an object or entity acted upon, or to the environment or circumstances in which the event occurs. In assessing causation, people examine patterns, discount given explanations when others are present, and judge facilitative explanations as more plausible than inhibitory explanations. Similarly, actions can be framed as controlled or uncontrolled, internally or externally originated, or as a result of stable or unstable conditions within an individual or environment.

Framing of responsibility involves various biased judgments identified by psychologists. *Fundamental attribution error* explains other people's actions based on stable personality characteristics and ignores external causes. *Actor–observer bias* is the tendency to attribute other people's behaviors to inherent characteristics, but to attribute one's own behavior to situational factors. *Self-serving bias* involves attributing one's own successes to personal strengths or abilities and failures to situational or external factors. *Personal control bias* suggests humans assign blame for disastrous occurrences in portion to the perceived severity of the consequences. Finally the *just-worth hypothesis* suggests evaluations of suffering increases in proportion to the degree that a victim's suffering is deemed unjustified.

Most Western cultures emphasize the importance and value of the individual and stress individual accomplishment and responsibility. What's more, most Americans believe that their overall political and social system is sound. As result, we immediately explain events in terms of the behavior of individuals. We blame villains and, in turn, sympathize with victims. This *personalization of responsibility* is evident in American laws, court system, and the media's obsession with personalization of the news (W. L. Bennett, 2008).

In one of the most important contributions to framing theory, Iyengar (1991) argued that news coverage of politics and other matters is predominated by episodic framing versus thematic framing. *Episodic framing* involves storytelling from the perspective of people and discrete events (episodes) where news can be easily explained by the specific actions of individuals or organizations. By contrast, media rarely engage in *thematic framing* where stories are told from a societal perspective using abstract concepts instead of case studies or exemplars. Episodic framing makes it easy to ascribe blame, while thematic framing does not.

Implications.   For politicians, society's penchant to ascribe responsibility for events to specific individuals or organizations provides opportunities for taking credit for accomplishments or for blaming others. However, political communicators should be conscious of the degree to which they engage in fundamental attribution error, actor–observer bias, self-serving bias, and personal control bias. They also must be able to recognize and respond when critics engage in potentially faulty attributions. The adroit denial of responsibility when falsely accused ("I was framed!") can be critical to the political survival of an officeholder, candidate, or cause if based on fact.

A particularly popular way to frame issues involves *oppositional framing* that juxtaposes the "bad guy" versus "good guy" and the "villain" versus the "victim." An unintended consequence of this phenomenon is the creation of a *culture of victimization* (Dershowitz, 1994). In responding to crisis situations, for example, politicians are often guarded in making any statements that suggest culpability, and depending on the circumstances have various options for explaining their responsibility (Coombs, 2010). This dichotomy was readily evident in the gigantic Deepwater Horizon oil spill in the Gulf of Mexico in April 2010. BP was immediately made the villain. Yet critics argued that faulty U.S. energy policy and lax governmental regulation were to blame for allowing drilling to take place in the first place and under inadequate oversight. The Obama administration was lionized for not being more aggressive in fixing the leak, but also for not attacking BP (whose cooperation was needed to fixed the problem).

As the BP incident suggests, an unintended consequence of our culture's penchant for episodic explanations is that we want to ascribe blame to specific people, organizations, or political parties when, in fact, the "system" or "society" might have created the situation. Thus, some events are wrongly dismissed as unfortunate accidents, even though they might have been prevented through government intervention or changes in cultural values. Various problems are framed as problems of *individuals* rather than problems of *society*, and modern culture even condones values or behaviors that contribute to those problems. This leads to the *medicalization* of problems (Conrad, 1992) where the typical solution is treatment rather than prevention. Ironically, blaming systemic factors creates a trap for public officials, who can quickly be accused of a lack of leadership in addressing important societal problems.

Framing of Stories (including News Framing)

The final context for framing in political communications involves the framing of stories, the telling of complex narratives that explain an idea or situation (Currie, 2007). Storytelling is a basic way that both information sources and intermediaries communicate information—through everyday conversations, oral accounts, speeches, lectures, letters, memoirs and diaries, blogs, articles, and multimedia. Storytelling can combine all of the framing forms discussed thus far.

Simply stated, a *story* is an account of an incident or event. Stories vary in terms of their complexity, can involve intrigue, and often include commentaries by the storyteller about story elements. However, most stories are linked together with a central organizing idea or frame that provides meaning to an unfolding strip of action (Gamson & Modigliani, 1989).

Stories follow familiar *formats* or *structures* based on the mode of communication. Storytelling also follows *conventions*, and people have expectations about how stories ought to be presented based on the genre, which is based on mental schemata or scripts. Central to effective storytelling is the use of culturally resonating meanings, norms, and values. Cultural themes can utilize *archetypes* representing ideal or prototypical *people* (such as the victim, the father figure), *mythical figures* who engage in identifiable behavior (David vs. Goliath), a *principle* (democracy, freedom of speech), or a familiar *narrative* or expression ("making a bargain with the devil"). Effective stories feature ideas that can be grasped quickly and easily. Central organizing ideas can be labeled *grand metaphors* (Lakoff, 2002), *master frames* (Snow & Benford, 1992), or *enduring cultural frames* (Gamson, Croteau, Hoyner, & Sasson, 1992).

Various rhetorical devices are deployed to convey meaning. Fairhurst and Sarr (1996) described seven framing techniques: *metaphors, stories (anecdotes), traditions, slogans, jargon and catchphrases, contrast,* and *spin.* In their classic explanation of framing devices used by media, Gamson and Modigliani (1989) identified *metaphors, exemplars, catch-phrases, depictions,* and *visual images.* These operate in tandem with three *reasoning devices* dealing with explicit and implicit statements about *roots* (causal analysis), *consequences* (effects), and *appeals to principles* (moral claims). Additional framing devices include figurative language beyond metaphors (such as *analogies, similes, personifications, hyperboles,* and *idioms*); the use of *symbols, celebrities,* and *large and official numbers* (Salmon, 1990); and reliance on *experts, man-on-the-street interviews,* and *documentary evidence* (Martz-Mayfield & Hallahan, 2009).

Storytelling and News. Much of our understanding of framing and storytelling is based on analyses of news coverage by newspapers, magazines, radio, and television (Entman, Matthes, & Pellicano, 2009; de Vreese, 2005a, 2005b; see also Chitty, 2000; Nesbitt-Larking, 2007; Pan & Kosicki, 1993; Stanton, 2007; Wicks, 2001). News reports are obviously important in political communication, but news stories are only one specific, albeit important category of storytelling. Table 9.2 inventories some key studies published since 2000 on news framing of political discussions. Table 9.3 lists major studies dealing with framing and elections.

Traditional news framing research focuses on framing as an activity of journalists grounded in their cognitive understanding of the world and their desire to arrange events into meaningful, organized stories or "interpretive packages" (Gamson, 1996; Graber, 1988; Tuchman, 1978). In this vein, news frames operate as "organizing principles that are socially shared and persistent over time, that work symbolically to meaningfully structure the social world" (Reese, 2001, pp. 10–11).

Importantly, news framing about a particular topic frequently changes over time and delineates stages in the life cycle of an issue (Baysha & Hallahan, 2004; Gamson & Modigliani, 1989; Jasperson, Shah, Watts, Faber, & Fan, 1998; M. Miller & Riechert, 2001; Shah, Watts, Domke, & Fan, 2002). Invariably, *values* play key roles in news (Nelson, Oxley, & Clawson, 1997; Nelson & Willey, 2001). Indeed, news reporting on the activities of public figures operates as a series of morality plays about what is good versus bad and important versus unimportant. Shah, Domke, and Wackman (2001) argue

TABLE 9.2 Selected Research Since 2000 on Framing of Politics

United States	International
Afghanistan war, support for (Edy & Meirick, 2007)	Advertising regulation-Australia (Henderson, Coveney, Ward, & Taylor, 2009)
American presidency (Holbert et al., 2005)	AIDS/HIV, support for international support (Bleich, 2007)
Civil defense (Grossman, 2001)	China—National image (J. Mann, 2000)
Civil rights movement (McAdam, 2000)	Cold War (Hammond, 2007)
Clinton-Lewinsky scandal (Kenski, 2003)	Croatian politics (Segvic, 2005)
Economic news (Lowry, 2008)	Economics in India (middle class) (Fernandes, 2006)
Federal spending (Sky, 2003)	Euro, launch of (de Vreese, Peter, & Semetko, 2001)
Foreign policy, U.S. (Entman, 2004)	European politics (Glenn, 2001; Semetko & Valkenburg, 2000; de Vreese, 2003)
Government officials (Gabrielson, 2005)	Film piracy in China (Wang, 2003)
Gun ownership (Downs, 2002)	Gulf War (Butler, 2009; Choi, 2004; Dimitrova & Strömbäck, 2005; King & Wells, 2009; Rajiva, 2005 ; Reese, 2003)
Hate group rallies (Chong & Druckman, 2007a; Druckman 2001a, b; Sniderman & Theriault, 2004)	Humanitarian relief (DeChaine, 2005)
Labor strike (Simon & Xenos, 2000)	Islamic expatriates (Salvatore, 2007)
Lobbying (McCrath, 2007)	Intervention, U..S. in Dominican Republic (Soderlund, 2001)
Motorcycle outlaws (Fugisang, 2001)	Malaysian politician (Tiung & Hasim, 2009)
Personal responsibility (Matthes, 2009a)	Missionary activities (Dixon, 2005)
Political correctness (Dickerson, 2001)	Muslim women (Amireh, 2002; Luthra, 2007)
Presidential speeches (Feldman, 2007)	Muslims in Britain (Pintak, 2006; Poole, 2002)
Public journalism and journalistic frames (Delli Carpini, 2005)	Palestinian conflict (Jamal, 2005)
Sexual/gendered politics (Heidensohn, 2000)	Peace protests (Cooper, 2002; Opp, 2009)
Tax expenditures (Nelson & Willey, 2001; Zelinsky, 2005)	Public opinion—Europe (Hagendoorn & Kantorova, 2000; Kentrova, 2000)
Weapons of mass destruction (Ritter, 2003)	Religious minorities in Greece (Bantimaroudis, 2007)
Welfare reform (Shen & Edwards, 2005)	SARS in China and United States (Luther & Zhou, 2005)
	Separatism (Hale, 2008; S.A.Jones, 2007)
	Somalia strife (Bantimoudis & Ban, 2001)
	Terrorism (Coaffee, 2003; Entman, 2003; Guiora, 2008; Kuypers, 2006; Montiel & Shah, 2008; Norris et al. 2003; Reynolds & Barrett, 2003; Sarabia-Panol, 2007; Schnell & Callaghan, 2005;
	Terrorism, victims of (Simpson, 2006)

TABLE 9.3 Selected Research Since 2000 on Framing and Elections (U.S. and International)

Advice to progressives (Hartmann, 2007; Lakoff, 2002, 2004, 2008; Morgan 2008; Yoos, 2007)
Alienation of young voters (Parmalee, Perkins, & Sayre, 2007)
Campaign finance reform (Grant & Rudolph, 2004)
Celebrity politicians (Drake & Higgins, 2006; Holmes & Redmond, 2006)
Comparing news media framing (Strömbäck & Dimitrova, 2006; Strömbäck & Kaid, 2008; Strömbäck & van Aelst, 2010)
E-mail (A.P. Williams, 2006)
Germany elections (Froehlich & Rüdiger, 2006)
Israeli elections (Werder & Golan, 2002)
Minority group responses (Perkins, 2005)
Negative advertising frames (Scheneck-Hamlin, Procter, & Rumsey, 2007)
Netherlands - Referendums (de Vreese & Semetko, 2004)
News v. ads in Brazil (Porto, 2002)
Political scientists. role of (Brewer & Sigelman, 2002)
Switzerland direct-democratic campaign (Hänggli & Kriesi, 2010)
Ukraine elections (Baysha & Hallahan, 2004)
U.S. Senate race 1992 (Fridkin & Kenney, 2005b)

there are two fundamental values in the news media's framing of politics: *ethical values* (incorporating beliefs about human and civil rights, religious morals or personal principles) and *material values* (including understanding of expedience, practicality and self-interest).

Storytelling and Poltical Advertising. Advertising also plays a critical role in politics (Baker, 2009; Richardson, 2008; Trent & Fridenberg, 2007). However, comparatively little research is devoted to storytelling or framing in advertising in general or political advertising in particular. Recent research on political advertising has focused mostly on two key factors: the use of negative advertising and the role of emotion (Brader, 2005). Importantly, both implicitly involve framing. The most notable studies about framing in political advertising were conducted by Biocca (1991a, 1991b). Subsequent research has suggested that several factors that moderate framing's effectiveness: incumbency (Fridkin & Kenney, 2005a); culture (Gevorgyan, 2010); valencing (Gunsch, Brownlow, Haynes, & Mabe, 2000), and appeals to specific audiences (Parmalee, Perkins, & Sayre, 2007). One international study suggests contradictory framing effects for constituents watching news versus advertising dealing with the same issues (Porto, 2007). Another study suggests that advertising effects might be explained indirectly based on the news coverage that advertising campaigns receive (Jasperson & Fan, 2004).

Implications. To be effective, politicians must be good storytellers who are able to capture the imagination of voters. Their ideas must resonate with the public, and storytelling can be a key to a politician's success. In the same way, the professional communicators must be able to tell stories in imaginative ways using both free media (publicity) and paid media (advertising).

Effective storytelling through publicity requires understanding what is newsworthy, basic formats and genres, the conventions of media storytelling and framing, and the routines, competitive concerns, and constraints confronting media workers (Hallahan, 2010). These and other factors shape media message production and *frame selection* (Shoemaker & Reese, 1996; Tewksbury & Scheufele, 2009).

Among the most important changes in the evolution of news framing research over the past decade has been recognition of the role of frame sponsorship and entrepreneurship by advocates (Andsager, 2000), the correspondence between advocacy frames and generic news frames (Tewksbury et al., 2000), and how journalists reconstruct *elite frames* (Callaghan & Schnell, 2005). Van Gorp (2007, p. 68) similarly makes the distinction between framing *through* the media and framing *by* the media. When seeking publicity, successful political communicators must frame issues and candidates in ways that reflect the values and norms of society but also resonate with the personal values of individual journalists (Callaghan & Schnell, 2005; Gamson et al., 1992). These differ by culture or region, so tailoring and localizing stories and adapting framing strategies might be essential.

Journalists' adoption of *issue-specific news frames* can be enhanced to the extent that a promoted frame fits within larger formulaic approaches to explaining the news and exploiting the mechanisms used by media to frame stories. *Generic news frames* have been used by some researchers to describe categories of narrative storytelling in the media (de Vreese, 2005b). In general, these reflect basic news values used by journalists to select and construct stories. For example, Cappella and Jamieson (1997) differentiated between *strategy-based framing* and *issue-based framing* as generic news frames that apply to elections. Strategic election framing focuses on news about which candidate is winning or losing; uses language suggesting war, games or competition; addresses a candidate's style and public reactions; and gives weight to candidate polls and standings. Strategy framing actually fits within an even broader news frame that might be labeled *competition* or *conflict*. Such framing unintentionally focuses attention on the election itself, not the underlying issues behind the election (Valentino, Beckmann, & Buhr, 2001).

Other generic news frames applicable to political communication include *human impact, powerlessness, economics, moral value,* and *conflict* (Neuman, Just, & Crigler, 1992; Semetko & Valkenburg, 2000); *human interest, consequence,* and *conflict* (Price & Tewksbury, 1997; Price, Tewksbury, & Powers, 1997); and *leadership* (Luther & Zhou, 2005). The *salvational frame* is a favorite variation on human-interest framing routinely featured on daytime TV talk shows where a person confesses and becomes rescued from a destructive lifestyle choice, indiscretion, or relationship (Lowney, 2008).

In creating advertising, political communicators have much more control over messaging than in news framing, but must still be aware of the genres of advertising and the conventions of storytelling. In both print and broadcast advertising, two basic storytelling approaches are used (Wells, 1989). *Lectures* involve a sponsor or spokesperson addressing an audience directly, usually making explicit comments and specifying a call to action. *Dramas* involve audiences eavesdropping on a scene in which actors demonstrate the central idea, but the audience might be left to impute the meaning and draw its own conclusions about how to respond.

Discussion

From this discussion, it is readily apparent that framing is integral to political communication and political public relations in at least seven contexts. Political communicators frame situations, attributes, risks, arguments supporting, issues, responsibility and stories.

The central idea that links each of these models of framing is *contextualization*. Framing puts political ideas into a context and establishes frames of reference so people can evaluate information, comprehend meanings, and take action. Framed messages are necessary to provide the clues necessary for people to make sense of the message and for it to be persuasive (Hallahan, 1999a). Importantly, particular approaches to framing might be appropriate in specific circumstances, but examples of multiple forms of framing might be evidenced in the same political materials.

Applying Framing in Political Communication

Framing is a valuable theoretical construct, but also has very practical applications in everyday politics. Framing subsumes many of the basic political communication tactics (image making, positioning, attacks on opponents, fear appeals, etc.) and provides a rationale for many of the practices used in political communications. Political public relations practitioners would therefore benefit from following published and proprietary framing research by academics and professionals.

Studying framed messages could be done through qualitative analyses of political materials (position papers, direct mail, speeches, advertisements, etc.) to identify examples of the seven forms of framing discussed here. Insights also can be gained by focusing upon those qualities attributed to people and political causes, the use of negative versus positive propositions, and the attribution of responsibility in disputes and elections. Particularly useful might be to analyze how political issues or activities are presented by the media; and the devices or mechanisms that support particular frames. (For useful discussions of how messages might be analyzed, see Callaghan, 2005; Durham, 2001; Gamson & Modigliani, 1989; Gamson et al., 1992; Hertog & McLeod, 2001; Kuypers, 2009; Matthes, 2009a, b; Reese, 2001, 2007; B. Scheufele, 2004; and Tankard, 2001.)

Political communicators also can analyze the impact of framing as part of research they are already conducting to assess their own work. For example, alternative framing approaches can be explored in focus groups in the same way that political communicators develop positions, gauge the positive and negative characteristics of candidates, and judge the potential effectiveness of campaign components. Critical experiments and quasi-experimental field tests can be used to pretest framing strategies. Finally, questions designed to gauge responses to the potential or actual framing of a candidate or issues can be incorporated into polls and surveys that measure knowledge, attitudes and opinions, and behavioral intent. (For discussions about studying framing effects using behavioral research, see Hertog & McLeod, 2001; Reese, 2001, 2007; D. Scheufele, 1999; Simon, 2001; Tewksbury & Scheufele, 2009; Vraga, Carr, Nytes, & Shah, 2010.)

Political Framing and Alternative Media

Although Entman (1993) described media framing as a "fractured paradigm," the broader concept of framing might be better described as a "fragmented puzzle." The borders have been mostly filled in, but of many of the interlocking pieces are yet to be turned over in full view and put in place in today's turbulent media environment.

Clearly public relations practitioners and political communicators need to think about framing in a variety of ways, not just in the context of issue and news framing. That's because political PR and political communication take place in a variety of contexts and employ a variety of media (Hallahan, 2010b). Besides *public media*, these include *one-on-one communications, events*, and *controlled media*. Each of the seven models in the typology presented here can be deployed in these various media, which remain untapped topics for future research.

In particular, the advent of new *interactive media* requires thinking about framing and media from new perspectives. Obviously, online news can extend the reach of media-produced news, and its potential influence on politics. However, the World Wide Web also provides a new forum for frame sponsors to deploy a full range of framing devices that may reach audiences directly through Web sites and other tools (Zoch, Collins, Sisco, & Supa, 2008). New media also provide journalists with opportunities to break out of the singular framing of stories (a process labeled *frame breaking*) through the use of hyperlinks in stories that encourage digressions and enable users to explore additional background about a story (Fredin, 2001). Although online news can provide background, evidence suggests that participants in online forums do not frame issues in the same way as the media (Boyles Tucey, 2010; Constantinescu & Tedesco, 2007). Other findings suggest that online discussions and media coverage might interact so that discussions followed by journalists shape media framing while also bolstering media framing effects (Zhou & Moy, 2007).

Framing and Political Relationships

If the purpose of political public relations is to establish and maintain mutually beneficial political relationships, as suggested by Strömbäck and Kiousis's definition in the introductory chapter, then clearly message framing is an essential tool in the process. Most discussions about relationships in public relations have focused on organizations rather than political figures or causes. Yet the principles of effective organizational–public relationships apply in the political arena as well: Government officials, political candidates, special interest groups, and social movements all seek and benefit from an ongoing, routine pattern of exchanges and interactions that helps advance their political goals while (one hopes) serving the interests of voters, constituents, or the public at large.

Positive relationships can alternatively be defined as *frame sharing*, or the development of common worldviews. Developing mutual perspectives involves experiencing the same situations (seeing the same strips of social reality) and sharing a common culture (beliefs, values, customs, and stories). Furthermore, it could be argued that people and entities in positive, mutually beneficial relationships agree about the attributes of the people and objects around them, make few risky relationship-based choices, recognize the need for cooperation, agree about potentially divisive issues, and assume responsibility for their actions. Thus, to the extent that message framing can attain these positive goals, framing can be viewed as a tool of relationship building and political reconciliation .

References

Adams, M., & Coltrane, S. (2007). Framing divorce reform: Media, morality, and the politics of family. *Family Process, 46*(1), 17–34.

Alexander, R. J. (2008). *Framing discourse on the environment: A critical discourse approach*. New York: Routledge.

Amireh, A. (2002). Framing Nawal El Saadaw: Arab feminism in a transnational world. In T. Saliba, C. Allen, & J. A. Howard (Eds.), *Gender, politics and Islam* (pp. 269–304). Chicago, IL: University of Chicago Press.

Andsager, J. L. (2000). How interest groups attempt to shape public opinion with competing news frames. *Journalism & Mass Communication Quarterly, 77*(3), 577–592.

Baer, K. S. (2005, January/February). Word games. *Washington Monthly*. Retrieved from http://www.washingtonmonthly.com/features/2005/0501.baer.html.

Bai, M. (2005, July 17). The framing wars. *New York Times Magazine*. Retrieved from http://www.nytimes.com/2005/07/17/magazine/17DEMOCRATS.html?pagewanted=all.

Baker, F. W. (2009). *Political campaigns and political advertising: A media literacy guide.* Westport, CT: Greenwood Press.

Bantimaroudis, P. (2007). Media framing of religious minorities in Greece: The case of the Protestants. *Journal of Media and Religion, 6*(3), 219–235.

Baptista, L. C. (2003). Framing and cognition. In J. A. Treveño (Ed.), *Goffman's legacy* (pp. 197–215). Lanham, MD: Rowman & Littlefield.

Bateson, G. (1972). *Steps to an ecology of mind: Collected essays in anthropology, psychology, evolution and epistemology.* San Francisco, CA: Chandler.

Bauer, M. W., & Gutteling, J. M. (2006). Issue salience and media framing over 30 years. In G. Gaskell & M. W. Bauer (Eds.), *Genomics and society: Legal, ethical and social dimensions* (pp. 113–130). Sterling, VA: Earthscan.

Baumeister, R. F., Bratslavsky, E., Finkenauer, C., & Vohs, K. D. (2001). Bad is stronger than good. *Review of General Psychology, 5*(4), 323–370.

Baysha, O., & Hallahan, K. (2004). Media framing of the Ukrainian political crisis, 2000–2001. *Journalism Studies, 5*(2), 233–246.

Beach, L. R., & Connolly, T. (2005). *The psychology of decision making: People in organizations.* Thousand Oaks, CA: Sage.

Beger, N. J. (2004). *Tensions in the struggle for sexual minority rights in Europe: Que(e)rying political practices.* Manchester, England: Manchester University Press.

Bell, J. S. C. (2006). Framing the AIDS epidemic: From "homo" geneous deviance to widespread panic. In L. Castañeda & S. B. Campbell (Eds.), *News and sexuality: Media portraits of diversity* (pp. 95–110). Thousand Oaks, CA: Sage.

Benford, R. D. (1997). An insider's critique of the social movement framing perspective. *Sociological Inquiry, 67*(4), 409–430.

Benford, R. D., & Snow, D. A. (2000). Framing processes and social movements: An overview and assessment. *Annual Review of Sociology, 26,* 11–39.

Bennett, C. J. (2008). *The privacy advocates: Resisting the spread of surveillance.* Cambridge, MA: MIT Press.

Bennett, W. L. (2008). *News: The politics of illusion* (8th ed.). New York: Longman.

Berns, N. (2004). *Framing the victim: Domestic violence, media and social problems.* Hawthorne, NY: Aldine de Gruyter.

Besley, J., & McComas, K. (2005). Framing justice: Using the concept of procedural justice to advance political communication research. *Communication Theory, 15*(4), 414–436.

Best, J. (1987). *Images of issues: Typifying contemporary social problems.* New York: Aldine de Gruyter.

Biocca, F. (1991a). *Television and political advertising: Vol. 1. Psychological processes.* Hillsdale, NJ: Erlbaum.

Biocca, F (1991b). *Television and political advertising: Vol. 2. Signs, codes and images.* Hillsdale, NJ: Erlbaum.

Bizer, G. Y., Larsen, J. T., & Pettty, R. E. (2011). Exploring the valence-framing effect: Negative framing enhances attitude strength. *Political Psychology, 32,* 59–80.

Bizer, G., & Petty, R. E. (2005). How we conceptualize our attitudes matters: The effects of valence framing on the resistance of political attitudes. *Political Psychology, 26*(4), 553–568.

Bleich, S. (2007). Is it all in a word? The effect of issue framing on public support for U.S. spending on HIV/AIDS in developing countries. *Harvard Institute for Global Health, 12*(2), 120–132.

Boardman, R. (2006). *The international politics of bird conservation: Biodiversity, regionalism and global governance.* Northampton, MA: Edward Elgar.

Bosman, J. (1987). Persuasive effects of political metaphors. *Metaphor and Symbol, 2*(2), 97–113.

Boyles Tucey, C. (2010, April). *Face-to-face vs. online deliberation on global warming and stem cell issues.* Paper presented to Western Political Science Association, San Francisco.

Brader, T. (2005). Striking a responsive chord: How political ads motivate and persuade voters by appealing to emotions. *American Journal of Political Science, 49*(2), 388–405.

Brewer, P. R. (2002). Framing, value words, and citizens' explanations of their issue opinions. *Political Communication, 19*(3), 303–316.

Brewer, P., & Sigelman, L. (2002). Political scientists as color commentators: Framing and expert commentary in media campaign coverage. *Harvard International Journal of Press/Politics, 7*(1), 23–35.

Broder, J. M. (2009, May 2). Seeking to save the planet, with a thesaurus. *New York Times.* Retrieved from http://www.nytimes.com/2009/05/02/us/politics/02enviro.html?_r=1& pagewanted=print.

Bruno, J., & Greenfield J. (1971). *The advance man.* New York: Morrow.

Brunsma, D., Overfelt, D., & Picou, J. S. (2007). *The sociology of Katrina: Perspectives on a modern catastrophe.* Lanham, MD: Rowman & Littlefield.

Burack, C. (2008). *Sin, sex and democracy: Antigay rhetoric and the Christian right.* Albany, NY: SUNY Press.

Burnett, B. (2008, August 7). Framing the election. Huffington Post. Retrieved from http://www.huffingtonpost.com/bob-burnett/framingtheelection_b_117420.html

Butler, J. (2009). *Frames of war: When is life grievable?* London: Verso.

Callaghan, K. (2005). Controversies and new directions in framing research. In K. Callaghan & F. Schnell (Eds.), *Framing American politics* (pp. 179–214). Pittsburgh, PA: University of Pittsburgh Press.

Callaghan, K., & Schnell, F. (2005). Framing political issues in American policies. In K. Callaghan & F. Schnell (Eds.), *Framing American politics* (pp. 1–20). Pittsburgh, PA: University of Pittsburgh Press.

Campbell, N. D. (2007). Framing the "opium problem": Protoscientific concepts of addiction. In *Discovering addiction: The science and politics of substance abuse research* (pp. 12–28). Ann Arbor: University of Michigan Press.

Cappella, J. N., & Jamieson, K. H. (1997). *Spiral of cynicism: The press and the public good.* New York: Oxford University Press.

Carragee, M., & Roefs, W. (2004). The neglect of power in recent framing research. *Journal of Communication, 54*((2), 214–233.

Chaiken, S., & Maheswaran, D. (1994). Heuristic processing can bias systematic processing: Effects of source credibility, argument ambiguity, and task importance on attitude judgment. *Journal of Personality and Social Psychology, 66*(3), 460–473

Chitty, N. (2000). A matrix model for framing news media. In A. Malken & A. P. Kavoori (Eds.), *The global dynamics of news: Studies in international news coverage and news agenda* (pp. 13–30). Stamford, CT: Ablex.

Choi, J. (2004). The framing of the "axis of evil." In R. D. Berenger (Ed.), *Global media go to war: The role of news and entertainment media during the 2003 Iraq war* (pp. 29–39). Spokane, WA: Marquette Books.

Chong, D., & Druckman, J. N. (2007a). Framing theory. *Annual Review of Political Science 10,* 103–126.

Chong, D., & Druckman, J. N. (2007b). A theory of framing and opinion formation in competitive elite environments. *Journal of Communication, 57*(1), 99–118.

Clawson, R. (2008). *Legacy and legitimacy: Black Americans and the Supreme Court.* Philadelphia, PA: Temple University Press.

Coaffee, J. (2003). *Terrorism, risk, and the city: The making of a contemporary urban landscape.* Aldershot, England: Ashgate.

Cobb, R. A., & Elder, C. D. (1972). *Participation in American politics: The dynamics of agenda building.* Boston, MA: Allyn & Bacon.

Conrad, P. (1992). Medicalization and social control. *Annual Review of Sociology 18,* 209–232.

Constantinescu, A. R., & Tedesco, J. C. (2007). Frame convergence between online newspaper coverage and reader discussion posts about three kidnapped Romanian journalists. *Journalism Studies, 8*(3), 444–464.

Coombs, W. T. (2010) Parameters for crisis communications In W. T. Coombs & S. Holladay (Eds.), *Handbook of crisis communications* (pp. 17–54). Malden, MA: Wiley-Blackwell.

Cooper, A. H. (2002). Media framing and social movement mobilization: German peace protest against INF missiles, the Gulf War and NATO peace enforcement in Bosnia. *European Journal of Political Research, 41*(1), 37–80.

Cooper, M. (2005). Thinking of jackasses. *The Atlantic, 295*(3), 99–103. Retrieved from www. theatlantic.com/magazine/archive/2005/04//thinking-of-jackasses/3838/.

Currie, G. (2007). Framing narratives. In D. D. Hutto (Ed.), *Narrative and understanding persons* (pp. 17–42). New York: Cambridge University Press.

D'Angelo, P. (2002). News framing as a multi-paradigmatic research program: A response to Entman. *Journal of Communication, 48*(4), 100–117.

DeChaine, D. R. (2005). *Global humanitarianism: NGOs and the crafting of community*. Lanham, MD: Lexington Books.

Delli Carpini, M. X. (2005). News from somewhere: Journalistic frames and the debate over "public journalism." In K. Callaghan & F. Schnell (Eds.), *Framing American politics* (pp. 21–53). Pittsburgh, PA: University of Pittsburgh Press.

De Martino, B., Kumaran, D., Seymour, B., & Dolan, R. J. (2006). Frames, biases, and rational decision making in the human brain. *Science, 313*(5787), 684–687.

Dershowitz, A. (1994) *The abuse excuse: And other cop-outs, sob stories, and evasions of responsibility*. Boston, MA: Little Brown.

de Vreese, C. H. (2003). *Framing Europe: Television news and European integration*. Amsterdam, the Netherlands: Aksant.

de Vreese, C. H. (2005a). News narrative and news framing: Constructing political reality. *International Journal of Public Opinion Research, 17*(3), 380–381.

de Vreese, C. H. (2005b). News framing: Theory and typology. *Information Design Journal + Document Design, 13*(1), 51–62

de Vreese, C. H., Peter, J., & Semetko, H. (2001). Framing politics at the launch of the Euro: A cross-national comparative study of frames in the news. *Political Communication, 18*(2), 107–122.

de Vreese, C. H., & Semetko, H. A. (2004). *Political campaigning in referendums: Framing the referendum issue*. London: Routledge.

Dickerson, D. L. (2001). Framing "political correctness" in the *New York Times*. In S. D. Reese, O. H. Gandy, Jr., & A. E. Grant (Eds.), *Framing public life: Perspectives on media and our understanding of the social world* (pp. 163–174). Mahwah, NJ: Erlbaum.

Dillard, J. P., & Anderson, J. W. (2004). The role of fear in persuasion. *Psychology & Marketing, 21*(11), 909–926.

Dimitrova, D. V., & Strömbäck, J. (2005). Mission accomplished? Framing of the Iraq War in the elite newspapers in Sweden and the United States. *Gazette, 67*(5), 399–417.

Dixon, D. (2005). Aid workers or evangelists, charity or conspiracy: Framing of missionary activity as a function of international political alliances. *Journal of Media & Religion, 4*(1), 13–25.

Downs, D. (2002). Representing gun owners: Frame identification as social responsibility in news media discourse. *Written Communication, 19*(1), 44–75.

Drake, P., & Higgins, M. (2006). "I'm a celebrity, get me into politics": The political celebrity and the celebrity politician. In S. Holmes & S. Redmond (Eds.), *Framing celebrity: New directions in celebrity culture* (pp. 87–100). New York: Routledge.

Druckman, J. (2001a). On the limits of framing effects: Who can frame? *Journal of Politics, 63*(4), 1041–1066.

Druckman, J. (2001b). The implications of framing effects for citizen competence. *Political Behavior, 23*(3), 225–256.

Durham, F. (2001). Breaching powerful boundaries: A postmodern critique of framing. In S. D. Reese, O. H. Gandy, Jr., & A. E. Grant (Eds.), *Framing public life: Perspectives on media and our understanding of the social world* (pp. 123–136). Mahwah, NJ: Erlbaum.

Edelman, M. (1967). *The symbolic uses of politics*. Urbana: University of Illinois Press.

Edelman, M. (1993). Contestable categories and public opinion. *Political Communication, 10*, 231–242.

Edy, J. A., & Meirick, P. C. (2007). Wanted, dead or alive: Media frames, frame adoption and support for the war in Afghanistan. *Journal of Communication, 57*(1), 119–141.

Elliott, C. S., & Hayward, D. M. (1998). The expanding definition of framing and its particular impact on economic experimentation. *Journal of Socio-Economics, 27*(2), 229–243.

Ensink, T., & Sauer, J. (Eds.) (2003). *Framing and perspectivising in discourse.* Philadelphia, PA: John Benjamins.

Entman, R. M. (1993). Framing: Toward a clarification of a fractured paradigm. *Journal of Communication, 43*(4), 51–58.

Entman, R. M. (2003). Cascading activation: Contesting the White House's frame after 9/11. *Political Communication, 20*(4), 415–432.

Entman, R. M. (2004). *Projections of power: Framing news, public opinion, and U.S. foreign policy.* Chicago, IL: University of Chicago Press.

Entman, R. M., Matthes, J., & Pellicano, L. (2009). Nature, sources and effects of news framing In. K. Wahl-Jorgensen & T. Hanitzsch (Eds.), *Handbook of journalism studies* (pp. 175–190). New York: Routledge.

Esacove, A. W. (2004). Dialogic framing: The framing/counterframing of "partial birth" abortion. *Sociological Inquiry, 74*(1), 70–101.

Fairhurst, G., & Sarr, R. (1996). *The art of framing.* San Francisco, CA: Jossey-Bass.

Feldman, J. (Ed.). (2007). *Framing the debate: Famous presidential speeches and how progressives can use them to change the conversation (and win elections).* Brooklyn, NY: Ig.

Fernandes, L. (2006). *India's new middle class: Democratic policies in an era of economic reform.* Minneapolis: University of Minnesota Press.

Fiske, S. T., & Taylor, S. E. (1991). *Social cognition* (2nd ed.). New York: McGraw-Hill.

Fredin, E. S. (2001). Frame breaking and creativity: A frame data base for hypermedia news. In S. D. Reese, O. H. Gandy, Jr., & A. E. Grant (Eds.), *Framing public life: Perspectives on media and our understanding of the social world* (pp. 269–294). Mahwah, NJ: Erlbaum.

Fridkin, K. L., & Kenney, P. J. (2005a). The dimensions of negative messages. *American Politics Research, 36*(5), 694–723.

Fridkin, K., & Kenney, P. J. (2005b). Campaign frames: Can candidates influence media coverage? In K. Callaghan & F. Schnell (Eds.), *Framing American politics* (pp. 54–75). Pittsburgh, PA: University of Pittsburgh Press.

Froehlich, R., & Rüdiger, B. (2006). Framing political public relations: Measuring success of political communication strategies in Germany. *Public Relations Review, 32*(1), 18–25.

Futrell, R. (2003). Framing processes, cognitive liberation and the NIMBY protest in the U.S. chemical-weapons disposal conflict. *Sociological Inquiry, 73*(3), 359–386.

Gabrielson, T. (2005). Obstacles and opportunities: Factors that constrain elective officials' ability to frame political issues. In K. Callaghan & F. Schnell (Eds.), *Framing American politics* (pp. 76–102) Pittsburgh, PA: University of Pittsburgh Press.

Gamson, W. A. (1996). Media discourse as a framing resource. In A. N. Crigler (Ed.), *The psychology of political communication* (pp. 111–132). Ann Arbor: University of Michigan Press.

Gamson, W. A., Croteau, D., Hoyner, W., & Sasson, T. (1992). Media images and social construction of reality. *Annual Review of Sociology, 18*, 373–393.

Gamson, W. A., & Modigliani, A. (1989). Media discourse and public opinion on nuclear power: A constructionist approach. *American Journal of Sociology, 95*(3), 1–37.

Gevorgyan, G. (2010). Does culture matter? Using accommodation, framing and Hofstede theories to predict Chinese voters' perceptions and attitudes toward culturally oriented online political advertising. *China Media Research, 6*(1). Retrieved from http://www.chinamediaresearch.net.

Gilliam, F. D., & Iyengar, S. (2005). Super-predators or victims of societal neglect? Framing effects in juvenile crime coverage. In K. Callaghan & F. Schnell (Eds.), *Framing American politics* (pp. 148–166) Pittsburgh, PA: University of Pittsburgh Press.

Gitlin, T. (1980). *The whole world is watching.* Berkeley: University of California Press.

Glenn, J. K., III. (2001). *Framing democracy: Civil society and civic movements in Eastern Europe.* Stanford, CA: Stanford University Press.

Goffman, E. (1974). *Frame analysis: An essay on the organization of experience*. Cambridge, MA: Harvard University Press.

Golden, J. L. (2005). *Message in a bottle: The making of fetal alcohol syndrome*. Cambridge, MA: Harvard University Press.

Graber, D. A. (1988). *Processing the news* (2nd ed.). New York: Longman.

Grant, J. T., & Rudolph, T. J. (2004). *Expression v. equality: The politics of campaign finance reform*. Columbus: Ohio State University Press.

Green, J. (2005). It isn't the message, stupid. *The Atlantic, 295*(4), 45–46. Retrieved from http://www.theatlantic.com/magazine/print/2005/ 05/it-isn-apos-t-the-message-stupid/3903/

Grossman, A. D. (2001). *Neither dead or nor red: Civilian defense and American political development during the early Cold War*. New York: Routledge.

Guiora, A. N. (2008). *Fundamentals of counterterrorism*. Austin, TX: Wolters Kluwer Law & Business.

Gunsch, M. A., Brownlow, S., Haynes, S. E., & Mabe, Z. (2000). Differential forms: Linguistic content of various political advertising. *Journal of Broadcasting & Electronic Media, 44*(1), 27–42.

Hagendoorn, L., & Kantorova, A. (2000). The effects of issues framing on public opinion formation. The trickery of political communication. In N. Schleicher (Ed.), *Communication culture in transition* (pp. 9–27). Budapest, Hungary: Akadémiai Kiadó.

Hale, H. E. (2008). *The foundations of ethnic policies: Separatism of states and nations in Eurasia and the world*. New York: Cambridge University Press.

Hallahan, K. (1999a). Seven models of framing: Implications for public relations. *Public Relations Review, 11*(3), 205–242.

Hallahan, K. (1999b). Content class as a heuristic cue in the processing of news versus advertising. *Public Relations Review, 11*(4), 293–320.

Hallahan, K. (2008). Strategic framing. In W. Donsbach (Ed.), *International encyclopedia of communication* (Vol. 10, pp. 4855–4860). Malden, MA: Blackwell.

Hallahan, K. (2010a). Being public: Publicity as public relations. In R. L. Heath (Ed.), *Handbook of public relations* (2nd ed., pp. 523–545). Los Angeles, CA: Sage.

Hallahan, K. (2010b). Public relations media. In R. L. Heath (Ed.), *Handbook of public relations*. (2nd ed., pp. 623–641). Los Angeles, CA: Sage.

Hammond, P. (2007). *Framing post-Cold War conflicts: The media and international intervention*. Manchester, England: Manchester University Press.

Hänggli, R., & Kriesi. H. (2010). Political framing strategies and their impact on media framing in a Swiss direct-democratic campaign. *Political Communication, 27*(2), 141–157.

Hansen, A. (2000). Claims-making and framing in British newspaper coverage of the "Brent Spar" controversy. In S. Allan, B. Adam, & C. Carter (Eds.), *Environmental risk and the media* (pp. 55–72). London: Routledge.

Hartmann, T. (2007). *Cracking the code: How to win hearts, change minds and restore America's original vision*. San Francisco, CA: Berrett-Koehler.

Haydarov, R. (2010). *Effects of attribute framing and goal framing on vaccinations* (Unpublished master's thesis). Kansas State University, Manhattan.

Heidensohn, F. (2000). *Sexual politics and social control*. Philadelphia, PA: Open University Press.

Henderson, J., Coveney, J., Ward, P., & Taylor, A. (2009). Governing child obesity: Framing regulation of fast food advertising in the Australian print media. *Social Science & Medicine, 69*(9), 1402–1408.

Hertog, J. K., & McLeod, D. M. (2001). Multiperspective approach to framing analysis: A field guide. In S. D. Reese, O. H. Gandy, Jr., & A. E. Grant (Eds.), *Framing public life: Perspectives on media and our understanding of the social world* (pp. 139–162). Mahwah, NJ: Erlbaum.

Hilgartner, S., & Bosk, C. L. (1988). The rise and fall of social problems: A public arenas model. *American Journal of Sociology, 94*(1), 53.

Holbert, R., Tschida, D., Dixon, M., Cherry, K., Steuber, K., & Airne, D. (2005). The West Wing and depictions of the American presidency: Expanding the domains of framing in political communication. *Communication Quarterly, 53*(4), 505–522.

Holmes, S., & Redmond, S. (2006). *Framing celebrity: New directions in celebrity culture.* New York: Routledge, 2006.

Hughes, A. (2003). Defining negative political advertising: Definition, features and tactics. Australian National University (Working paper). Retrieved from http:// smib.vuw.ac.nz:8081/ WWW/ANZMAC2003/.../ADV21_hughesa.pdf

Iyengar, S. (1991). *Is anyone responsible?* Chicago, IL: University of Chicago Press.

Iyengar, S., & Kinder, D. R. (1987). *News that matters: Television and American opinion.* Chicago, IL: University of Chicago Press.

Jamal, A. (2005). *Media politics and democracy in Palestine: Political culture, pluralism and the Palestinian Authority.* Portland, OR: Sussex Academic Press.

Jasperson, A. E., & Fan, D. P. (2004). The news as molder of campaign ad effects. *International Journal of Public Opinion Research, 16*(4), 417–436.

Jasperson, A. E, Shah, D. V., Watts, M., Faber, R. J., & Fan, D.P. (1998). Framing the public agenda. Media effects on the importance of the federal budget deficit. *Political Communication, 15*(2), 205–224.

Jenness, V. (2006). Social movement growth, domain expansion and framing processes: The gay/ lesbian movement and violence against gays and lesbians as a social problem. In D. Schneer & C. Aviv (Eds.), *American queer, now and then* (pp. 198–209). Boulder, CO: Paradigm.

Johnson-Cartee, K. S. (2005). *News narratives and news framing: Constructing political reality.* Lanham, MD: Rowman & Littlefield.

Jones, S. A. (2007). *Framing the violence in southern Thailand: Three ways of Malay–Muslim separatism* (Unpublished master's thesis). Ohio University, Athens. Retrieved from http://etd.ohiolink. edu/send-pdf.cgi/Jones%20Sara%20A.pdf?ohiou1179351296

Jones, S. L. (2010). *Coalition building in the anti-death penalty movement: Privileged morality, race realities.* Lanham, MD: Lexington Books.

Kahneman, D., & Tversky, A. (1979). Prospect theory: An analysis of decision under risk. *Econometrica, 47*(2), 263–291.

Kelley, H. H. (1967). Attribution social psychology. In D. Lewis (Ed.), *Nebraska symposium on motivation* (Vol. 14, pp. 192–240). Lincoln: University of Nebraska Press.

Kellstedt, P. M. (2003). *The mass media and the dynamics of American racial attitudes.* New York: Cambridge University Press.

Kellstedt, P. M. (2005). Media frames, core values, and the dynamics of racial policy preferences. In K. Callaghan & F. Schnell (Eds.), *Framing American politics* (pp. 167–178). Pittsburgh, PA: University of Pittsburgh Press.

Kendall, D. E. (2005*). Framing class: Media representations of wealth and poverty in America.* Lanham, MD: Rowman & Littlefield.

Kensicki, L. (2001, April). Deaf President Now! Positive media framing of a social movement within a hegemonic political environment. *Journal of Communication Inquiry, 25*(2), 147–166.

Kenski, K. M. (2003). The framing of network news coverage during the first three months of the Clinton–Lewinsky scandal. In R. E. Denton Jr. & R. L. Holloway (Eds.), *Images, scandal and communication strategies of the Clinton presidency* (pp. 247–270). Westport, CT: Praeger.

Kinder, D. R., & Nelson, T. E. (2005). Democratic debate and real opinions. In K. Callaghan & F. Schnell (Eds.), *Framing American politics* (pp. 103–122). Pittsburgh, PA: University of Pittsburgh Press.

King, E. G., & Wells, R. A. (2009). *Framing the Iraq War endgame: War's denouement in an age of terror.* New York: Palgrave Macmillan.

King, P., & McCombs, M. (1994). The party agendas in the 1992 Taiwan legislative election: A content analysis of the television political party advertisings (TPPA). *Asian Journal of Communication, 4*(1), 77–98.

Kiousis, S. (2008). Priming. In *Encyclopedia of political communication.* Retrieved from http://0-www.sage-rereference.com/catalog.library.colostate.edu/politicalcommunication/Article_n539.html.

Kiousis, S., Kim, S., McDevitt, M., & Ostrowski, A. (2009). Competing for attention: Information subsidy influence in agenda building during election campaigns. *Journalism & Mass Communication Quarterly, 86*(3), 545–562.

Kitzinger, J. (2004). *Framing abuse: Media influence and public understanding of sexual violence against children.* Ann Arbor, MI: Pluto.

Kitzinger, J. (2006). Ultimate neighbour from hell? Stranger danger and the media framing of pedophilia. In C. Critcher (Ed.), *Critical readings: Moral panics and the media* (pp. 135–147). New York: Open University Press. (Original work published in 1999)

Klandermans, B. (1997). *The social psychology of protest.* Oxford, England: Blackwell.

König, T. (2005). Frame analysis: Theoretical preliminaries. Retrieved from http://www.ccsr. ac.uk/methods/publications/frameanalysis/

Kosicki, G. (2002). The media priming effect: News media and considerations affecting political judgment. In J. P. Dillard & M. Pfau (Eds.), *The persuasion handbook: Developments in theory and practice* (pp.63–81). Thousand Oaks, CA: Sage.

Kuypers, J. A. (1997). *Presidential crisis rhetoric and the press in the post-Cold War world.* Westport, CT: Praeger.

Kuypers, J. A. (2002). *Press bias and politics: How the media frame controversial issues.* Westport, CT: Praeger.

Kuypers, J. A. (2006). *Bush's war: Press bias and framing of the war on terror.* Lanham, MD: Rowman & Littlefield.

Kuypers, J. A. (Ed.). (2009). *Rhetorical criticism: Perspectives in action.* Lanham, MD: Lexington Press.

Lakoff, G. (2002). *Moral politics: How liberals and conservatives think.* Chicago, IL: University of Chicago Press.

Lakoff, G. (2004). *Don't think of an elephant: Know your values and frame the debate: The essential guide for progressives.* White River Junction, VT: Chelsea Green.

Lakoff, G. (2008). *The political mind.* New York: Viking Press.

Levin, I. P., Schneider, S. L., & Gaeth, G. J. (1998). All frames are not created equal: A typology and critical analysis of framing effects. *Organizational Behavior and Human Decision Processes, 76*(2), 149–188.

Levy, J. S. (2003). Applications of prospect theory to political science. *Synthese, 35*(2), 215–241.

Lewicki, R. J., Gray, B., & Elliott, M. (Eds.). (2003). *Making sense of intractable environmental conflicts: Frames and cases.* Washington, DC: Island Press.

Lippmann, W. (1961). *Public opinion.* New York: Macmillan. (Original work published 1922)

Loue, S., Lloyd, L. S., & O'Shea, D. (2003). *Community health advocacy.* New York: Kluwer Academic.

Lowney, K. S. (2008). Claims-making, culture and the media in the social construction process. In J. A. Holstein & J. F. Gubrium (Eds.), *Handbook of constructionist research* (pp. 331–354). New York: Guilford Press.

Lowry, D. (2008). Network TV news framing of good vs. bad economic news under democratic and republican presidents: A lexical analysis of political bias. *Journalism & Mass Communication Quarterly, 85*(3), 483–498.

Luntz, F. (2006). New American lexicon [memorandum]. Retrieved from http://www.political-cortex.com/special/Luntz_NAL_Introduction.

Luntz, F. (2007). *Words that work: It's not what you say, it's what people hear.* New York: Hyperion.

Luther, C., & Zhou, X. (2005). Within the boundaries of politics: News framing of SARS in China and the United States. *Journalism & Mass Communication Quarterly, 82*(4), 857–872.

Luthra, R. (2007). Framing gender in Afghanistan and Iraq: Unveiling the gaze of empire. In A. Sreberny & P. Sonwalkar (Eds.), *Media and political violence* (pp. 325–340). Cresskill, NJ: Hampton Press.

Lytton, T. D. (2008). *Holding bishops accountable: How lawsuits helped the Catholic Church confront clergy sexual abuse.* Cambridge, MA: Harvard University Press.

Maher, T. M. (2001). Framing: An emerging paradigm or a phase of agenda setting? In S. D. Reese, O. H. Gandy, Jr., & A. E. Grant (Eds.), *Framing public life: Perspectives on media and our understanding of the social world* (pp. 83–94). Mahwah, NJ: Erlbaum.

Manheim, J. (1987). A model of agenda dynamics. *Communication yearbook 10*, 449–516.

Mann, C. R., Zatz, M. S., & Rodriguez (Eds.). (2006) *Images of color, images of crime* (3rd ed.). Los Angeles, CA: Roxbury.

Mann, J. (2000). Framing China. In D. A. Graber (Ed.), *Media power in politics* (4th ed., pp. 44–47). Washington, DC: CQ Press.

Martz-Mayfield, M., & Hallahan, K. (2009). Filmmakers as social advocates: A new challenge for issues managers. *Public Relations Journal, 3*(4), Article 2. Retrieved from http://www.prsa.org/SearchResults/download/6D-030404/0/Filmmakers_as_Social_Advocates_A_New_Challenge_for

Matthes, J. (2009a). Framing responsibility for political issues: The preference for dispositional attributions and the effects of news frames. *Communication Research Reports, 26*(1), 82–86.

Matthes, J. (2009b). What's in a frame? A content analysis of media framing studies in the world's leading communication journals, 1990–2005. *Journalism and Mass Communication Quarterly, 86*(2), 349–367.

McClure, J., White, J., & Sibley, C. G. (2009). Framing effects on preparation intentions: Distinguishing actions and outcomes. *Disaster Prevention and Management, 18*(2), 187–199.

McCombs, M. (2004). *Setting the agenda: The news media and public opinion.* Malden, MA: Blackwell.

McCombs, M., & Ghanem, S. I. (2001). Convergence of agenda-setting and framing. In S. D. Reese, O. H. Gandy, Jr., & A. E. Grant (Eds.), *Framing public life: Perspectives on media and our understanding of the social world* (pp. 67–82). Mahwah, NJ: Erlbaum.

McCright, A. M., & Dunlap, R. E. (2000). Challenging global warming as a social problem: An analysis of the conservative movement's counter-claims. *Social Problems, 47*(4), 499–522.

McDermott, R., Fowler, J. H., & Smirnov, O. (2008). On the evolutionary origin of prospect theory preferences. *Journal of Politics, 70*(2), 335–350.

Mercer, J. (2005). Prospect theory and political science. *Annual Review of Political Science 8*, 1–21.

Miller, C.A. (2006). Framing shared values: Reason and trust in environmental governance. In J. Bauer (Ed.), *Forging environmentalism: Justice, livelihood and contested environments* (pp. 377–396). Armonk, NY: M. E. Sharpe.

Miller, M. M., & Riechert, B. P. (2001). Spiral of opportunity and frame resonance: Mapping the issue cycle in news and public discourse. In S. D. Reese, O. H. Gandy, Jr., & A. E. Grant (Eds.), *Framing public life: Perspectives on media and our understanding of the social world* (pp. 107–122). Mahwah, NJ: Erlbaum.

Montiel, C., & Shah, A. (2008). Effects of political framing and perceiver's social position on trait attributions of a terrorist/freedom fighter. *Journal of Language & Social Psychology, 27*(3), 266–275.

Morgan, A. (2008). *The price of right: How the conservatives' agenda has failed America (and always will).* New York: Sterling & Ross.

Nash, K., & Bell, V. (2007). The politics of framing. *Theory, Culture & Society, 24*(4), 73–86.

Nelson, T. E., Oxley, Z. M., & Clawson, R. A. (1997). Toward a psychology of framing effects. *Political Behavior, 19*(3), 221–246.

Nelson, T. E., & Willey, E. A. (2001). Issues frames that strike a value balance: A political psychology perspective. In S. D. Reese, O. H. Gandy, Jr., & A. E. Grant (Eds.), *Framing public life: Perspectives on media and our understanding of the social world* (pp. 245–266). Mahwah, NJ: Erlbaum.

Nesbitt-Larking, P. (2007). *Politics, society and media.* Orchard Park, NY: Broadview Press.

Neuman, W. R., Just, M., & Crigler, A. N. (1992). *Common knowledge: News and the construction of political meaning.* Chicago, IL: University of Chicago Press.

Nisbet, M., Brossard, D., & Kroepsch, A. (2003). Framing science: The stem cell controversy in an age of press/politics. *Harvard International Journal of Press/Politics, 8*(2), 36.

Nisbet, M. C., & Huge, M. (2007). Where do science debates come from? Understanding attention cycles and framing. In D. Brossard, J. Shanahan, & T. C. Nesbitt (Eds.), *The media, the public and agricultural biotechnology* (pp. 193–230). Cambridge, MA: CABI.

Norris, P., Kern, M., & Just, M. (Eds.). (2003). *Framing terrorism: The news media, the government and the public.* New York: Routledge.

Opp, K. (2009). *Theories of political protest and social movements: A multidisciplinary introduction, critique and synthesis.* New York: Routledge.

Ott, B., & Aoki, E. (2002). The politics of negotiating public tragedy: Media framing of the Matthew Shepard murder. *Rhetoric & Public Affairs, 5*(3), 483–505.

Pan, Z., & Kosicki, G. (1993). Framing analysis: An approach to news discourse. *Political Communication, 10*(1), 59–79.

Pan, Z., & Kosicki, G. (2001). Framing as a strategic action in public deliberation. In S. D. Reese, O. H. Gandy, Jr., & A. E. Grant (Eds.), *Framing public life: Perspectives on media and our understanding of the social world* (pp. 35–66). Mahwah, NJ: Erlbaum.

Parmalee, J. H., Perkins, S. C., & Sayre, J. J. (2007). What about people our age? Applying qualitative and quantitative methods to uncover how political ads alienate college students. *Journal of Mixed Research Methods, 1*(2), 183–199.

Parrott, J. B. (2009, August 2). Obama, Gates and Lakoff: The perils of "framing." *American Thinker.* Retrieved from http://www.americanthinker.com/2009/08/obama_and_gates_lakoff_theper.html

Patton, T. O. (2006). Through whose lens? (Re)framing the race and gender divide in journalism. In B. A. Muse & C. J. Price (Eds.), *Emerging issues in contemporary journalism* (pp. 243–264). Lewiston, NY: Edwin Mellen Press.

Perkins, S. C. (2005). Un-presidented: A qualitative framing analysis of the NAACP's public relations response to the 2000 presidential election. *Public Relations Review, 31*(1), 63–71.

Petty, R. E., & Cacioppo, J. T. (1986). *Communication and persuasion: Central and peripheral routes to attitude change.* New York : Springer-Verlag.

Piñon, A., & Gambara, H. (2005). A meta-analytic review of framing effect: Risky, attribute and goal framing. *Psicothema, 17*(2), 325–337.

Pintak, L. (2006). Framing the other: Worldview, rhetoric and media dissonance since 9/11. In E. Poole & J. E. Richardson (Eds.), *Muslims and the news media* (pp. 188–198). New York: I.B. Tauris.

Poole, E. (2002). *Reporting Islam: Media representations of British Muslims.* London: I. B. Tauris.

Porto, M. P. (2007). Framing controversies: Television and the 2002 presidential election in Brasil. *Political Communication, 24*(1), 19–36.

Pratto, F., & John, O. P. (1991). Automatic vigilance: The attention-grabbing power of negative social information. *Journal of Personality and Social Psychology, 61*(3), 380–391.

Price, V., & Tewksbury, D. (1997). News values and public opinion: A theoretical account of media primary and framing. In G. Barnett & F. J. Boster (Eds.), *Progress in communication science* (pp. 173–212). Greenwich, CT: Ablex.

Price, V., Tewksbury, D., & Powers (1997). Switching trains of thought: The impact of news frames on readers' cognitive responses. *Communication Research, 24*(5), 481–506.

Priest, S. H., & Eyck, T. T. (2004). Peril or promise: News media framing of the biotechnology debate in Europe and the U.S. In N. Sterh (Ed.), *Biotechnology: Between commerce and civil society* (pp. 175–178). New Brunswick, NJ: Transaction.

Rajiva, L. (2005). *The language of empire: Abu Ghraib and the American media.* New York: Monthly Review Press.

Reese, S. D. (2001). Framing public life: A bridging model for media research. In S. D. Reese, O. H. Gandy, Jr., & A. E. Grant (Eds.), *Framing public life: Perspectives on media and our understanding of the social world* (pp.7–32). Mahwah, NJ: Erlbaum.

Reese, S. D. (2004). Militarized journalism: Framing dissent in the Gulf Wars. In S. Allan & B. Zellzer (Eds.), *Reporting war: Journalism in wartime* (pp. 247–265). New York: Routledge.

Reese, S. D. (2007). The framing project: A bridging model for media research revisited. *Journal of Communication, 57*(1), 148–154.

Reese, S. D., Gandy, O. H., Jr., & Grant, A. E. (Eds.) (2001). *Framing public life: Perspectives on media and our understanding of the social world*. Mahwah, NJ: Erlbaum.

Reynolds, A., & Barnett, B. (2003). "America under attack": CNN's visual and verbal framing of September 11. In S. Chermak, F. Y. Bailey, & M. Brown (Eds.), *Media representations of September 11* (pp. 85–102). Westport, CT: Praeger.

Rhodes, J. (2007). *Framing the Black Panthers: The spectacular rise of a Black power icon*. New York: New Press.

Richardson, G. W. (2008). *Pulp politics: How political advertising tells the stories of American politics* (2nd ed.). Lanham, MD: Rowman & Littlefield.

Ries, A., & Trout, J. (1981). *Positioning: The battle for your mind*. New York: McGraw-Hill.

Ritter, S. (2003). *Frontier justice: Weapons of mass destruction and the Bushwhacking of America*. New York: Context Books.

Rohlinger, D. A. (2002). Framing the abortion debate: Organization resources, media strategies and movement-countermovement dynamics. *Sociological Quarterly, 43*(4), 479–507.

Roizen, R. (2004). How does the nation's "alcohol problem" change from era to era? Stalking the social logic of problem-definition transformation since repeal. In S. W. Tracy & C. J. Acker (Eds.), *Altering American consciousness: The history of alcohol and drug use in the United States, 1800–2000* (pp. 61–90). Amherst: University of Massachusetts Press.

Roskos-Ewoldsen, D. R., Roskos-Ewoldsen, B., & Dillman Carpentier, R. F. (2002). Media priming: An updated synthesis. In J. Bryant & M. B. Oliver (Eds.), *Media effects: Advances in theory and research* (3rd ed., pp. 74–93). New York: Routledge.

Ross, R. J. S. (2004). *Slaves to fashion: Poverty and abuse in the new sweatshops*. Ann Arbor, University of Michigan Press.

Rove, K. (2010). *Courage and consequence: My life as a conservative in the fight*. New York: Threshold.

Ruiter, R. A. C., Abraham, C., & Kok, G. (2001). Scary warnings and rational precautions: A review of the psychology of fear appeals. *Psychology and Health, 16*(6), 613–630

Ryan, C. (1991). *Prime time activism*. Boston, MA: South End Press.

Ryan, C., & Gamson, W. A. (2006). The art of reframing political debates. *Contexts, 5*(1), 13–18.

Salmon, C. T. (1990, Spring). God understands when the cause is noble. *Gannett Center Journal, 4*(2), 23–34.

Salovey, P., Schneider, T. A., & Apanovitch, A. M. (2002). Message framing and the early prevention and detection of illness. In J. P. Dillard & M. Pfau (Eds.), *The persuasion handbook: Developments in theory and practice* (pp. 391–406). Thousand Oaks, CA: Sage.

Salvatore, A. (2007). The exit from a Westphalian framing of political space and the emergence of a transnational Islamic public. *Theory, Culture & Society, 24*(4), 45–52.

Sarabia-Panol, M. Z. (2007). The 9/11 terrorist attacks on America: Media frames from the Far East. In T. Pludowski (Ed.), *How the world's news media reacted to 9/11: Essays from around the globe* (pp. 169–185). Spokane, WA: Marquette Books.

Scheneck-Hamlin, W. J., Procter, D. E., & Rumsey, D. J. (2006). The influence of negative advertising frames on political cynicism and politician accountability. *Human Communication Research, 26*(1), 53–74.

Scheufele, B. (2004). Framing-effects approach: A theoretical and methodological critique. *Communications. The European Journal of Communication Research, 29*(4), 401–428.

Scheufele, D. (1999). Framing as a theory of media effects. *Journal of Communication, 49*(4), 103–122.

Scheufele, D. (2000). Agenda-setting, priming, and framing revisited: Another look at cognitive effects of political communication. *Mass Communication & Society, 3*(2/3), 297–316.

Scheufele, D. (2008). Framing effects. In W. Donsbach (Ed.), *The international encyclopedia of communication*. Malden, MA: Blackwell. doi 10.1111/b.9781405131995.2008.x

Schneider, J. W. (1985). Social problems theory: The constructionist view. *Annual Review of Sociology 11*, 209–229.

Schnell, F. D., & Callaghan, K. (2005). Terrorism, media frames and framing effects: A macro- and micro-level analysis. In K. Callaghan & F. Schnell (Eds.), *Framing American politics* (pp. 123–147). Pittsburgh, PA: University of Pittsburgh Press.

Schroedel, J. R. (2000). *Is the fetus a person? A comparison of policies across the fifty states.* Ithaca, NY: Cornell University Press.

Segvic, I. (2005). The framing of politics: A content analysis of three Croatian newspapers. *Gazette: International Journal for Communication Studies, 67*(5), 469–488.

Semetko, H., & Valkenburg, P. (2000). Framing European politics: A content analysis of press and television news. *Journal of Communication, 50*(2), 93–109.

Seymour, F. (2008). Framing the millennium ecosystem assessment messages for political resonance. In J. Ranganathan, M. Munasinghe, & F. Irvin (Eds.), *Policies for sustainable governance of global ecosystem services* (pp. 296–314). Northhampton, MA: Edward Elgar.

Shah, D., Domke, D., & Wackman, D. B. (2001). Effects of value-framing on political judgment and reasoning. In S. D. Reese, O. H. Gandy, Jr., & A. E. Grant (Eds.), *Framing public life. Perspectives on media and our understanding of the social world* (pp. 227–246). Mahwah, NJ: Erlbaum.

Shah, D., Watts, M., Domke, D., & Fan, D. (2002). News frames and cueing of issue regimes: Explaining Clinton's public approval in spite of scandal. *Public Opinion Quarterly, 66*(3), 339–370.

Shen, E. (2004). Effects of news frames and schemes on individual's issue interpretation and attitudes. *Journalism and Mass Communication Quarterly, 81*(2), 400–416.

Shen, E., & Edwards, H. H. (2005). Economic individualism, humanitarianism and welfare reform: A value-based account of framing effects. *Journal of Communication, 55*(4), 795–809.

Sherif, M. (1967). *Social interaction: Processes and products.* Chicago, IL: Aldine.

Shoemaker, P. J., & Reese, S. D. (1996). *Mediating the message: Theories of influences on mass media content* (3rd ed.). New York: Longman.

Simon, A. F. (2001). A unified method for analyzing media framing. In R. P. Hart & D. R. Shaw (Eds.), *Communication in U.S. elections: New agendas* (pp. 75–90). Lanham, MD: Rowman & Littlefield.

Simon, A. F., & Xenos, M. (2000). Media framing and effective public deliberation. *Political Communication, 17*(4), 363–376.

Simon, A. F., & Jerit, J. (2007). Toward a theory relating political discourse, media and public opinion. *Journal of Communication, 57*(1), 254–271.

Simpson, D. (2006). *The culture of commemoration.* Chicago, IL: University of Chicago Press.

Sky, T. (2003). *To provide for the general welfare: A history of the federal spending power.* Newark, DE: University of Delaware Press.

Sloan, J. (2006). *Learning to think strategically.* Boston, MA: Elsevier/Butterworth-Heinemann.

Sniderman, P. M., & Theriault, S. M. (2004). The structure of political argument and the logic of issue framing. In W. E. Saris & P. M. Sniderman (Eds.), *Studies in public opinion* (pp. 133–165). Princeton, NJ: Princeton University Press.

Snow, D. A. (2004). Framing processes, ideology and discursive fields. In D. A. Snow, S. A. Soule, & H. Kriesi (Eds.), *The Blackwell companion to social movements* (pp. 380–412). Malden, MA: Blackwell.

Snow, D. A., & Benford, R. D. (1992). Master frames and cycles of protest. In A. D. Morris & C. M. Mueller (Eds.), *Frontiers in social movement theory* (pp. 133–155). New Haven, CT: Yale University Press.

Snow, D. A., Rochford, E. B., Worden, W. K., & Benford, R. D. (1986). Frame alignment processes, micromobilization and movement participation. *American Sociological Review, 51*(4), 464–481.

Soderlund, W. C. (2001). Press framing of the 1965 U.S. intervention in the Dominican Republic: A test of the propaganda model. In W. C. Soderlund (Ed.), *Media definitions of Cold War reality: The Caribbean basin, 1953–1992* (pp. 43–58). Toronto: Canadian Scholars' Press.

Spector, M., & Kitsuse, J. I. (1987). *Constructing social problems.* New York: Aldine de Gruyter.

Squires, J. (2000). *Gender in political theory.* Malden, MA : Blackwell

Stanton, R. (2007). *Media relations.* South Melbourne, Australia: Oxford University Press.

Strömbäck, J., & Dimitrova, D. V. (2006). Political and media systems matter. A comparison of election news coverage in Sweden and the United States. *Harvard International Journal of Press/Politics, 11*(4), 131–147.

Strömbäck, J., & Kaid, L. L. (Eds.). (2008). *Handbook of election news coverage around the world*. New York: Routledge.

Strömbäck, J., Mitrook, M. A., & Kiousis, S. (2010). Bridging two schools of thought: Applications of public relations theory to political communication. *Journal of Political Marketing, 9*(1–2), 73–92.

Strömbäck, J., & van Aelst, Peter (2010). Exploring some antecedents of the media's framing of election news: A comparison of Swedish and Belgian election news. *International Journal of Press/Politics, 15*(1), 41–59.

Swain, C. M. (2002). *The new white nationalism in America*. New York: Cambridge University Press.

Tadlock, B. L., Gordon, C. A., & Popp, E. (2007). Framing the issue of same-sex marriage: Traditional values versus equal rights. In C. A. Riggerman & C. Wilcox (Eds.), *The politics of same-sex marriage* (pp. 193–214). Chicago, IL: University of Chicago Press.

Tankard, J. W. (2001). The empirical approach to the study of media framing. In S. D. Reese, O. H. Gandy, & A. E. Grant (Eds.), *Framing public life: Perspectives on media and our understanding of the social world* (pp. 95–106). Mahwah, NJ: Erlbaum.

Tewksbury, D., Jones, J., Peske, M. W., Raymond, A., & Vig W. (2000). The interaction of news and advocate frames: Manipulating audience perceptions of a local public policy issue. *Journalism and Mass Communication Quarterly, 77*(4), 804–829.

Tewksbury, D., & Scheufele, D. A. (2009). News framing theory and research. In J. Bryant & M. B. Oliver (Eds.), *Media effects: Advances in theory and research* (3rd ed., pp. 17–33). New York: Routledge.

Thornburgh, D., & Lin, H. S. (Eds.). (2002). *Youth, pornography and the Internet: Report of Committee to Study Tools and Strategies for Protecting Kids from Pornography and Their Applicability to Other Inappropriate Internet Content, Computer Science and Telecommunications Board, National Research Council*. Washington, DC: National Academy Press.

Thrall, A. T. (2006). The myth of the outside strategy: Mass media news coverage of interest groups. *Political Communication, 23*(4), 407–420.

Tiung, L., & Hasim, M. S. (2009). Media framing of political personality: A case study of a Malaysian politician. *European Journal of Social Science, 9*(3), 408–424.

Trent, J. S., & Friedenberg, R. (2007). *Political campaign communication: Principles and practice*. Lanham, MD: Rowman & Littlefield.

Tuchman, G. (1978). *Making news: A study in the construction of social reality*. New York: Free Press.

Tversky, A., & Kahneman, D. (1981). The framing of decisions and the psychology of choice. *Science, 211*(4481), 453–458.

Valentino, N. A. Beckmann, M. N., & Buhr, T. A. (2001). A spiral of cynicism for some: The contingent effects of campaign news frames on participation and confidence in government. *Political Communication, 18*(4), 347–367.

Van Gorp, B. (2007). The constructionist approach to framing: Bringing culture back in. *Journal of Communication, 57*(1), 6–78.

Vraga E. K., Carr, D. J., Nytes, J. P., & Shah, D. V. (2010). Precision v. realism on the framing continuum: Understanding the underpinnings of message effects. *Political Communication, 27*(1), 1–19.

Wang, S. (2003). *Framing piracy: Globalization and film distribution in greater China*. Lanham, MD: Rowan & Littlefield.

Watkins, M., Edwards, M., & Thakar, U. (2001). *Winning the influence game: What every business leader should know about government*. New York: Wiley.

Weaver, D. H. (2007). Thoughts on agenda setting, framing and priming. *Journal of Communication, 57*(1), 142–147.

Wells, W. D. (1989). Lectures and dramas. In P. Cafferata & A. M. Tybout (Eds.), *Cognitive and affective responses to advertising* (pp. 13–20). Lexington, MA: Lexington Books.

Werder, O., & Golan, G. (2002). Sharon wins: News coverage and framing of the 2001 Israeli prime minister election in ten western print media. *Global Media Journal, 1*(1). Retrieved from http://lass.calumet.purdue.edu/cca/gmj/fa02/graduatefa02/gmj-fa02-werder-golan.htm

Weyland, K. (2002). *The politics of market reform in fragile democracies: Argentina, Brazil, Peru and Venezuela.* Princeton, NJ: Princeton University Press.

White, W. L. (2004). Lessons of language: Historical perspectives on the rhetoric of addiction. In S. W. Tracy & C. J. Acker (Eds.), *Altering American consciousness: The history of alcohol and drug use in the United States, 1800–2000* (pp. 33–60). Amherst: University of Massachusetts Press.

Wicks, R. H. (2001). *Understanding audiences: Learning to use the media constructively.* Mahwah, NJ: Erlbaum.

Wiggins, E. L. (2001). Frames of conviction: The intersection of social frameworks and standards of appraisal in letters to the editor regarding a lesbian commitment ceremony. In S. D. Reese, O. H. Gandy, Jr., & A. E. Grant (Eds.), *Framing public life: Perspectives on media and our understanding of the social world* (pp. 207–214). Mahwah, NJ: Erlbaum.

Williams, A. P. (2006). Self-referential and opponent-based framing: Candidate e-mail strategies in campaign 2004. In A. P. Williams & J. C. Tedesco (Eds.), *The Internet election: Perspectives on the Web in campaign 2004* (pp. 83–98). Lanham, MD: Rowman & Littlefield.

Williams, G. I., & Williams, R. H. (2003). Framing the fathers' rights movement. In D. R. Loeske & J. Best (Eds.), *Social problems: Constructivist readings* (pp. 93–100). New York: Aldine de Gruyter.

Wong, C. O., & McMurray, N. E. (2002). Framing communication: Communicating the anti-smoking message effectively to all smokers. *Journal of Community Psychology, 30*(4), 433–447.

Yeo, E., Park, K., & Arabi, A. (2007). News framing West Nile virus—An outbreak of a new health hazard. *Journal of Humanities & Social Sciences, 1*(2).Retrieved from http://www.scientificjournals.org/journals2007/articles/1152.pdf

Yoos, G. E. (2007). *Reframing rhetoric: A liberal politics without dogma.* New York: Palgrave Macmillan.

Zelinsky, E. A. (2005, April 1). Do tax expenditures create framing effects? Volunteer firefighters, property tax exemptions and the paradox of tax expenditure analysis. *Virginia Tax Review, 24, 797.* Retrieved from http://www.allbusiness.com/accounting/3584666-1.html

Žeželj, I., Škoić, B., Hristić, D., & Stokić, D. (2007). Valence framing of political preferences and resistance to persuasion. *Psihologija, 40*(3), 356–385.

Zhou, C., & Moy, P. (2007). Parsing framing processes: The interplay between online public opinion and media coverage. *Journal of Communication, 57*(1), 79–98.

Zoch, L. M. (2001). What's really important here? Media self-coverage in the Susan Smith murder trial. In S. D. Reese, O. H. Gandy, Jr., & A. E. Grant (Eds.), *Framing public life: Perspectives on media and our understanding of the social world* (pp. 195–206). Mahwah, NJ: Erlbaum.

Zoch, L. M., Collins, E. L. Sisco, H. F., & Supa, D. H. (2008). Empowering the activist: Using framing devices on activist organizations' web sites. *Public Relations Review, 34*(4), 351–358.

10

POLITICAL PUBLIC RELATIONS AND CRISIS COMMUNICATION

A Public Relations Perspective

W. Timothy Coombs

Crisis communication represents a rapidly growing body of research that draws from a number of domains, including public relations, corporate communication, organizational communication, marketing, presidential rhetoric, and political communication. We can separate crisis communication into two broad contexts: (a) corporate crisis communication and (b) political crisis communication. Corporations and politicians both face crises, but while the two areas share similarities, there are subtle differences that lead to differences in conceptualization and application of crisis communication. At times political and corporate communication can look very similar while at other times it can appear radically different. This chapter explores how and why the similarities and differences between crisis communication in the corporate and political realms emerged. Ideally, this exploration will reveal how the two areas of crisis communication might inform one another and where unique aspects of crisis communication reside. The chapter will also offer a number of research propositions related to differences and similarities between crisis communication in the corporate and political realms. The search for answers begins with a review of crisis communication research in the two areas. Comprehensive literature reviews for each area could fill entire volumes. For brevity, the reviews are here abbreviated and limited to key research in each area.

Corporate Crisis Communication Research

Corporate crisis communication has become a dominant line of research in public relations (Kent, 2010). In corporate crisis communication, a crisis can be defined as "the perception of an unpredictable event that threatens important expectations of stakeholders and can seriously impact an organization's performance and generate negative outcomes" (Coombs, 2007b, pp. 2–3). This definition emphasizes the perceptual nature of crises from a stakeholder perspective. If stakeholders believe there is a crisis resulting from violations of expectations, a crisis does exist and there will be negative consequences if the situation is not addressed. The term *crisis* should, however, be reserved for only those events that have the potential to seriously impact the organization or actually do so. Many times we call events crises that really do not require assembling the crisis management team.

Methodologically, the corporate crisis communication research can be divided into rhetorical and quantitative approaches, and the literature reviewed in this section will be divided between these research lines. The rhetorical crisis communication research covers corporate apologia, image restoration theory, focusing events, and the rhetoric of renewal. The quantitative crisis communication research includes situational crisis communication theory (SCCT) and contingency theory.

Rhetorical Crisis Communication Approaches

Rhetoric provides common roots for some approaches to corporate crisis communication as well as some approaches to political communication. Therefore, the potential for integration with political communication is high for rhetorical approaches. Corporate crisis communication has strong ties to apologia, the rhetoric of self-defense. Apologia was applied to political discourse well before the offshoot of corporate apologia developed in the late 1980s. Dionisopolous and Vibbert (1988) created the first arguments for corporate apologia. They held that corporations, like individual human beings, have public personas that are subject to attack and in need of defense. Ware and Linkugel's (1973) apologia strategies became the early foundation for corporate crisis response strategies. Later, Hearit (1994, 2006) elaborated on the ways apologia could be adapted and applied to the analysis of corporate crisis rhetoric. The key element remained the need to determine which strategy or combination of strategies would be most effective in protecting a public persona/organizational reputation. A crisis triggers questions of social legitimacy, which threatens the organizational reputation. Corporate crisis response strategies were then used to rebuild the social legitimacy and organizational reputation (Hearit, 1994).

Working from apologia in conjunction with Burke and coupled with the notion of accounts from interpersonal communication, Benoit developed image repair theory (IRT) (1995). Image repair or image restoration theory is later referred to as image repair discourse. Consistent with apologia, a crisis threatens an organization's reputation when the organization is held responsible for the crisis. Image restoration theory was originally a broad theory that was not limited to organizations nor was it designed specifically for crisis communication. Image repair theory was applicable any time there was a threat to a public persona/reputation. In fact, image repair theory has been applied to politicians as well as to corporations and celebrities (Benoit, 1995, 1997; Benoit & Brinson, 1994). The rhetor/crisis manager selects crisis response strategies (image restoration strategies) that can afford the greatest reputational protection. Table 10.1 lists the various crisis response strategies developed by Benoit.

Fishman (1999), drawing upon the work of Birkland (1997), emphasizes the focusing event in corporate crisis communication. A focusing event occurs when the situation is "sudden and unpredictable" and becomes widely known very rapidly. There are type 1 and type 2 focusing events. Type 1 focusing events include natural disasters and are considered "normal." Type 2 focusing events result when a novel event violates expectations thereby creating uncertainty and public attention. Fishman's (1999) premise is that some crises rise to the level of a type 2 focusing event when they become widely known during a short time frame. The unique nature of focusing events permits them to help shape the public agenda and possibly even the policy agenda. Crisis communication becomes a part of issues management because the crisis triggers and can influence a policy discussion (Fishman, 1999).

The discourse of renewal focuses on the future, not the current crisis. Crisis managers talk about how things will be better in the future rather than trying to parse blame and dwell on the crisis. Renewal's focus on the future involves

TABLE 10.1 Benoit's (1995) Image Restoration Strategies

Denial

    Simple denial: claim there is no crisis

    Shifting the blame: blame someone or something else for the crisis

Evading Responsibility

    Provocation: react to someone else's actions

    Defeasibility: lack of control over the situation or lack of information

    Accident: did not mean for the event to occur

    Good intentions: expected the outcome to be positive not negative

Reducing Offensiveness of Event

    Bolstering: remind people of past good acts

    Minimization: argue the event created little damage

    Differentiation: make act look better by comparing it to similar acts

    Transcendence: place the act is a new, more favorable context

    Attack accuser: attack those who say there is a crisis

    Compensation: offer people goods or money

Corrective action: promise to change and not repeat the act and/or return the situation to its pre-event status

Mortification: admit guilt, express regret, and ask of forgiveness issues of repairing damage and improving on the past as a way to prevent future crises. However, not all organizations have the option to employ the discourse of renewal. To effectively use the discourse of renewal, an organization must have: (a) precrisis ethical standards that are high, (b) precrisis relationships with stakeholders that are strong, (c) a concentration on life beyond the crisis rather than on blame, and (d) a desire to engage in effective crisis management (Ulmer, Seeger, & Sellnow, 2007b). Stakeholders begin to feel better when they hear about the positive future and forget about the problems created by the current crisis. Hope and a bright future are common themes found in political rhetoric as well. For example, President Reagan's campaign rhetoric in the 1980 election drew heavily on the bright future. Again, the similarities suggest a potential overlap in how corporate crisis communication can be applied to political crises.

Quantitative Crisis Communication

A growing body of corporate crisis communication has applied experimental methods to the study of crisis communication. This research is spearheaded by situational crisis communication theory (SCCT) and contingency theory. Experiments are used to test crisis communication ideas and to prove that specific suggestions about when to use certain crisis response strategies hold true. The rhetorical corporate crisis communication does inform the quantitative research by supplying crisis response strategies and suggestions about when certain strategies might be more or less effective. However, the rhetorical corporate crisis communication is speaker-centric. The focus is on what the crisis manager says and does while assuming how people will react to the crisis and crisis response strategies. The quantitative research is, in contrast, audience-centric. There is an effort to understand how stakeholders perceive the crisis and how they will react to the crisis response strategies (Lee, 2004).

Situational crisis communication theory research is based upon organizational managers being the crisis managers. The theory is built specifically for corporations as the crisis manager. For instance, the constraints for the theory include the financial constraints corporations may face during a crisis that involve legal issues and tensions between corporate financial and social responsibilities (Coombs, 2007b). Crisis responsibility, that is, stakeholder attributions of how responsible the organization is for the crisis, is the pivotal variable. Various situational factors, such as crisis type and crisis history, are identified as influencing perceptions of crisis responsibility. In turn, the level of crisis responsibility guides the selection of the crisis response. Situational crisis communication theory recommends the perceived amount of accepting crisis responsibility in the crisis response should be comparable to the perceptions of crisis responsibility. The increased perception of crisis acceptance is needed to protect the organization's reputation from the increased risk of damage and related negative behavior such as reduced purchase intention and increased likelihood of negative word-of-mouth (Coombs & Holladay, 2007).

Contingency theory is a grand theory of public relations driven by conflict and the variables that shape the communicative responses in crisis. Contingency theory has been applied to crisis communication with a strong focus on emotion. Jin, Pang, and Cameron (2007) integrated the appraisal model of emotion with contingency theory to create the integrated crisis mapping model (ICM). This model is constructed around four emotions: (a) anger, an offense has occurred; (b) fright, face uncertainty, and threat; (c), anxiety, face immediate danger; and (d) sadness, sense of loss develops. The integrated crisis mapping model crosses the two dimensions to form four quadrants. The first dimension is the public coping strategy ranging from problem-focused (take action) to cognitive-focused coping (change interpretation of relationship). The second dimension is the level of organizational engagement and indicates the amount of resources devoted to the crisis.

The quadrants are utilized to anticipate the emotional reactions of stakeholders to a crisis. Quadrants1 (high engagement and conative coping) creates reputational damage leading to anger then anxiety. Quadrant 2 (high engagement and cognitive coping) includes natural disasters and leads to sadness then fright. Quadrant 3 (low engagement and cognitive coping) includes, for example, terrorism and leads to fright and sadness. Quadrant 4 (low engagement and conative coping) involves, for example, security issues, and leads to anxiety then anger. Research has demonstrated that Quadrant 1 is connected to anger while Quadrants 2 to 4 are dominated by anxiety (Jin, 2009; Jin & Pang, 2010; Jin, Pang, & Cameron, 2007). The next step in the research is to determine how best to respond to the emotions generated by the crises (Jin & Pang, 2010).

Summary

Some basic premises can be drawn from the corporate crisis communication research. When crises occur, they threaten the organization's reputation and related assets. Crises often induce anger and anxiety among stakeholders. Crises with internal causes (high crisis responsibility) can inflict more reputational damage and generate more anger than those with external causes (low crisis responsibility). How crisis managers communicate in response to a crisis determines the amount and nature of the damage the crisis inflicts on the organization and its stakeholders. Crises have a strong perceptual component. Crisis communication efforts must consider how stakeholders define the crisis situation and how they react to the crisis response strategies—what management says and does in response to the crisis. The crisis response element of crisis communication is reactive as managers respond to the crisis event.

Political Crisis Communication

Political crisis communication research can trace its origins to presidential crisis rhetoric. Researchers were interested in how presidents strategically used crises in their communication. The focus was more on the use of the term *crisis* than on the nature of political crisis communication. As interest shifted to the content of political crisis communication, the framing of crises took center stage. Research examined the efforts of political crisis managers to frame and to exploit crises.

Presidential Crisis Communication

Political crisis communication is rooted in rhetoric as well. Windt (1973) pioneered presidential crisis rhetoric. His belief was that presidents defined situations as crises, and that save for violent confrontations, political crises did not just emerge: "Situations do not create crises. Rather, the president's perceptions of the situation and the rhetoric he used to describe it mark an event as a crisis" (Windt, 1973, p. 7). The term *crisis* was a political weapon. Terming a situation as a crisis framed the situation and allowed presidents to pursue political objectives. As Bostdorff (1994) observed, "Because a crisis terminology has particular implications, rhetors can use it to their persuasive advantage" (p. 5). At its base, a crisis can create fear and the need for policies. Crises create advantages, including: (a) people attend to a threat, (b) urgency legitimizes need for swift action, (c) crises encourage people to unite in response to the crisis, and (d) crises create recognition of the need for short-term sacrifice. Hence, presidents might engage in crisis promotion in order to achieve a political victory. Presidents do have an advantage when trying to promote international situations as crises. Successful crisis promotion can build personal credibility, create a reserve of power, justify enacting or winning support for policies, divert attention from another problem, or make a presidential appear presidential. However, there is no guarantee of success with crisis promotion. The president's rhetorical skills are one of the key elements in crisis promotion (Bostdorff, 1994).

Kuypers (1997) develops more fully the idea of presidential crisis rhetoric as framing. Working from Entman (1993), a frame makes certain elements of reality more salient "in such a way as to promote a particular problem, definition, causal interpretation, moral evaluation, and/or treatment recommendations for the item descried" (p. 53). Clearly, political crisis communication does include crisis frames designed to define the problem and how best to resolve the problem. When presidents evoke the crisis frame, decisive action is required and people should support, not debate, it. Crises create a sense of immediacy and urgency (Kiewe, 1994). Presidential crisis rhetoric is thus composed of a statement of fact, a melodrama with the United States as the hero against some villain, and a policy that is framed as a moral act. Presidential crisis rhetoric then becomes a means of advancing policy changes. However, some crises are event driven. In those situations presidents can only try to shape interpretation of the events (Dow, 1989). Framing is easiest when a crisis develops slowly and is ambiguous. People will seek clarification and the crisis frame can provide clarity. Crises that develop quickly are more difficult to frame (Young & Launer, 1988). It could be argued that the fast moving crises are the ones where the situation defines the crisis—people will perceive a crisis before the president has an opportunity to craft and to present a frame.

Beyond Presidents: Politicians, Policies, Crisis Framing, and Exploitation

Framing has emerged as the central feature of political crisis communication. Strömbäck and Nord (2006) used frames in their examination of perceived crisis management. They posited that political fortunes can be tied to how politicians are perceived to manage the crisis and stated: "perceptions are more important than reality with regard to how public confidence is affected" (p. 795). Their research examined a fast moving crisis involving the Swedish government's reaction to the 2004 tsunami. The results found that even though political confidence was low, people still expected an effective response. Effectiveness was being evaluated in terms of the speed of the response and recognition that the crisis was serious. The media analysis showed the government was viewed as slow and that governmental efforts to shift the blame created a backlash (Strömbäck & Nord, 2006).

Boin, t'Hart, and McConnell (2008, 2009) drew upon the earlier political crisis communication research to build their theory of crisis exploitation. The theory of crisis exploitation is the most detailed articulation of political crisis communication at this point in time. The theory was born from the question of why some crises create political change while others do not. Agenda building has long recognized that crises can trigger policy changes (Cobb, Ross, & Ross, 1976). In fact, Birkland (1997) built his concept of focusing events around the belief that crises draw attention to issues/concerns and can facilitate policy changes. The theory of crisis exploitation examines "the purposeful utilization of crisis-type rhetoric to significantly alter levels of political support for public office-holders and public policies" (Boin et al., 2009, p. 83).

Framing remains an important element in the theory of crisis exploitation. Crisis exploitation is a contest between competing frames. The competition is between incumbents/status quo and their opposition. Three crisis frames were identified: (a) denial, claims there is no crisis; (b) threat, crisis does exist and is a threat; and (c) opportunity, crisis exists and offers a chance for change. The three frames have different effects on the political stance and policy stance. Table 10.2 summaries those effects.

Crisis framing involves both significance and causality. The denial frame tries to minimize the significance of the crisis, the threat frame recognizes the

TABLE 10.2 Crisis Frames: Political and Policy Stance Effects

Crisis Frame	Political Stance	Policy Stance
No crisis	No blame	Business as usual
Crisis as threat	Diffuse blame	Defend status quo
Crisis as opportunity	Focus Blame	Attack status quo

event is significant, and the opportunity frame seeks to maximize the event's significance. Strategies for framing causality for a crisis can be to (a) endogenize, the blame rests with particular politicians or policies, or (b) exogenize, outside forces (nature or human) were the causes making the event uncontrollable. The threat frame favors the exogenize causality while the opportunity frame favors the endogenize causality. It is natural for there to be multiple, competing frames because politics is marked by multiple interests. The prevailing frame is the one that becomes widely accepted. The nature of the frame will have political and policy implications (Boin et al., 2009).

Crisis framing contests encompass two political spheres: (1) policy game and (2) political game. The policy game is a struggle between those wanting policy change and those wanting the status quo. The political game is the struggle between government officials and their opposition. In the policy game, change advocates can seek a paradigm shift or incremental change. The status quo (incumbents) resists any change or attempt to contain the policy change (incremental). Incremental change is the most likely result (Boin et al., 2009) and often is no more than symbolic actions designed to create quiescence among irate publics (Coombs & Holladay, in press). The political game involves the opposition trying to blame incumbents or just to tarnish their reputations. Incumbents choose among deflecting, diffusing, or accepting responsibility. Accepting responsibility is unlikely if opponents are bent on attacking over the crisis. One advantage for incumbents is the ability to delay investigations (Boin et al., 2009).

The policy implications are the degree of changes to the beliefs that generate policy. Those changes range from deep core beliefs to secondary aspects. Deep core beliefs represent fundamental normative and ontological beliefs. These can include the nature of human beings, power, freedom, and justice. Core beliefs emerge from the deep core and are the policy positions and ways to achieve those positions. The secondary aspects are instrumental decisions that seek to implement specific policies (Sabatier, 1988). The political implications can be: (a) elite damage, careers and reputations decline; (b) elite reinvigoration, politicians benefits from the crisis; and (c) elite escape, blame is avoided or diffused across a number of actors (Boin et al., 2009). Crisis exploitation is not simply a matter of frames and actions by politicians. Crisis exploitation can be affected by the mass media, commission inquiries, situational factors, and temporal factors. The mass media can present its own frame that competes with those forwarded by political actors. Commission inquiries can be political or expert-led. In some situations blame is obvious, thus making other frames irrelevant. Crises are more damaging the nearer they are to an election.

Incumbents fair best when they: (a) have a reserve of precrisis political capital, (b) effectively communicate their frames, (c) have been in office a short time, and (d) an expert-led commission investigates. Opposition fairs best when (a) there is an endogenous cause for the crisis, (b) incumbents have been in office a long time, (c) incumbents had recent bad press, and (d) the commission is political-led. Efforts to exploit crises do matter: "Skillful office-holders can manage to politically 'contain' crises and thereby insulate themselves and their colleagues from sanctions and reputation losses" (Boin et al., 2008, p. 100).

Summary

Some basic premises can be drawn from the political crisis communication research. Situations can become crises because political actors choose to define them as such. Crises can be a political weapon used to damage political careers, enhance political careers, or promote policy change. Crises are a matter of framing and that framing process is contested. Winning the framing contest is an essential element of crisis communication. Crises can evoke fear and anxiety. Crises with an internal cause are more damaging to politicians than crises with an external cause.

The Search for Intersections

While the domains differ, we can identify some basic points of overlap between political and corporate crisis communication. The points of intersection include "political" research in the corporate crisis communication literature and conceptual overlap between the dominant research lines. From these points of intersection we can identify opportunities for how the two crisis communication research streams can inform one another.

Politicians in the Corporate Crisis Communication Research

There is extant research in the larger body of corporate crisis communication works that have a political focus. However, this research was not designed to examine political crisis communication as a unique entity but as part of the "corporate" crisis communication research in the public relations literature. In addition, the existing corporate crisis communication research focuses on individual politicians as the crisis managers.

Image repair theory has had the greatest application to political crises. As noted earlier, image repair theory was created as a general theory of image restoration and not for specific application to crisis communication in a corporate setting. As such, image repair theory is the best suited crisis communication theory for the case analysis of political crises. Researchers have examined a wide range of cases using image repair theory, including Kenneth Starr, President Clinton, President Reagan, Clarence Thomas, and Gary Condit (Benoit & Anderson, 1996; Benoit, Guillifor, & Panici, 1991; Benoit & McHale, 1999; Benoit & Nill, 1998; Benoit & Wells, 1998; Len-Rios & Benoit, 2004). The case study analyses favor the use of mortification (full apology) as the way for government officials to restore their reputations after a crisis. An example of apology's favored role is the advice from the Condit case. Gary Condit was a congressman from California who had an affair with an intern. She was later found murdered and the affair was publicly revealed during the investigation. Condit was not charged with the crime. The article argues that had Condit apologized, he would likely have been reelected to Congress instead of suffering defeat (Len-Rios & Benoit, 2004).

Huang (2006) used content analysis and an attribution theory framework (Bradford & Garrett, 1995), similar to situational crisis communication theory, to examine crisis responses and media coverage of political crises in Taiwan. Four different crises were examined to determine the effect of the crisis responses. The effect was assessed by examining the media coverage of the crises. All four crises were tied in some way to ethical violations. The comparative case study found support for the attribution theory-based model of how best to respond to ethical violations. In this study, the corporate recommendations appeared to hold true for the political arena as well. The one exception was that concession was not received positively in any of the four crisis situations (Huang, 2006). This literature analysis provides a foundation for understanding how corporate crisis communication might inform political crisis communication and vice versa.

Conceptual Overlap: Frames and Crisis Responsibility

There is a conceptual overlap between corporate and political crisis communication in the use of frames and crisis responsibility. The difference lies in the emphasis placed on the two concepts.

Frames are a critical aspect of political crisis communication. Politicians seek to frame crises, and success or failure in crisis communication is often a matter of whose crisis frame comes to dominate the situation (Boin, McConnell, & t'Hart, 2008; Kuypers, 1997). Frames are discussed in corporate crisis communication as well. Crisis types are taken as frames that suggest how stakeholders should interpret the situation (Coombs, 2007a). Moreover, Heath (2004) treats crisis communications as narratives. This focus fits perfectly with practitioner advice that crisis managers must tell their side of the story during a crisis; that is, must communicate and communicate quickly in a crisis (Coombs, 2007b). Political crisis communication emphasizes the ambiguity that creates a battle

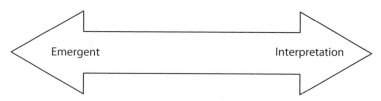

FIGURE 10.1 Crisis frame continuum.

for crisis frames. Situational factors that serve to define the crises are viewed as a constraint (Boin, t'Hart, & McConnell, 2009). Corporate crisis communication focuses more on the way situational factors define the crisis. Situational factors (data about the event) emerge thereby creating a frame, although oftentimes, crisis frames are open to debate (Hearit, 2006). We can place views of crisis frames on a continuum from emergent to interpretation. Figure 10.1 visually depicts the crisis frame continuum. Corporate crisis communication leans toward the emergent while political crisis communication favors interpretation. For an emergent crisis frame, a crisis exists and is driven by stakeholder perceptions, not crisis manager frames. For an interpretation crisis frame, crisis managers shape how stakeholders perceive the situation.

Crisis responsibility links the crisis to events external to the crisis manager or events related to the crisis manager. For instance, exogenized crises are beyond the control of the crisis manager thereby mitigating crisis responsibility. Endogenized crises are linked to the crisis managers—something that was done or not done precipitated the crisis (Boin, McConnell, & t'Hart, 2008). Conceptually there is a link between frames and crisis responsibility. In terms of the theory of crisis exploitation, crisis responsibility is *one* of the factors to consider, while it is *the* driving factor in situational crisis communication theory. Again, the two crisis communication literatures utilize the same concept but differ in the importance it plays in theory development and practice. This suggests that political crisis managers can gain insight into the factors that shape perceptions of crisis responsibility while corporate crisis managers can learn strategies for attempting to frame crises and what factors influence the ability to frame a crisis.

Conceptual Overlap: Crisis Promotion

Promotion of a crisis offers an even greater contrast. Politicians, especially presidents, might exploit a crisis for political advantage. For instance, a politician engages in crisis exploitation in hopes of winning passage of particular legislation or an election. The politician seeks to label a situation a *crisis* because the term has power and potential political utility. In contrast, corporate leaders actively shun the term *crisis*. In external discourse you may hear the terms *situation* and *incident*, but rarely is there a public discussion of a crisis. In corporations, the term *crisis* has power as well because it means resources will be mobilized and employed. But the term *crisis* is largely reserved for internal use. Managers do not go looking for a crisis to help validate or to win support for new policies.

However, in the corporate realm, stakeholders often engage in crisis exploitation as a means of forcing an organization to change policies and practices. Challenge crises can be viewed as crisis exploitation. If stakeholders can prove a crisis exists, or that the organization operates in an immoral or dangerous manner, the organization may be forced to change. Challenges are won by stakeholders when organizations fear the reputational damage the challenge may inflict upon them. If it appears other stakeholders will support a challenge, managers are likely to change policies and practices in order to preserve their reputational assets. For example, the Immokalee workers, a small union of agricultural workers in Florida, won a major concession from major fast food corporations because they promoted the issue of worker exploitation, which created a reputational threat for Yum! brand, McDonald's, and Burger King. Challenges are threatening when they have legitimacy, stakeholders pursue the challenge with a sense of urgency, and stakeholders can muster power resources such as the ability to communicate the challenge to others (Coombs & Holladay, 2007). In challenge crises, corporate managers play the role of incumbents trying to protect the status quo.

A common point in the crisis management literatures is a crisis having the potential to shape public policy. There is a recognized link between corporate crisis management and issues management. Poorly managed crises can trigger issues management and the application of new policies for corporations to follow. Effective crisis management reassures people the situation is fine and requires no further action. In other words, effective crisis management can diffuse an issue. Birkland's (1997) focusing event is a common reference for corporate and political crisis management. A focusing event brings attention to some problem/deficiency in society. Natural disasters are common focusing events, but Fishman (1999) argued that some corporate crises are focusing events. The attention creates the opportunity for policy action. An issue is thrust into the media spotlight and potentially catapulted on to the policy agenda. Once on the policy agenda, the issue may even produce policy change. However, as in crisis exploitation, there is no guarantee that a focusing event will produce new public policy (Fishman, 1999). Moreover, the policy change may only be symbolic and designed to reassure a nervous populace (Coombs & Holladay, in press). There is a strong match between how corporate crisis communication uses issues management and political crisis communication utilizes crisis exploitation. This suggests that corporate crisis managers can gain insight into how stakeholders might exploit crises to create change, and that political crisis managers can gain insights into how to derail political change efforts.

Conceptual Overlap: Negative Affect

Political and corporate crisis communication research share an interest in the negative affect generated by crises as well. Politicians attempt to use the fear and anxiety evoked by a crisis to pursue political objectives. Corporate crisis managers generally try to reduce the anxiety and anger generated by a crisis. The negative affect experienced by stakeholders can result in negative behaviors toward an organization such as reducing purchase intentions. Moreover, affect may be a barrier to effective corporate crisis communication. This suggests that corporate crisis managers might learn how to harness the benefits of negative affect while political crisis managers could understand how negative affect might hinder the pursuit of political objectives.

Exploration of Differences

There are four critical comparison points for exploring the differences between political and corporate crisis communication: (a) crisis managers, (b) crisis types, (c) constraints on the crisis communicators, and (d) what constitutes success in crisis management. The crisis type is an important driver in corporate crisis communication. The crisis type has significant implications for the selection of crisis response strategies. Constraints on crisis communicators can vary from corporate to the political arenas placing different limitations on the crisis communicators. Finally, what counts as success for crisis managers can vary between the two arenas. How one evaluates success and failure has implications for the selection of crisis response strategies.

Crisis Managers

Political crisis communication is complicated by the different types of potential crisis managers. On a base level, there are elected and appointed officials. Elected officials are "politicians" and have the constraint of seeking reelection. Appointed officials are "bureaucrats" and must follow their guidelines and please those with the appointment power. There is also the distinction between agencies and individuals. The crisis could be one that belongs to a specific agency or one involving an individual elected official. We can cross the two factors to create the 2 × 2 matrix in Table 10.3. Agencies would more closely parallel corporations, especially those with appointed leadership. In the U.S. case, appointed agencies would include the Food and Drug Administration (FDA) and Environmental Protection Agency (EPA). Elected agencies would include the Senate and the House of Representatives. Individual politicians would be akin to individual businesspeople accused of wrongdoing. While an individual's behavior can have some effect on the organization, the crisis is primarily for the individual not the organization. In such a case, there are two crisis managers, the individual and the organization. Hearit's (1994) individual/group dissociation illustrates quite clearly how organizations can separate

TABLE 10.3 Political Crisis Manager Matrix

	Elected	Appointed
Individual	Politicians	Bureaucrats
Agency	Elected Agencies	Bureaucratic Agencies

themselves effectively from miscreant individuals during a crisis. The organization claims one or a few employees are responsible for the crisis (individual) and do not reflect the true nature of the organization or group (Hearit, 1994).

Origins of Crises

For corporate crisis managers, the focus has been on handling crises that have origins within the organization. The origins are rooted in crisis types. Situational crisis communication theory divides crisis types into three categories: victim, accidental, and intentional. The specific types are listed in Table 10.4. Corporations and agencies can share any of the crisis types found in Table 10.4. Politicians and bureaucrats face a more limited range of crises involving

TABLE 10.4 Crisis Types

Victim crises: Stakeholder attribute minimal crisis responsibility to the organization

    Natural disasters: acts of nature such as hurricanes

    Rumors: false information about an organization spreads and can damage its reputation

    Workplace violence: attack on employees by current or former employee

    Product tampering: external actor damages the organization in some manner

Accident crises: Stakeholders attribute low crisis responsibility to the organization

    Challenges: some group claims the organization is operating in an immoral manner

    Technical error accidents: industrial accident is caused by equipment or technological failure

    Technical error product harm: product is defective or potentially harmful due to equipment or technological failure

Preventable crises: Stakeholders attribute strong crisis responsibility to the organization

    Human-error accident: industrial accident caused by improper job performance

    Human-error product harm: product is defective or potentially harmful as a result of improper job performance

    Organizational misdeed: management violates the law and/or willfully places stakeholders at risk (Coombs, 2007a).

challenges, human error accidents (ineffective execution of duties), and management misconduct. It is important to separate management misconduct further for politicians and bureaucrats. Management misconduct can include legal or moral violations. The difference is critical because legal violations provide additional constraints.

Most crises are a result of the organization's actions, and include organizational misdeeds, accidents, and product harm. Victim and challenge crises are external in locus and forced upon an organization. Managers must decide how they will handle these external threats and whether or not the threat even rises to the level of crisis. Crisis type matters because of its effect on attributions of crisis responsibility. Crisis responsibility is a constant variable across corporate crisis communication. In victim crises, the organization suffers collateral damage as external factors force the crisis onto the organization. Victim crises are the easiest to manage because of the minimal crisis responsibility they generate. A challenge crisis has external origins as well. The difference is that some external actor claims organizational behaviors are inappropriate and qualify as a crisis. A challenge is a framing contest, especially if the organization chooses to deny there is a problem.

Political crises are frequently external situations that the politicians step in to manage. Clearly, there is some connection between the politician and the crisis, but the origins are external/exogenize. Oftentimes, the politician is expected to be the "hero" and enters to rescue people. Examples would be government involvement in cases of dangerous pharmaceuticals or food poisoning outbreaks. Crisis responsibility is not an issue, rather, the politicians are judged on their ability to manage the crisis—a focus on performance. The Federal Emergency Management Agency (FEMA) being evaluated on its performance in Hurricane Katrina illustrates performance evaluation. Internal political crises do occur and include scandals and poor job performance. In such crises responsibility is an important factor. Internal/endogenized crises pose a much greater threat to politicians and institutions. Congressman Condit's affair with a staff member is an example of an internal/endogenized crisis. Consider how the Swedish government was expected to take action on a tsunami crisis halfway around the world (Strömbäck & Nord, 2006).

It is rare for corporations to be placed in the hero role during a crisis. Natural disaster may, however, create the opportunity for a corporate hero. Organizations that provide vital services, such as utilities, have a responsibility to return operations to normal as quickly as possible after a crisis. Stakeholders may have expectations for how quickly the vital services are restored. In such cases, the perceived crisis management skill found in political crisis communication is relevant. However, corporations as heroes seem to be a very limited occurrence. This discussion leads to the first proposition for further research:

Proposition 1: Political crisis managers are much more likely to manage "outside" crises and to attempt the hero role in crisis management.

Crisis Constraints

Stakeholders have expectations for how corporations should behave. In fact, stakeholder expectations are a defining characteristic of a crisis (Coombs, 2007b). Stakeholders hold organizations accountable for a variety of behaviors, including those related to social responsibility (Coombs & Holladay, 2010). Stakeholders hold expectations for government officials and agencies as well (Strömbäck & Nord, 2006). Tax money pays salaries so there is a clear sense of public accountability for government officials and agencies, and the media have both a professional and commercial interest in holding governmental officials, agencies, and politicians accountable. In turn, stakeholders have expectations that government officials and agencies will address many external threats as well as governmental failures. Both corporate and governmental crisis managers will feel the pressure to address failures to meet stakeholder expectations.

In the corporate context, organizations face financial constraints during a crisis. Apologies are extremely expensive crisis responses because they admit guilt. The admission of guilt means lawsuits stemming from the crisis will be won by the plaintiffs (crisis victims). Legal departments thus frequently want crisis managers to remain silent so as not to provide any evidence to be used against the organization during trials (Fitzpatrick & Ruben, 1995; Tyler, 1997). Thus, organizations may avoid apologies because they cannot absorb the financial burden associated with it (Coombs, 2007a; Tyler, 1997). Moreover, poor crisis communication results in reputational damage and loss of supportive behaviors that can have negative financial consequences for an organization, such as a drop in sales or stock price.

In political contexts, crisis victims can also sue politicians and agencies. However, the bureaucratic agency will probably still exist, elected agencies with definitely survive, and most politicians will keep their jobs. Appointed officials run the greatest risk of losing their jobs when crises result in lawsuits. Governments may go bankrupt for a time, but they continue to operate, which is not the case for most corporations. The reduced financial constraint should result in greater use of apologies among politicians. The situation is such that the crisis managers have little to lose but still face a strong need for public accountability. In fact, image restoration theory's bias toward apology as a default response fits well within the political context, and better in the political than in the corporate realm. This suggests a second proposition:

Proposition 2: In similar crises, political crisis responses will demonstrate a greater use of apology than corporate crisis communication.

However, legal crises are the same regardless of crisis manager type when guilt can result in prison terms. Managers, politicians, and bureaucrats will all follow legal strategies of releasing as little information as possible when they are at risk of being convicted of a crime (Fitzpatrick & Rubin, 1995). This suggests a third proposition:

Proposition 3: There should be no difference in how legal crises involving potential prison terms are managed in the political and corporate arenas.

Measure of Crisis Communication Success

The constraints is crisis communication have a direct relationship to measures of success in crisis communication. For a corporation, success is measured in terms of survival and financial performance. A corporation survives a crisis by being able to continue operations. Business continuity is a discipline closely akin to crisis management and concentrates on how to keep a business running after a crisis. Business continuity prepares for disruptions caused by various crises with contingency plans on how to keep operations going either at full or reduced capacity. Clearly, survival is a financial concern. Most corporations fail after a crisis because they could not operate thereby losing revenue and eventually ceasing to exist.

There are both direct and indirect indicators of financial performance. Direct measures include sales, stock price, and market share. Significant drops in any of these financial indicators are harmful to an organization and eventually could threaten its survival. In part, crisis communication seeks to reassure and to retain customers and investors. Such reassurance must be provided quickly, hence, the emphasis in corporate crisis communication on a fast response. Poorly handled crisis communication can exacerbate a crisis. Speed is not enough if the wrong message is delivered to stakeholders, however (Coombs, 2007b). Therefore, corporate crisis managers are under pressure to react fast and effectively to a crisis. A slow reaction or inattention to a crisis can intensify the financial damage from a crisis.

One reason a quick response is beneficial relates to the anger generated by a crisis. Both the situational crisis communication theory and contingency theory have examined how crises create anger among stakeholders. A crisis violates stakeholder expectations. The nature of those violations of expectations determines the anger felt by stakeholders. Research based on the situational crisis communication theory found that attributions of crisis responsibility are strongly correlated with anger. Stakeholders are much angrier when the crisis involves human error or management misconduct than for crises that produce weak attributions of crisis responsibility, such as product tampering or natural disasters (Coombs & Holladay, 2005). Moreover, the angrier the stakeholders following a crisis, the more likely they are to not purchase a product or to engage in negative word-of-mouth about an organization (Coombs & Holladay, 2007). By communicating quickly, crisis managers can diffuse the anger and prevent additional financial damage.

Reputation is an indirect financial indicator. Research has consistently proven that a strong, favorable corporate reputation creates financial benefits, including attracting customers, generating investment interest, motivating employees, and gaining positive media coverage (Fombrun & van Riel, 2004). Image repair theory and situational crisis communication theory both devote a considerable amount of attention to reputational concerns. Both emphasize that crisis communication is critical to repairing the reputational damage inflicted by the crisis. Corporations invest a great deal of resources into building their reputations so they want to protect this valuable intangible asset during and after a crisis.

For individual bureaucrats and politicians, the measure of success is retaining one's job. The bureaucrat keeps the appointed position and the politician wins reelection. Agencies have some concern over reputation as it may relate to funding, while elected agencies have little concern about reputation save for how it might affect elections. However, the reputation does not have the acuteness or time pressure experienced by corporations. For instance, the U.S. Senate and the House of Representatives will not disappear. Also note how after repeated, high-profile failures, FEMA still receives funding. Government and institutions are under little pressure to perform successfully in a crisis but individual political actors are. Those who are the face of the institution are at risk of job loss but the institution and those comprising it will survive.

Bureaucrats in danger of losing their positions and politicians facing elections are similar to corporate crisis managers except for the financial concern. They are under pressure to act quickly. A failure to respond quickly and effectively to the crisis can damage their reputations and result in loss of their office. Agencies and people behind the scenes, on the other hand, are unlikely to face immediate consequences for how they handle a crisis. The exception for bureaucratic agencies is if the crisis involves a public health threat. This is because a public health threat creates new expectations and possible loss of life, which demands a fast response (Ulmer, Sellnow, & Seeger, 2007a). This discussion suggests two additional propositions:

Proposition 4: Government officials under job pressure will react with the same speed as corporate crisis managers.

Proposition 5: Bureaucratic agencies will react more slowly than corporate crisis managers except when the crisis is a public health emergency.

Political officials, especially those facing elections, often look to the future. Political rhetoric has addressed this future orientation in research including Bormann's (1977) "fetching good out of evil" and the application of the jeremiad to political discourse. The jeremiad warns of doom but also can be used to present an alternative, bright future. Murphy (1990) notes how Robert Kennedy used the jeremiad after the assassination of Martin Luther King Jr. to create change. Murphy (1990) noted the jeremiad was used "as a means to restore social harmony in a time of crisis" (p. 402). The rhetoric of renewal shares this focus on a different and better future. Corporate crisis managers are limited by certain situational factors when they seek to use the rhetoric of renewal. Politicians seem to be less constrained when seeking to use the rhetoric of renewal. This leads to the final proposition suggested in this chapter:

> **Proposition 6**: Political crisis managers will use the rhetoric of renewal more frequently than corporate crisis managers.

Conclusion

Corporate and political crisis communication research have had limited intermixing of ideas when looking at references. The reference similarity is primarily corporate crisis communication research being cited by political crisis communication scholars. The separation is not unusual for crisis communication because the topic draws researchers from many different fields. A scholarly Tower of Babel emerges, creating fragmentation in the crisis communication research. A focal point of this chapter is to build a more developed bridge between the corporate and political crisis communication research. Toward that end, the chapter has sought to identify (a) important conceptual overlaps and (b) why unique differences exist between the two areas.

The conceptual overlap provides an opportunity for political and corporation crisis communication researchers and practitioners to learn from one another. Lessons learned in political crisis communication can be adapted to corporate crisis communication and vice versa. The unique aspects of political and corporate crisis communication provide the opportunity to execute comparative research to determine the validity and extent of these unique aspects. Each of the six propositions presented in this chapter offers an opportunity for comparative crisis communication research. This chapter overviews the fertile ground for research designed specifically to address the unique aspects of political crisis communication and how that may differ from its corporate counterpart. Researchers will stake their claims I hope and determine what insights can be gained by applying corporate crisis communication to political crisis communication, and vice versa.

References

Benoit, W. L. (1995). *Accounts, excuses, and apologies: A theory of image restoration*. Albany, NY: SUNY Press.

Benoit, W. L. (1997). Hugh Grant's image restoration discourse: An actor apologizes. *Communication Quarterly, 45*(3), 251–267.

Benoit, W. L., & Anderson, K. K. (1996). Blending politics and entertainment: Dan Quayle versus Murphy Brown. *Southern Communication Journal, 62*(1), 73–85.

Benoit, W. L., & Brinson, S. (1994). AT&T: Apologies are not enough. *Communication Quarterly, 42*(1), 75–88.

Benoit, W. L., Gullifor, P., & Panici, D. (1991). President Reagan's defensive discourse on the Iran–Contra affair. *Communication Studies, 42*(4), 272–294.

Benoit, W. L., & McHale, J. (1999). "Just the facts, ma'am": Starr's image repair discourse viewed in 20/20. *Communication Quarterly, 47*(3), 265–280.

Benoit, W. L., & Nill, D. M. (1998). A critical analysis of Judge Clarence Thomas's statement before the Senate Judiciary Committee. *Communication Studies, 49*(3), 179–195.

Benoit, W. L., & Wells, W. T. (1998). An analysis of three image restoration discourses on Whitewater. *Journal of Public Advocacy, 3*(1), 21–37.

Birkland, T. A. (1997). *After disaster: Agenda setting, public policy, and focusing events*. Washington, DC: Georgetown University Press.

Boin, A., 't Hart, P., & McConnell, A. (2009). Crisis exploitation: Political and policy impacts of framing contests. *Journal of European Public Policy, 16*(1), 81–106.

Boin, A., McConnell, A., & t'Hart, P. (2008). Governing after a crisis. In A. Boin, A. McConnell, & P. 't Hart (Eds.), *Governing after crisis: The politics of investigation, accountability and learning* (pp. 3–32). Cambridge, England: Cambridge University Press.

Bormann, E. (1977). Fetching good out of evil: A rhetorical use of calamity. *Quarterly Journal of Speech, 65*(2), 130–139.

Bostdorff, D. M. (1994). *The presidency and the rhetoric of foreign crisis*. Columbia: University of South Carolina Press.

Bradford, J. L., & Garrett, D. E. (1995). The effectiveness of corporate communicative responses to accusations of unethical behavior. *Journal of Business Ethics, 14*(11), 875–892.

Cobb, R. W., Ross, J. K., & Ross, M. H. (1976). Agenda building as a comparative political process. *American Political Science Review, 70*(1), 126–138.

Coombs, W. T. (2007a). Attribution theory as a guide for post-crisis communication research. *Public Relations Review, 33*(2), 135–139.

Coombs, W. T. (2007b). *Ongoing crisis communication: Planning, managing, and responding* (2nd ed.). Los Angeles: Sage.

Coombs, W. T., & Holladay, S. J. (2005). Exploratory study of stakeholder emotions: Affect and crisis. In N. M. Ashkanasy, W. J. Zerbe, & C. E. J. Hartel (Eds.), *Research on emotion in organizations: Vol. 1. The effect of affect in organizational settings* (pp. 271–288). New York: Elsevier

Coombs, W. T., & Holladay, S. J. (2007). The negative communication dynamic: Exploring the impact of stakeholder affect on behavioral intentions. *Journal of Communication Management, 11*(4), 300–312.

Coombs, W. T., & Holladay, S. J. (2010). *PR strategy and application: Managing influence*. Malden, MA: Wiley-Blackwell.

Coombs, W. T., & Holladay, S. J. (in press). Self-regulatory discourse: Corrective or quiescence? *Management Communication Quarterly*.

Dionisopolous, G. N., & Vibbert, S. L. (1988). CBS vs Mobil Oil: Charges of creative bookkeeping. In H. R. Ryan (Ed.), *Oratorical encounters: Selected studies and sources of 20th century political accusation and apologies* (pp. 214–252). Westport, CT: Greenwood.

Dow, B. J. (1989). The function of epideictic and deliberative strategies in presidential crisis rhetoric. *Western Journal of Speech Communication, 53*(3), 294–310.

Entman, R. M. (1993). Framing: Toward clarification of fractured paradigm. *Journal of Communication, 43*(4), 51–58.

Fishman, D. A. (1999). ValuJet flight 592: Crisis communication theory blended and extended. *Communication Quarterly, 47*(4), 345–375.

Fitzpatrick, K. R., & Rubin, M. S. (1995). Public relations vs. legal strategies in Organizational crisis decisions. *Public Relations Review, 21*(1), 21–33.

Fombrun, C. J., & van Riel, C. B. M. (2004). *Fame and fortune: How successful companies build winning reputations*. New York: Prentice-Hall Financial Times.

Hearit, K. M. (1994). Apologies and public relations crises at Chrysler, Toshiba, and Volvo. *Public Relations Review, 20*(2), 113–125.

Hearit, K. M. (2006). *Crisis management by apology: Corporate response to allegations of wrongdoing.* Mahwah, NJ: Erlbaum.

Heath, R. L. (2004). Telling a story: A narrative approach to communication during crisis. In R. L. Heath & D. P Millar (Eds.), *Responding to crisis: A rhetorical approach to crisis communication* (pp. 167–188). Mahwah, NJ: Erlbaum.

Huang, Y. H. (2006). Crisis situations, communication strategies, and media coverage: A multicase study revisiting the communication response model. *Communication Research, 33*(3), 180–205.

Jin, Y. (2009). The effects of public's cognitive appraisal of emotions in crises on crisis coping and strategy assessment. *Public Relations Review, 35*(3), 310–313.

Jin, Y., & Pang, A. (2010). Future directions of crisis communication research: Emotions in crisis—the next frontier. In W. T. Coombs & S. J. Holladay (Eds.), *Handbook of crisis communication* (pp. 677–682). Malden, MA: Blackwell.

Jin, Y., Pang, A., & Cameron, G. T. (2007). Integrated crisis mapping: Towards a public-based, emotion-driven conceptualization in crisis communication. *Sphera Publica, 7*(1), 81–96.

Kent, M. L. (2010). What is a public relations "crisis"? Refocusing crisis research. In W. T. Coombs & S. J. Holladay (Eds.), *Handbook of crisis communication* (pp. 705–712). Malden, MA: Blackwell.

Kiewe, A. (Ed.) (1994). *The modern presidency and crisis rhetoric.* Wesport, CT: Praeger.

Kuypers, J. A. (1997). *Presidential crisis rhetoric and the press in the post-cold war world.* Westport, CT: Praeger.

Lee, B. K. (2004). Audience-oriented approach to crisis communication: A study of Hong Kong consumers' evaluations of an organizational crisis. *Communication Research, 31*(5), 600–618.

Len-Rios, M. E. & Benoit, W. L. (2004). Gary Condit's image repair strategies: Determined denial and differentiation. *Public Relations Review, 30*(1), 95–106.

McConnell, & P. t'Hart (Eds.), *Governing after crisis: The politics of investigation, accountability, and learning* (pp. 3–32). New York: Cambridge University Press.

Murphy, J. M. (1990). "A time of shame and sorrow": Robert F. Kennedy and the American jeremiad. *Quarterly Journal of Speech, 76*(4), 401–414.

Sabatier, P. (1988). An Advocacy coalition model of policy change and the role of policy-oriented learning therein. *Policy Sciences, 21*, 129–168.

Strömbäck, J., & Nord, L. W. (2006). Mismanagement, mistrust and missed opportunities: a study of the 2004 tsunami and Swedish political communication. *Media Culture and Society, 28*(5), 789–800

Tyler, L. (1997). Liability means never being able to say you're sorry: Corporate guilt, legal constraints, and defensiveness in corporate communication. *Management Communication Quarterly, 11*(1), 51–73.

Ulmer, R. R., Seeger, M. W., & Sellnow, T. L. (2007a). *Effective crisis communication: Moving from crisis to opportunity.* Thousand Oaks, CA: Sage.

Ulmer, R. R., Seeger, M. W., & Sellnow, T. L. (2007b). Post-crisis communication and renewal: Expanding the parameters of post-crisis discourse. *Public Relations Review, 33*(2), 130–134.

Ware, B. L., & Linkugel, W. A. (1973). They spoke in defense of themselves: On the generic criticism of apologia. *Quarterly Journal of Speech, 59*(2), 273–283.

Windt, T. O., Jr. (1973). The presidency and speeches on international crises: Repeating the rhetorical past. *Speaker and Gavel, 2*(2), 6–14.

Young, M. J., & Launer, M. K. (1988). KAL 007 and the superpowers: An international argument. *Quarterly Journal of Speech, 74*(3), 271–295.

11

POLITICAL PUBLIC RELATIONS AND RELATIONSHIP MANAGEMENT

John A. Ledingham

In 1984 Ferguson presented a review of public relations research from the previous 9 years. She concluded that the core of public relations is the relationship between an organization and its publics, and insisted that:

> the unit of study [of public relations research] should not be the organization, nor the public, nor the communication process [but] rather, the unit of study should be the relationship between an organization and its publics.

> (p. ii)

Ferguson's admonition represented a call for a new perspective of public relations, a foundation that would provide the best opportunity for public relations to cast off the confines of "journalism with a business orientation," or "the conscience of the corporation" and develop an overarching theory based on the relationship between an organization and its key publics. Specifically noting that the communication process should not be the unit of study, her manifesto was nothing less than a reordering of the field, a sea change in the way public relations should be thought of, and a move to elevate the discipline from a craft to a strategic management function crucial to the successful interaction of organizations and publics. Today, we see the results of Ferguson's insight in the discipline that has evolved; a management function that derives its goals from analysis, with plans appropriate to those goals, and evaluation strategies consistent with those of other disciplines.

Ferguson's thesis has found recognition under the label of "relationship management," a concept of public relations in which the discipline's historic near-compulsive focus on communication is replaced with the broader perspective that communication is one—but not the only—strategic tool used in managing an organization–public relationship (Cutlip, Center, & Broom, 1985).

Defining Relationship Management and Political Public Relations

As noted in the introductory chapter by Strömbäck and Kiousis, public relations is often defined as the *management of communication*, with the distinction between modern PR and past practice being the notion of PR as a *management* function. Others define PR as the management of organization–public relationships *through* communication (Cutlip, Center, & Broom, 1994). However, both perspectives reflect the notion that the core focus and defining imperative of public relations is communication. In fact, there are numerous initiatives and activities that are a part of public relations practice that are not communication per se. For example, a special event is not in and of itself communication, nor are open houses, walkathons, or the activities of a speakers' bureau. The same can be said of lobbying, stockholder relations, and development; which are *practice applications*, not communication. Thus, the notion of relationship management (RM) differs from other perspectives in that it is concerned with the management of organization–public relationships (OPRs) not only through communication, but also through activities and practice applications, in short, *behaviors.*

That some define public relations as a field primarily concerned with communication, rather than relationships, reflects the difficulty public relations practitioners have with specifying what public relations *is*. As has been previously noted (Ledingham 2001; Ledingham & Bruning, 1998), when public relations practitioners are asked what public relations *is*, they generally respond by recalling what public relations *does*.

Q. *"What is public relations?"*

A. *"We do publicity, press relations, and produce the annual report and such."*

In fact, the primary function of public relations is to manage organization–public relationships. This is achieved through both symbolic behavior (communication) *and* actual behaviors in an ongoing exchange between organizations and publics, organizations and organizations, and publics and other publics. Moreover, focusing on the interests and goals shared by the entities in the relationship, and striving to ensure mutual understanding and mutual benefits, is a *strategy* that supports the practical and theoretical benefits of long-term relationships. Accordingly, I have offered the following definition of relationship management:

> Public relations is the ethical and efficient management of organization–public relationships, focused over time on common interests and shared goals in support of mutual understanding and mutual benefit.

(Ledingham, 2003, p.190)

Thus "relationship management," or "the relational perspective of public relations" (Ledingham & Bruning, 1998) can be compared with the notion of political public relations proposed by Strömbäck and Kiousis in the introductory chapter of this collection, and defined as follows:

> Political public relations is the management process by which an organization or individual actor for political purposes, through purposeful communication and action, seeks to influence and to establish, build, and maintain relationships and reputations with its key publics to help support its mission and achieve its goals.

The above definition underscores the importance of relationships in political public relations; and further suggests that relationships are formed not only through communication, but also through action. In this regard, political public relations and relationship management share a similar perspective.

Both relationship management and political public relations have undergone tremendous growth in recent years, spurred by the extraordinary amounts of money poured into political campaigns and as a part of the evolution of public relations. Also, a number of practice applications—including lobbying, issues management, and crisis communication—have been revisited in light of the relational perspective. However, the relational perspective has yet to be applied to political public relations.

This chapter contributes to the body of knowledge by identifying the similarities and differences between relationship management and political public relations, and the results of viewing political public relations through the lens of relationship management. In the process, the literature of both relationship management and political public relations is reviewed, and a number of theories that explain and predict organizational and stakeholder behavior are discussed, including social exchange, selectivity, stakeholder loyalty, and effects theory. We begin with a review of the literature of relationship management.

Review of Literature of Relationship Management

A content analysis of *Public Relations Review* and the *Journal of Public Relations Research* for the years 1985 through 2004 found that the literature on relationship management "virtually exploded" (Ki & Hon, 2006). During that period, 39 articles concerning relationship management were reported published in the two premier public relations journals. An audit, which included additional scholarly journals, expanded the number of relationship management publications to more than 50 (Ledingham, 2006).

The literature on relationship management starts, not surprisingly, with the search for a definition. In Broom, Casey, and Ritchey's (1997) article, the authors called for a definition of an organization–public relationship (OPR), and Ledingham and Bruning (1998) quickly responded with the following:

[an organization–public relationship is] the state that exists between an organization and its key publics in which the actions of one can impact the social, economic, or political well-being of the other.

(p. 62)

Broom, Casey, and Ritchey (2000) then offered their definition, setting forth an agenda for further research. Their definition is seen below:

Organization–public relationships are represented by patterns of interaction, transaction, exchange, and linkage between an organization and its publics. These relationships have properties that are distinct from the identities, attributes and perceptions of the individuals and social collectivities in the relationships. Though dynamic in nature, organization–public relationships can be described at a single point in time and tracked over time.

(p. 18)

Broom and Dozier (1990) then suggested coorientational measurement as a way of capturing the views of both an organization's members and those of stakeholders regarding an organization–public relationship. Coorientation asks both organization members and stakeholders to rate a set of variables concerning the organization. Both organization members and stakeholders also are then asked to predict the way in which the other entity will rate the variables. In this way, measures of *agreement* and *accuracy* are generated. The notion of *agreement* refers to the degree to which the ratings of the organization members and those of the stakeholder group are similar. And, the notion of *accuracy* refers to the ability of each entity to predict the way in which the other entity rated the variables. In this system, the more positive is the relationship the higher the degree of *agreement* and *accuracy*.

The literature also includes a study of the impact of time in a relationship on the quality of that relationship (Ledingham, Bruning, & Wilson, 1999), which noted that in some instances it might take decades for a relationship to solidify. In addition, an edited text concerning public relations as relationship management (Ledingham & Bruning, 2000) provided public relations scholars with the opportunity to contribute chapters that reflected their thinking in regard to relationship management. For example, Broom et al. (2000) provided an update of their earlier (1997) model of an organization–public relationship, while Grunig and Huang (2000) contributed an amended version of the earlier Broom et al. model with relationship maintenance strategies added. Coombs (2000) took advantage of the opportunity to further the notion of "relational history" as a determinant of organizational–public relationship status, while Bridges and Nelson (2000) concluded that: "[an] effective commitment to ongoing stakeholder relations … may help mitigate the outcome of conflicts… with regard to managing issues" (p. 111). Wilson (2001) explored the notion of "stakeholder loyalty" and concluded that the theory: "...provides an exciting new direction of inquiry in the field of public relations" (p. 144). Kruckeberg (2000) called on public relations experts to "reconcile their organizations' ongoing relationship with a range of...publics that are evolving within [a] global ... society" (p. 146). Toth (2000) offered a model that positions public relations as an interpersonal function operating between an organization and its stakeholders, while Dimmick, Bell, Burgiss, and Ragsdale (2000), advanced a "professional" model of public relations impressive in both its breadth and depth. And, Thomlison (2000)—an interpersonal and intercultural scholar— contributed a review of social exchange theory in relationship research, focusing particularly on its usefulness in explaining stakeholder behavior. Ledingham and Bruning (2000) demonstrated how perceptions of the quality of an organization– public relationship could impact stakeholders' decision making, while Bruning and Ledingham (2000) reported that organization–public relationships operate much the same in a business-to-business context as they do in an organization– stakeholder context. And, Esposito and Koch (2000) explored the idea of relationship within the context of network news programs.

Separate from the edited collection, Hallahan (1999) had revisited the notion of "community" as a foundation for building and managing relationships. Wise's (2007) more recent review of lobbying in Washington, DC underscored the importance of relationships in building trust between lobbyists and those they seek to influence, noting that lobbyists "regularly used words such as 'important,' 'critical,' and 'essential' when speaking of relationships" (p. 366).

Moreover, Ledingham (2003) contributed a summary of the contribution of relationship management to the literature of public relations, as follows:

> ...programs designed to generate mutual understanding and benefit—the desired outcome of management of organization–public relationships— can contribute to attainment of an organization's social, economic, and political goals when those programs focus on the common wants, needs, and expectations of organizations and interacting publics.
>
> (pp. 193–194)

The literature also highlighted the historic problem of justifying the cost of public relations initiatives. Traditionally, some practitioners have looked to message production as the solution to every public relations problem, often without fully considering the consequences of the messaging (Broom, 1986; Ledingham & Bruning, 1998, 2000). Consequently, those practitioners sometimes justified expenditures by citing the number of messages produced or press releases sent to the media, a procedure unacceptable to organizational managers seeking documented results rather than production metrics.

The review also brought to the foreground a series of other issues that concern relationship management scholars. For example, Grunig (1993) had early on suggested that a focus on communication (*symbolic behaviors*) to the detriment of activities (*behavioral relationships*) negatively impacts the ability of the organization "to demonstrate that their efforts contribute to the goals of ... organizations by building long-term *behavioral* relationships with strategic publics" (p. 136). More recently, Ledingham (2006) had called for organizations to not only "talk the talk," but also "walk the walk" by not merely communicating, but also supporting relationships with behavior.

The existence of two different views of what public relations ought to be trying to accomplish also is found in the literature (Grunig, 1992). One view sees public relations as a way to earn a return on investment, carry out the policies of upper management, and act as a "buffer" between an organization and its stakeholders. In that scenario, public relations has no real role in policy setting, and functions simply as an instrument of implementation. An alternative perspective—that of "strategic management"—involves public relations in the decision-making process, and as a part of the strategic team responsible for identifying the consequences of policy.

Another report from the literature concerns the notion of stakeholder loyalty, in which members of a stakeholder group were found to be favorably disposed toward an organization. That disposition may take the form of a tendency to accept the behaviors, position, or communication of an organization in the face of opposing positions (Ledingham & Bruning, 1998). The researchers found that those who perceive that an organization is committed to mutual understanding and mutual benefit tend more often to view the organization favorably (Ledingham & Bruning, 1998). Stakeholder loyalty also has been linked to a number of other relationship dimensions, including trust, openness, and time in the relationship (Bruning & Ledingham, 1999; Ledingham & Bruning, 1998).

The literature also contains several additional reports of varying interest, including a "planning pyramid" which seeks to ensure that cultural imperatives are included in PR campaigns (Ledingham, 2009a) and a chronology of relationship management research (Ledingham, 2009b). Moreover, the research literature indicates that an organization's historical linkage to a community and contributions to its well-being are associated with higher relationship ratings (Ledingham & Bruning, 2000). Local governmental sponsorship of community activities also have been found to play a role in the decision of residents to remain in a declining community (Ledingham, 2003). And, higher levels of satisfaction occurred among reporters when media relations practitioners adapted their practices to meet the needs and expectations of those reporters (Ledingham & Bruning, 2007).

Review of Political Public Relations Literature

The literature of political public relations addresses the rise of political public relations and its impact on the news media and on political news

(Davis, 2002), and contains reports concerning corporate decision making in selecting a political campaign strategy (Hillman & Hitt, 1999), and increases in corporate political communication activity (Wilson, 1994). In addition, there are suggestions that community integration and mass and interpersonal communication can predict local citizen participation (McLeod, Scheufele, & Moy, 1999). There are also reports of research on new public communicative services, and linkages between political communication and civic malaise (Strömbäck & Shehata, 2010).

Further, the literature also includes articles that deal with the notion of political marketing; that is, the application of marketing principles to politics. That concept affords the opportunity to apply public relations theory, particularly that of relationship management, to political campaigns. Marketing, of course, holds that consumers have needs and that the role of marketing is to satisfy those needs, reflected in the common-language description of marketing as "meeting consumers' needs at a profit." Accordingly, a marketing orientation toward political activities can be expected to follow a marketing model (Strömbäck, Mitrook, & Kiousis, 2010). That is, (a) intelligence is gathered that identifies what consumers want (analyze the environment), (b) strategies are developed to ensure awareness and availability of the product (plan), (c) the product is made available throughout the marketplace (implement the plan), and (d) the efficiency of the process is evaluated (evaluate).

According to the literature, a campaign that is *market oriented* grows out of a political party that seeks to know what is important to voters and tries to meet those needs (Strömbäck, 2007). However, as has been pointed out, being market *oriented* and using marketing *techniques* are not the same thing. Rather, a campaign can employ marketing techniques such as advertising, PR, direct mail (or e-mail) marketing, and the like, but if the campaign is not grounded in finding what voters need and making efforts to satisfy those needs, it is not "market oriented" (Strömbäck, Mitrook, & Kiousis, 2010).

A *product-oriented party*, on the other hand, develops its beliefs, promises, pledges, and platform internally and presents them for an up or down vote (Strömbäck, 2007). Sales techniques are used to "sell" ideas that the party feels are superior. If voters reject the positions, it is assumed that is because they were not sold correctly, because it could not be that the positions were incorrect or unattractive (Strömbäck, Mitrook, & Kiousis, 2010). In this approach, the notion of *product positioning* is key. If the candidate is a newcomer to politics, like a product new to the marketplace, the initial task of the campaign is to create awareness ("Now, for the first time XXX is available..."). When facing competition, the task is to show how the candidate/product is better by emphasizing a *product differential* ("...XXX has little green cleansing chips/a superior voting record"). Relationships in this context are an investment to be called upon at election time.

The Rise of Political Parties and the Emergence of the Mass Media

Political communication—a basic component of political public relations—has been around as long as there have been candidates and issues. Roman candidates painted campaign slogans on the walls of their cities. Later, "town criers" sang paid political "commercials" to London residents set to the melody of popular songs. Broadsides in medieval Europe carried the political messages of those who paid for printing. Yet, it is interesting that there is no provision in the U.S. Constitution for political parties. Rather, the Founding Fathers must have hoped that the innate wisdom of the citizenry would lead to harmonious decisions without the need for the contentiousness that often characterizes political parties. Nonetheless, the ink on the U.S. Constitution was barely dry before the newly formed government's plan to provide infrastructure in the form of roads and canals led to a split between merchants and farmers, which resulted in the formation of the Federalist Party (favoring) and the Democratic-Republican Party (opposed). The debate between the two political philosophies was carried out in a series of publications that were, in fact, an early example of political public relations.

While some newspapers trace their beginnings to being the "house organ" of a political party, others were the result of the dedication of a person or cause. For example, Benjamin Lundy (1789–1839) was a leather goods maker residing in St. Clairsville, Ohio. In spring 1820, Lundy loaded the leather goods he had produced over the winter on a raft and poled down the Ohio River to St. Louis to sell them as he did every spring. Seeing families of slaves sold on the docks at St. Louis so affected Lundy that after selling his goods and the raft in St. Louis, he returned to St. Clairesville, sold his leather-making tools and used the money to create an abolitionist newspaper entitled *The Genius of Universal Emancipation*, which lasted until his death (Clark, 2008).

Lundy's *Emancipation* was but one of many "special interest" newspapers increasingly available to growing metropolitan populations. By the 1820s, the Industrial Revolution had spawned population centers around factory sites, and as the cities grew, so also grew a commitment to free, universal, compulsory public education. Thus, increased literacy, political discourse, the needs of immigrant populations, and an emerging merchant class spurred the growth of newspapers (Biagi, 2007). The "tipping point" came when Benjamin Day imported the concept of the "Penny Press" from England and in 1833 began selling the *New York Sun* for one cent (Campbell, 2001). Merchants took advantage of the increase in circulation to promote their goods and services through newspaper advertising, changing the source of revenue for newspapers from subscription to space sales (Eksterowicz & Roberts, 2000). A number of other factors contributed to the growth of newspapers including a dramatic drop in the cost of newsprint, and new Hoe & Company presses that could print up to 4,000 copies of a newspaper per hour.

The penny press ended around 1860 and was succeeded by the era of yellow journalism, a period characterized by rabid competition between the then giants of journalism, Joseph Pulitzer and William Randolph Hearst (Campbell, 2001). Their circulation wars generated sensationalized "reporting," which probably sparked the Spanish-American War. The competing newspapers carried tales of "monkey men" living in "golden cities" on the moon, and reported political scandals, exploitation, and malfeasance wildly exaggerated or simply false. By the mid-1890s, the situation had gotten so bad that the *New York Times,* the *Christian Science Monitor,* and the *Wall Street Journal* led a charge for a new set of journalistic standards, including the then-novel concept of "balanced reporting" (Connery, 1992). As the 20th century progressed, an economically powerful and Constitutionally protected free press alternately attacked and colluded with politicos to mobilize public sentiment against a series of scoundrels *de jour,* including at various times the North (or the South), Spain, France, England (if it were a slow news decade), the indolent rich, socialists, "fellow travelers," Europe, liberals, "leftists," "card-carrying members of the Communist Party," "one-worlders," "socialized medicine," "peaceniks," and so on.

The nation's first public relations practitioners used the press to raise the money needed to carry on World War I (Cutlip, Center, & Broom, 1994). Franklin Delano Roosevelt broadcast his "fire side chats" over the "new" medium of radio (Baum & Kernell, 2001) and became the first U.S. President to appear on television (at the World's Fair in 1939). The presidential election of 1948 concluded with winner Harry S. Truman photographed grinning and holding high a copy of the *Chicago Tribune* that, in its early editions, had headlines trumpeting the "victory" of Thomas Dewey (Sitkoff, 1971). By the presidential campaign of 1952 and the catchy Republican slogan "I Like Ike," televised political advertising had arrived and produced a permanent change in political campaigning (Devlin, 1986). Political public relations had now morphed into a major part of the American political scene, and it remains so today.

Relationship Management and Political Public Relations: Differences and Similarities

There are several similarities between *political public relations* and relationship management. Both focus on building relationships with key stakeholder groups, and both mimic the four-step management process. However, there are also substantial differences.

- Market-oriented political public relations identifies what stakeholders want and offers it, whereas relationship management identifies jointly held interests and goals as the basis for relationships.
- Relationship management seeks to build lasting relationships that are mutually satisfying. Market-oriented political public relations employs short-term strategies to reach the limited goal of winning an election.

- Relationship management is more likely to result in a *sharing* of power, access, and community support, whereas market-oriented political public relations is about *controlling* power.
- Product-oriented parties have a mantra (cut taxes, smaller government, reduce benefits) driven not by the electorate, but by a rigid ideology. In practice, market-oriented parties may in fact be far less flexible than are most market-oriented organizations. Other differences include the following:
- "Traditional PR," with notable exceptions, functions as a support mechanism for organizational policy, and uses purchased and "free" or "earned" media to promote and protect the policies of an organization, as decided by senior management. Sales (or product)-oriented political public relations has a viewpoint, and seeks to "sell" that viewpoint.
- The relationship management perspective is inexorably linked to building enduring relationships, whereas product-oriented public relations, as a function of political public relations, is just as firmly fixed on the gaining of power.
- The intent, exchanges, and processes of relationship management and political public relations can be strikingly different, primarily because the locus of each is different.
- The locus of relationship management—by definition and emerging practice—is relationships. For political public relations the locus—partly by definition but even more by practice—is power and stability.
- Effective relationship management results in a quality relationship, whereas effective political public relations results in gaining or maintaining power within the political system.
- Whereas relationship management seeks mutuality, political public relations seeks victory.
- Philosophically, relationship management seeks balance, whereas political public relations seeks dominance.
- Whereas public relations effectiveness is seen in the quality of the relationship, that of political public relations is seen in behavior, including voter registration, donations, and voting.

Political stakeholders could benefit from political public relations practitioners adopting some of the concepts of relationship management, such as shared interests, mutuality, and the idea of building relationships over time. Adopting these concepts to political public relations could promote greater attention to substantive issues, solidify long-term relationships and help to establish overbridging political philosophies rather than relying on the short-term strategy of scare tactics or the shock value of pseudo issues that are more or less typical of campaign sloganeering.

Three more specific theories are helpful in explaining organization–stakeholder relationships and are discussed below:

Social Exchange Theory

A number of theories are valuable in explaining organizational and stakeholder behavior, but none more so than social exchange theory. Social exchange conceptualizes the social environment in terms of exchanges and expectations. The success or failure of an organization–public relationship can be determined by whether those exchanges meet expectations. For example, a crisis can often be traced to an organization's "failure to meet the social norms and expectations of stakeholders" (Coombs, 2000, p. 77). Social exchange portends a *comparison level of alternatives* in which individuals choose behaviors that promise the most benefit (Thomlison, 2000). Stakeholders consistently make decisions based on the comparison level of alternatives (Bruning & Ledingham, 1999; Ledingham & Bruning, 1998).

Moreover, social exchange theory suggests that relationships thought to provide the most benefit are more likely to flourish, a notion supported by research (Ledingham & Bruning, 1998; Bruning & Ledingham, 2000). Other factors include loyalty (Ledingham & Bruning, 1998), convenience (Bruning & Ledingham, 2008), satisfaction (Bruning Castle, & Schrepfer, 2004), community leadership (Ledingham, 2003), and mutual understanding and mutual benefit (Ledingham & Bruning, 1998, 2000). The organization (or candidate) that best positions itself as providing the most benefit usually will win out. However, benefit can be offset by the quality, duration, or loyalty associated with an organization–public relationship.

Effects Theory

Because the practice both of public relations and political public relations frequently involves the mass and the social media—both as disseminators of communication and as reporters of events—it is appropriate that the matter of media effects, or "effects" theory be explored. Effects theory tells us that the primary impact of communication is to reinforce that which we already believe (Littlejohn, 2003) and that to gain maximum efficiency, mediated and interpersonal communication should be used in tandem, with each supporting the other, "intertwined like the strands of a rope" (Grunig, 1993).

Nonetheless, the mass media are a double-edged sword. Procandidate communication is effective in reinforcing support for a candidate. However, the same message when viewed by a person opposed to that candidate may well reinforce negative feelings toward that candidate. Also, there is little evidence for the idea that mass mediated messages have the ability to change the support of uncommitted recipients, or especially those who have already decided on a candidate, except in instances of calamity (Littlejohn, 2003).

Similarly, internal messages designed to encourage organizational loyalty, or fidelity to an organization's way of doing things, will not be successful if they are not in keeping with the sentiment of that internal stakeholder group. Internal campaigns will consequently run into major problems if they fail to understand that communication—mediated or interpersonal—mainly tends to reinforce the predispositions of message recipients. Thus, the most important "effect" of mediated messages may be to strengthen support rather than to change minds.

Selectivity Theory

Selectivity theory helps us to understand how we process messages. The average American household is exposed to several hundred mediated messages each week (Toffler, 1971). Selectivity theory posits three components in the way we unconsciously filter messages. The first is "selective attention." That is, we attend to some messages we are already interested in. If not interested, we tend not to process a message. We also are selective in the way in which we interpret a message. If the message is consistent with our values, we tend to assign higher value to it than we would if it ran counter to our views. Finally, we are selective in what we retain, also based on our interests (Littlejohn, 2003).

Selectivity theory helps us to understand that, in somewhat the same way effects theory operates, the "impact" of messages is mostly seen with those who already are disposed to act (or vote) one way or another, and are best thought of as useful in mobilizing support rather than changing minds.

Implications

Throughout this review, it is important to keep in mind that not all organization–public relationships are the same, any more than all interpersonal relationships are the same (Hutton, Goodman, Alexander, & Genest, 2001). Some are more important to the actors involved than are others. Some require more maintenance. The balance of any number of factors in a relationship—access, trust, control—may shift, impacting the state of the organization–public relationship (Broom et al., 2000).

It also helps to recall what the participants bring to the relationship. For organizations that includes knowing what is important to stakeholders, supporting activities important to both entities, mutual understanding and benefit, and shared control. Stakeholders need to appreciate the requirements of the organization, support the interests they have in common, and work together to pursue the goals they share.

Moreover, management does not mean manipulation. Indeed, the idea of *ethics and balance* can be traced to the symmetrical model of public relations developed by Grunig and Hunt (1984). The notion of *common interests and shared goals* provides the organization–public relationship with focus and draws on persuasion theory (Littlejohn, 1995). It also is important to keep in mind that the notion of an *organization–public relationship* is grounded in interpersonal relationship building, and that the literature of interpersonal relationships can provide clues as to expected organizational behavior (Grunig, Grunig, & Ehling, 1992; Ledingham, Bruning, Thomlison, & Lesko, 1997; Thomlison, 2000).

To recap, relational theory holds that relationship management is the ethical and efficient management of organization–public relationships focused, over time, on common interests and shared goals in support of mutual understanding and benefit. In this case, *ethical management* is self-explanatory. The term *efficient management* refers to following a process of analysis, planning, implementation and evaluation, and *correction* in constructing a campaign plan and carrying it out. However, when it comes to focusing on common interests and shared goals—basics of relationship management—political public relations could benefit from the experiences of relationship management, where a growing body of research indicates the importance of focusing on interests and goals shared by organizations and stakeholders when choice decisions are being made by stakeholders. The decision of residents to stay in a community and the decision of utility subscribers to remain with a traditional service provider are evidence of the advantages of this approach.

Product-oriented political public relations, on the other hand, makes no mention of efforts to operationalize organization–public relationship dimensions to fit the situation at hand, or to identify common concerns, but instead puts its platform together without (external) stakeholder input and dogmatically is not inclined to change. Even market-oriented political public relations does not seek to operationalize organization–public relationships or build on common interests, but tends to use one-sided approaches in which stakeholder input is not balanced against the needs of the political party or other sponsoring group.

In that same way, the perception of mutuality—including mutual access, sharing of power, input and so on—and especially of mutual benefit—is a major driver in the choice behavior of stakeholders. Somewhat surprisingly, mutuality is not a major tenet of political public relations. Thus, political parties and political communication and campaigns could benefit from (a) operationalizing relationship dimensions so that they have meaning for stakeholders, (b) following the four-step planning paradigm, (c) identifying and acting on interests and goals important both to stakeholders and sponsoring organizations, and (d) ensuring action with regard to promises of mutual understanding and mutual benefit.

Discussion

Political campaigns have been a mainstay of American life since colonial patriots found they could mobilize a willing population to support independence. Today, the populous is inundated with a combination of grassroots efforts and televised political commercials, augmented by the use of social media. Yet, we do not seem to have moved much from long-held positions. The reality is that we are in control of what we hear and see, what it means to us, and what we retain. We are prewired to largely pay attention to those matters that we are already interested in. We interpret the meaning of messages depending on our particular makeup, and we only retain information that interests us. Moreover, the effect of most communication is to *reinforce the views* we already hold. And, all else being equal, we are swayed not so much by ideology as by the best return we can get for the investment of our time or behavior.

This is not to say that political public relations campaign messages do not have any effects, but that the impact is limited. Pouring millions of dollars into a single state, or even a single city seldom moves the electoral meter more than a few percentage points, and it often is difficult to attribute those directly to campaign activity. However—and this has been the case from colonial times to today—the media have the ability to mobilize the electorate to do what it is already predisposed to do.

Conclusions

How, then, can relationship management be helpful to those practicing political public relations? First, to paraphrase former Speaker of the House Tip O'Neill, *all politics are relational.* Political public relations should focus more on identifying the relationship dimensions relevant to stakeholders and using them as the basis of its political public relations campaign. Political public relations, instead, tends to either ask voters what they want, or to develop its "product" internally, without voter input. Neither political public relations approach works as well as basing relationship building on common interests and shared goals, a relationship management fundamental.

Recommendations

Identify relevant relationship dimensions and construct political public relations around the dimensions.

Relationship dimensions must be operationalized to targeted voters. The literature is replete with examples of successful relationship management initiatives following this technique. Political public relations campaign messaging needs to fit the differences one finds geographically and socioeconomically with regard to perceptions, values, and mindset.

Build relationships. Relationship management almost never depends on television commercials, yet the literature shows the success of relationship management initiatives in overcoming a decline in community conditions and a competitor's lower costs for telephone service, both by building relationships with stakeholders.

Make interpersonal communication the centerpiece of the campaign. Although grassroots mobilizing has become more important, many political campaigns still go the easy route of pouring huge amounts of money into television advertising and undervaluing personal contact. There is no doubt that *interpersonal communication* is immensely more effective than mediated communication, with social media the next best approach, supported by mass media, rather than the other way around.

Use both symbolic and actual behaviors. Effective relationship management initiatives have demonstrated the value of not just talking, but also of doing. Still, many campaigns continue to give short shrift to actual activities. The campaigns may say they are market oriented, but they perform more as if they were product oriented.

Again, the literature shows the importance of behavioral relationships coupled with symbolic relationships. Moreover, political communication cannot be viewed only through the lens of media relations, but must—if it is to have any meaningful impact—be part of an overall strategy that involves relationship building at every juncture of the campaign, including precampaigning planning and postcampaign analysis.

Moreover, multiple relationships require an organization to prioritize its relationships and allot resources in keeping with the importance of each relationship. Multiple stakeholders also require consistency and coordination and messages must be built around the operationalization of the relationship dimensions most important to stakeholders.

The literature also contains repeated references to how *changes in the media impact the practice* of political communication and political public relations. For example, the fragmentation of the mass media and the resultant proliferation of specialized media—both print and electronic—are providing increased opportunities for political public relations. And, the power of the media is moving from mass media to social media, a more personal and in many ways a more powerful form. How political public relations reacts to these changes will impact the future of the practice. In short, as go the media, so will go that portion of political public relations that thrives on media relationships.

Need for Further Research

It is counterproductive to argue whether the function of public relations is to create awareness, position the organization, or manage mutually beneficial relationships: It is all of those and more. However, no two relationships are the same and all are not of the same intensity (Hutton et al., 2001). Moreover, relationships may progress through degrees of intensity. Certainly, in some cases, the function of the public relations practitioner is to create awareness, that which Duck (1991) contends is the first requirement of a relationship. In other cases, stakeholders may only know of an organization because of what they have heard, an early stage of Knapp and Vangelisti (2008) phases of relationship development and decline.

At some point, however, a relationship may intensify because of the importance those in the relationship assign to it or for other reasons. Altman and Taylor's social penetration theory (1973) suggests two relationship dimensions for gauging organization–public relationship quality, *breadth* and *depth*. *Breadth* refers to the number of topics shared by the actors in the relationship. *Depth* refers to the level of topic detail shared by the actors. Altman and Taylor suggest that in the early development of relationships, communication patterns are less personal that those exhibited in the later development of the relationship. Obviously, then, an organization–public relationship may exhibit increased frequency of interaction, or be altered in some other way involving shared interests and goals or perceptions of mutual understanding and mutual benefit. Research into not only relationship quality, but also *relationship breadth* and *depth* could be enlightening, as could identifying the process a stakeholder may move through—if indeed they do so—from awareness to other more intimate levels of a relationship. In addition, Hutton et al. (2001) suggest that cultivating and managing a relationship is very important when the group is involved with an issue, but for groups not so involved, perceptions based simply on what stakeholders may have heard seem to be more important. More specifically, the construct of reputation may be critical in understanding situations of low stakeholder involvement. Thus, research exploring a *continuum* of stakeholder engagement is central to expanding our knowledge of political public relations depending on the level of involvement between political actors and their various constituencies.

However, after reviewing the relationship management literature, we feel the most impactful relationship dimensions—and, therefore, the ones that ought to be included in relationship scales—are trust, openness, satisfaction, access, mutual control, and responsiveness, and that it is doubtful that additional research into relationship dimensions will yield anything new.

In sum, the relational approach to public relations theory sees the organization–public relationship as a joint relationship, a partnership of sorts, existing in that part of a continuum that is favoring neither the organization nor stakeholders. It implicitly endorses the concept of mutuality, mutual understanding, mutual benefits, and mutual gain, while recognizing that at any given time, one of the entities may be experiencing more gain than the other. Through its communication, activities, and practice applications, relationship management builds long-term relationships between organizations and stakeholders.

Political public relations, on the other hand, could benefit greatly from a two-way approach to party membership and campaigns, beyond the usual "fruits of victory" of employment, favored treatment and the like. The politico-party faithful-voter relationship could be expected to function more effectively if it were approached as a partnership, based on mutuality, and less of a one-sided, product-oriented but focus group tested process which essentially seeks to *gain* favor, not *share* it.

References

Altman, I., & Taylor, D. (1973). *Social penetration: The development of interpersonal relationships*. New York: Holt, Rinehart & Winston.

Baum, M., & Kernell, S. (2001). Economic class and popular support for Franklin Roosevelt in war and peace. *Public Opinion Quarterly, 65*(2), 198–229.

Biagi, S. (2007). *Media/impact: An introduction to mass media*. Belmont, CA: Thompson.

Bridges, J., & Nelson, R. A. (2000). Issues management: A relational approach. In J. A. Ledingham & S. D. Bruning (Eds.), *Public relations as relationship management: A relational approach to public relations* (pp. 95–116). Mahwah, NJ: Erlbaum.

Broom, G. (1986, May). *Public relations roles and systems theory: Functional and historical causal models*. Paper presented at the meeting of the International Communication Association, Chicago, IL.

Broom, G., Casey, S., & Ritchey, J. (1997). Toward a concept and theory of organization-public relationships, *Journal of Public Relations Research, 9*(2), 83–98.

Broom, G., Casey, S., & Ritchey, J. (2000). Toward a concept and theory of organization–public relationships: An update. In J. A. Ledingham & S. D. Bruning (Eds.), *Public relations as relationship management: A relational approach to public relations* (pp. 3–22). Mahwah, NJ: Erlbaum.

Broom, G., & Dozier, M. D. (1990). *Using research in public relations: Applications in program management*. Englewood Cliffs. NJ: Prentice Hall.

Bruning, S. D., Castle, J. D., Schrepfer, E. (2004, Fall). Building relationships between organizations and publics: Examining the linkage between organizatrion-public relationships, evaluations of satisfaction, and behavioral intent. *Communication Studies, 55*(3), 117–128.

Bruning, S. D., & Ledingham, J.A. (1999). Relationships between organizations and publics: Development of a multi-dimensional organization-public relationship scale. *Public Relations Review, 25*(2), 157–170.

Bruning, S. D., & Ledingham, J. A. (2000). Organization and key public relationships: Testing the influence of the relationship dimensions in a business-to-business context. In J. A. Ledingham & S. D. Bruning (Eds.), *Public relations as relationship management: A relational approach to public relations* (pp. 159–173). Mahwah, NJ: Erlbaum.

Campbell, W. J. (2001), *Yellow journalism: Puncturing the myths, defining the legacies*. Santa Barbara, CA: Praeger.

Clark, C. E. (2008). William Llyod Garrison. In S. L. Vaughn (Ed.), *Encyclopedia of American journalists* (pp. 194–196). New York: Taylor & Francis.

Connery, T. B. (1992). *A sourcebook of American literary journalism: Representative writers in an emerging genre*. New York: Greenwood Press.

Coombs, T. (2000). Crisis management: Advantages of a relational perspective. In J. A. Ledingham & S. D. Bruning (Eds.), *Public relations as relationship management: A relational approach to public relations* (pp. 73–93). Mahwah, NJ: Erlbaum.

Cutlip, S. M., Center, A. H., & Broom, G. M. (1985). *Effective public relations* (6th ed.). Englewood Cliffs, NJ: Prentice-Hall.

Cutlip, S. M., Center, A. H., & Broom, G. M. (1994). *Effective public relations* (7th ed.). Englewood Cliffs, NJ: Prentice-Hall.

Davis, A. (2002). *Public relations democracy: Public relations, politics and the mass media in Britain*. Manchester, England: Manchester University Press.

Devlin, L. P. (1986). An analysis of presidential television commercials 1952–1984. In L. L. Kaid,

D. Nimmo, & K. R. Sanders (Eds.), *New perspectives on political advertising* (pp. 21–54). Carbondale: Southern Illinois University Press.

Dimmick, S., Bell, T. E., Burgiss, S. G., & Ragsdale, C. (2000). Relationship management: A new professional model. In J. A. Ledingham & S. D. Bruning (Eds.), *Public relations as relationship management: A relational approach to public relations* (pp. 117–136). Mahwah, NJ: Erlbaum.

Duck, S. (1991). *Psychology.* New York: Guilford Press.

Eksterowicz, A. J., & Robert, R. N. (Eds.). (2000). *Public journalism and political knowledge.* Lanham, MD: Rowman & Littlefield.

Esposito, S., & Koch, S. (2000) Relationship news. In J. A. Ledingham & S. D. Bruning (Eds.), *Public relations as relationship management: A relational approach to public relations* (pp. 221–238). Mahwah, NJ: Erlbaum.

Ferguson, M. A. (1984, August). *Building theory in public relations: Inter-organizational relationships.* Paper presented to the Public Relations Division, at the annual conference of the Association for Education in Journalism and Mass Communication, Gainesville, FL.

Grunig, J. E. (1992). Communiccation, public relations and effective organizations: An overview of the book. In J. E. Grunig (Ed.), *Excellence in public relations and communication management* (pp. 1–28). Hillsdale, NJ: Erlbaum.

Grunig, J. E. (1993). Image and substance: From symbolic to behavioral relationships. *Public Relations Review, 19*(2), 121–139.

Grunig, J. E., & Huang, Y-H. (2000). From organizational effectiveness to relationship indicators: Antecedents of relationships, public relations strategies, and relationship outcomes. In J. A. Ledingham & S. D. Bruning (Eds.), *Public relations as relationship management: A relational approach to public relations* (pp. 23–54). Mahwah, NJ: Erlbaum.

Grunig, J. E., & Hunt, T. (1984). *Managing public relations.* New York: Holt, Rinehart & Winston.

Grunig, L. A., Grunig, J. E., & Ehling, W. P. (1992). What is an effective organization? In J. E. Grunig (Ed.), *Excellence in public relations and communication management* (pp. 65–90). Hillsdale, NJ: Erlbaum.

Hallahan, K. (1999). Seven models of framing: Implications for public relations. *Journal of Public Relations Research, 11*(3), 205–242.

Hillman, A. J., & Hitt, M. A. (1999). Corporate political strategy formulation: A model of approach, participation, and strategy decisions. *Academy of Management Review, 24*(4), 825–842.

Hutton, J., Goodman, M. B., Alexander, J. B., & Genest C. M. (2001). Reputation management: The new face of corporate public relations? *Public Relations Review, 27*(3), 247–261.

Ki, E., & Hon, L. (2006). Relationship maintenance strategies on fortune 500 company web sites. *Journal of Communication Management, 10*(1), 27–43.

Knapp, M. L., & Vangelisti, A. L. (2008). *Interpersonal communication and human relationships.* Boston, MA: Allyn & Bacon.

Kruckeberg, D. (2000). Public relations: Toward a global profession. In J. A. Ledingham & S. D. Bruning (Eds.), *Public relations as relationship management: A relational approach to public relations* (pp. 145–158). Mahwah, NJ: Erlbaum.

Ledingham, J. A. (2001). Government-community relationships: Extending the relational perspective of public relations. *Public Relations Review, 27*(3), 285–295.

Ledingham, J. A. (2003). Explicating relationship management as a general theory of public relations. *Journal of Public Relations Research, 15*(2), 181–198.

Ledingham, J. A. (2006). Relationship management: A general theory of public relations. In C. Botan & V. Hazelton, Jr. (Eds.), *Public relations theory II* (pp. 465–483). Mahwah, NJ: Erlbaum.

Ledingham, J. A. (2009a). Cross-cultural public relations: A review of existing models with suggestions for a post-industrial public relations pyramid. *Journal of Promotional Management, 14*(3-4), 225–241.

Ledingham, J. A. (2009b).A chronology of organization-stakeholder relationships with recommendations concerning practitioner adoption of the relational perspective. *Journal of Promotional Management, 14*(3-4), 243–262.

Ledingham, J. A., & Bruning, S. D. (1998). Relationship management and public relations: Dimensions of an organization–public relationship. *Public Relations Review, 24*(1), 55–65.

Ledingham, J. A., & Bruning, S. D. (2000). A longitudinal study of organization–public relationship dimensions: Defining the role of communication in the practice of relationship management. In J. A. Ledingham & S. D. Bruning (Eds.), *Public relations as relationship management: A relational approach to public relations* (pp. 55–69). Mahwah, NJ: Erlbaum.

Ledingham, J. A., & Bruning, S. D. (2007). The media audit: A tool for managing media relationships. *Journal of Promotion Management, 13,*189–202.

Ledingham, J. A., Bruning, S. D., Thomlison, T. D., & Lesko, C. (1997). The applicability of the interpersonal relationship dimensions to an organizational context: Toward a theory of relational loyalty; a qualitative approach. *Academy of Managerial Communication Journal, 1*(1), 23–43.

Ledingham, J. A., Bruning, S. D., & Wilson, L. J. (1999). Time as an indicator of the perceptions and behavior of members of a key public: Monitoring and predicting organization–public partnerships. *Journal of Public Relations Research, 11*(2), 167–183.

Littlejohn, S. (1995). *Theories of human communication* (5th ed.). Belmont, CA: Wadsworth.

Littlejohn, S. (2003). *Theories of human communication.* Belmont, CA: Wadsworth.

McLeod, J. M., Scheufele, D. A., & Moy, P. (1999). Community, communication, and participation: The role of mass media and interpersonal discussion in local political participation. *Political Communication, 16,* 315–336.

Presbrey, F. (2000). The history and development of advertising. *Advertising & Society Review, 1*(1), 1–13.

Sitkoff, H. (1971). Racial militancy and interracial violence in the Second World War. *The Journal of American History, 58*(3), 661–681.

Strömbäck, J. (2007). Political marketing and professionalized campaigning: A conceptual analysis. *Journal of Political Marketing, 6*(2/3), 49–67.

Strömbäck, J., Mitrook, M. A., & Kiousis, S. (2010). Bridging two schools of thought: Applications of public relations theory to political marketing. *Journal of Political Marketing, 9*(1/2), 73–92.

Strömbäck, J., & Shehata, A. (2010). Media malaise or a virtuous circle? Exploring the causal relationships between news media exposure, political news attention and political interest. *European Journal of Political Research, 49*(5), 575–597.

Thomlison, T. D. (2000). An interpersonal primer with implications for public relations. In J. A. Ledingham & S. D. Bruning (Eds.), *Public relations as relationship management: A relational approach to public relations* (pp. 177–203). Mahwah, NJ: Erlbaum.

Toffler, A. (1971). *Future shock.* New York: Random House.

Toth, E. (2000). From personal influence to interpersonal influence: A model for relationship management. In J. A. Ledingham & S. D. Bruning (Eds.), *Public relations as relationship management: A relational approach to public relations* (pp. 205–220). Mahwah, NJ: Erlbaum.

Wilson, L. J. (1994). Excellent companies and coalition building among the Fortune 500: A value and relationship-based theory. *Public Relations Review, 20*(4), 333–343.

Wilson, L. J. (2001). Relationships within communities: Public relations for the new century. In R. L. Heath (Ed.), *Handbook of public relations* (pp. 521–526). Thousand Oaks, CA: Sage.

Wise, K. (2007). Lobbying and relationship management: The K Street connection. *Journal of Public Relations Research, 19*(4), 357–376.

12

POLITICAL PUBLIC RELATIONS AND GOVERNMENT COMMUNICATION

Karen Sanders

Introduction

In the 2008 December issue of the *Journal of Communication*, its editor, Michael Pfau (2008), laid down a number of challenges to communication scholars. He stated:

> Too often we write for others within specific narrow niches of our own discipline and as a result, our output is not read by most communication scholars, let alone by scholars in allied fields.

> (p. 597)

Pfau's twofold explanation for this state of affairs is apposite for understanding the situation of government communication research. First, he points to the fragmentation and specialization of the communication discipline. Of course, specialization is by no means a bad thing and real world complexity demands it. However, it can have negative effects and, in terms of government communication research I would suggest that this is the case. On the one hand, until now there has been little cross-fertilization of ideas between areas such as political communication, public relations, political marketing, public affairs, and management theory, all of which are working on issues related to government communication. On the other hand, this lack of interdisciplinary conversation has left government communication research not only bereft of robust theoretical models but also of common meanings and understandings of the precise nature of government communication. The challenge set out by the editors of this book regarding the theoretical development of political public relations is, then, timely, and in this chapter my first aim will be to respond to it.

Returning to Pfau, the second explanation he gives for the apparent irrelevance of the communication discipline is the kind of research questions its practitioners ask (2008, pp. 599–600). He suggests that communication scholars principally address what he calls "peripheral" issues, those focused on specific niches such as communication content (economic or health communication, for instance), the structure of communication transactions (e.g., interpersonal or political communication), or classes of people (e.g., women or ethnic minorities). Of interest in themselves, the knowledge they produce is of less wide relevance. Pfau (2008) argues that research should tackle what he calls "functional issues" defined as "questions about communication processes or end states" (p. 600) that provide knowledge of interest across disciplines. Pfau's definition suggests that "government communication" falls into the category of a peripheral issue. However, as he also explains, it is possible "to address functional issues within a peripheral context. When this happens, research output is of interest not just to others in that specific niche, but to scholars across the communication field and to those in allied disciplines" (Pfau, 2008, p. 600). For example, examining processes of building message consistency would be of broad concern to communication scholars. The second aim of this chapter, then, will be to identify the significant functional questions that government communication research should be addressing so that scholarship in this field matters beyond "the narrow niches of our own discipline."

Government Communication Research: What Is It and Where Is It Published?

The first issue, however, is what is our own discipline? The introductory chapter to this volume sets out arguments to suggest that there is an emerging field known as "political public relations" defined as

> the management process by which an organization or individual for political purposes, through purposeful communication and action, seeks to influence and to establish, build, and maintain beneficial relationships and reputations with its key publics to help support its mission and achieve its goals.

The Strömbäck and Kiousis definition draws on a review chiefly of the political communication and public relations literature and is a useful starting point for considering the location of government communication studies. It is helpful because it addresses core disciplinary concerns, thus fulfilling Pfau's recommendation regarding the need for research that explores functional, substantive issues that cross disciplinary boundaries. Government communication research could, then, serve as a testing ground for some of the theoretical assumptions and conceptual definitions found in the editors' understanding of political public relations.

This prompts a set of questions regarding the state of government communication studies. How do those who study it define it? Where do they publish or present their findings? What do they write about and what theoretical models and methodologies do they apply? Can government communication be considered a peripheral issue or is there an argument for it to be considered as a new emergent field? I will consider the first two questions next and deal with the remaining questions later in the chapter.

Taking first the question of definition, a review of the major relevant communication journals and related books over the last 10 years together with Google Scholar searches using *government communication* as the search term, reveals no common understanding of what "government communication" means.[1] As we shall see, for political communication scholars, government communication has been equated with chief executive—presidential or prime ministerial—communication. Scholars working within the fields of public relations and public affairs have ranged some way beyond this narrow focus, examining local and regional government communication. However, so far as this writer can discover, there has been no systematic consideration of how government communication should be defined. Indeed, government communication is rarely considered as a field in and of itself. A Google Scholar search reveals Deutsch's classic 1963 study *The Nerves of Government; Models of Political Communication and Control* as the first and most cited study for government communication followed by one 2007 study (Liu & Horsley, 2007). In other words, in almost 50 years practically no prominent work has addressed government communication as a discrete area of research.

Researchers working on government communication have no specific scholarly venue to showcase their work and generally have presented it within the political communication, public relations, or media and politics sections of, for example, the *International Communication Association*, the *International Association for Mass Communication Research*, the *Political Studies Association*, the *American Political Studies Association*, and the *European Public Research Association*. Exceptionally, the *International Public Relations Symposium* spotlighted government communication research at its annual meeting in 2010.

On the other hand, those writing on government communication have no shortage of possible publishing venues, although there is no specific journal for the field. Government communication research can be found, for example, in the *International Journal of Press/Politics, Political Communication, European Journal of Communication, Journal of Public Affairs* and the *Journal of Communication Management*. Most of this work is being produced by political communication scholars, followed by those working in public relations, organizational communication, and public affairs. I will examine their principal approaches and themes in the following sections, beginning first with the contribution of political communication.

Political Communication Perspectives: *The West Wing Approach*

The West Wing, the U.S. television series created by Aaron Sorkin and originally broadcast between 1999 and 2006, brilliantly showed the "rhetorical presidency" in action (Tulis, 1987). Based in the west wing of the White House, the
world it depicts is one of frantic decision making, combative media relations,
a heroic president, and haggling inside the Beltway. *The West Wing's* depiction
of the relationship between politics, media, and the public neatly captures some
of the achievements and challenges for political communication scholarship's
approach to the study of government communication, as I shall explain next.

Focusing first on the achievements, the field of political communication
draws on a rich intellectual heritage, including influences from psychology, lin-
guistics, sociology, rhetorical studies, journalism, and political science (Bennett
& Iyengar, 2008), that has enhanced our understanding of three key themes for
government communication: the role of power; the relationship to and role of
news media, and normative questions related to government communication's
purpose and performance in constitutional democracies.

Where Power Lies: Who Wears the Crown?

To take first the issue of power: how power is achieved and exercised through
communicational means has always been a major concern for political communication scholars. Early work in political communication was heavily skewed
toward election studies and media effects research; these continue to be central areas of interest in the field (Bennett & Iyengar, 2008). Classic political
communication studies have examined issues such as voter opinion formation
and reinforcement (Katz & Lazarsfeld, 1955), agenda setting (McCombs &
Shaw, 1972), and framing (Goffman, 1959, 1974; Iyengar, 1991). Scholars have
explored the cognitive, affective, and behavioral effects of strategic political
communication. More broadly, political communication research has excelled
in charting the systemic shifts in the balance of power among governments,
media, and public. Key thematic areas such as rhetorical analysis of political
discourse (Zarefsky, 2004) and its influence on audiences (Edwards, 2003), voting and propaganda studies (McChesney, 2008), mass media effects, and the
flow of influence among government, press, and public opinion (see Graber,
2005; Lin, 2004 for overviews of the field), chart the workings of political
power and influence through communication. This, after all, is how Swanson
(2000) defines political communication's overall approach, suggesting that it is
the analysis of "the role of communication in political processes and institutions
associated with electoral campaigning and governing" (p. 190).

I will take two contrasting examples of how political communication scholars have conceptualized government communication's role in the power game.
First, Blumenthal's (1980) notion of the "permanent campaign" examines how

governing partly becomes a process of combining "image-making with strategic calculation" in order to ensure the politicians' public popularity (p. 7). The application of election campaign or political marketing techniques to the business of governing, such as gathering intelligence, targeting audiences, promoting messages, or rapid rebuttal, has been explored as a structural, institutional, and personal response to contemporary media demands that often short changes the public (e.g., Franklin, 2004). The most radical form of this analysis suggests that media and government power work together to "manufacture consent" (Hermann & Chomsky, 1988) from a powerless public to the prevailing economic hegemony.

To take a contrasting example of government communication's role, a number of scholars have pointed to a "third age of political communication" (Blumler & Kavanagh, 1999) where digital media can be used to enhance democratic processes. Developments in e-democracy and e-government that permit interactivity, and within the right institutional frameworks, improved transparency and accountability, are viewed as capable of releasing the democratic energies of the people (e.g., Axford & Huggins, 2001; Chadwick, 2006; Saco, 2002). According to this analysis, digital media leach power from senior politicians and the mainstream political media, increasing the potential of citizens' power (Coleman & Blumler, 2009).

In conclusion, common to many of these analyses are questions about who has power, how power is distributed, and how power is lost and gained. The adversarial and competitive nature of communication relationships is stressed particularly, as we shall see, in regard to the media. In other words, in relation to the study of government, political communication research ensures that the issue of power is kept firmly in view. *The West Wing* and its staffers who vie with political opponents, lobby groups, and media critics to maintain the momentum that will ensure policy delivery are the televisual correlate of the work of political communication scholars who address issues of structural, symbolic, and institutional power in charting the development of strategic communication at the service of governments (e.g., Cottle, 2003; Davis, 2002; Edelman, 1964, 1988).

It takes Two to Tango: The Relationship Between Politicians and Journalists

The focus on power suggests what I consider to be a second major contribution of political communication studies to understanding government communication, namely, the exploration of government's relationship with news media. *The West Wing*'s focus on press relations, on finding the right tactics and the right narratives, on image construction, on issues of trust, and on the salience of scandal are all themes which have been explored in the political communication literature in relation to government communication (Canel &

Sanders, 2006; Cox, 2001; Hacker, 2004). Research has focused on areas such as communication strategies, commonly known by the pejorative term *spin*; or on source relationships to explain the ebb and flow of power between politicians and journalists (Davis, 2002). In the view of some scholars "the indexing hypothesis—selecting content patterns that are cued by the positions of decisive actors in a political conflict—still explains most routine political reporting" (Bennett, 2004, p. 292; see also Arnold, 2004). Other scholars have looked to the model of "primary definition" to explain the dynamics of the source–reporter relationship (Gitlin, 1980). Here sources are identified as the forces that hold the balance of power, using their institutional might as well as logistical and ideological resources to ensure that certain stories are told and others are not. Source power is also explored in agenda setting and agenda building studies of the media, a major area of political communication research initiated by McCombs and Shaw's pioneering study (1972) that examined the relationship between public and media agendas (see also Weaver, McCoombs, & Shaw, 2004). Media have increasingly come to be seen as political actors in their own right so that in Cook's view, "news media today are not merely part of politics: they are part of government" (Cook, 2005, p. 3).

The importance of the relationship with news media has pointed to the logistical and operational issues of how governments organize their communication as a significant area of research and debate, although thus far work has centered mainly on the organizational chart, roles, functions, and decision making processes of White House communication (Kumar 2003, 2007; Kumar & Sullivan, 2003).

In sum, themes such as the news media considered as a political institution and the development of the "mediapolis," the space of appearance in which democratic politics takes place (Silverstone, 2007), have received considerable attention from political communication researchers in contrast to their virtual exclusion from work in political science.[2]

The Democracy Question

Finally, the third major contribution of political communication research has been a normative concern with how communication "performs its civic functions at the center of social and political life, and also to point the way toward shaping communication to better serve democratic processes" (Swanson, 2000, p. 200). The health and quality of democracy and citizenship are at the heart of the concerns explored in a number of studies (e.g., Patterson, 1994, 2003), particularly at times of crisis when events and issues such as war, scandal, and terrorism become of vital public interest (Norris, Kern, & Just, 2003; Taylor, 1997).

The civic usefulness of the information environment or the way in which government communication can subvert citizenship through the practice of spin are well-rehearsed themes (Barnett & Gaber, 2001). Linked to these concerns, the examination of government communication practices associated with the development of electronic technology and its impact on political practices and institutions and, more especially, the quality of democratic life has, as we saw earlier, been a growing theme of political communication research (Coleman & Blumler, 2009).

Limitations of Political Communication Research

Political communication's privileging of the themes of power, the media, and the normative context for communication are key contributions to the understanding of government communication. However, it is clear too that political communication research has not engaged with the area of government communication in anything like the detail and scope with which electoral communication, for example, has been addressed. In addition, it is questionable whether the field's dominant theoretical paradigms are sufficient for adequately exploring research questions related to government communication. I will give four examples of significant gaps in or shortcomings of political communication research for understanding government communication.

First, there are key conceptual questions that, as far as I can judge, are barely addressed in the literature. To take the most egregious example, there is little attempt to define what is meant by government communication. Generally, political communication scholars have examined only chief executive (presidential or prime ministerial) communication, neglecting the multiple instances of government communication at ministerial as well as local and regional levels.[3] U.S. presidential communication has been the main area of study from Neustadt's classic study *Presidential Power* (1960) and continuing with work by Denton and Hahn (1986), Tulis (1987), Smith and Smith (1994), and Denton and Holloway (1996). Chief executive communication has also been explored in a number of other national contexts including Argentina (de Masi, 2001), Australia (Young, 2007), and Britain (Seymour Ure, 2003; Franklin, 2004). Chief executive communication strategies in relation to political scandal and to terrorism have been examined in work investigating Spain and Britain (Canel & Sanders, 2006, 2009). References to chief executive communication can also be found in more generalist literature (Canel, 2007; McNair, 2007; Oates, 2008; Sanders, 2009; Stanyer, 2007).

A second gap and thus obstacle to creating adequate theoretical frameworks for government communication research is the overwhelming emphasis on U.S. data. Presidential communication occupies the lion's share of government communication studies. Basic data about government communication management across the world, how it is organized, its institutional and regulatory contexts, are extremely limited.

In third place, political communication's emphasis on strategic communication's instrumental role in government's maintenance or struggle for power appears to theorize the exercise of power as a zero sum game where there can only be winners and losers. Governments spin and media seek conflict. This is linked, in fourth place, to what I consider to be a necessary focus on the media's role in government communication but one that appears in some accounts to have pushed the public out of the picture. In general terms, political communication research often seems colored by an intellectual pessimism about the possibility of creating the conditions for civic conversation in contemporary media democracies (Sanders, 2009, pp. 229–233).

Surveying the Communication Map

Reviewing the literature on government communication from public affairs, political marketing, public relations, and organizational communication research reveals a similar picture to that for political communication studies: there is little work specifically addressing the subject of government communication.

Organizational Communication and the Public Sector

Taking first organizational communication, this methodologically and theoretically diverse field is, in Monge and Scott Poole's words (2008) "an intersection ... between the study of human communication and the study of human organization" (p. 679). Researchers have paid some attention to communication in public sector organizations, most notably in Garnett and Kouzmin's (1997) *Handbook of Administrative Communication*, Graber's (2003) comprehensive analysis of managing communication in public organizations, and Lee's (2008) collection of articles and essays on government public relations. Graber (2003) points to the need for the incorporation of the area of communication into the management functions and processes of public sector organizations and puts out a call for "major studies and experiments in public-sector organizational communication" as a research priority (p. 276). Seven years on, however, organizational communication has yet to pay systematic attention to the subject.

Public Affairs: Looking Toward Government

Public affairs studies offers a more promising panorama given the field's commitment to "interpreting and making sense of the complexity of external relationships, particularly with government and community groups" and understanding "the task of managing key issues that arise out of such stakeholder relationships through the use of lobbying and other representational activities" (Harris & Moss, 2001, p. 7) and through the use of issue management (Jaques, 2006). However, public affairs has chiefly centered on a model of public affairs understood as communication managed from the corporate or voluntary sector toward government. Indeed, in the 10 years of the existence of the *Journal of Public Affairs*, there has been only one published study explicitly focused on government communication (Fairbanks, Plowman, & Rawlins, 2007).

Political Marketing and the Management Function

Political marketing's focus on the application of marketing and management theory to politics has produced a rich vein of studies (see Henneberg, 2008 for an overview) that have increased our understanding of the market-oriented strategic thinking that underlies part of political decision making and behavior. According to this perspective, the logic of communication strategies has increasingly come to obey the logic of the market. Election campaigns are run in a similar way to commercial marketing campaigns that seek to provide products that consumers want, and, similarly, governments continue to campaign when in power. Again, as is the case for political communication research, political marketing scholars have largely centered on election campaigns (Baines, Brennan, & Egan, 2003; Lees-Marshment, Strömbäck, & Rudd, 2010), with some attention being paid to political parties (Wring, 2005). In addition, in Henneberg's (2008) words, a research bias toward marketing in campaigns (p. 157) has obscured "more general and theoretical discussions" and created a narrow understanding of political marketing theory as integrating "an (initial) descriptive understanding of political marketing management with a prescriptive theory (i.e., one that can help political actors to apply political marketing management techniques effectively and efficiently)" (p. 159) that he considers insufficient to capture the richness of politics.

For others, the application of marketing management to politics has either used overly system-specific theoretical starting points (Strömbäck, 2007) or a number of questionable theoretical assumptions about the nature of politics, chiefly in relation to the adoption of neoclassical economic assumptions (Savigny, 2007). On two counts, then, political marketing's contribution to understanding government communication is limited: first, it simply has paid little attention to the subject (although see Lees-Marshment, 2004); second, it has generally used narrow theoretical models for understanding politics. However, political marketing has placed the spotlight on management functions within politics and on the application of marketing strategy and techniques to some areas of political decision making, which implies the use of public relations strategies and techniques and a shared interest in managing relationships with publics and in strategic communication (Strömbäck, Mitrook, & Kiousis, 2010).

Public Relations: Ways Forward

The public relations literature (and I include corporate communication in this category) provides a somewhat richer hunting ground both in terms of research related to government communication and the availability of theoretical approaches. Researchers have initiated work in public sector communication (Gregory, 2006, 2009; Killingsworth, 2009; Liu & Horsley, 2007; Vos, 2006; Vos & Westerhoudt, 2008), although the overwhelming majority of public relations research continues to be centered on the corporate world. As we shall see, researchers have applied models that could usefully inform theoretical and conceptual development of the field.

Developing Research in Government Communication Management

Despite the paucity of work specifically on government communication, there are, as Strömbäck and Kiousis suggest in their introductory chapter, useful theoretical insights to be gained from studying some of the literature reviewed above and, in particular, that found in the field of public relations. These include first, the approach of relationship theory and, linked to this, a distinctive conceptualization of the public; second, the application of management theory to the communication function and third, fresh ideas about performance and its evaluation through applying the concept of reputation to governments.

Putting the Public into Government Communication Management

Relationship management theory centers the analysis of communication on the establishment of relationships with diverse publics or stakeholders. The construction of relationships between organizations and publics is posited as the core aim of public relations (Ferguson, 1984). Scholars have sought to operationalize dimensions of organization–public relationships in measurable scales. Ledingham and Bruning (1998), for example, suggested that this relationship could be quantified along the dimensions of trust, openness, involvement, investment, and commitment with increased presence of these dimensions acting as an indicator of communication quality and efficacy. Hon and Grunig (1999) considered that the dimensions of control mutuality, trust, satisfaction, commitment, exchange relationship, and communal relationship were those that would allow both PR researchers and practitioners to measure the impact of communication activities.

Relationship management theory places publics at the center of analytical frameworks and in a way that is not always the case in, for example, political communication research. It allows government communication to be conceived of as the cultivation of long-term relationships oriented to developing specific relationship dimensions. This is the approach exemplified, for instance, in public diplomacy's conceptualization of government communication (Signitzer & Wamser, 2006).

Relationship management theory is linked to a two-way model of communication exemplified by Grunig's symmetrical/excellence model of public relations (Grunig & Grunig, 1992; Grunig & Hunt, 1984) that has provided one of the major analytical frameworks for public relations scholarship over the last 30 years (Botan & Hazleton, 2006). It suggests that longer-term mutual understanding rather than just short-term electoral or strategic gain may be a helpful way of analyzing government communication management.

Government Communication as a Management Function

One enduring theme across communication literature has been that of the "professionalization" of communication. From the political communication perspective, professionalization has sometimes (Hamelink, 2007), albeit not always (McNair, 2007; Negrine, 2008), been cast in a negative light. For critics, the role of expert communicators and the introduction of the marketing concept into political communication have been considered to impact negatively on democratic politics. For example, the UK government's introduction of professionalized government communication management during Tony Blair's time in office (1997–2007) was considered to have damaged public trust in their governors (Sanders, 2009).

However, considering government communication from a management approach, as some public relations scholars have done using the strategic planning and quality management literature (Cutlip, Center, & Broom, 2000; Gregory, 2006; Vos, 2006),[4] can help in the development of an analytical framework and set of indicators for measuring professionalization, or better "professionalism," in a way that allows greater conceptual precision, rigorous operationalization, and normative clarity (Pandey & Garnett, 2006). On this latter point, it is, in my view, not possible to avoid dealing with ethical considerations when considering government communication. For example, we can develop standards and indicators of professional government communication flowing from management theory that are applicable cross-nationally. However, I believe we would want to argue that truly "professional" communication entails normative standards. This means that the government communication management of some regime types (authoritarian systems, for example), could never be considered truly professional, however well organized they were.

Performance and Reputation

The management of intangibles and, more particularly, of corporate reputation has increasingly become the guiding philosophy of communication departments and public relations research (Argenti, 2003; Van Riel & Fombrun, 2007). Walker (2010, pp. 369–370) identifies five key attributes for the definition of corporate reputation:

1. Reputation is based on perception. In other words, it is a socially constructed phenomenon that is not necessarily completely factual.

2. Reputation is the aggregate perception of all stakeholders, internal and external, related to specific issues.
3. Reputation is inherently comparative in relation to other companies, specified standards, or as assessed in longitudinal terms.
4. Reputation can be positive or negative.
5. Reputation is established through time and, although prey to its vagaries, is relatively stable.

Walker (2010) offers a definition of corporate reputation as: "a relatively stable, issue specific aggregate perceptual representation of a company's past actions and future prospects compared against some standard" (p. 370). Reputation is distinct from the concept of "identity"—what the organization is—and "image"—stakeholders' perceptions of the organization. It is a construct based on perceived behavior through time. Because of its reliance in part on communication it may be a useful conceptual tool for developing analytical approaches to understand the effectiveness of government communication.

Defining Government Communication

Returning to the question of defining government communication, at the outset it is worth underlining a number of characteristic features of government communication.

First, government communication is *multilayered*. As we have seen, the term *government communication* is often used to refer solely to top-level executive communication. It should, however, also be used to refer to communication in political executive institutions at national, regional, and local levels: examples might include the German *Länder* governments, Canadian municipal government (Killingsworth, 2009), Dutch local government (Vos & Westerhoudt, 2008), or Colombian mayoral communication (Singhai & Greiner, 2008).

Second, government communication implies a degree of *publicness* that can be understood in two senses. On the one hand, regardless of the political realities, it is almost always claimed that government is constituted on the basis of the people's direct or indirect consent and charged to enact their will (Puddington, 2009). On the other hand, the organizational or institutional setting is public in that it is directed to external audiences and played out partly in the space of appearance with important implications for the operational conditions for communication (Liu & Horsley, 2007, p. 378). Of course, government communication management is not always public: it partly involves the organization of internal processes and structures; and government communicators may privately brief journalists.

Third, the public sector, and more specifically government communication, wrestles with considerable *complexity* in terms of goals, needs, audiences, definition, and resources. Graber's (2003, pp. 3–18) examination of public sector organizations suggests differences from private sector organizations with regard to internal structures and processes, to transactions between the organization and its environment, and to the environment itself (see also Rainey, 2003). In general terms, she judges public sector organizations to be more constrained by legal and regulatory frameworks and with more diversity and uncertainty about objectives and decision-making criteria.

Fourth, public sector communication and, in particular, government communication, operates in a *political environment*. Politics structure resources, personnel, and goals. Heads of communication, for example, may be appointed on the basis of partisan rather than professional criteria. Communication budgets may grow as elections approach.

With these distinguishing characteristics in mind, does the overarching definition of political public relations capture the key elements for understanding government communication management (i.e., "the management process by which an organization or individual for political purposes, through purposeful communication and action, seeks to influence and to establish, build, and maintain beneficial relationships and reputations with its key publics to help support its mission and achieve its goals")? I would argue that this depends on how we define the term *political*.

The review of cognate communication fields suggests first that government communication management should take a wide view of relevant stakeholders and, more particularly, pay more attention to publics beyond the media. It has also pointed to the creation of relationships and of reputation as being significant functions of government communication management. Political communication research underlines, among other things, a normative concern with how communication "performs its civic functions at the center of social and political life, and also to point the way toward shaping communication to better serve democratic processes" (Swanson, 2000, p. 200). This turns our attention to notions of purpose and performance, and it is here that the definition of political public relations may fall short in relation to understanding government communication management. While not wishing to be overly prescriptive about the purposes of government communication, it may be misleading to suggest that it is for "political purposes" alone. In other words, we need to be clear that there is a distinction between communication managed to achieve a government's political goals and communication managed in line with overarching government obligations in relation to the common civic good. In practice, this means we can debate, for example, whether and how government communication is "politicized" or what it means for it to be "professional." For these reasons, and at the risk of being accused of pedantry, I would argue either for clarification of what is meant by the word *political* or, to avoid misunderstanding, the inclusion of the notion of *civic* purposes as well as political ones in the definition of government communication management.

Conclusions

This review of scholarship in the area of government communication suggests that there are a number of attractive challenges for the future. First, it is clear that there is a need for more theoretically sophisticated frameworks that can draw on developments in the diverse communication subfields that make up the communication discipline. Second, we must look to found concepts on data not drawn mainly from U.S. research. This links to a third challenge which involves assembling adequate data sets that will allow us to operationalize concepts, questions, and hypotheses. This will allow us to formulate micro-, meso-, and macrolevel questions and hypotheses. For example, at the mesolevel, we might be interested in whether organizational size matters for communication performance (Pandey & Garnett, 2006). At the macrolevel, exploring indicators relating to the media landscape (infrastructure capacity, level of press freedom, etc.) and government communication performance might similarly provide pointers toward future policy priorities.

Government Communication Management: An Emerging Field?

Can we argue that government communication research is an emergent field? Certainly, as researchers we have much work to do to chart the diverse levels at which government communication takes place including national or federal, regional, and local levels; examining the relationships between these levels; and taking into account variables such as legal contexts and electoral and political systems. We also need to examine the definition and content of, as well as the relationships between the diverse communication functions found in government communication including corporate communication; that is, communication related to the government entity (mayoral or presidential office, for example); policy communication, which is related to policy goals (environmental or health targets, for instance); and organizational communication, such as internal or crisis communication) (Vos, 2006).[5]

Take policy communication: This occurs in many different guises including, for example, political advertising, an area that has been a major research focus of political communication scholars, but principally in the field of election campaign advertising (Kaid & Holtz Bacha, 2006). Government advertising in general and the area of government social marketing communication in particular (health campaigns; environmental change, driving behavior, etc.) have generated a considerable body of research by scholars mainly from a marketing perspective (Rice & Atkin, 2001). Research in this area would be enriched by bringing to bear insights from political communication scholarship that pay proper attention to the importance of context and to the reality of power disparities, sometimes underplayed or even ignored by public relations work (Gower, 2006). On the other hand, understanding policy communication to include foreign policy goals, the area known as "public diplomacy," could test the propositions of analysts such as Leonard, Small, and Rose (2005), who have argued for a communication approach based on "mutuality" and on long-term trust-building rather than short-term image-building (Signitzer, 2008; Signitzer & Wamser, 2006;).

Focusing on government communication *management* means, as Vos puts it (2006): "paying attention to quality and increasing the added value of communication within an organisation" (p. 256). This implies a concern with performance, something already present in the management, political marketing, and public relations literature, and therefore, with the development of performance indicators and standards, a trend that is present in some political communication work (Norris, 2009). This does not mean we have to go up epistemological blind alleys, uncritically either adopting theory that purports to be analytical but has in fact a prescriptive, positivist undergirding (Savigny, 2007), or naïve versions of symmetrical communication (Gower, 2006). However, government communication research can hardly avoid discussion of normative issues, nor would it be desirable to do so if our research is to engage with issues that matter not only to the wider scientific community but also to policy makers and our fellow citizens.

To conclude, an overarching frame for much Anglo-American political communication research has been the civic crisis of trust in government. President Bush's communication management of the "war on terrorism" after September 11, 2001, has been characterized as "propaganda of all shades" (Hiebert, 2003, p. 243). Similarly, the aftermath of Tony Blair's attempts to persuade the British public of the case for the Iraq war from 2002 to 2003 was allegedly a deepening cynicism about government communication and the installation of the term *spin*, which had begun to be widely used in the British political lexicon from 1997. Even Barack Obama, who campaigned partially on the promise of restoring public trust in government, came under intense criticism for his failure to communicate a sense of urgency and concern in relation to the BP oil spill catastrophe in the Gulf of Mexico. A sympathetic commentator criticized Obama's lack of engagement, stating (Rich, 2010): "Obama's press conference…—explaining in detail the government's response, its mistakes and its precise relationship to BP—was at least three weeks overdue. It was also his first full news conference in 10 months."

Research that matters will tackle core issues relating to how trust is generated with government's multiple stakeholders. The hackneyed but nevertheless key watchwords of *transparency* and *accountability* are central to this research enterprise: we need to understand more clearly what they mean and how and when they enhance civic life. It can be research that translates into policy recommendations about structures, resources, processes, and outcomes, not driven by managerial imperatives but by normative concerns about the quality of civic life.

Notes

1 I reviewed the following journals from 2001 to 2010 selected for their prominence in scholarly debates and citation indices: for communication research generally, the *Journal of Communication*; for political communication, the (Harvard) *International Journal of Press/Politics and Political Communication*; for political marketing, the *Journal of Political Marketing*; for public relations, the *Journal of Public Relations Research, Public Relations Review*, the *Corporate Reputation Review*, and the *Journal of Communication Management*; for government communication, the *Government Information Quarterly* and the *Journal of Information, Technology and Politics* (until 2007, the *Journal for E-Government*); for public affairs, the *Journal of Public Affairs*; and for organizational communication, the *Journal of Organizational Communication* and the *Journal of Organizational Studies*.

2 This neglect is illustrated by the lack of any references to the political communication literature in the volume edited by Colin Hay on *New Directions in Political Science* (2010).

3 There are exceptions (e.g., Franklin & Richardson, 2002).

4 The strategic planning approach was used in the establishment of a training and development framework for UK government communicators known as EVOLVE (see Gregory, 2006) and Dutch researchers have formulated instruments inspired by Kaplan and Norton's "balanced scorecard" or the European Foundation for Quality Control to 'help government organizations to communicate more effectively with their citizens (Vos, 2006, p. 250).

5 There has been notable work in this area mainly from a public relations perspective (see Coombs, 2009).

References

Argenti, P. (2003). *Corporate communication* (3rd ed.). New York: McGraw-Hill.

Arnold, R. D. (2004). *Congress, the press, and political accountability*. Princeton, NJ: Princeton University Press.

Axford, B., & Huggins, R. (Eds.). (2001). *New media and politics*. London: Sage.

Baines, P. R., Brennan, R., & Egan, J. (2003). "Market" classification and political campaigning: Some strategic implications. *Journal of Political Marketing, 2*(2), 47–66.

Barnett, S., & Gaber, I. (2001). *Westminster tales: The twenty-first century crisis in political journalism*. London: Continuum.

Bennett, W. L. (2004). Gatekeeping and press-government relations: A multigated model of news construction. In L. L. Kaid (Ed.), *Handbook of political communication research* (pp. 283–314). Mahwah, NJ: Erlbaum.

Bennett, W. L., & Iyengar, S. (2008). A new era of minimal effects? The changing foundations of political communication. *Journal of Communication, 58*(4), 707–731.

Blumenthal, S. (1980). *The permanent campaign*. New York: Simon & Schuster.

Blumler, J. G., & Kavanagh, D. (1999). The third age of political communication: Influences and features. *Political Communication, 16*(3), 209–230.

Botan, C., & Hazleton, V. (2006). Public relations in a new age. In C. Botan & V. Hazleton (Eds.), *Public relations theory II* (pp. 1–18). Mahwah, NJ: Erlbaum.

Canel, M. J. (2007). *Comunicación de las instituciones públicas* [Communication for public institutions]. Madrid, Spain: Tecnos.

Canel, M. J., & Sanders, K. (2006). *Morality tales: Political scandals and journalism in Britain and Spain in the 1990s*.Cresskill, NJ: Hampton Press.

Canel, M. J., & Sanders, K. (2009). Crisis communication and terrorist attacks: Framing a response to the 2004 Madrid bombings and 2005 London bombings. In T. Coombs (Ed.), *Handbook of crisis communication* (pp. 449–466). Oxford, England: Blackwell.

Chadwick, A. (2006). *Internet politics: States, citizens and new communication technologies*. Oxford, England: Oxford University Press.

Coleman, S., & Blumler, J. (2009). *The Internet and democratic citizenship: Theory, practice and policy.* Cambridge, England: Cambridge University Press.

Cook, T. (2005). *Governing with the news: The news media as a political institution* (2nd ed.). Chicago, IL: University of Chicago Press.

Coombs, T. (Ed.). (2009). *Handbook of crisis communication.* Oxford, England: Blackwell.

Cottle, S. (Ed.). (2003). *News, public relations and power.* London: Sage.

Cox H. L. (2001). *Governing from center stage: White House communication strategies during the age of television politics.* Cresskill, NJ: Hampton Press.

Cutlip, S., Center, A. H., & Broom, G. (2000). *Effective public relations* (8th ed.). Upper Saddle River, NJ: Prentice-Hall.

Davis, A. (2002). *Public relations democracy: Public relations, politics and the mass media in Britain.* Manchester, England: Manchester University Press.

De Masi, O. A. (2001). (Ed.). *Comunicación gubernamental* [Govermental communication]. Barcelona, Spain: Paidos.

Denton, R. E., & Hahn, D. (1986). *Presidential communication: Description and analysis.* Westport, CT: Praeger.

Denton, R. E., & Holloway, R. L. (1996). Clinton and the town hall meetings: Mediated conversation and the risk of being "in touch." In R. E. Denton & R. L. Holloway (Eds.), *The Clinton presidency: Images, issues and communication strategies* (pp. 17–41). Westport, CT: Praeger.

Deutsch, K. (1963). *The nerves of government: Models of political communication and control.* New York: Free Press.

Edelman, M. (1964). *The symbolic uses of politics.* Urbana: University of Illinois Press.

Edelman, M. (1988). *Constructing the political spectacle.* Chicago,IL: University of Chicago Press.

Edwards, G. C., III (2003). *On deaf ears: The limits of the bully pulpit.* New Haven, CT: Yale University Press.

Fairbanks, J., Plowman, K., & Rawlins, B. (2007). Transparency in government communication. *Journal of Public Affairs, 7*(1) 23–37.

Ferguson, M. A. (August, 1984). *Building theory in public relations: Interorganizational relationships.* Paper presented at the Association for Education in Journalism and Mass Communication, Gainesville, FL.

Franklin, B. (2004). *Packaging politics: Political communications in Britain's media democracy.* London: Edward Arnold.

Franklin, B., & Richardson, J. (2002). Priming the parish pump. *Journal of Political Marketing, 1*(1), 117–147.

Garnett, J. L. & Kouzmin, A. (1997). *Handbook of administrative communication.* New York: Dekker.

Gitlin, T. (1980). *The whole world is watching: Mass media and the making and unmaking of the new left.* Berkeley: University of California Press.

Goffman, E. (1959). *The presentation of self in everyday life.* Garden City, NY: Doubleday.

Goffman, E. (1974). *Frame analysis: An essay on the organization of experience.* New York: Harper & Row.

Gower, K. K. (2006). Public relations research at the crossroads. *Journal of Public Relations Research, 18*(2), 177–190.

Graber, D. (2003). *The power of communication: Managing information in public organizations.* Washington, DC: CQ Press.

Graber, D. (2005). Political communication faces the 21st century. *Journal of Communication, 55*(3), 479–507.

Gregory, A. (2006). A development framework for government communicators. *Journal of Communication Management, 10*(2), 197–210.

Gregory, A. (2009). The competencies of senior communicators in the UK National Health Service. *Journal of Communication in Healthcare, 2*(3), 282–293.

Grunig, J. E., & Grunig, L. (1992). Models of public relations and communication. In J. Grunig (Ed.), *Excellence in public relations and communication management* (pp. 285–326). Hillsdale, NJ: Erlbaum.

Grunig, J. E., & Hunt, T. (1984). *Managing public relations.* New York: Holt, Rinehart & Winston.

Hacker, K. L. (Ed.). (2004). *Presidential candidate images.* Lanham, MD: Rowman & Littlefield.

Hamelink, C. (2007). The professionalisation of political communication: Democracy at stake? In R. Negrine, P. Mancini, C. Holtz-Bacha, & S. Papathassopoulos (Eds.), *The professionalization of political communication* (pp. 179–187). Bristol, England: Intellect.

Harris, P., & Moss, D. (2001). [Editorial] Understanding public affairs. *Journal of Public Affairs, 1*(1), 6–8.

Hay, C. (Ed.) (2010). *New directions in political science.* Basingstoke, England: Palgrave Macmillan.

Henneberg, S. C. (2008). An epistemological perspective on research in political marketing. *Journal of Political Marketing, 7*(2), 151–182.

Herman, E., & Chomsky, N. (1988). *Manufacturing consent.* New York: Pantheon.

Hiebert, E. R. (2003). Public relations and propaganda in framing the Iraq war: A preliminary review. *Public Relations Review, 29*(3), 243–255.

Hon, C. L., & Grunig, J. E. (1999). *Guidelines for measuring relationships in public relations.* Gainesville, FL: The Institute for Public Relations.

Iyengar, S. (1991). *Is anyone responsible? How television frames political issues.* Chicago, IL: University of Chicago Press.

Jaques, T. (2006). Issue management: Process versus progress. *Journal of Public Affairs, 6*(1), 69–74.

Kaid, L. L., & Holtz-Bacha, C. (Eds). (2006). *The Sage handbook of political advertising.* Thousand Oaks, CA: Sage.

Katz, E., & Lazarsfeld, P. F. (1955). *Personal influence: The part played by people in the flow of communication.* New York: Free Press.

Killingsworth, C. (2009). Municipal government communications: The case of local government communications. *The McMaster Journal of Communication, 6*(1), 61–79.

Kumar, M. J. (2003). The contemporary presidency: Communications operations in the White House of President George W. Bush: Making news on his terms. *Presidential Studies Quarterly, 33*(2), 366–393.

Kumar, M. J. (2007). *Managing the president's message: The White House communications operations.* Baltimore, MD: John Hopkins University Press.

Kumar, M. J., & Sullivan, T. (Eds.). (2003). *The White House world: Transitions, organization, and office operations.* College Station: Texas A &M University Press.

Ledingham, J. A., & Bruning, S. D. (1998). Relationship management in public relations: Dimensions of an organization–public relationship. *Public Relations Review, 24*(1), 55–65.

Lee, M. (Ed.). (2008). *Government public relations: A reader.* Boca Raton, FL: CRC Press.

Lees-Marshment, J. (2004). *The political marketing revolution: Transforming the government of the UK.* Manchester, England: Manchester University Press.

Lees-Marshment, J., Strömbäck, J., & Rudd, C. (Eds.). (2010). *Global political marketing.* London: Routledge.

Leonard, M., Small, A., with Rose, M. (2005, February). *British public diplomacy in the "age of schisms."* London: Foreign Policy Centre.

Lin, Y. (2004). Fragmentation of the structure of political communication research: diversification or isolation? In L. L. Kaid (Ed.), *Handbook of political communication research* (pp. 69–108). Mahwah, NJ: Erlbaum.

Liu, B. F., & Horsley, J. S. (2007). The government communication decision wheel: toward a public relations model for the public sector. *Journal of Public Relations Research, 19*(4), 377–393.

McChesney, R. (2008) *The political economy of media: Enduring issues, emerging dilemmas.* New York: Monthly Review Press.

McCombs, M., & Shaw, D. (1972). The agenda-setting function of mass media. *Public Opinion Quarterly, 36,* 176–187.

McNair, B. (2007). *An introduction to political communication* (4th ed.). London: Routledge.

Monge, P., & Scott Poole, M. (2008). The evolution of organizational communication. *Journal of Communication, 58*(4), 679–692.

Negrine, R. (2008). *The transformation of political communication.* Basingstoke, England: Palgrave Macmillan.

Neustadt, R. (1960). *Presidential power: The politics of leadership with reflections on Johnson and Nixon.* Cambridge, MA: Harvard University Press.

Norris, P. (Ed.). (2009). *The public sentinel: News media and governance reform.* Washington, DC: World Bank.

Norris, P., Kern, M., & Just, M. (Eds.). (2003). *Framing terrorism: The news media, the government and the public.* New York: Routledge.

Oates, S. (2008). *Introduction to media and politics.* London: Sage.

Pandey, S., & Garnett, J. (2006). Exploring public sector communication performance: Testing a model and drawing implications. *Public Administration Review, 66*(1), 37–51.

Patterson, T. E. (1994). *Out of order.* New York: Vintage Books.

Patterson, T. E. (2003). *The vanishing voter: Public involvement in an age of uncertainty.* New York: Vintage Books.

Pfau, M. (2008). Epistemological and disciplinary intersections. *Journal of Communication, 58*(4), 597–602.

Puddington, A. (2009). Freedom in the world 2009: Setbacks and resilience. Freedom House. Retrieved from http://www.freedomhouse.org/template.cfm?page=130&year=2009.

Rainey, H. G. (2003). *Understanding and managing public organizations* (3rd ed.). San Francisco, CA: Jossey-Bass.

Rice, R., & Atkin, C. (Eds.). (2001). *Public communication campaigns* (3rd ed.). Thousand Oaks, CA: Sage.

Saco, D. (2002). *Cybering democracy.* Minnesota: University of Minnesota Press.

Sanders, K. (2009). *Communicating politics in the 21st century.* Basingstoke, England: Palgrave Macmillan.

Savigny, H. (2007). Ontology and epistemology in political marketing. *Journal of Political Marketing, 6*(2), 33–47.

Seymour Ure, C. (2003). *Prime ministers and the media: Issues of power and control.* Oxford, England: Blackwell.

Signitzer, B. (2008). Public relations and public diplomacy: Some conceptual explorations. In A. Zerfass, B. van Ruler, & K. Sriramesh (Eds.), *Public relations research: European and international perspectives and innovations* (pp. 205–216). Wiesbaden, Germany: VS Verlag.

Signitzer, B., & Wamser, C. (2006). Public diplomacy: A specific governmental public relations function. In C. Botan & V. Hazleton (Eds.), *Public relations theory II* (pp. 435–464). Mahwah, NJ: Erlbaum.

Silverstone, R. (2007). *Media and morality: On the rise of the mediapolis.* Cambridge, MA: Polity.

Singhai, A., & Greiner, K. (2008). Performance activism and civic engagement through symbolic and playful actions. *Journal of Development Communication, 19*(2), 43–53.

Smith, C. A., & Smith, K. (1994). *The White House speaks: Presidential leadership as persuasion.* Westport, CT: Praeger.

Stanyer, J. (2007). *Modern political communication: Mediated politics in uncertain times.* Cambridge, MA: Polity Press.

Strömbäck, J. (2007). Political marketing and professionalized campaigning: A conceptual analysis. *Journal of Political Marketing, 6*(2/3), 49–67.

Strömbäck, J., Mitrook, M., & Kiousis, S. (2010). Bridging two schools of thought: applications of public relations theory to political marketing. *Journal of Political Marketing, 9*(1), 73–92.

Swanson, D. (2000). Political communication research and the mutations of democracy. *Communication Yearbook, 23*, 189–205.

Taylor, P. (1997). *Global communications, international affairs and the media since 1945.* London: Routledge.

Tulis, J. (1987). *The rhetorical presidency.* Princeton, NJ: Princeton University Press.

Van Riel, C., & Fombrun, C. (2007). *Essentials of corporate communication: Implementing practices for effective reputation management.* New York: Routledge.

Vos, M. (2006). Setting the research agenda for governmental communication. *Journal of Communication Management*, *10*(3), 250–258.

Vos, M., & Westerhoudt, E. (2008). Trends in government communication in the Netherlands. *Journal of Communication Management*, *12*(1), 18–29.

Walker, K. (2010). A systematic review of the corporate reputation literature: Definition, measurement, and theory. *Corporate Reputation Review*, *12*(4), 357–387.

Weaver, D., McCombs, M., & Shaw, D. (2004). Agenda-setting research: Issues, attributes, and influences. In L. L. Kaid (Ed.), *Handbook of political communication research* (pp. 257–282). Mahwah, NJ: Erlbaum.

Wring, D. (2005). *The politics of marketing the Labour Party*. Houndsmill, England: Palgrave Macmillan.

Young, S. (Ed) (2007). *Government communication in Australia*. Cambridge, England: Cambridge University Press.

Zarefsky, D. (2004). Presidential rhetoric and the power of definition. *Presidential Studies Quarterly*, *14*(3), 607–619.

13

GLOBAL POLITICAL PUBLIC RELATIONS, PUBLIC DIPLOMACY, AND CORPORATE FOREIGN POLICY

Juan-Carlos Molleda

Introduction

This chapter discusses the interplay between public relations and public diplomacy from the perspectives of governments, nongovernmental organizations, and transnational corporations (TNCs). The trend of nonstate actors' participation in public diplomatic efforts is addressed. Subsequently, emphasis is placed on the role of TNCs as actors that increasingly have the power to influence or reinforce host government socioeconomic priorities, decisions, and actions, as well as the ways in which host governments and the citizenry define their relationship with TNCs.

More specifically, the chapter uses the literature of global public relations, public diplomacy, international business, and international strategic management to define the constructs of corporate foreign policy and corporate diplomacy. Mike Eskew (2006), former CEO of UPS, has said that one of the lessons he learned about corporate diplomacy was that long-term commitments are rewarded. By this he meant that corporation heads must take a long-term view of their business commitments. For example, UPS Europe took a long time to see profits, but in the long run having the patience needed to allow adaptation to other countries' cultures paid off (Eskew, 2006). Also, when working at UPS Asia, Eskew (2006) learned that sometimes the corporation must give up some control to gain greater flexibility and knowledge along the way, and think locally but act globally. He recommended putting international business operations in the hands of locals because they are the ones who know what practices work in their culture. Doing this will help the corporation to eventually achieve the long-term goals it hopes to accomplish in the host country. He also said that it was necessary to let acquired companies assimilate at their own pace. When companies are rushed into complying with a new regime, it does not help them to adapt or lead to success in a new environment. Lastly, Eskew (2006) argued that a corporation must be perceived as an integrator rather than an exploiter. Integration is a two-way street: The country and corporation are dependent upon each other for success. One way a corporation can help with this process is to practice good corporate citizenship and environmental responsibility every day in every country in which it operates (Eskew, 2006). Eskew's lessons learned are much of what academics point to as the keys to success for practicing corporate diplomacy. TNCs' actions and operations in business, politics, and sustainability are closely scrutinized on a continuing basis. These three interdependent areas determine the policies and values TNCs set to guide their relationship with home and host stakeholders.

The multidisciplinary theoretical framework for corporate diplomacy and corporate foreign policy is illustrated in this chapter with a discussion on corporate social responsibility (CSR) as a political practice. Similarly, the documentation of public relations techniques and efforts of U.S.-based TNCs in Latin America are addressed. For instance, corporate social responsibility programs and actions are analyzed from a political viewpoint, in which the role of transnational businesses, especially in developing countries, is that of a political actor. The association between a TNC and its country of origin's foreign policy also is discussed as an element that determines corporate diplomacy and strategic communication policies. For example, the United States faces various degrees of anti-American sentiments and activism in Latin America because of the effect of U.S. foreign policy, both in global and in regional terms. This situation forces U.S.-based TNCs to actively seek strategic engagements with host governments, businesses, and communities.

An Overview of Public Diplomacy in Public Relations

Public diplomacy has been defined as "the process by which direct relations are pursued with a country's people to advance the interests and extend the values of those being represented" (Sharp, 2007, p. 106). This definition implies strategic relationship-building efforts, advocacy, and the articulation of identities and the achievement of legitimacy and reputation by a variety of state and nonstate actors among segments of the population of a country in which those actors are guests. The direct component of the relationship entails engagement and dialogue in which personal and mediated communications have primary roles to play.

The associations between diplomacy and mass communication, and public diplomacy and public relations have been subjects of study (Gilboa, 2000; E. Signitzer & Coombs, 1992, respectively). In particular, public diplomacy has been conceptualized as a specific governmental public relations function (B. Signitzer & Wamser, 2006). This function entails government-to-public and public-to-public relationships to articulate national identity and to explain government policies to nonstate actors. However, as we will learn later in this chapter, nonstate actors have the power to influence host and home governmental policies and priorities. Using communication and public relations theories, the topic has been analyzed by approaching Habermas's communicative action theory (Wehrenfenning, 2008), coorientation in international relations (Verčič, Verčič, & Laco, 2006), contingency theory (Zhang, Qiu, & Cameron, 2004), and image restoration theory (Zhang & Benoit, 2004).

Public diplomacy techniques and efforts include information activities, international broadcasting, and educational and cultural exchanges (B. Signitzer & Wamser, 2006). Internet communications are being studied as tools and channels of public diplomacy and global political public relations (Curtin & Gaither, 2004; Searson & Johnson, in press). Other traditional conceptualizations of public diplomacy comprise image cultivation, advocacy of national interests, and promotion of mutual understanding (Zhang & Swartz, 2009a). An additional dimension includes promotion of global public goods (GPG), which is relevant at times when global environmental and economic or trade concerns force the international community to address these challenges collectively. The Asian tsunami relief campaigns coordinated by the United Nations represent the enforcement of GPG and offered positive lessons of governments, TNCs, and international nongovernmental organizations (NGOs) working together toward a common goal (Zhang, 2004). Other UN international communication policies and localized public information strategies in favor of peace in Central America have also been documented (Alleyne, 2008).

Public diplomacy and global public relations seem to be used together to promote political and socioeconomic models of a market economy (Ławniczak, 2007). This is an extension of "transitional" strategies and instruments carried out by the major global players, China, the European Union (EU), and the United States. The EU communication infrastructure and global and cultural communication techniques have been the subject of study among scholars (Fawkes & Moloney, 2008; Valentini, 2007). More specifically, L'Etang (1998) documented the beginnings of UK public relations in the 20th century with the exploration of state propaganda and the intelligence services.

In terms of specific public diplomatic efforts directed by governments, Wang (2006a) discussed the association between national reputation and public diplomacy, including three basic assumptions: public diplomacy as policy-driven, the primacy of nation-state governments in public diplomatic structure and processes, and the focus on mass mediated communication. National reputation has been a byproduct of and associated to the extent and tone of domestic and international news coverage about a foreign country in national environments. In particular, news coverage of foreign nations in industrialized markets has been found to be related to global public relations efforts conducted by foreign governments or agencies (i.e., public relations, lobbying, advertising, and legal counsel), which have been found to reduce negative coverage instead of increase positive news (Kiousis & Wu, 2008; Lee, 2006) and to influence public perceptions of foreign nations (Kiousis & Wu, 2008). In a related topic, the U.S. Foreign Agents Registration Unit, which comes under the U.S. Department of State, registers representatives of foreign interests in the United States who use lobbying or strategic communication in their countries' or organizations' interests. The registry has been the particular focus of research to assess the impact of strategic representation of foreign countries and media and perceptual outcomes (Lee, 2006; Zhang, 2005).

State and nonstate diplomatic efforts cover an array of topics of global concern; for example, health diplomacy involves activities that improve global health while strengthening relationships between the United States and populations abroad (Wise, 2009). U.S. public diplomatic efforts have been analyzed from a historical perspective (Wang, 2007), along with Arab–U.S. relations (Hiebert, 2005), post–September 11 (Zhang, 2007), and the North Korean nuclear threat (Hwang & Cameron, 2008). Additionally, commercial diplomacy entails activities by foreign affairs ministries, or in the case of the United States, the Department of State, as well as embassies and consulates around the world that support their country's business, trade, and financial sectors (Melissen, 2007a).

Emergent economies such as Brazil, Russia, India, and China (the BRIC countries) become the focus of research and the practice of public diplomacy and political public relations; for example, Bardhan and Patwardhan (2004) write about public relations of TNCs' subsidiaries in India. Lately, China has been at the center of public diplomacy studies with an emphasis on political public relations, including the impact of official head-of-state visits on local news coverage (Wang & Chang, 2004), image repair efforts during and after a transnational crisis (Peijuan, Ting, & Pang, 2009), media representation of a Chinese product crisis (Li & Tang, 2009), agenda building and image polishing (Zhang & Cameron, 2003), and the U.S.–China conflict resolution model (Zhang, Qiu, & Cameron, 2004). China's public diplomacy and global public relations efforts reached a climax before and during the Beijing 2008 Olympic Games. The country took advantage of the high-profile global event to strengthen its national identity; to consolidate a global reputation as an emergent but benevolent power; to advance its economic interests worldwide; and to reduce the impact of criticism concerning its questionable human rights records, and the seemingly contradictory economic and political systems, and in particular the quality of "Made in China" products and services (Loo & Davies, 2006; Manzenreiter, 2010). However, Manzenreiter (2010) questioned the effectiveness of China's soft power or public diplomatic efforts.

Nonstate actors are playing a greater role in public diplomacy and global public relations. Nongovernmental organizations (NGOs) as news creators and disseminators affecting international discussions on political, social, and economic issues were studied by Zhang and Swartz (2009a). They conceptualized a model to describe the core values, operations, effectiveness, and factors affecting effectiveness of a NGO news service. In sum, NGOs, national governments, and multilateral organizations use public diplomacy and global political public relations to achieve individual and collective goals. Other nonstate actors involved in public diplomacy are TNCs, and because of their size and power are greatly impacting international relations and strategic communication.

Definitions of Corporate Diplomacy

Corporate diplomacy is first about people, second about people who understand, and third about people who exercise the highest diplomatic qualities in organizations (Herter, 1966). Herter suggested asking a question when practicing corporate diplomacy: "Is the corporate policy in the foreign interest?" This is important because Herter said the interests of the U.S. government and U.S. business abroad must be mutually responsive. He suggested also asking questions about the corporation's practices that will make sure the host country, its people, and resources are treated appropriately. These questions should assess fairness, honesty, practicality, and flexibility.

Answering these questions appropriately is important for corporate success (Herter, 1966). In order to make a profit, corporations must consider the host countries' desires and act ethically. Wang (2006b) agreed on the importance of respecting other countries when practicing corporate diplomacy. He said there are three main objectives for corporate diplomacy. They are to promote the goals of the nation-state, communicate the nation's values, and create a sense of mutual understanding and trust between all countries and people.

Scherer and Palazzo (2007) and Palazzo and Scherer (2008) take a different approach when examining corporate diplomacy. They defined the role of corporations as political actors by evaluating positivist and postpositivist corporate social responsibility (CSR). When the schools within business and society research are analyzed, positivist CSR is enacted by a corporation because it will lead to increased profits (Scherer & Palazzo, 2007). Postpositivist CSR is more idealistic, according to Scherer and Palazzo (2007), and businesses do not necessarily base their philanthropic activities on the agenda of major public interest groups or other organizations with real or perceived economic, social, or political power; otherwise, businesses mainly consider powerless stakeholders whose interests are rarely considered under the positivist approach. Herter (1966) and Wang (2006b) would probably argue that postpositivist CSR is the ideal, but corporations appear to be mainly practicing positivist CSR. Husted and Allen (2006) explained that "institutional pressures, rather than strategic analysis of social issues and stakeholders, are guiding decision-making with respect to CSR" (p. 838).

Essentially, most academics would agree that public diplomacy is a growing trend among nonstate actors when they become involved with state actors. This involvement enhances the corporation's own initiatives, while often simultaneously benefiting the host country. This public diplomacy takes place despite the greater emphasis on institutional as opposed to societal or political priorities (Husted & Allen, 2006). Governments are willing to welcome TNCs to their countries because TNCs offer a variety of benefits to the host country, which include optimal use of production factors, use of unemployed resources, upgrading of resource quality, and the generation of economic growth (Steiner & Steiner, 2003). However, the presence of TNCs may not benefit the host country. For example, there may be a fear that TNCs could replace local companies, take the best natural and human resources, destroy local entrepreneurship, and decrease local research and development (R&D) (Steiner & Steiner, 2003). Thus, there is a fine line between benefits and drawbacks of TNCs' economic and political interventions in host countries.

TNCs are influenced and regulated by both the home and host governments, both of which put their interests at the front of any transaction and agreement. However, TNCs have some bargaining strengths they can use to their advantage in negotiations and relations with host governments, such as technology, strategic communication expertise (i.e., public affairs, public relations, corporate communication, advertising, and marketing), ability to export output, local product diversity, and value of foreign direct investment (FDI) (Steiner & Steiner, 2003). The ideal situation is to avoid conflicts over incompatibility of goals between host and home governments and TNCs. Some public perceptions about TNCs may steer the conflict. Host countries may suspect that TNCs are foreign-policy instruments of their home-country government, are independent of any government with supranational powers, or are agents of their host-country government or coalition within the host government (Steiner & Steiner, 2003). These public perceptions may raise political concerns, such as the potential for TNCs to exercise influence over or disrupt local politics, and with respect to foreign control of sensitive sectors of the local economy. For instance, the Ogaden National Liberation Front in Ethiopia argued that:

> It is the policy of the current Ethiopian regime to lure and involve multinationals, especially oil companies in the conflict in order to take advantage of the power and political influence of these multinationals, whose lobby can sway international opinion in order to mute voices of conscience, hence annul any international action against the war crimes and crimes against humanity Ethiopia is committing in Ogaden.
>
> ("Ethiopian Ogaden Rebels," 2007, ¶ 4)

Chen (2004) studied the bargaining power of TNCs in China from a public affairs perspective and formulated a conceptual model of TNC–government bargaining strategies. She articulated a set of practices for an effective public affairs function in an emergent economy:

> 1) practicing issues management, 2) constantly and systematically analyzing the MNC's [multinational corporation] bargaining power with the host government, 3) selecting public affairs strategies based on the emphasis of MNC-government bargaining, 4) exercising relationship management and 5) being ethical in practice.

> (p. 408)

Although this research focused on an emergent market economy, the need for and practice of corporate diplomacy and global political public relations began decades ago.

The Need for Corporate Diplomacy: Its Beginnings

Corporate diplomacy is not a new concept. The language used regarding corporate diplomacy and the theories supporting it are mentioned as early as a 1966 in a speech made at the National Institute of Petroleum Economics by Herter, then General Manager of the Government Relations Department at Socony Mobil Oil Company. He pinpointed three reasons that he believed suggested a need for corporate diplomacy in the postwar era. First Herter (1966) noted that after the war the new nations that emerged distrusted Western capitalism, and second there were new global competitors, the majority in Europe and Japan, and many were government owned or funded. Lastly, the attitude toward U.S. investment had changed in the minds of other countries. He concluded that "a varied and frustrating political climate, the intensity and nature of foreign competition, and growing protectionism have made the international scene much more crowded and complicated than it used to be" (Herter, 1966, p. 408). TNCs navigate these uncharted waters by means of the use of coordinated and controlled public relations and communication strategies between headquarters and subsidiaries (Molleda & Laskin 2010).

Muldoon (2005) extended Herter's principles for the need of corporate diplomacy to deal effectively with today's issues:

> Over the course of the last twenty years, global capitalism has become the most influential "ideology" in the world, catapulting firms and their leaders onto the world stage as influential players in international political, economic, and social relations. Increasingly, business is shaping the fundamental values and norms of society and defining public policy and practice.

> (p. 341)

Globalization has elevated the clout of TNCs among nonstate actors as corporations and NGOs are now challenging the traditional state-centric hierarchical structure of the international system (Muldoon, 2005). Budd (2001) has explained how the times are changing: Foreign policy is playing a greater role in the internal politics of nation-states, and there is more emphasis on raising societal responsibilities to correspond to shareholder expectations. Moreover, perceptions of corporate reputation are becoming as important as financial performance; the false conviction that beliefs are universal and that democracy is synonymous with free-market capitalism are being challenged (Budd, 2001). This latter assumption may not hold true because "[d]espite the rise of other nations and continents," Zakaria argued (2008), "the shadows of the West will be long and its legacies deep for decades to come, perhaps longer" (p. 52).

Goodman (2006) agreed that business is expanding into a global realm. Milton Friedman defined business as "an entity that creates wealth for its owners within the rules" (cited in Goodman, 2006, p. 5). Goodman has said, however, that business has expanded beyond this definition. Business now includes: "NGOs who are investors, investors who are employees, employees who are customers, consumers who are also local business partners, business partners who are also local stakeholders, local stakeholders who are also media, consumers who are also media, and media who are also NGOs" (pp. 5–6). As business expands, Goodman (2006) emphasized the importance of corporations respecting public opinion and expectations. To support his point, Goodman quoted Arthur W. Page who said, "[a]ll business begins with public permission and exists by public approval" (cited in Goodman, 2006, p. 6). Goodman stated that corporations must be transparent and ethical. They must follow universal values in four areas: human rights, labor rights, environmental standards, and anticorruption and transparency.

Durham (2002) summed up Muldoon's call for corporate diplomacy by pointing out that "corporate diplomacy answers a need created by globalization." Globalization has created this need by pushing corporations into conflict with NGOs and pressure groups. This has also in turn created a need for supranational regulators like the World Trade Organization. He mentioned the current needs for corporate diplomacy, many of which are similar to those enumerated by Herter in the 1960s. Durham (2002) said that the justifications for corporate diplomacy are found in an upsurge of joint ventures, recent mergers and acquisitions, the rise of NGOs defending human rights and the environment, and the shift of regulatory power from governments to global organizations such as the WTO and the World Intellectual Property Organization, among other multilateral institutions.

Responsibilities are Changing Hands

Corporations are becoming increasingly important to many nation-states, and their relationships are going through major changes. After the 2004 and 2005 global disasters—the Indian Ocean Tsunami, Hurricanes Katrina and

Rita, and the earthquake in Pakistan—corporations and NGOs were in fact the quickest to respond (Goodman, 2006). Governments followed suit but they would have had trouble staying afloat if it were not for TNCs and NGOs. One debated question relates to whether TNCs should take on international responsibilities, but it appears that many corporations have already done so (Durham, 2002). Goodman said that corporations often touch many more lives than governments possibly can. Relationships are also changing between corporations and NGOs. Most TNCs now have corporate responsibility programs set up (Durham, 2002). Many corporations hope that these developing programs will help them to avoid future confrontations with NGOs. Numerous corporations also donate to NGOs in an attempt to maintain good relationships with them.

Wang (2006b) argued that countries with poor foreign relations may suffer the consequence of decreased business deals and transactions. He stated that public diplomacy is less in the hands of governments today and is emerging as a responsibility of corporations. Therefore, some national economies will suffer if corporations do not choose to incorporate those countries in their business plans. According to Muldoon (2005) though, the rising power of TNCs is both positive and negative, which means the countries may not suffer as much as Wang predicted. Muldoon (2005) said companies have abused their power in the past and he mentioned an ongoing cycle of abuse of power followed by reform. Hart (2004), on the other hand, seemed to think that at this time it is difficult to evaluate the effects of corporations in politics, even in U.S. politics. He said, "[w]e need to do more work, both theoretical and empirical, on businesses as actors in American politics" (p. 65). Hart argued that businesses are often forgotten when counting organizations that are active at the national level, but they actually outnumber other politically active organizations. This fact can become apparent when examining TNCs' CSR efforts in their host countries.

Corporate Citizenship, Corporate Social Responsibility, and Sustainability

Globalization has resulted in an altered interpretation of CSR (Palazzo & Scherer, 2008), which has become more political as the divisions between nations blur and as TNCs grow in number. The emergence of CSR programs during the politically turbulent 1960s and 1970s, for example, points to the origins of CSR as a defense mechanism or reaction to crisis and its overemphasis as an unambiguously ethical model of managerial effectiveness (Brown, 2008).

Palazzo and Scherer (2008) assessed the alternate term for CSR, *corporate citizenship*, and said that the separation of the economic and political spheres needs to be further evaluated. Scherer has suggested deliberative democracy, an approach to CSR inspired by Jürgen Habermas. This political theory incorporates the positivist principles of economic return with the purely ethical motives of postpositivist CSR and accounts for the changing roles of corporations and the interactions between NGOs and governments; it also admits to the limits of CSR and corporate abilities.

Many corporations are feeling a burden of power (Muldoon, 2005). Corporations are feeling pressure to be more socially responsible, and are being pushed to practice some form of CSR. Many TNCs are now looking for a way to maintain autonomy while government organizations bombard them with requests to be environmentally and socially responsible. Muldoon also quoted Daniel Litvin, a senior research fellow at Chatham House and author of *Empires of Profit: Commerce, Conquest & Corporate Responsibility,* who said that some corporations are unsure of the benefits of CSR: "[c]ompanies that have taken up the CSR agenda have often continued to face severe public criticism" (cited in Muldoon, 2005, p. 351). Muldoon instead suggested partnering with NGOs. He said,

> [c]learly, multi-sector partnerships are the most visible approach to corporate citizenship for many corporations, but they are also considered an innovative approach for governments, international governmental organizations and civil society groups to overcome their "capacity constraints"—resources, expertise, and legitimacy—for dealing with social, economic and environmental public policy problems.
>
> (p. 353)

Partnering with host governments and domestic NGOs is more challenging when a TNC is associated with a country of origin that has unsettled and conflicting relationships with the public and nonprofit hosts.

Anti-Americanism as a Factor Affecting Corporate Diplomacy

This section of the chapter places the political relationships between TNCs and host governments and institutions in the larger context of an international relations environment in which foreign policies and decisions may mold corporate pursuits and operations. The relationship between a U.S.-based TNC and a host government is determined by the each party's goals. The similarity or divergence of goals could have a positive or negative effect on the TNC–government relationship. However, there are some environmental and contextual factors that may impact entry-level negotiations and operations in a host country and may even affect exit strategies. One of these factors is the relationship between the host country and the TNC's home country.

After the events of September 11, 2001, anti-American sentiment flourished in many parts of the world, among them in Latin America because U.S. foreign policy seemingly ignored the subcontinent. This region's governments and populations, in particular, felt left out of foreign priorities because of the emphasis that was being placed on the Middle East and the war against terrorism. This section describes how anti-Americanism has affected the relationship between U.S. business interests and national governments, institutions, and populations in Latin American countries. Although the focus is on Latin America (the author's specialty), the issues can easily be translated to other parts of the world that are experiencing a changing scenario for relations with the government of the United States, as well as U.S.-based businesses and other national contexts.

What is Anti-Americanism?

Anti-Americanism is the psychological tendency to hold negative views of the United States and of U.S. society in general (Katzenstein & Keohane, 2007). It "rests on the singular idea that something associated with the United States, something at the core of American life, is deeply wrong and threatening to the rest of the world" (Ceaser, 2003, p. 4). Anti-Americanism has been referred to as antiyanquismo, anti-U.S. resistance, and yankeephobia (McPherson, 2006).

Anti-Americanism can be considered more of a response to U.S. policy than a priori ideology (McPherson, 2006). McPherson explained, "Latin American rich and poor turned most anti-US when policies supporting dictatorship and repression contradicted Washington's promises of democracy and freedom" (p. 272). Just because anti-American sentiments are being held does not mean that they are applied the same way to U.S. citizens as they are to activities of the U.S. government (McPherson, 2006). Some have appreciated the "US people as 'good' while berating their government's actions as 'bad'—*norteamericanos* fooled by *yanqui* imperialism [emphasis in original]" (McPherson, 2006, p. 272).

Sources of Anti-Americanism

Antipathy toward the United States can be driven by numerous factors, including but not limited to the political system and the view that "US economic self-interest was the primary reason for any US presence in Latin America" (McPherson, 2006, p. 272). The sources for this sentiment around the world can be better divided into fundamental sources and ephemeral sources. Fundamental sources for anti-Americanism (disliking what the United States of America is) include the fact that the United States has enjoyed unchallenged military superiority since the end of the Cold War (Katzenstein & Keohane, 2007) and that the United States has intervened militarily in different scenarios around the world. Other fundamental factors include the clear differences in public attitudes toward social welfare, the death penalty, and human rights. Other possible sources include resentment of the dominant U.S. role in economic and social globalization and its wealth (Katzenstein & Keohane, 2007). The ephemeral sources for anti-Americanism (disliking what the United States of America does) are linked to foreign and domestic policies and the effects these policies have on people around the world.

Types of Anti-Americanism

There are four types of anti-Americanism: liberal, social, sovereign-nationalist, and radical (Katzenstein & Keohane, 2007). Liberal anti-Americanism, which is prevalent in liberal societies of highly industrialized countries, criticizes the United States for not living up to its own values as a country. The United States parades itself under the banner of its ideals, but is seen as too self-interested and hypocritical to defend them in "words or deeds," much more so than other liberal countries may be (Katzenstein & Keohane, 2005, p. 35). Such behavior opens the United States to charges of hypocrisy from people who share its ideals but disagree with its actions.

Social anti-Americanism comes from a set of political institutions that include liberal values in a larger set of social and political arrangements. They help define market processes and outcomes that are left more autonomous in the United States. It is characterized by a support for a variety of social programs that are possible in the United States but are not undertaken. A more genuinely value-based conflict exists here over the preference given to the wealthy over the poor through U.S. policies, higher esteem placed in the sanctity of international treaties, greater desire for "generous social protections," death penalty use, and the preference of multilateral versus unilateral action (Katzenstein & Keohane, 2005, pp. 38–39).

Sovereign-nationalist anti-Americanism "focuses on two values: the importance of not losing control over the ways policies are inserted in world politics and the importance and value of collective national identities" (Katzenstein & Keohane, 2007, p. 32) or more specifically on the ideas of nationalism, sovereignty, and power. This type of anti-Americanism resonates in countries with strong traditions and where U.S. actions are perceived as detrimental to nationalism, sovereignty, or the exercise of power (Katzenstein & Keohane, 2005, p. 40).

Latin America, for example, has been noted to reflect sovereign-nationalist anti-Americanism more than any other type of anti-Americanism (Katzenstein & Keohane, 2005). Some parts of the Middle East and Asia, especially China, are also characterized by strong sovereign-nationalist anti-Americanism sentiments. These are likely to build when issues such as Google's recent challenge to sovereignty arise. Google has been in China and abiding by China's Internet legal norms for 4 years. Now, Google is seeking to break ties with those rules and abide by the "pretext of Internet freedom" claiming that "business is business" ("The Biggest Loser," 2010, p. 6).

The last form of anti-Americanism is radical. It is built around "the belief that U.S. identity, as reflected in the economic and political power relations and institutional practices of the United States, ensures that its actions will be hostile to the furtherance of good values, practices and institutions throughout the world" (Katzenstein & Keohane, 2007, p. 33). For progress toward a better world to take place, the U.S. economy and society will have to be transformed by any means necessary. Not all radical groups that are anti-American advocate violence, but they do argue for the weakening, destruction, or transformation of the political and economic institutions of the United States. Radical anti-Americanism is the second most commonly seen form of anti-Americanism in Latin America.

Expressions of Anti-Americanism in Latin America

Anti-Americanism sentiments can be found all over the world including Europe (Ewing, Scott, & Fishbein, 2008), the Middle East (Walker, 2007), and even in the United States of America itself (Scruton, 2007). However, the region of the world that has recently displayed its deep hatred for the United States is one of its closest neighbors, Latin America and the Caribbean. Headlines in *The Wall Street Journal* such as "Free Markets Spur Protest: Across Latin America, Many Feel Let Down by Economic Changes" (Luhnow, 2005) highlight the spread of rising frustrations.

Cuba has been a big player in developing anti-American sentiments in Latin America. There are numerous reasons for the subcontinent's attitude toward the United States, and there is a long history between the two regions. For example, the United States has held a negative relationship with Cuba which has affected their trade policies (Lengell, 2008). Anti-American sentiments also started emerging with Hugo Chávez. The president of Venezuela has been pushing for the development of a Latin American organization to stand up against free trade, and has positioned himself as a world leader from Iran to China and across the Americas (Geyer, 2006). Chávez has managed to tap into growing discontent throughout Latin America, where citizens have lost faith in traditional political parties and feel that U.S.-advocated reforms only benefit the elite (Smith, 2005b).

However, most of the anti-American sentiments in Latin America began in 2001 when George W. Bush was elected president of the United States. Even though he vowed that Latin America would be his top foreign policy priority (Smith, 2005a), it seemed to become an after-thought for Washington after the events of September 11, 2001 (Smith, 2005a). Washington would only pay attention to Latin America when the issues of drugs, guerrillas, hurricanes, or currency became relevant in terms of U.S. interests (Smith, 2005a). Even so, the United States has been seen to limit its help to Latin America on these issues. For example, the United States reduced its funds to Mexico for the Mérida Initiative—a package meant to help Mexico fight drug trafficking—by 25% (Chris, 2009).

For the last few years, Latin America has been struggling with its admiration for the United States. Much of that admiration turned to resentment

(Smith, 2005a), which was also fueled by former President Bush and his administration's aggressive unilateralism; Washington's actions caused people in the region, rich and poor, to condemn Washington's disregard for international institutions and norms (Geyer, 2006). For instance, as a result of Washington's involvement with the Middle East, more specifically the war in Iraq, Latin America boycotted U.S. products in 2003 ("No Money," 2003). Labor unions in the largest port in Brazil as well as other Latin American countries planned a 24-hour boycott of ships and goods that were associated with the United States ("No Money," 2003). "We are proposing that no adherent to the strike drink a Coca-Cola or go into a McDonald's for lunch," Duarte, president of the Urban Unions of Santos, the largest port of Brazil and Latin America, said ("No Money," 2003, p. 3). Boycotts like these have affected companies such as Dunkin' Donuts, McDonald's, Burger King, Starbucks, Sears, Krispy Kreme, and Wal-Mart ("In Mexico," 2006; "May 1st," 2006).

United States involvement in the Middle East has not been the only reason for Latin Americans to boycott U.S. products and services. On May 1, 2006, a boycott similar to that of the "Great American Boycott of 2006: No Shopping, No School, No Work" took place in Mexico and other parts of Central America. This boycott was a way to express anti-U.S. sentiments because of cross-border tensions and immigration policies ("In Mexico," 2006).

Although the Bush administration's policies led to further deterioration of relations with Latin America, many of these problems existed before he took office. In the mid-1980s, when communism faded as a potential threat, Washington urged Latin American governments to introduce market reforms and promised privatizations and free trade would raise millions out of poverty (Smith, 2005a). Latin Americans became disillusioned with Washington's push for democracy linked to free trade as the answer to poverty (Geyer, 2006).

Now, Latin Americans blame the United States for pushing them into believing "political phantasms" (Geyer, 2006). This has caused many Latin Americans to become distrustful of others, especially government figures (Sands, 2008). This remains a major cultural hindrance for Latin America and the potential for democracy.

Anti-Americanism is never going to disappear, and U.S. leaders, business executives, and even citizens will always have enemies who do not support its views, actions, and values. Such conflicted attitudes could pose a challenge for the current U.S. president, who is in charge of charting a course in a region where President Bush had a low rating in public opinion polls (Sands, 2008). For Washington to counter Chávez's influence, it would have to start paying attention to Latin America after virtually ignoring it following September 11 (Smith, 2005b). Washington needs to repair the relationship and focus on programs to aid education, health care, and justice systems because the people of Latin America want to be treated as equals (Smith, 2005a). This indicates the ongoing nature of the relationships between nations and regions with foreseeable implications for TNC–government relations and TNCs' social and business partnering efforts to, for instance, implement CSR programs or achieve commercial alliances.

From Theory to Practice and Vice Versa

Transnational corporations engage in government relations at home and host countries. Their behaviors and operations are regulated by national, regional, and global governmental and trade institutions. They are also political actors who may impact legislation or government priorities in terms of foreign affairs, for the home country, or trade and foreign direct investment (FDI) promotion for the host countries. Here the management of the international public relations function is guided for political purposes, which supports the definition of political public relations articulated by the editors of this volume in the introductory chapter. Moreover, the purposeful corporate efforts and communication techniques are aimed to influence home and host policies and relational outcomes.

TNCs have political agendas and through strategic communication and lobbying attempt to influence political processes and decisions. Therefore, attending to the expectations and legislation of multiple governments requires the use of public relations and public affairs techniques and efforts in complex political environments and for strategic political goals and objectives. The maneuver over unstable and ever-changing water currents should be guided by a corporate foreign policy, which should state the core values to initiate, develop, and maintain relationships with government authorities, agencies, and other institutions. Budd (2001) stated the components of a corporate office of foreign policy:

> (a) an internal directorate charged with monitoring, assessing, reporting on noncommercial trends in those parts of the world pivotal to the company's interest; (b) principally serving as a resource for the CEO and ... the board, alerting to the public mood shifts, political swings and implications thereof; and (c) targeting those more discernible 'trends-beneath-trends' that stand to engender direct and potential threats against corporate actions.

> (p. 132)

"Large and small nonstate actors, and supranational and subnational players develop public diplomacy policies of their own," Melissen explained (2007b, p. 12). Management and global public relations executives have this added responsibility to fulfill. Budd (2001) described the expansion of the global CEO's role, which entails a new level of corporate statesmanship and strategic and tactical diplomacy. He said the highest level of management should pay attention, among other business-related aspects, to nonfinancial issues, such as the significance of social and political trends; the perceptions of host public and governments; nation-state cultural, social, and political biases; all cultural customs, traditions, values, and attitudes of people within the area of operation; foreign affairs literacy; and the positive and negative aspects of globalism. Management should be able to articulate their thoughts on the latter subject.

In terms of the global political public relations profession and the professional, and the comprehensive literature review in this chapter, the following are considerations that could be used to develop principles of corporate diplomacy:

1. Corporate foreign policy should strive to strike a balance between institutional and contextual forces.
2. Historical environmental forces, such as anti-Americanism, need to be understood and studied in terms of sources and types to strategize potential threats, opportunities, and responses to facilitate legitimacy of the TNC and its actions and operations in host countries.
3. TNCs are affected by home and host regulations and expectations. Therefore public relations and public affairs professionals are advised to assess both perceptions and legislation, as well as to develop communication plans and programs to engage home and host stakeholders and persuasively make the connection between host and home expectations and realities.

Topics for future research in corporate diplomacy and corporate foreign policy and a subset of global political public relations can also be drawn from this chapter:

1. Corporate social responsibility efforts as a political function of TNCs, especially the association between the matching of CSR programs and the orientation and priorities of host governments.
2. The degrees and forms of institutionalization of corporate foreign policy and its insertion in strategic communication plans, including the variations of models according to industry types, country of origin, and economic and political orientation of host countries.
3. Influence of sources and types of contextual phenomenon such as anti-Americanism on corporate policy, strategies, and tactics to establish and maintain relationships with host governments in regions with various degrees of anti-Americanism and perhaps, antiglobalism and anticapitalism.

The political function of global public relations demands a deep knowledge of goals and potential benefits of TNCs actions and operations for the home and host countries. The political orientation and domestic and foreign policies determine the acceptance or rejection of TNCs' presence in specific markets. The corporate foreign policy and, subsequently, corporate diplomatic techniques and efforts have to be articulated by considering a long-term view of relationship-building strategies and mutually beneficial outcomes for home and host stakeholders, including governments. Public relations theories and teachings are easy to extrapolate to the global political environments with progressive reasons for interdependence and collective action.

References

Alleyne, M. (2008). Manufacturing peace through international communication policies: United Nations public information strategy in Guatemala 1996–2004. *Communication, Culture & Critique, 1,* 163–178.

Bardhan, N., & Patwardhan, P. (2004). Multinational corporations and public relations in a historically resistant host culture. *Journal of Communication Management, 8*(3), 246–263.

The biggest loser. (2010). *China Daily.* Retrieved from http://www.chinadaily.com.cn/opinion/2010-03/22/content_9620293.htm

Brown, R. (2008). Sea change: Santa Barbara and the eruption of corporate social responsibility. *Public Relations Review, 34*(1), 1–8.

Budd, J. F. Jr. (2001). Opinion … foreign policy acumen needed by global CEOs. *Public Relations Review, 27*(2), 123–134.

Ceaser, J. W. (2003, Summer). A genealogy of anti-Americanism. *The Public Interest, 152,* 3–18.

Chen, Y. R., (2004). Effective public affairs in China: MNC-government bargaining power and corporate strategies for influencing business policy formulation. *Journal of Communication Management, 8*(4), 395–413.

Chris, H. (2009, March 23). Clinton to address trade and turmoil in Mexico. *USA Today,* 1.

Curtin, P. A., & Gaither, T. K. (2004). International agenda-building in cyberspace: A study of Middle East government English-language websites. *Public Relations review, 30,* 25–36.

Durham, T. (2002). Business buys into deals with diplomacy. *Times Higher Education Supplement, 1524,* 20.

Eskew, M. (2006). Corporate diplomacy. *Leadership Excellence, 23*(4), 5–6.

Ethiopian Ogaden rebels warn foreign firms not to venture in region. (2007, September 17). BBC Worldwide Monitoring. Retrieved from LexisNexis Academics.

Ewing, J., Scott, M, & Fishbein, J. (2008, March 10). More fodder for the yank-haters: The spreading U.S. credit crisis is turning up the heat on Europe's simmering anti-Americanism. *Business Week,* (4074), 35.

Fawkes, J., & Moloney, K. (2008). Does the European Union (EU) need a propaganda watchdog like the US Institute of Propaganda Analysis to strengthen its democratic civil society and free market? *Public Relations Review, 34,* 207–214.

Geyer, G. A. (2006, November 7). Split opens hemisphere to world; Latin Americans cast aside U.S. to take more ominous shadow. *The Washington Times,* A12.

Gilboa, E. (2000). Mass communication and diplomacy: A theoretical framework. *Communication Theory, 10*(3), 275–309,

Goodman, M. B. (2006). The role of business in public diplomacy. *Journal of Business Strategy, 27*(3), 5–7.

Hart, D. (2004). Business is not an interest group: On the study of companies in American national politics. *Annual Review of Political Science, 7*(1), 47–69.

Herter, C. A. (1966, March 11). Corporate diplomacy in foreign countries. *Vital Speeches of the Day, 32*(13), 407–409.

Hiebert, E. (2005). Commentary: Challenges for Arab and American public relations and public diplomacy in a global age. *Public Relations Review, 31*(3), 317–322.

Husted, B. W., & Allen, D .B. (2006). Corporate social responsibility in the multinational enterprise: strategic and institutional approaches. *Journal of International Business Studies, 37,* 838–849.

Hwang, S., & Cameron, G. T. (2008). The elephant in the room is awake and takes things personally: The North Korean nuclear threat and the general public's estimation of American diplomacy. *Public Relations Review, 34*(1), 41–48.

In Mexico, "nothing gringo on May 1." (2006, April 14). Associated Press. Retrieved from http://sweetness-light.com/archive/may-1st-boycott-gringos-day

Katzenstein, P. J., & Keohane, R. (2005). *Varieties of anti-Americanisms: Framework for analysis.* Paper presented at the annual meeting of the American Political Science Association, Washington, DC.

Katzenstein, P. J., & Keohane, R. (2007). *Anti-Americanisms in world politics.* Ithaca, NY: Cornell University Press.

Kiousis, S., & Wu, X. (2008). International agenda-building and agenda-setting: Exploring the influence of public relations counsel on US news media and public perceptions of foreign nations. *International Communication Gazette, 70*(1), 58–75.

Ławniczak, R. (2007). Public relations role in a global competition "to sell" alternative political and socio-economic models of market economy. *Public Relations Review, 33,* 377–386.

Lee, S. (2006). An analysis of other countries' international public relations in the U.S. *Public Relations Review, 32*(2), 97–103.

Lengell, S. (2008, March 8). U.S. not to loosen policies on Cuba; Bush cites rights abuses.. *The Washington Times,* Nation section.

L'Etang, J. (1998). State propaganda and bureaucratic intelligence: The creation of public relations in 20th century Britain. *Public Relations Review, 24*(4), 413–441.

Li, H., & Tang, L. (2009). The representation of the Chinese product crisis in national and local newspapers in the United States. *Public Relations Review, 35*(3), 219–225.

Loo, T., & Davies, G. (2006). Branding China: The ultimate challenge in reputation management? *Corporate Reputation Review, 9*(3), 198–213.

Luhnow, D. (2005, September 7). Free markets spur protest: Across Latin America, many feel let down by economic changes. *The Wall Street Journal,* A18.

Manzenreiter, W. (2010). The Beijing Games in the Western imagination of China: The weak power of soft power. *Journal of Sport & Social Issues, 34*(1), 29–48.

May 1st To Be "Boycott Gringos" Day Across US." (2006). Retrieved from http://sweetness-light.com/archive/may-1st-boycott-gringos-day.

McPherson, A. (Ed.). (2006). *Anti-Americanism in Latin America and the Caribbean.* New York: Berghahn Books.

Melissen, J. (2007a). Introduction. In J. Melissen (Ed.), *The new public diplomacy: Soft power in international relations* (pp. xvii–xxii). Basingstoke, England: Palgrave Macmillan.

Melissen, J. (2007b). The new public diplomacy: Between theory and practice. In J. Melissen (Ed.), *The new public diplomacy: Soft power in international relations* (pp. 3–27). Basingstoke, England: Palgrave Macmillan.

Molleda, J. C., & Laskin, A. (2010). Coordination and control of global public relations to manage cross-national conflict shifts: A multidisciplinary perspective for research and practice. In G. J. Golan, T. J. Johnson, & W. Wanta (Eds.), *International media communication in a global age* (pp. 319–344). New York: Routledge.

Muldoon, J. (2005). The diplomacy of business. *Diplomacy & Statecraft, 16*(2), 341–359.

No money for war: Consumers around the globe boycott US. (2003). Retrieved from The Canadian Centres for Teaching Peace. http://www.peace.ca/boycottUSA.htm.

Palazzo, G., & Scherer, A. G. (2008). Corporate social responsibility, democracy, and the politicization of the corporation. *Academy of Management Review, 33*(3), 773–775.

Peijuan, C., Ting, L. P., & Pang, A. (2009). Managing a nation's image during crisis: A study of the Chinese government's image repair efforts in the "Made-in-China" controversy. *Public Relations Review, 35*(3), 213–218.

Sands, D. R. (2008, April 15). Latin American's complex dance with democracy. *The Washington Times,* A13.

Scherer, A. G., & Palazzo, G. (2007). Toward a political conception of corporate responsibility: Business and society seen from a Habermasian perspective. *Academy of Management Review, 32*(4), 1096–1120.

Scruton, R. (2007, September). Anti-Americanism. *American Spectator, 40*(7), 40–42.

Searson, E. M., & Johnson, M. A. (in press). Transparency laws and interactive public relations: An analysis of Latin American government Web sites. *Public Relations Review,* doi: 10.1016/j. pubrev.2010.03.003

Sharp, P. (2007). Revolucionary states, outlaw regimes and the techniques of public diplomacy. In J. Melissen (Ed.), *The new public diplomacy: Soft power in international relations* (pp. 106–123). Basingstoke, England: Palgrave Macmillan.

Signitzer, E., & Coombs, T. (1992). Public relations and public diplomacy: Conceptual convergences. *Public Relations Review, 18,* 137–147.

Signitzer, B., & Wamser, C. (2006). Public diplomacy: A specific governmental public relations function. In C. H. Botan & V. Hazleton (Eds.), *Public relations theory II* (pp. 435–464). Mahwah, NJ: Erlbaum.

Smith, G. (2005a, November 21). Why Latin Americans detest Uncle Sam. *Business Week Online.* Retrieved from http://www.businessweek.com/bwdaily/dnflash/nov2005/ nf20051121_6027.htm

Smith, G. (2005b, December 26). Chavez: Trading oil for influence. *Business Week Online. Retrieved from http://www.businessweek.com/print/magazine/content/05_52/b3965071.htm?chan=gl*

Steiner, G. A., & Steiner, F. F. (2003). *Business, government, and society: A managerial perspective text and cases* (10th ed.). New York: McGraw-Hill Irwin.

Valentini, C. (2007). Global versus cultural approaches in public relationship management: The case of the European Union. *Journal of Communication Management, 11*(2), 117–133.

Verčič, D., Verčič, A. T., & Laco, K. (2006). Coorientation theory in international relations: The case of Slovenia and Croatia. *Public Relations Review, 32*(1), 1–9.

Walker, J. (2007, July 15). Truly democratic—and anti-American. *The Jerusalem Post,* 13.

Wang, J. (2006a). Managing national reputation and international relations in the global era: Public diplomacy revisited. *Public Relations Review, 32*(2), 91–96.

Wang, J. (2006b). Public diplomacy and global business. *Journal of Business Strategy, 27*(3), 41–49.

Wang, J. (2007). Telling the American story to the world: The purpose of U.S. public diplomacy in historical perspective. *Public Relations Review, 33*(1), 21–30.

Wang, J., & Chang, T.K. (2004). Strategic public diplomacy and local press: How a high-profile "head-of-state" visit was covered in America's heartland. *Public Relations Review, 30*(1), 11–24.

Wehrenfenning, D. (2008). Conflict management and communicative action: Second-track diplomacy from a Habermasian perspective. *Communication Theory, 18,* 356–376.

Wise, K. (2009), Public relations and health diplomacy. *Public Relations Review, 35*(1), 127–129.

Zakaria, F. (2008). *The post-American world.* New York: Norton.

Zhang, J. (2004). Public diplomacy as symbolic interactions: A case study of Asian tsunami relief campaigns. *Public Relations Review, 30*(1), 26–32.

Zhang, J. (2005). World system and its agents: Analysis of the registrants of Foreign Agent Registration Act (FARA). *Public Relations Review, 31,* 47–54.

Zhang, J. (2007). Beyond anti-terrorism: Metaphors as message strategy of post-September 11 U.S. public diplomacy. *Public Relations Review, 33*(1), 31–39.

Zhang, J., & Benoit, W.L. (2004). Message strategies of Saudi Arabia's image restoration campaign after 9/11. *Public Relations Review, 30*(2), 161–167.

Zhang, J., & Cameron, G. T. (2003). China's agenda building and image polishing in the US: Assessing an international public relations campaign. *Public Relations Review, 29*(1), 13–28.

Zhang, J., Qiu, Q., & Cameron, G.T. (2004). A contingency approach to the Sino-U.S. conflict resolution. *Public Relations Review, 30*(4), 391–399.

Zhang, J., & Swartz, B. C. (2009a). Public diplomacy to promote global public goods (GPG): Conceptual expansion, ethical grounds, and rhetoric. *Public Relations Review, 35*(4), 382–387.

14

DIGITAL POLITICAL PUBLIC RELATIONS[1]

Kaye D. Sweetser

With the increased use of digital communication tools, public relations has been noted to return to a more personal "relationship" with key publics. As outlined in the definition of political public relations that Strömbäck and Kiousis articulate as a basis of this book, relationship is a prime aspect of both the definitions of political communication and public relations. Indeed, a focus on relationships may have been even more present in political public relations than general public relations, as political communication has always taken a personal approach to connecting with its publics. That is, political public relations has traditionally sought to make candidates appear more personal through tactics such as wearing less formal attire in certain situations and choreographing campaign events that allow candidates to personally interact with constituents.

From the voter's standpoint, the rise of digital communication has facilitated an act that has been around as long as elections—the act of talking politics. From connecting with politicians to talking about politics with peers, voters have long engaged in political discourse. So the evolution of digital political public relations is not surprising when one considers the opportunity campaigns have had to mass produce the process where candidates connect with constituents and the benefits to voters whose circle of friends expanded.

Even the terms associated with digital communication speak to the foundations of public relations. The word *interactivity* in digital media represents the ability to either contribute to content or create one's own nonlinear path through information (McMillian, 2002). In public relations, interactivity harkens ideas of dialogic communication where two-way conversations occur between the organization and key publics (Kent & Taylor, 1998). Similarly, the en vogue umbrella term *social media* refers to the ability of groups of people to connect and share information. Looking at the term *social media* from a public relations perspective, one can't help but think of relationships, a key theoretical approach to creating meaningful connections with an organization's publics (Sweetser, 2010). As such, digital political public relations spans the boundaries of more traditional public relations in that it also informs, engages, and has the potential to mobilize publics through the use of digital tools and to take the cocreational approach to the next level (Boton & Taylor, 2004).

This chapter will examine the use of digital political public relations from multiple perspectives. First, the chapter will examine campaign use of digital public relations. Second, constituents' use of digital tools will be explored. The third section will review the e-government literature to describe how governments have integrated digital tools. Finally, general political talk online will be examined.

Campaign and Politicians' Use of Digital Tools

Since the earliest campaigns, candidates have looked for ways to connect with voters and spread information. Historically, such information dissemination could occur through public relations-planned pseudo-events like a debate or even through public relations-arranged media coverage. With regard to connecting to one's publics, candidates could host a political rally, which would give constituents a chance to meet the politician in person. As technology developed, politicians and campaigns started to use telephones and the airwaves, broadcasting essentially the same events through radio or television (Kaid, 2004; Selnow, 1998). With the ubiquitous adoption of the Internet, politicians have integrated digital communication tools and successively developed their use to a much more interactive and engaging style of communication.

Thinking of online political communication from a public relations perspective, Foot and Schneider (2006) point out that "the adoption and strategic use of information and communication technologies precedes the digital era" (p. 7). To this point, Tedesco (2004) suggests that campaigns can benefit from Grunig and Hunt's (1984) two-way symmetrical model, and that public relations used in campaign communications represent the greatest areas for potential and development. The creation of a digital presence requires strategic thinking about how to connect this tool with other publicity tools. Indeed, the messages and candidate image should align both in terms of content and quantity with the goals of the overall communication plan. Given that Benoit and Hansen (2004) suggested that "new technologies provide alternate sources of information about the presidential campagn that now compete with newspapers and television news" (p. 168), campaigns are now able to better communicate with a wider audience of constituents without the filter of the traditional media. To this point, the first use of the Internet in a political campaign in the United States was traditional public relations, as the 1992 Clinton campaign used the first-ever campaign Web site to post press releases and general interest information (Whillock, 1997).

History

The integration of campaign Web sites has increased exponentially since first introduced in the early 1990s. As more people got access to the Internet, broadband improved speed, digital communication became more ubiquitous, and campaigns saw the benefits of using this medium as a key public relations tool.

When campaign Web sites were first introduced during the 1992 presidential election cycle, Bimber and Davis (2003) suggested that this was primarily done as a way to reinforce messages conveyed in other media. The Clinton campaign, the first to distribute text over the Internet (Tedesco, 2004; Whillock, 1997), employed e-mail to some degree during this election cycle (Casey, 1996). In the 1994 election, Senators Dianne Feinstein and Edward M. Kennedy were the first congressional candidates to use campaign Web sites (Foot & Schneider, 2006).

Web use grew during the next campaign cycle, which Kaid and Bystrom (1999) termed the *electronic election*. Not only did all "serious candidates" (Tedesco, 2004) running for president have a digital presence, one even announced his candidacy online (LaPointe, 1999). According to D'Alessio (1997), nearly half of Senate and around 15% of House candidates had Web sites in 1996. Even with this wider adoption, scholars suggest Web sites were nothing more than electronic versions of campaign brochures (Foot & Schneider, 2006; Tedesco, 2004). This "virtual billboard" approach dominated campaign approaches to Web sites until the 2000 election. As Foot and Schneider (2006) suggest, "for most candidates in 1996, merely being on the Web, or demonstrating knowledge of the Web, *was* Web campaigning [emphasis added]." Evolving from that election, campaigns in the United States and abroad grew with each election cycle, offering more content, interactivity, donation, and mobilization opportunities.

The 2004 election cycle in the United States saw greater gains in integration, capitalizing on the lessons learned in the previous cycles. The focus in 2004 was on what is now called social media, as campaign blogs were introduced and more tailored content was offered to Web site visitors. Notable milestones of digital adoption are the use of blogs in the 2004 election, social networks during the 2006 midterm election, as well as better integration of viral video sharing, and the multiple platform approach taken during the 2008 election.

This historical look at the integration of digital communication tools into the campaign suggests a process where campaigns appear to test out technology at lower-level election cycles (midterm elections) or wait until the masses have adopted a tool before implementing it. Though not discussed extensively here, this type of evolution from brochure-ware to a more interactive repository of limitless campaign information was mirrored in other nations such as Chile (Boas, 2008). Early digital integration was challenged when campaigns were not able to fully operate the technology within the community standards, but campaigns have made positive strides to improve in this area and appear more organic and congruent in their communication.

Approaches

The personal, interactive, and instant elements of digital communication make it a unique medium through which to communicate. Underlying each approach is the goal of the campaign to strengthen the relationship with target publics: Schneider and Foot (2006) note that such practices revolve around relationship building with other political actors. Though speaking about blogs, Garrett's (2004) suggestions for a digital political presence hold true for a multitude of online tools: campaigns should write content in a personal voice, update several times a day, encourage comments, moderate comments, hyperlink to internal and external sources, hyperlink to other interactive sites, and call the readers into action. As such, it is easy to see that a single tool rarely has a single purpose. And certainly that purpose needs to operate in concert with the entire campaign strategy, as one of many tools in the political public relations arsenal. Along these lines, Trammell, Williams, Postelnicu, and Landreville (2006) looked at campaign blogs in the 2004 election and determined that the campaign public relations team aimed to involve voters in the campaign, share publicity materials and information about the campaign, and encourage donations or volunteering to actively support the campaign.

The most successful integrations of technology in the campaign communication plan focuses on multiple approaches. On one hand, Banwart (2002) found that campaigns deploy different issue strategies based on medium, which indicates that campaigns in theory understand optimizing the medium as a strategic tool. On the other hand, Sweetser Trammell (2007) found that when it came to communicating messages of interest tailored to a specific group (e.g., young people) in the spaces primarily used by that group (e.g., social media), campaigns failed to harness digital tools in a targeted manner.

Personalization online can have several different manifestations. It may refer to the ability for the user to personalize information. That is, RSS feeds and similar technology allow users to either deliver information to which they've subscribed or drill down to information most pertinent to them. The rise of subscription-based services, such as signing up for campaign e-mail or text alerts, has created a richness of constituent data not previously realized. By the end of his campaign, it was said that the Obama campaign had unbridled segmentation to specifically tailor their messages based on the recipient's interests, demographic characteristics, and donor level. Using an analytics team to track what e-mail was opened most, the Obama campaign developed an e-mail marketing strategy capable of generating campaign donations, driving the candidate's message, and mobilizing supporters.

(Waite, 2010, pp. 108–109)

One way that candidates have personalized and tailored messages in digital spaces has been targeted communication in social networks. During the 2008 election, both main party candidates John McCain and Barack Obama hosted the requisite Web page along with a social presence in several subculture specific social networks for Latino/a Americans and Asian Americans (Schnably, 2009). This act of tailoring the message to a specific target public to make the experience more personal is classic public relations.

Personalization may also refer to the informal level of communication. For campaigns, it may mean calling the candidate by his or her first name or showing the candidate in a more approachable manner. It has also been shown that many candidates on their Web sites feature, for example, pictures of the candidate's family and dog, and the candidate's favorite cookie recipe (Tedesco, Miller, & Spiker, 1999).

A more commonly thought of means of personalization is the act of making communication appear as if it is coming from the candidate. Campaign e-mail messages, while written by campaign staff, are often worded and sometimes signed as if they are coming directly from the candidate himself or herself (Trammell & Williams, 2004).

Looking at interactivity, McMillian (2002) first defined interactivity in three ways as allowing: user-to-system (e.g., clicking on a hyperlink), user-to-user (e.g., two-way communication between users such as chat or "volunteer" options on a site), and user-to-document interactivity (e.g., add or modify content). Later, Endres and Warnick (2004) added text-based interactivity to this typology, touching on the fact that rhetorical devices can also create a spirit of interactivity. This development paved the way for textual calls to action—engagement-driven prose—to be considered a real part of interactivity.

Having said this, early in campaign adoption of digital tools, campaign communication staff admitted avoiding interactivity (Stromer-Galley, 2000). Threatened by what others had touted as benefits to online interaction and social media, this led to what Baker and Stromer-Galley (2000) later called a façade of interactivity. That is, the researchers found campaigns integrated political discourse tools such as allowing comments on blog campaign blog posts, but the campaign staff would rarely respond to the comments and certainly not incorporate the feedback into the campaign strategies.

It is through interactivity, however, that the prime benefit of digital communication is realized for the campaign as the technology connects and mobilizes people. Bimber and Davis (2003) noted this as being a highly important and effective use of the technology, and Trammell et al. (2006) pointed out calls to action asking for volunteering, donation, or other activities that should be considered text-based interactivity. Indeed, these calls to action—be it donate, subscribe, or volunteer—translate online activity into traditional tangible benefits for the campaign.

During the 2004 Democratic primary in the United States, candidate Howard Dean became well-known for mobilizing his supporters through a series of grassroots initiatives. According to Hull (2006), the Dean campaign decentralized the involvement process by pushing it into local hands rather than managing it within the campaign. That is, Dean transferred the power to get involved directly to his supporters to let them manage the process—and they did so on the local level nationwide in record numbers, mainly by connecting through MeetUp.com (Hull, 2006). Gibson and McAllister (2008) suggest that the Dean campaign ignited a spark that then spread around the globe, as more international campaigns saw the benefit of e-campaigning after his use of digital tools.

The Obama campaign experimented with mobile communication during the 2008 election. That campaign established mobile phone applications that allowed supporters to download ringtones or custom wallpapers, and to receive text messages from the campaign (Hendricks & Denton, 2010; Mackay, 2010). The campaign also created an iPhone and iTouch application that would classify contacts in users' address books as to whether that contact lived in a battleground state (Hendricks & Denton, 2010).

Some campaign rallies during the 2008 election also featured opportunities for attending supporters to text in messages that would appear on screens at the rally. This text-to-screen interactivity not only made the rally attendee feel connected to the event and the campaign, but the campaign then had contact information (mobile phone number) for that supporter (Mackay, 2010). This database of supporters could then be used by the campaign to send campaign information (Mackay, 2010). This suggests that the use of mobile technology may afford campaigns great opportunities to create a rather detailed database of supporters, and the ability to instantly mobilize voters into action.

A host of interactive tools can be used for political public relations. Under the backdrop of the 2008 presidential election, Schnably (2009) found that both campaigns used 7 of 41 possible digital tools, including Facebook, an official blog, LinkedIn, Action Center, MySpace, YouTube, and an official Web site. Among these, social networking tools were the most common digital tools for the candidates. These sites not only allowed the campaigns the opportunity to connect with their constituents, but for the first time created that opportunity to connect within spaces the prospective voters were already hanging out. That is, constituents did not have to go to a candidate Web site but could be pushed to campaign content while spending time on his or her social network of choice. This also created a greater potential for virality, in that when one person participates on a social site it often pushes that information out to that person's entire list of contacts (e.g., the Facebook wall and status feed).

Sweetser, Golan, and Wanta (2008) considered how campaign-created content might fit into the information system and whether instant campaign communication might influence the media through an agenda setting effect, and analyzed two forms of campaign-released communication (campaign blog posts and campaign ads) and major media coverage in the 2004 election. The data showed that campaign blogs still followed the media agenda, and there was no correlation between ads and the other agendas. This indicated that the campaign blog was a place for instant rebuttal to criticism and breaking news. Taking the approach of intercandidate agenda setting, Kiousis and Shields (2008) also used campaign Web content to determine whether one candidate's agenda impacted another's, which they found some support for, including the idea that the candidate agenda could be carried across information subsidies, which in modern elections can be seen as different social media platforms.

Understanding this agenda-setting potential via blogs, campaigns turned political bloggers into communication consultants during the 2006 midterm election cycle by putting bloggers on the payroll (Davis, 2009). This strategy of using the voice of the blogger to communicate the messages of the campaign continued into the 2008 election cycle in the United States (Davis, 2009).

The assumption to this point has been that campaigns have been primarily using digital communication as a means of focused promotion (Tedesco, Miller, & Spiker, 1999). Yet, just as in advertising, the communication can also be targeted at an opponent in an attack. Early on, Williams, Trammell, Postelnicu, Landreville, and Martin (2005) found few instances of attacking the opponent in blogs. Later analyses by Trammell (2004, 2006) noted a higher level of attack blog posts against the opponent. Cho and Benoit (2006), who analyzed campaign press releases during the same period, also noted an increase in negativity as the campaign waged on. During the 2008 election, the Republican National Committee created an attack site spoofing Facebook with "BarackBook" which showed a list of other less-than-savory political figures to whom Barack Obama was linked (Mackay, 2010). The Obama campaign responded by posting a series of policy documents on social networking site Scribd, a site typically used to share longer-form documents (Mackay, 2010). Not surprisingly, major campaigns in the 2008 election also enlisted YouTube for opponent and issue attacks.

Constituents' Use of Campaign Political Digital Tools

As discussed above, campaigns have extended their overall communication strategy into digital spaces as a means to take advantage of the features of various digital tools and improve their ability to reach their constituents. But to what effect? How do prospective voters use the campaign political digital tools?

History

With each election cycle, the numbers of consumers of online political information have steadily increased. Usage rose from 23% of all U.S. Internet users in 2000, to 34% in 2004, and to 46% in January 2008 (Pew, 2008a). These numbers indicate that American voters have been supplementing mainstream media as sources for political information with online sources, including campaign and citizen-produced content. For public relations, this shows that the mass media are no longer the sole source of information, and that publics are both going directly to the source (campaigns) and becoming sources themselves (peer-to-peer). According to Pew (2008b), the most prominent online political activities in 2008 were watching online political videos, using social network Web sites, and making political contributions. Additionally, Pew (2009) reported one in three Internet users forwarded political information to another person.

Perception of Tools and Effects

The ultimate desired effect with any campaign communication is to provide information that spurs a prospective voter into going to the polls and casting that vote in favor of the candidate. Getting constituents to the digital tools is the first step. Informing the constituents is the second step. Finally, spurring the constituents to action is the last step.

From a uses and gratifications perspective, scholars are able to not only understand why one selects a particular source for political information but why one would avoid the source as well (Blumler & McQuail, 1969; McLeod & Becker, 1974). Sweetser, Lariscy, and Tinkham (2010) found using digital campaign content (for example, friending a candidate on Facebook) had a significant and negative correlation with age, meaning younger people were more likely to approach digital campaign material than their older counterparts. Related to this, the researchers found that younger people believed these online interactions with the campaign and candidate could be classified as "political participation" (Sweetser et al., 2010). Given this, Sweetser et al. (in press) suggest: "As campaigns engage more online with constituents and this group who sees political participation online as a legitimate form, the worldview may shift and tactics we considered tried and true today (e.g., attending a debate, posting a sign in the front yard) will no longer be relevant." For campaigns, this means a greater emphasis on deploying meaningful online opportunities to mobilize and inform prospective voters.

Most general uses and gratifications research in political communication surrounds how people use the Internet in general for political information. From a public relations perspective, it is imperative to understand not just how people use general political information but how they use content created by the campaign. Via uses and gratifications theory, Ancu and Cozma (2009) examined the motivations of accessing candidate profiles on MySpace during the 2008 primary season. Users were driven to this campaign content mainly by the desire for social interaction with like-minded supporters, information seeking, and entertainment. Profiles in these social networking sites is a prime way to connect with voters, as the public relations communication and relationship-building occurs in the spaces constituents are already hanging out in online.

Next consider the process of informing prospective voters about the candidate. Positively informing voters about the candidate's stance is paramount. As such, the campaign–voter agenda setting effect is a key component of winning an election. Along these lines, Ku, Kaid, and Pfau (2003) measured the transfer of issue salience from candidate Web sites during the 2000 U.S. presidential campaign. The researchers found evidence supporting the premise that visiting a campaign Web site may have an agenda setting effect on potential voters. In addition, research suggests that the use of Internet for political information may have a positive impact on people's political efficacy and knowledge (Kaid, McKinney, & Tedesco, 2007).

Social networks, in particular, create a feeling of proximity between the constituent and the candidate. Applying a dialogic method of content analysis to comments left on the Facebook walls of candidates in the midterm 2006 election, Sweetser and Weaver Lariscy (2008) found that constituents' language toward candidates was very informal and similar to how one would speak to a friend. Half of more than 5,000 Facebook wall comments featured the constituent calling the candidate "you" or using the candidate's first name only (Sweetser & Lariscy, 2008). The researchers concluded that even though the mere social networking presence was a dialogic feature within the overall campaign, the lack of candidate/campaign interaction on Facebook indicated unrealized potential with regard to two-way symmetrical interaction.

E-Government

E-Government is defined as the use of information technology to facilitate the business of government (United Nations [UN] & American Society for Public Administration [ASPA], 2002). With billions of tax dollars invested into the concept, government hopes to provide better customer orientation, efficiency, and effectiveness. Here e-government can refer to the overall concept, as well as specific digital services such as filing taxes or renewing car registration online.

E-government is heralded as a way to improve government transparency, responsiveness, and accountability (Bèlanger & Carter, 2008). The presence of a public relations variable as a prime motivation for adopting e-government initiatives suggests that the concept is not solely about technology and efficiency, but also driven by the desire to improve relationships with citizens. Tapscott and Agew (1999) suggest that e-government is not merely about putting services online for citizens, but rather about harnessing digital technology in order to remain relevant in a more interactive and informational era. As such, Goodman and Kiousis (1998) aptly point out that a chief decision with the creation of any e-government initiative is the decision regarding what role citizens will play in the political process, asking whether the purpose of any single initiative is intended to merely inform people or somehow allow them to participate in a government process. Based on their case study of e-government initiatives, Goodman and Kiousis (1998) suggested that future initiatives should aim to (a) educate citizens, (b) define conceptual goals of projects, (c) match interactive attributes of technology with conceptual objectives, (d) assure universal access, (e) create symbiotic relationships among participants, (f) offer access and initiatives free of charge, (g) have an assessment plan, and (h) consult with institutions of higher learning to tap into academic expertise. In the end, it is expected that e-government initiatives would lead to improved relationships with stakeholders, better delivery of service to citizens, and a more efficient means of doing business.

History

It has been estimated that with e-government projects growing 6.9% annually, the United States had invested a total of $5.8 billion by 2009 (Pulliam, 2005). In 2005, approximately 19% of all government organizations worldwide offered online services (West, 2005). This level of worldwide implementation includes a large variety of different programs, engaging various types of stakeholders to include government-to-business, government-to-internal employees, government-to-other-institutional government organizations, and citizen-to-citizen initiatives (Carter & Belanger, 2003).

The specific use of tools and number of tools used in e-government initiatives are many. Dating back to 1978, electronic town hall meetings were conducted in Hawaii and a similar two-way conferencing system in Alaska allows legislators to hold hearings with constituents (Goodman & Kiousis, 1998). Straddling the line between official state and elected official use, the Obama administration has run a very robust digital public relations program by actively managing a Twitter account, engaging Facebook presence, regular YouTube addresses from the president, and a blog updated daily.

All e-government initiatives are not equally successful, however. Applying stakeholder theory to e-government use, Chan and Pan (2008) argue for successful e-government implementation, noting that the organization must (a) engage intermediaries when the end-user cannot be engaged, (b) understand that users should not just be convinced to use e-government, but rather be encouraged to take ownership, (c) know that users might be coerced to use e-government services, but that will not equal satisfaction, and (d) realize that sustained user engagement is paramount to tweak technology to meet user needs. Knowing that trust is a central piece of the relationship, Bélanger and Carter (2008) focused on users' initial trust in e-government. The researchers found that people must trust the mechanisms (e.g., Internet, mobile) and that the e-government service can assist users by posting privacy policies and seals. Next, users must trust the government entity sponsoring the service.

Today, e-government initiatives use digital tools ranging from blogs to Twitter, to allow their populace the ability to stay abreast of information or submit feedback. Perhaps the most ambitious initiative was launched by Barack Obama who, only weeks after having been elected president, launched the first e-government Web site of its scale in the United States with the Change.gov site. *Wired Magazine* called it "the beginning of a new era in government communication and transparency" (Ratliff, 2009). Though challenged by some privacy issues unique to digital communication on government Web sites, the Obama administration prevailed in still solidly claiming the rights to the first successful instance of federal-level digital e-government.

Elected and Appointed Officials' Use of Digital Tools

Given that political talk is occurring organically and candidates use digital tools to win votes, many elected officials continue an online presence after the campaign. Looking at the factors that predispose an elected official to adopt digital tools, Ward, Lusoli, and Gibson (2007) suggested that micro (personal), meso (institutional/organizational), and macro (systemic) factors are critical. Ward et al. (2007) argue that digital political public relations tools allow elected officials to personalize a party message and create a real connection with those who elected them. On the other hand, officials might find the amount of feedback from constituents overwhelming and difficult to monitor (Ward et al., 2007). A piece of this concern also stems from the many-to-many communication ability, which creates a concern that there will be greater scrutiny of the politician or issue stance as nonparty participants begin to engage within the digital tools offered. In this regard, elected officials face many of the same issues as corporate organizations when using digital public relations tools.

Sheffer (2003) examined elected officials' use of e-mail as a means to communicate with constituents. E-mail provides many benefits in e-government, including inexpensive, personal, and faster communication compared to traditional correspondence through mail or telephone. However, survey results of elected officials showed that e-mail was not being integrated as a political tool. Legislators reported considering information from constituents that came in via e-mail, but said those opinions did not impact the elected officials' opinions and expressed difficulty in sorting through which e-mail senders were constituents (Sheffer, 2003). Ward et al. (2007) examined the extent to which elected officials in Australia used digital public relations tools to engage their constituents. Focusing on members of parliament, the researchers suggested that these digital tools would allow elected officials to "draw on the interactive elements of new media technologies to create a new style of personalized, accessible and ongoing relationship with voters" (p. 211). Even so, their research found that engagement opportunities occurred on MP Web sites less often than informational offerings. Features that offered higher levels of interactivity, such as online meetings or discussion boards, were virtually absent (Ward et al., 2007).

There are other examples, however. After assembling a list of reportedly more than 13 million subscribers to the campaign e-mail listing following the 2008 presidential election in the United States, the Obama team continued to employ the tool moving Barack Obama from candidate to president (Waite, 2010). Barack Obama used the richly populated database to target e-mail messages to his most active supporters from the campaign days and underwent state-by-state mobilization efforts to spur supporters into letter writing and support campaigns for his top agenda items (Waite, 2010).

Political Talk and Information Seeking on Noncampaign Sites

Political public relations has always been aided by technology as a means to widen the reach of a message and better communicate with one's publics. Though communication opportunities are limitless, McDevitt, Kiousis, and Wahl-Jorgensen (2003) found online political discourse may trigger what they call a spiral of moderated opinion expression, pointing out the difference between what it means to speak up and contribute to a conversation thread and speaking out providing an opinion. Tedesco (2004) suggested that what "delineates the Internet from traditional print and broadcast media, at least in theory, is that the communication network offers ordinary citizens unrestricted access and ability to voice their political agenda to a worldwide audience" (p. 510). A key piece of this voice is that it allows people to engage with others not only as peers, but as influencers, and in some cases agenda setters. Though journalists do not always attribute content reported on in traditional media to bloggers as sources, Davis (2009) contends that political bloggers may function as agenda setters, and uses an instance of an image posted on the U.S. blog Drudge Report showing then-campaigning Barack Obama in a turban dressed as a Kenyan tribal leader as anecdotal evidence to support this after traditional media repeated the story. Some bloggers also claimed responsibility for making possible key election wins, and government officials admit that their daily reading now includes political blogs throughout the day to keep current on the pulse of American politics (Davis, 2009).

Uses and Effects

Knowing that people talk online about politics, the next logical question is "from where do they get their knowledge"? Research suggests several sources. Campaign communication, as earlier discussed, is one key source. Additionally, the media serves as an information source to fuel digital political discourse. Along these lines, Roberts, Wanta, and Dzwo (2002) found that news media content informs discussion on the electronic bulletin boards in that participants used information learned from the media to elaborate on the topics discussed in the online political forums. Like all things online, the speed at which this occurred was fast compared to traditional processes, and the transfer of salience from the media to the electronic bulletin board participants ranged from 1 to 7 days (Roberts et al., 2002).

Looking at the motivations for why one would use digital tools for political information lies a rich line of uses and gratifications research. Kaye and Johnson (2002a) found the primary motivations for using digital political information to be guidance, information seeking and surveillance, entertainment, and social utility. Linking media use to political attitudes and behaviors, they reported that information seeking and surveillance are associated with higher interest in politics (Kaye & Johnson, 2002a). Using the political media gratifications scale, Sweetser and colleagues shed light on generational differences and why some avoid political information online (Sweetser, Lariscy, & Tinkham, 2008, 2010). Kaid, McKinney, and Tedesco (2007) found that 71% of young voters consulted online political information sources during an election. Results also indicated that young citizens were more likely to use the Internet when compared to older voters.

Credibility is another important construct when thinking of peer-to-peer political talk. Citizens rate online sources of political information as credible (Johnson & Kaye, 1998, 2000, 2004). Johnson and Kaye (2000) suggested that Internet users "may judge online information as credible because they can get the information they want from a wide variety of places when they want it and without having that information filtered by the media" (p. 874). For political public relations, this is a key concept to understand because now practitioners must be able to assess which noncampaign and nonmedia sources have influential voices among their constituents.

Along these lines, Johnson and Kaye (2004) surveyed political blog readers asking them to rate credibility of content from blogs. Perhaps not surprisingly, blog readers rated blogs as being more credible than some online versions of traditional media. Looking at YouTube, English, Sweetser, and Ancu (2010) conducted an experiment examining whether the persuasive approach (source/pathos, logic/logos, and emotion/ethos) used in a political YouTube video would impact the credibility of the video, and the subsequent political effects of the video. The study found no relationship between political information efficacy or political cynicism with appeals, and results indicated that political video viewers resist being swayed by emotion or statistics.

Mobilization among like-minded people, outside of the context of the campaign, is another act facilitated by digital communication. Since early on activists have used the Internet to communicate and mobilize themselves. From a public relations perspective, it is important to understand how activist publics use digital tools and monitor activities related to the organization or campaign. Using digital technology, like-minded people are able to connect and join forces for a common cause (McCaughey & Ayers, 2003). A myriad of political issue groups that may not have agreed on all points can join forces for a large-scale protest planned completely via the Internet. Here, small and large groups come together on a common issue (generalized to meet the goals of each organization) and can create a much larger voice than each could have done through individual protests.

During the 2004 election in the United States, grassroots campaigning on the national level took off as major party candidates hosted and posted content from supporters' blogs within the confines of the campaign site. In an attempt to employ this grassroots coverage, digital political public relations for the two main party campaigns seemingly embraced the changing media relations landscape when they credentialed bloggers to "cover" the nominating conventions. Sweetser (2007) found that while these nonmedia credentialed bloggers were more biased compared to traditional media, bloggers primarily used factual statements. In sum, this experiment yielded positive coverage of the conventions, but mostly resulted in bloggers doing what they did best: talking about their day. Most importantly, perhaps, is that credentialing bloggers created a buzz for an event whose ability to garner mainstream media coverage and public interest had languished.

Constituents, opponents, detractors, or even the media can share content about the campaign online, which could have far-reaching impact if the content "goes viral" and spreads to millions of voters quickly. In some cases, social media content shared by constituents then becomes so talked about in digital spaces that the media pick up the story, sharing it with an entirely new audience. One example may be the "macaca incident," where Republican Virginia Senate candidate George Allen was captured on video calling a college student of Indian descent "macaca," an ethnic slur. The video quickly became one of the most viewed videos on YouTube (Gueorguieva, 2008), and forced Allen out of the race. Internationally, political parody sites from outside the campaign occur regularly and represent another element that political public relations must monitor (Gibson & McAllister, 2008). In situations when consumer-generated content attempts to tell the story of the campaign or issue, political public relations is now responding to media crises brought on or into the spotlight by their constituents. In these cases it is difficult for the campaigns to control the portrayal of the candidate or issue, which is important because everyone is now a potentially a media producer.

However, in more cases than not, viral videos created by those outside of the campaign are examples of strategic wins by the campaign in that others understand and believe in the campaign message enough to talk about it online. Such messages have the potential to carry even more weight, taking advantage of the peer-to-peer nature and the credibility of third-party endorsement. And if that message is presented in a catchy way then it has all the more potential. Take, for example, Obama Girl, as she became known. Though unaffiliated with the campaign, the song "I've Got a Crush … On Obama" helped raise awareness of the candidate during the early days and received much media attention (Powell, 2010). During the 2008 presidential campaign, McCain supporters uploaded 330 videos and Obama supporters uploaded more than 1,800 videos to each campaign's video channel (Mackay, 2010).

Looking at the pure effects of political talk online, Sweetser and Kaid (2008) investigated what they called "stealth" political messages. The researchers surveyed readers of three different blogs: a blog that openly made political statements, a blog that made masked "stealth" political statements wrapped in personal stories, and a blog that did not make political statements. The results indicated that readers of nonpolitical blogs were more confident in their level of political information and their ability to participate in politics. Additionally, this study found that people who read the "stealth" political messages would not avoid the blog when the political messages appeared though they would not approach a nonpolitical blog for such messages (Sweetser & Kaid, 2008). These findings are important because as more people become content producers, and more messages are presented in a more personal manner, consumers may be exposed to political messages when they least expect it.

Concluding Thoughts

Digital political public relations is already a crucial factor, and will become even more important in the future. The next phase will involve moving beyond the campaign context to examine how citizens use and are impacted by digital political messages on a daily basis. This type of ongoing political discourse is important to public relations practitioners if they are to understand the history and context of the issues, and will enable a longer lasting relationship with publics.

Strategically, this involves several different opportunities for political public relations, many of which harken back to the definition of political public relations outlined earlier by Strömbäck and Kiousis. Recall their explication of political public relations as being:

the management process by which an organization or individual for political purposes, through purposeful communication and action, seeks to influence and to establish, build, and maintain beneficial relationships and reputations with its key publics to help support its mission and achieve its goals.

Now consider two foci of this definition in relation to digital political public relations. First, the management function as an enabler to purposeful communicating and action is paramount, because digital communication should not happen in a void. Digital dissemination is yet another tool for communicating the message, and it should be done in complete alignment with other efforts. If digital is only regarded as usable at lower levels within the organization, then the entire communication strategy is in jeopardy if communication efforts contradict the message or if inappropriate levels of attention are given to one of the organizational issues. The management function ensures that communication, including digital communication, is congruent and prioritized according to the overall strategy.

Second, the understanding that relationships are central to successfully maintaining reputation, support, and a level of influence is perhaps better realized through digital political public relations than other embodiments of the practice. Relationship-building has been noted by public relations scholars as a significant attribute afforded through digital tools, as organizations are able to connect with their publics in the same spaces where one might meet a friend. Considering this, digital political public relations face the greatest opportunity through integrating relationship building into specific strategies. Digital tools can be employed for the purpose of influence and persuasion efforts, but in order to achieve such goals, the recipient has to be attuned to the source and content. Relationships set the condition for these effects, and facilitate other important actions that also demonstrate support. For example, relationships can be one piece of a holistic approach to improve digital fundraising efforts with the understanding that online presence alone will not increase donations; mobilization efforts aimed at connecting publics and organizing them into real-world support activities beyond the Internet are also needed (Hull, 2006).

None of this, however, is possible if political public relations does not operate in a completely ethical and open environment. Achieving the level of transparency and ethical vigor needed to be successful in digital communication is a moving target whose "ideal" is constantly evolving as fast as technology. Take for instance the use of bloggers as campaign consultants in the 2006 and 2008 campaigns in the United States. At that time the pay-for-post approach was not completely endorsed in digital public relations practice or by the public—but it was not illegal. However, recent regulation from the Federal Trade Commission now governs such acts as commercial endeavors and requires complete disclosure by both parties (Federal Trade Commission, 2009). This underscores the need for practitioners to operate close to the practice's many ethical codes in order to avoid becoming a case study of what not to do or damaging a relationship with one's constituents (Sweetser, 2010). With regard to transparency, political public relations practitioners must consider how transparent and open their entire program is, and not just their use of digital tools. Here, as in other contexts, consistency is central.

With regard to digital technology, mobiles appear to be the next horizon for development. Used to some extent in the Obama campaign during the 2008 election, digital forecasters predict that mobiles will continue to grow, as will the number of applications and tasks that one can do on a mobile device. The increase in mobile means by which to communicate to and connect with publics will likely place an even heavier emphasis on relationships because one is not likely to subscribe to mobile messaging and interaction opportunities without a relationship.

Regardless of the technology, one thing will remain constant in digital political public relations. Communication that does not appear organic and which is not engaging will not yield results. Public relations, political and otherwise has always been about the relationships with one's publics, and the development of digital tools has only emphasized the potential for developing those relationships on a larger basis.

Note

1   The author would like to thank Khali V. Adams for her assistance on this chapter.

References

Ancu, M., & Cozma, R. (2009). MySpace politics: Uses and gratifications of befriending candidates. *Journal of Broadcasting and Electronic Media, 53*(4), 567–583.

Baker, A., & Stromer-Galley, J. (2006). Joy and sorrow on interactivity on the campaign trail: Blogs in the primary campaign of Howard Dean. In A. Williams & J. Tedesco (Eds.), *The Internet election* (pp. 111–131). Lanham, MD: Rowman & Littlefield.

Banwart, M. C. (2002). *Video style and webstyle in 2000: Comparing the gender differences of candidate presentation in political advertising on the Internet* (Unpublished doctoral dissertation). University of Oklahoma, Norman.

Bélanger , F., & Carter, L. (2008). Trust and risk in e-government adoption. *Strategic Information Systems, 17*(2), 165–176.

Benoit, W. L. & Hansen, G. J. (2004). The changing environment of presidential campaigns. *Communication Research Reports, 21*(2), 164–173.

Bimber, B. A., & Davis, R. (2003). *Campaigning online: The Internet in U.S. elections.* New York: Oxford University Press.

Blumler, J. G., & McQuail, D. (1969). *Television in politics: Its uses and influence.* Chicago, IL: University of Chicago Press.

Boas, T. C. (2008). Chile: Promoting the personal connection—The Internet and presidential election campaigns. In S. Ward, D. Owen, R. Davis, & D. Taras (Eds.), *Making a difference: A comparative view of the role of the Internet in politics* (pp. 15–34). Lanham, MD: Lexington Books.

Botan, C. H., & Taylor, M. (2004). Public relations: State of the field. *Journal of Communication, 54*(4), 645–661.

Carter, L., & Belanger, F. (2003). The influence of perceived characteristics of innovating on e-government adoption. *Electronic Journal of e-Government, 2*(1), 11–20.

Casey, C. (1996). *The Hill on the Net: Congress enters the information age.* Boston: AP Professional.

Chan, C. M. L., & Pan, S. L. (2008). User engagement in e-government systems implementation: A comparative case study of two Singaporean e-government initiatives. *Strategic Information Systems, 17*(2), 124–139.

Cho, S., & Benoit, W. (2006). 2004 Presidential campaign messages: A functional analysis of press releases from President Bush and Senator Kerry. *Public Relations Review, 32*(1), 47–52.

D'Alessio, D. (1997). Use of the World Wide Web in the 1996 U.S. election. *Electoral Studies, 16*(4), 489–500.

Davis, R. (2009). *Tying politics: The role of blogs in American politics.* New York: Oxford University Press.

Endres, D., & Warnick, B. (2004). Text-based interactivity in candidate campaign websites: A case study from the 2002 elections. *Western Journal of Communication, 68*, 322–342.

English, K., Sweetser, K. D., & Ancu, M. (2010). YouTube-ification of political talk: An examination of persuasion appeals in viral video. *American Behavioral Scientist.*

Federal Trade Commission. (2009, October 5). FTC publishes final guides governing endorsements, testimonials: Changes affect testimonial advertisements, bloggers, celebrity endorsements. Press release. Retrieved from http://www.ftc.gov/opa/2009/10/endortest.shtm.

Foot, K. A., & Schneider, S. M. (2006). *Web campaigning.* Cambridge, MA: MIT Press.

Garrett, J. J. (2004). *User experience analysis: Presidential campaign sites.* Report prepared for Adaptive Path. Retrieved from http://www.adaptivepath.com/aboutus/pr/archives/012604/

Gibson, R., & McAllister, I. (2008). Australia: Potential unfulfilled? The 2004 election online. In S. Ward, D. Owen, R. Davis, & D. Taras (Eds.), *Making a difference: A comparative view of the role of the Internet in politics* (pp. 35–56). Lanham, MD: Lexington Books.

Goodman, R., & Kiousis, K. (1998). *Teledemocracy: Using new media technology to enhance civic education.* Paper presented to Southwest Symposium of the Southwest Education Council for Journalism and Mass Communication, El Paso, TX.

Grunig, J. E., & Hunt, T. (1984). *Managing public relations.* Belmont, CA: Thomson Wadsworth.

Gueorguieva, V. (2008). Voters, MySpace, and YouTube: The impact of alternative communication channels on the 2006 election cycle and beyond. *Social Science Computer Review, 26*(3), 288–300.

Hendricks, J. A., & Denton, R. E. (2010). Political campaigns and communicating with the electorate in the twenty-first century. In J. A. Hendricks & R. E. Denton (Eds.), *Communicator-in-chief: How Barack Obama used new media technology to win the White House* (pp. 1–18). Lanham, MD: Lexington Books.

Hull, C. C. (2006). Online organization: Dean, Kerry, and the Internet politicking in the 2004 Iowa caucus. In A. Williams & J. Tedesco (Eds.), *The Internet election* (pp. 57–66). Lanham, MD: Rowman & Littlefield.

Johnson, T. J., & Kaye, B. K. (1998). Cruising is believing? Comparing media and traditional sources on media credibility measures. *Journalism & Mass Communication Quarterly, 75*, 325–340.

Johnson, T. J., & Kaye, B. K. (2000). Using is believing: The influence of reliance on the credibility of online political information among politically interested Internet users. *Journalism & Mass Communication Quarterly, 77*, 865–879.

Johnson, T. J., & Kaye, B. K. (2004). Wag the blog: How reliance on traditional media and the Internet influence credibility perceptions of Weblogs among blog users. *Journalism & Mass Communication Quarterly, 81*(3), 622–642.

Kaid, L. L. (2004). Political advertising. In L. Kaid (Ed.), *Handbook of political communication research* (pp. 155–202). Mahwah, NJ Erlbaum.

Kaid, L. L., & Bystrom, D. (1999). *The electronic election: Perspectives on the 1996 campaign communication.* Mahwah, NJ: Erlbaum.

Kaid, L. L., M. McKinney, & J. Tedesco (2007). Political information efficacy and young voters. *American Behavioral Scientist, 50*(9), 1093–1111.

Kaye, B. K. & Johnson, T. J. (2002a). Online and in the know: Uses and gratifications of the web for political information. *Journal of Broadcasting and Electronic Media, 46*(1), 54–71.

Kaye, B. K., & Johnson, T. J. (2002b). Webelievability: A path model examining how convenience and reliance on the Web predict online credibility. *Journalism and Mass Communication Quarterly, 79*(3), 619–642.

Kent, M. L., & Taylor, M. (1998). Building a dialogic relationship through the World Wide Web. *Public Relations Review, 24*(3), 321–340.

Kiousis, S., & Shields, A. (2008). Intercandidate agenda-setting in the presidential elections: Issue and attribute agendas in the 2004 campaign. *Public Relations Review, 34*(4), 325–330.

Ku, G., Kaid, L., & Pfau, M. (2003). The impact of Web campaigning on traditional news media and public information processing. *Journalism & Mass Communication Quarterly, 80*, 528–547.

LaPointe, M.E. (1999). *Cyber campaigning for the United States Senate: A content analysis of campaigning Web sites in the 1998 Senate elections.* Unpublished manuscript, University of Nevada, Reno.

Mackay, J. B. (2010). Gadgets, gizmos, and the Web 2.0 Election. In J. A. Hendricks & R. E. Denton (Eds.), *Communicator-in-chief: How Barack Obama used new media technology to win the White House* (pp. 19–35). Lanham, MD: Lexington Books.

McCaughey, M., & Ayers, M. D. (2003). *Cyberactivism: Online activism in theory and practice.* New York: Routledge.

McDevitt, M., Kiousis, S., Wahl-Jorgensen, K. (2003). Spiral of moderation: Opinion expression in computer-mediated discussion. *International Journal of Public Opinion Research, 15*(4), 454–470.

McLeod, J. M., & Becker, L. B. (1974). Testing the validity of gratifications measures through political effects analysis. In J. G. Blumler & E. Katz (Eds.), *The uses of mass communications: Current perspectives on gratifications research* (pp. 137–164). Beverly Hills, CA: Sage.

McMillan, S. J. (2002). Exploring models of interactivity from multiple research traditions: Users, documents, and systems. In L. Lievrouw & S. Livingston (Eds.), *Handbook of new media* (pp. 162–182). London: Sage.

Pew Internet and American Life Project. (2008a). The Internet gains in politics. Retrieved from http://pewinternet.org/pdfs/Pew_MediaSources_jan08.pdf.

Pew Internet and American Life Project. (2008b). The Internet and the 2008 election. Retrieved from http://www.pewinternet.org/PPF/r/252/report_display.asp.

Pew Internet and American Life Project. (2009). The Internet's role in campaign 2008. Retrieved from http://pewinternet.org/Reports/2009/6--The-Internets-Role-in-Campaign-2008.aspx.

Powell, L. (2010). Obama and Obama Girl: YouTube, viral videos, and the 2008 presidential election. In J. A. Hendricks & R. E. Denton (Eds.), *Communicator-in-chief: How Barack Obama used new media technology to win the White House* (pp. 83–104). Lanham, MD: Lexington Books.

Pulliam, D. (2005). E-gov spending expected to rise, despite congressional dissatisfaction. Retrieved from http://www.govexec.com/dailyfed/1204/010605p1.htm.

Ratliff, E. (2009, January 19). The wired presidency: Can Obama really reboot the White House? *Wired Magazine.* Retrieved from http://www.wired.com/politics/onlinerights/magazine/17-02/ff_obama?currentPage=all.

Roberts, M., Wanta,W., & Dzwo, T. (2002). Agenda setting and issue salience online. *Communication Research, 29*, 452–465.

Schnably, C. (2009). Internet tools in the 2008 presidential election: A dialogic approach. (Unpublished master's thesis). Grady College of Journalism and Mass Communication, University of Georgia, Athens.

Schneider, S. M., & Foot, K. A. (2006). Web campaigning by U.S. presidential primary candidates in 2000 and 2004. In A. Williams & J. Tedesco (Eds.), *The Internet election* (pp. 21–36). Lanham, MD: Rowman & Littlefield.

Selnow, G. W. (1998). *Electronic whistle stops: The impact of the Internet on American politics.* Westport, CT: Praeger.

Sheffer, M. L. (2003). State legislators' perceptions of the use of e-mail in constituent communication. *Journal of Computer-Mediated Communication, 8*(4). Retrieved from http://jcmc.indiana.edu/vol8/issue4/sheffer.html.

Stromer-Galley, J. (2000). Online interaction and why candidates avoid it. *Journal of Communication, 50*(4), 111–132.

Sweetser, K. D. (2007). Blog bias: Reports, inferences, and judgments of credentialed bloggers at the 2004 nominating conventions. *Public Relations Review, 33*(4), 426–428.

Sweetser, K. D. (2010). A losing strategy: The impact of nondisclosure in social media on relationships. *Journal of Public Relations Research, 22*(3), 288–312.

Sweetser, K. D., Golan, G. J., & Wanta, W. (2008). Intermedia agenda setting in television, advertising, and blogs during the 2004 election. *Mass Communication & Society, 11*(2), 197–216.

Sweetser, K. D., & Kaid, L. L. (2008). Stealth soapboxes: Political information efficacy, cynicism, and uses of celebrity Weblogs among readers. *New Media & Society, 10*, 67–91.

Sweetser, K. D., & Lariscy, R. W. (2008). Candidates make good friends: An analysis of candidates' use of Facebook. *International Journal of Strategic Communication, 2*(3), 175–198.

Sweetser, K. D., Lariscy, R. W., & Tinkham, S. F. (2008). The dabblers, devoted, developing, and disinterested: Examining political uses and gratifications, Internet political sophistication, political information efficacy and cynicism. Paper presented to Political Communication Division, National Communication Association, San Diego, CA.

Sweetser, K. D., Lariscy, R. A., & Tinkham, S. F. (in press). Kids these days: Examining differences in political uses and gratifications, Internet political participation, political Information efficacy, and cynicism based on age. *American Behavioral Scientist.*

Tapscott, D., & Agnew, D. (1999). Governance in the digital economy—The importance of human development. *Finance and Development, 36*(4), 84–87.

Tedesco, J. (2004). Changing the channel: Use of the Internet for communicating about politics. In L. L. Kaid (Ed.), *Handbook of political communication research* (pp. 507–532) Mahwah, NJ: Erlbaum.

Tedesco, J. C., Miller, J. L., & Spiker, J. A. (1999). Presidential campaigning on the information superhighway: An exploration of content and form. In L. L. Kaid, & D. G. Bystrom (Eds.), *The electronic election: Perspectives of the 1996 campaign communication* (pp. 51–63). Mahwah, NJ: Erlbaum.

Trammell, K. D. (2004, November). *Year of the blog: Webstyle analysis of the 2004 presidential candidate blog posts and reader comments.* Paper presented at the Political Communication Division, National Communication Association Annual Conference.

Trammell, K. D. (2006). Blog offensive: An exploratory analysis of attacks published on campaign blog posts from a political public relations perspective. *Public Relations Review, 32*(4), 402–406.

Trammell, K. D., & Williams, A. P. (2004). Beyond direct mail: Evaluating candidate e-mail messages in the 2002 Florida gubernatorial campaign. *Journal of eGovernment, 1*(1), 105–122.

Trammell, K. D., Williams, A. P., Postelnicu, M., & Landreville, K. D. (2006). Evolution of online campaigning: Increasing interactivity in candidate Web sites and blogs through text and technical features. *Mass Communication & Society, 9*(1), 21–44.

Trammell, S., & Kaye, D. (2007). Candidate campaign blogs: Directly reaching out to the youth vote. *American Behavioral Scientist, 50*(9), 1255–1263.

United Nations (UN) & American Society for Public Administration (ASPA). (2002). Benchmarking e-government: A global perspective. Retrieved from http://unpan1.un.org/intradoc/groups/public/documents/un/unpan021547.pdf

Waite, B. C. (2010). E-mail and electoral fortunes: Obama's campaign Internet insurgency. In J. A. Hendricks & R. E. Denton (Eds.), *Communicator-in-chief: How Barack Obama used new media technology to win the White House* (pp. 105–121). Lanham, MD: Lexington Books.

Ward, S., Lusoli, W., & Gibson, R. (2007). Australian MPs and the Internet: Avoiding the digital age? *The Australian Journal of Public Administration, 66*(2), 210–222.

West, D. M. (2005). Fifth annual global e-government study: U.S. and four Asian nations are world's five best online governments. Retrieved from http://www.brown.ed/Administration/News_Bureau/2005-06/05-024.html.

Whillock, R. K. (1997). Cyber-politics: The online strategies of '96. *American Behavioral Scientist, 40*(8), 1208–1225.

Williams, A. P., Trammell, K. D., Postelnicu, M., Landreville, K. D., & Martin, J. D. (2005). Blogging and hyperlinking: Use of the Web to enhance viability during 2004 U.S. campaigns. *Journalism Studies, 6*(2), 177–186.

15
POLITICAL PUBLIC RELATIONS RESEARCH IN THE FUTURE

Spiro Kiousis and Jesper Strömbäck

As shown throughout the chapters in this volume, the emerging topic of political public relations is a vibrant one that merits additional theoretical development and empirical scrutiny. Based on the conceptualizations presented throughout the previous chapters, political public relations is clearly an interdisciplinary subject lying at the crossroads of public relations, political communication, political science, and political marketing scholarship. While much work in this area has been isolated and independent in the past, we strongly advocate for the integration and convergence of theories, concepts, and principles in contemporary and future research. This is largely based on the notion that political public relations has a rich scholarly history that has developed in isolation in multiple fields.

Indeed, the Martinelli chapter in this book traces its complex roots to the literature on activism, agenda setting, critical studies, rhetoric, media effects, persuasion, and uses and gratifications to name a few. Over time, scholars have noted that public relations and politics are closely intertwined (Cutlip, Center, & Broom, 2000; McKinnon, Tedesco, & Lauder, 2001; Xifra, 2010). As a consequence, the final chapter of this volume aims to identify some common themes across the previous chapters that can be used to inform future researchers of potential domains calling for further attention in political public relations.

As a starting point, we begin with our definition that "political public relations is the management process by which an organization or individual for political purposes, through purposeful communication and action, seeks to influence and to establish, build, and maintain beneficial relationships and reputations with its key publics to help support its mission and achieve its goals." A major assumption behind our explication is that political public relations is a *management function* that should help organizations advance their mission and objectives (e.g., Seitel, 2001; Xifra, 2003). As underscored by Xifra (2010), "Strategies used by political parties and leaders, both during election and non-election periods, respond clearly to the concept established in the doctrine of strategic public relations" (p. 168). In particular, we contend that it should guide not only organizational communication, but organizational action and behavior as well. Thus, we see political public relations as a proactive and strategic endeavor rather than a reactive and merely technical one.

Also important is that the concept of political organizations is broader than that of political parties. Political organizations certainly include political parties, but also government offices, interest groups, think tanks, nongovernmental organizations, and even corporations to the extent that they attempt to influence political issues, processes, or public opinion related to political matters. In this context, an analysis of political marketing and stakeholder engagement by Hughes and Dann (2009) is instructive. Following their analysis and depending on the type of organization involved in political marketing or political public relations, at least 17 stakeholder groups can be identified: alternative political providers; electoral commissions, parliaments, government offices; industry lobby groups; issue competitors; media organizations; party donors; party members and supporters; political candidates; political opponents; private lobbyists; social pressure lobby groups; citizens and society at large; splinter interest groups; voters at election time; and voters between elections. While this may not be the definitive list because it depends on the organization and thus is contextual, it illustrates that a large number of organizations and groups are relevant in the context of political public relations.

A related point is that political public relations should not be confined to examinations of political campaigning, one major area for political public relations as both theory and practice, as highlighted in the chapter by Baines. It is not the only area, however, just as political parties are not the only relevant organizations in the context of political public relations. It is therefore crucial that political public relations also include the contexts of, for example, governing, policy making, relationship building, issues management, and opinion formation. The same is true of political marketing and political market orientation, as discussed by Lilleker and Jackson. As demonstrated in their chapter, political public relations and political marketing have several features in common, yet because of different academic roots—largely following the differences and sometimes turf wars between public relations and commercial marketing—appear largely separate in the literature. From both a theoretical and practical perspective this is unfortunate, because there are great similarities and because both disciplines could be used to inform and strengthen each other (Strömbäck, Mitrook, & Kiousis, 2010). Thus, we would encourage future scholars to bridge the gap between public relations and political marketing when investigating political public relations strategies, tactics, or processes.

Building on this point is the notion of grand strategy as articulated by Botan and Hazelton (2006), which offers a relevant backdrop for linking the tactical arenas of political public relations to the strategic levels of policy making and legislative action. In particular, they assert that "grand strategy is the policy-level decisions an organization makes about goals, alignments, ethics, and relationship with publics and other forces in the environment" (p. 198). The Eshbaugh-Soha chapter on presidential communications addresses such issues by examining how White House messages and organizational information infrastructure are used to advance policy and legislative priorities, but also have an important listening function that is employed to respond and change priorities based on input from citizens, interest groups, business, politicians, and other stakeholder groups (see also Sellers, 2010).

To be effective, political public relations cannot be reduced to mere technical tasks of disseminating messages, but should be part of the "dominant coalition" (Dozier & L. Grunig, 1992; L. Grunig, J. Grunig, & Ehling, 1992) responsible for grand strategy and strategy, and assigned the task not only of representing the organization to the publics, but also the publics to the organization. As noted by Kelley more than 50 years ago (1956), "the public relations man should be able to put his imprint most strongly on the political process if he can participate in more basic policy decisions—selection of issues and of the groups to which appeals will be directed—and if he can do this in a semi permanent association with particular parties and politicians" (p. 211).This may be even more important today than when Kelley wrote his book because permanent campaigning has become an increasingly ubiquitous feature of contemporary politics and governing (Blumenthal, 1980; Ornstein & Mann, 2000).

As important as the role of the presidency is in political public relations, it is but a part of the broader area of government communications. The Sanders chapter on government public relations underscores the role of political public relations in driving what can be thought of as grand strategy. Specifically, the notion that political public relations management inherently entails concerns with performance and evaluation is noteworthy, yet this is not merely to be determined at the organizational level. Her chapter is careful to also include assessment at the normative level of impacting democracy and political participation due to the unique nature of government communication in society. In this spirit, we encourage future scholars to not only consider the implications of political public relations at the organizational level, but at broader national and societal levels as well. Given that most research on political public relations has focused on political campaigns and elections, the extent to which it affects actually policy making and governing is strikingly underdeveloped. Consequently, the Sanders chapter makes a critical contribution toward filling this void in the literature. Coupled with the insights from the chapter on presidential communication, we suggest future research that examines the similarities and differences between government communication management at the executive level compared to other levels and branches of government in democracies.

From a stakeholder perspective, our definition also emphasizes the role of both *reputation* and *relationship* development and maintenance as a core part of the practice of political public relations. Applying the ideas of Hutton, Goodman, Alexander, and Genest (2001) to a political context, we see political public relations as critical to all stages of stakeholder engagement, whether it involves an adolescent first developing an allegiance to a political party all the way to a lifelong volunteer for civic organizations aiming to recruit new voters. Important in this context is also the multiplicity of publics that are relevant for political organizations, broadly conceived. As such, we reject views of political public relations as only focusing either on short-term *or* long-term interactions between organizations and key publics, and views that reduce political public relations to media relations, news management, or voter relations. The concepts of reputation and relationship management are *both* paramount to capturing this short-term and long-term orientation regarding the engagement of political organizations and the multiplicity of their key publics.

From this perspective, political public relations is not limited to simple information dissemination and exchange for peripherally involved publics, but it is also not important just solely for engagement of highly involved stakeholder groups such as major donors or special interest groups. Conceptualizing political public relations along a continuum of stakeholder engagement with reputation and relationship quality at each end can be a useful tool for understanding its study and practice. Figure 15.1 outlines this conceptualization.

For example, the Lieber and Golan chapter on news management explores many of the traditional tools of political media relations and introduces the idea of agenda indexing as a way to explain how certain topics receive extensive mass media coverage while others do not. On the other hand, the Tedesco chapter explores agenda building processes, and stresses that successful media relations and agenda building require skill at relationship cultivation. Hence, when considering the higher level of involvement and engagement between political news sources and journalists, a relationship management perspective can be offered to explain the convergence or divergence of content between government communications and news media content. On the other hand,

Low Engagement   High Engagement

(Reputation Quality)   (Relationship Quality)

FIGURE 15.1 Stakeholder engagement in political public relations.

the perspective of the political landscape by uninterested voters may best be explained via a reputational framework.

When considering the concept of media relations, traditional distinctions among television, radio, and print have become increasingly blurred. Indeed, the trend toward multimedia and cross-platform content raises new questions concerning the processes of media relations in a political context. In addition, the range of media in the traditional sense has greatly expanded and led to fragmented audiences on the one hand, yet at the same time, more viewers and users are consuming public affairs information through different venues than ever before. A useful framework for defining media that embraces the impact of digital communications is offered by Richard Edelman, president and CEO of Edelman Worldwide, who suggests the following media categories: mainstream, new media, social media, and owned media (Edelman, 2010).

While traditional media relations could be restricted to major newspapers, broadcast entities, and traditional journalistic publications—that is, traditional mass media—news management efforts in the digital age must also include efforts for engaging new media (bloggers), social media (social networking sites), and owned media (mobile communications). As a result, future investigations of political media relations should move beyond mainstream media analyses and include comparisons with all different types of media in order to broaden our understanding of news management processes in politics.

As noted above, a relationship management perspective to the study of political public relations can also offer a useful conceptual framework for theoretical advancement and empirical testing. Ledingham's chapter in this volume identifies the dimensions of trust, openness, satisfaction, access, mutual control, and responsiveness as arguably the most important in determining relationship quality in a political public relations setting. The long-term orientation of organizational stakeholder engagement in this chapter is compatible with the far end of our continuum in Figure 15.1. It is also noteworthy that this approach goes beyond defining political public relations as communication to include actions and behaviors, which is consistent with the definition provided in the introductory chapter.

As such, one application of the proposed model is that the aforementioned dimensions can be used for assessing relationship quality for highly engaged stakeholder groups while reputational dimensions may be more appropriate for groups on the lower end of the scale (Yang, 2005). Some relevant dimensions of reputation in political public relations may include vision and leadership, social responsibility, and emotional appeal (Fombrun, Gardberg, & Sever, 1999; Kiousis, Popescu, & Mitrook, 2007). Unlike many perspectives in the literature, it is important to recognize that we do not see the concepts of persuasion as incompatible with a relationship management approach because persuasion processes go beyond simple opinion and attitude change to include formation and reinforcement as core outcomes (Pfau & Wan, 2006). In fact, we suggest that persuasion is a critical part of both reputation and relationship management processes.

Beyond the continuum of stakeholder engagement outlined above, another pervasive theme throughout the chapters involves the role of interactive media and digital communications in political public relations. Unlike traditional communication disciplines, a public relations approach may be best equipped to understand the impact on emergent media technologies because of its emphasis on dialogic communication and recognition of a web of stakeholder relationships with organizations, a point also emphasized in the Sweetser chapter on digital political public relations. Specifically, she notes that "as such, digital political public relations spans the boundaries of more traditional public relations in that it also informs, engages, and has the potential to mobilize publics through the use of technology tools and takes the cocreational approach to the next level."

A chief linkage identified in this chapter is that digital political public relations can impact participation beyond prompting online or offline action. For example, the overview of e-government initiatives reminds us of this expanded potential. The growing influence of social media and technology in political public relations merits additional scholarly consideration. The 2008 Obama campaign was considered groundbreaking in its use of social media for mobilization of volunteers and for fund-raising (Hendricks & Denton, 2010), yet the tremendous changes in mobile communications remain understudied in the ongoing communications landscape.

Another trend raised in discussions of digital communications is that the range of communication tactics and tools used in political public relations efforts has significantly increased in the last two decades. To be brief, online efforts can potentially include e-mail, blogs, Web sites, RSS feeds, YouTube videos, Facebook posts, text messages, and so forth to name a few, yet traditional scholarship typically examines only one type of communication tool. Consequently, we suggest future research consider multiple message forms not just for online communication efforts, but offline communication activities as well. Returning to Eshbaugh-Soha's chapter on presidential public relations, for instance, the discussion regarding the influence of presidential speeches is insightful and can serve as a foundation for examining other types of presidential messages in political public relations. Indeed, recent research suggests that message form impacts the dynamics of political public relations efforts (Kiousis & Strömbäck, 2010). The Tedesco chapter identifies many of the common tactics and tools used in agenda building efforts in political public relations.

As such, we suggest future research should explore the influence of various message types to consider the full spectrum of communication activities in political public relations programs and campaigns, particularly those involving the executive branch of government. While the focus in Eshbaugh-Soha's chapter was on the U.S. presidency, investigations of executive political leadership in other countries and settings is also paramount for verifying patterns and trends observed in the U.S. system versus others around the globe, and for identifying factors that may condition the strategies or tactics of political public relations by the executive branch. This is, of course, equally true when examining other facets of political public relations. Only through comparative research will it become possible to identify and understand the structural and semistructural determinants and factors that shape the practice of political public relations. As noted by Blumler and Gurevitch (1995), comparative research "can serve as an effective antidote to unwitting parochialism" and has an unparalleled "capacity to render the invisible visible" (p. 76).

Because many efforts of political public relations focus on issues, the process by which issues are selected, prioritized, and acted upon is central to contemplating its impact on governing and democracy. This is true not only of narrowly defined political organizations, but also of corporations that operate in a political environment and thus have to respond to and adjust to political processes. As highlighted by Heath and Waymer in their chapter on issues management, this is a discipline that "unites the tensions and struggles of the marketplace with the wrangle of the public policy arena. Politics is part of the business agenda, as the business agenda is part of politics." The inclusion of corporate issues management in our understanding of political public relations offers additional interdisciplinary opportunities for scholars from business and related areas to add to its ongoing explication.

Connected to issues communication and issues management is the role of information subsidies and the concept of agenda building, discussed in several chapters of this volume. For example, the Tedesco chapter explores how politicians, news media, and citizens influence one another to determine the priorities and issues of major concern in the political arena. In addition, the role of framing contributes significantly to the agenda building process not only in terms of media coverage, but also how candidates and parties portray issues and policies, as well as how voters perceive them (Schaffner & Sellers, 2010). Interest groups, businesses, nonprofit organizations, activists, and lobbyists use framing strategies via messages and organizational actions to affect the political process.

The distinction regarding objects and attributes in the agenda building and agenda setting literature (McCombs, 2004) is important to our understanding of issues management and related processes (see Tedesco chapter for discussion). For example, much of what occurs in political public relations efforts concerns the transfer of salience from one agenda to another among various stakeholder groups. By using the object metaphor, this process of salience formation and transfer goes beyond issues, but can include organizations, politicians, and stakeholder groups themselves. Additional research exploring these distinctions is central to assessing the broader role of political public relations on organizational effectiveness and democracy. Returning to the continuum mentioned earlier, for example, does a common set of priorities between a political organization and multiple stakeholder groups lead to stronger relationships and reputations?

The Hallahan chapter contributes to this explication by identifying seven contexts in which framing is crucial for political public relations, including situations, risks, supporting arguments, issues, responsibility, and stories. In contrast to some perspectives of framing as a top-down phenomenon, he emphasizes that framing processes involve the shared development of meaning among politicians, news media, voters, and other stakeholder groups. The notion of frame sharing stressed at the conclusion of the chapter highlights the role of framing via political public relations in building consensus and community. We suggest more research in this area to move beyond looking at framing as a strategic process but also consider its normative impacts on the political process. This is consistent with the suggestion from the Sanders chapter regarding government communication management.

Given our view that political public relations should guide organizational behavior and action, another major theme throughout the book is the importance of ethics, professional values, and standards. Both professionals and scholars alike should be cognizant of concerns regarding the potential positive and negative impacts of political public relations at both the normative and practical levels. For example, questions such as how does political public relations affect the marketplace of ideas and political participation should be addressed as well as how does it assist candidates in winning elections or interest groups in staging political protests? A single model of ethics or professional values is unlikely to emerge, yet we propose here a potential framework for pursuing the study of ethics in political public relations. Specifically, we suggest research that looks at intentions, means, and ends. Most ethical theory and systems fall into one of these three arenas so this could serve as a starting point for ethical analyses in political public relations contexts.

A major setting of political public relations where ethics is often most prominent is in crisis communication. Although much of the crisis communication literature has focused on corporations, the Coombs chapter underlines the contributions of studying political crises when investigating crisis communication. In particular, he suggests that they be conceptualized differently in some ways but also seeks to find points of convergence to enhance our knowledge of political public relations. Many of the six propositions offered for empirical testing deal with stakeholders at different levels of engagement in a crisis. Consequently we suggest that the continuum introduced earlier may be instructive for understanding the influence of political public relations to the antecedents, processes, and consequences of crisis management and communication.

As much as any other area of communication, political public relations has increasingly become an international endeavor as gaining the support and understanding of global stakeholders is central to advancing political objectives for many types of organizations and groups. The growth of multinational companies, NGOs, and government entities are a testament to this expanded role of international political public relations. Public diplomacy efforts are recognized as a major part of successful international relations among nations and political public relations activities are a key component of these activities. The Molleda chapter specifically details the role of transnational corporations (TNC) in such efforts using the constructs of corporate foreign policy and corporate diplomacy to explain how TNCs can affect host government priorities and actions. Thus, it charters new territory in outlining the influence of nonstate actors in public diplomacy processes, an influence meriting additional attention in future scholarly research.

To sum up then, this volume has suggested many areas for additional exploration within the context of political public relations. While disconnected in previous scholarship, it is our hope that future research will continue our efforts to integrate perspectives from different fields to better understand the dynamics of political public relations. As with any book, this volume was only able to cover certain areas, but it is our intention that it can serve as a starting point. For example, while limited attention was given to the role of nonprofit organizations, fundraising, and activism in political public relations, we believe these are fruitful arenas for future scholarship.

Given the major trends in globalization and digital communications, the importance of political public relations in society will continue to expand. It is our hope that empirical research and theoretical models will keep pace to improve our understanding of this critical component in democracy and civil society. As a heuristic device, we propose the continuum of stakeholder engagement introduced earlier suggesting that reputation and relationship management perspectives offer useful frameworks for studying the phenomena depending on the level of interaction between political organizations and target publics (Hutton et al., 2001). In conclusion, a major aim of this volume was to serve as springboard for additional research in this interdisciplinary area of public relations, political communication, and political science. The expansion of knowledge awaits.

References

Blumenthal, S. (1980). *The permanent campaign: Inside the world of elite political operatives*. Boston, MA: Beacon Press.

Blumler, J. G., & Gurevitch, M. (1995). *The crisis of public communication*. London: Routledge.

Botan, C. H., & Hazleton, V. (Eds.). (2006). *Public relations theory II*. Mahwah, NJ: Erlbaum.

Cutlip, S. M., Center, A. H., & Broom, G. M. (2000). *Effective public relations* (8th ed.). New York: Prentice-Hall.

Dozier, D. M., & Grunig, L. A. (1992). The organization of the public relations function. In J. E. Grunig (Ed.), *Excellence in public relations and communication management* (pp. 395–418). Mahwah, NJ: Erlbaum.

Edelman, R. (2010). *The third way: Public engagement*. Paper presented to the New Media Academic Summitt, New York, NY.

Fombrun, C. J., Gardberg, N. A., & Sever, J. M. (1999). The reputation quotient: A multi-stakeholder measure of corporate reputation. *The Journal of Brand Management, 7*(4), 241–255.

Grunig, L. A., Grunig, J. E., & Ehling, W. P. (1992). What is an effective organization? In J. E. Grunig (Ed.), *Excellence in public relations and communication management* (pp. 65–90). Mahwah, NJ: Erlbaum.

Hendricks, J. A., & Denton Jr., R. E. (Eds.). (2010). *Communicator-in-chief: How Barack Obama used new media technology to win the White House*. Lanham, MD: Lexington Books.

Hughes, A., & Dann, S. (2009). Political marketing and stakeholder engagement. *Marketing Theory, 9*(2), 243–256.

Hutton, J. G., Goodman, M. B., Alexander, J. B., & Genest, C. M. (2001). Reputation management: The new face of corporate public relations? *Public Relations Review, 27*(3), 247.

Kelley Jr., S. (1956). *Professional public relations and political power*. Baltimore, MD: John Hopkins Press.

Kiousis, S., Popescu, C., & Mitrook, M. (2007). Understanding influence on corporate reputation: An examination of public relations efforts, media coverage, public opinion, and financial performance from an agenda-building and agenda-setting perspective. *Journal of Public Relations Research, 19*, 147–165.

Kiousis, S., & Strömbäck, J. (2010). The White House and public relations: Examining the linkages between presidential communications and public opinion. *Public Relations Review, 36*(1), 7–14.

McCombs, M. (2004). *Setting the agenda: The mass media and public opinion*. Cambridge, England: Polity.

McKinnon, L. M., Tedesco, J. C., & Lauder, T. (2001). Political power through public relations. In R. L. Heath (Ed.), *Handbook of public relations* (pp. 557–563). Thousand Oaks, CA: Sage.

Ornstein, N., & Mann, T. (Eds.). (2000). *The permanent campaign and its future*. Washington, DC: AEI Press.

Pfau, M., & Wan, H-H. (2006). Persuasion: An intrinsic function of public relations. In C. H. Botan & V. Hazleton (Eds.), *Public relations theory* II (pp. 101–136). New York: Erlbaum.

Schaffner, B. F., & Sellers, P. J. (Eds.). (2010). *Winning with words: The origins and impact of political framing*. New York: Routledge.

Seitel, F. (2001). *The practice of public relations* (8th ed.). Upper Saddle River, NJ: Prentice-Hall.

Sellers, P. (2010). *Cycles of spin: Strategic communication in the U.S. Congress*. New York: Cambridge University Press.

Strömbäck, J., Mitrook, M. A., & Kiousis, S. (2010). Bridging two schools of thought: Applications of public relations theory to political marketing. *Journal of Political Marketing, 9*(1/2), 73–92.

Xifra, J. (2003). *Teoria y estructura de las relaciones publicas* [Theory and structure of public relations]. Madrid, Spain: McGraw-Hill.

Xifra, J. (2010). Linkages between public relations models and communication manager's roles in Spanish political parties. *Journal of Political Marketing, 9*(3), 167–185.

Yang, S.-U. (2005). *The effect of organization-public relationships on reputation from the perspective of publics* (Unpublished doctoral dissertation). University of Maryland, College Park.

CONTRIBUTORS

Paul Baines (PhD The University of Manchester, 2001) is Reader in Marketing, Cranfield School of Management, Bedford, UK, Managing Editor, Europe, of the *Journal of Political Marketing*, and the author or coauthor of numerous articles, book chapters, and books on marketing and political marketing issues. His latest books include: with Robert Worcester and Roger Mortimore, *Explaining Labour's Landslip* (Politicos, 2005) and with Chris Fill and Kelly Page, *Marketing* (Oxford University Press, 2008/2011). Paul's marketing research consultancy experience includes research/strategy development projects for large and medium sized enterprises in both the public and private sectors.

W. Timothy Coombs (PhD Purdue University) is a Professor in the Nicholson School of Communication. He is the 2002 recipient of the Jackson, Jackson & Wagner Behavioral Science Prize from PRSA. His research has led to the development and testing of the situational crisis communication theory. He has published a number of books, book chapters, and articles in journals, including the *Journal of Public Relations Research, Public Relations Review, Management Communication Quarterly, Journal of Business Communication, Journal of Communication Management, International Journal of Strategic Communication, Ethical Space, International Journal of Sustainable Strategic Management,* and *Corporate Reputation Review.*

Matthew Eshbaugh-Soha (PhD Texas A&M University, 2002) is currently Associate Professor of Political Science at the University of North Texas. His research agenda focuses broadly on the American presidency, with current research projects exploring the effectiveness of the president's public communications on news coverage and public opinion. He has published numerous articles in several journals and is also the author of *The President's Speeches: Beyond "Going Public"* (Lynne Rienner).

Guy J. Golan is an Associate Professor in the Newhouse School of Communication at Syracuse Univeristy. He has focused his research (Florida, 2003) on political communication, public diplomacy, digital advertising, and social media. He has published more than two dozen peer reviewed journal articles in such publications as *Journalism and Mass Communication Quarterly, Mass Communications and Society, Newspaper Research Journal, Journalism Studies,* and *Journal of Computer-Mediated Communication.* Before joining academia, Golan served as a political communication professional in Israel.

Kirk Hallahan, APR, Fellow PRSA, is Professor in the Department of Journalism and Technical Communication at Colorado State University. His research interests include strategic communication, message and channel strategies, and applications of technology in public relations. He is recipient of the Jackson, Jackson & Wagner Behavioral Science Prize from the PRSA Foundation (2001), the Pathfinder Award from the Institute for Public Relations (2007), and the Outstanding Educator of the Year Award from the Public Relations Society of America (2010).

Robert L. Heath (PhD, University of Illinois, 1971) is Professor Emeritus at the University of Houston. He has written several books and many articles as well as chapters on communication, rhetoric, public relations, activism, crisis, risk, corporate social responsibility, issues management, and stakeholder participation. His work has developed and championed many theoretical advances based on dialog, reflective and critical management, rhetorical enactment, narrative as shared sense making, and risk management and communication as the rationale for community in a fully functioning society.

Nigel Jackson is a Lecturer at the Plymouth Business School, University of Plymouth. Prior to returning to academia he spent a number of years working first in politics and then in public relations. His experience in both this fields has influenced his research. He is the editor, with Darren Lilleker and Richard Scullion of *The Marketing of Political Parties* (Manchester University Press, 2006). He also wrote, with Steve Tansey, *Politics: The Basics* (Routledge, 2008). Nigel has focused in recent years on online political communication and has written with Darren Lilleker, *Political Campaigning, Elections and the Internet* (Routledge, 2011).

Spiro Kiousis, PhD, APR, is a Professor and Chair, Department of Public Relations, University of Florida, Director of Distance Education for the College of Journalism and Communications, and a University of Florida Research

Foundation Professor. He holds a BA in mass media from the University of San Francisco, an MA in media studies from Stanford University, and a PhD in journalism from the University of Texas at Austin. His current research interests include political communication, political public relations, and new media. Specifically, this interdisciplinary research explores the interplay among political public relations efforts, news media content, and public opinion in traditional and interactive mass mediated contexts. Dr. Kiousis has had articles published in several leading journals and has presented papers to numerous academic and professional associations.

John A. Ledingham (PhD Ohio State University, 1980) is a Professor in the School of Communication, Capital University, Columbus, Ohio. Dr. Ledingham joined academe following professional experience in print and broadcast communication, advertising–public relations firms, political campaigning, and consulting in Europe and the Pacific Rim. Dr. Ledingham's specialization is relationship management. He is the editor of a collection of papers concerning relationship management as well as over 100 articles, chapters, and convention papers.

Paul S. Lieber's research emphasis mirrors his decade long professional practice in global strategic communication, centered on creating valid, predictive models of persuasion within interactive or advanced technology environments. He is an Associate Professor in Public Relations at the University of Canberra, and was previously the Command Writer for U.S. Special Operations Command, head of information operations research for U.S. Central Command, and has held agency, corporate, and consulting positions in public and investor relations, as well as on the faculties of the University of South Carolina and Emerson College.

Darren G. Lilleker is Director of the Centre for Public Communication and Senior Lecturer in The Media School, Bournemouth University, Chair of the PSA Political Marketing Specialist Group, and Convenor for Political Communication for the European Consortium for Political Research. Dr. Lilleker has published widely on political marketing communication including the textbook *Key Concepts in Political Communication* (Sage, 2006), and *Political Campaigning, Elections and the Internet* (Routledge, 2011).

Diana Knott Martinelli spent nearly 15 years working in public relations, including positions in broadcasting, health care, and federal government organizations, before earning a Park Fellowship to the University of North Carolina at Chapel Hill, where she completed her PhD in mass communication. As the Widmeyer Professor in Public Relations at the P. I. Reed School of Journalism at West Virginia University, she teaches advanced public relations and graduate research courses and spends time each summer at Widmeyer Communications in Washington, DC. Her research has been published internationally, and she regularly gives communication seminars to government audiences.

Juan-Carlos Molleda is Associate Professor and Graduate Coordinator in the Department of Public Relations, College of Journalism and Communications, University of Florida. He is affiliated to the University of Florida's Center for Latin American Studies and the Paris Research Center. Molleda received a BS in social communication (1990) from Universidad del Zulia, Venezuela, a MS in corporate and professional communications (1997) from Radford University, Virginia, and a PhD in journalism and mass communications with an emphasis on international public relations and international business (2000) from the University of South Carolina. He is a founding member of the Institute for Public Relations' Commission on Global Communication Research. Molleda's research interests are in global corporate public relations; professionalism and social roles in Latin America, and the interplay between authenticity and strategic communication.

Karen Sanders is Professor of Communication at CEU San Pablo University (Madrid) and Chair of its Department of Advertising and Institutional Communication. She is also visiting professor at IESE Business School. She is a specialist in political communication and ethics and journalism, publishing *Ethics and Journalism* (Sage, 2003) and *Communicating Politics in the 21st Century* (Palgrave Macmillan, 2009) as well as numerous articles and chapters. In 2002 she cofounded the *Institute of Communication Ethics*. Together with other colleagues in Spain, in 2006 she launched the Association of Political Communication.

Jesper Strömbäck (PhD Stockholm University) is Professor of Media and Communication and Ludvig Nordstrsm Professor and Chair in journalism at Mid Sweden University, Sundsvall Campus. He is also Research Director at the Center for Political Communication Research at Mid Sweden University. He has published numerous articles in journals such as the *Journal of Communication, International Journal of Press/Politics,* and *Public Relations Review.* His most recent books are *Handbook of Election News Coverage Around the World,* coedited with Lynda Lee Kaid (Routledge, 2008) and *Global Political Marketing,* coedited with Jennifer Lees-Marshment and Chris Rudd (Routledge, 2010).

Kaye D. Sweetser, PhD, APR, has more than a decade of public relations experience. Since 1996 she has been practicing military public affairs, first as an active duty enlisted Navy mass communication specialist and then as a commissioned Navy Public Affairs Officer. In 2007, she worked as Media

Officer on a campaign that earned PRSA's highest honor, the Silver Anvil, in the government crisis communication category. As an academic, Dr. Sweetser believes the strongest assets she brings into her classroom are the experiences from her own practice of public relations. In 2010, she advised the winning team of students in PRSSA's Bateman Case Study Competition.

John C. Tedesco (PhD, University of Oklahoma, 1996) is Associate Professor and Director of Research and Outreach for the Virginia Tech Department of Communication, where he teaches courses in research methods, communication theory, public relations, and political communication. His research articles on political communication and public relations have been published in *International Journal of Press/Politics, Journal of Advertising, Argumentation and Advocacy, Journal of Broadcasting and Electronic Media, American Behavioral Scientist, Journalism Studies, Communication Studies*, and book chapters he has authored have appeared in numerous edited volumes. Tedesco is coauthor of *Civic Dialogue in the 1996 Presidential Campaign* (Hampton Press, 2000) and coeditor of *The Millennium Election* (Rowman & Littlefield, 2003), and *The Internet Election* (Rowman & Littlefield, 2006). He is a research coordinator with UVote and the National Election Research Team, which focuses on young adult political engagement. Tedesco is former Chair of the political communication divisions of the National Communication Association and the Eastern Communication Association. He is also track chair for Communication and Technology with the International Academy of Business Disciplines. Tedesco is a former reporter with the Times-Herald Record in Middletown, NY.

Damion Waymer (PhD Purdue University) is Assistant Professor of Communication at Virginia Tech, where he researches and teaches in the areas of public relations, public affairs, and issues management. More specifically, his research explores the ways that marginalized or underrepresented publics can and do enter their perspectives into the public arena, as well as what strategies are available to those publics to challenge various issues they may encounter. He has studied public policy issues related to gentrification, urban renewal, inner-city crime, the government response to Hurricane Katrina, and organizational family-leave policies.

INDEX